ESSAYS PRESENTED
TO C. G. SELIGMAN

W. Rothenstein Nov 1924

ESSAYS PRESENTED
TO C. G. SELIGMAN

Edited by

E. E. EVANS-PRITCHARD
RAYMOND FIRTH
BRONISLAW MALINOWSKI
and
ISAAC SCHAPERA

NEGRO UNIVERSITIES PRESS
WESTPORT, CONNECTICUT

Originally published in 1934
by Kegan Paul, Trench, Trubner & Co., Ltd., London

Reprinted in 1970 by Negro Universities Press
A Division of Greenwood Press, Inc.
Westport, Connecticut

Library of Congress Catalogue Card Number 70-106834

SBN 8371-3456-0

Printed in the United States of America

CONTENTS

v

LIST OF PLATES

C. G. Seligman, *from a drawing by* Sir William Rothenstein

Frontispiece

PREFACE

In handing over this volume of essays written in honour of Professor C. G. Seligman, F.R.S., to the anthropological world, the editors have but little to add.

An appreciation by Dr. A. C. Haddon, F.R.S., gives as good an idea of the personality and contributions of Seligman as could come from the pen of any living anthropologist, for Haddon gave him his first introduction to field anthropology in the famous Cambridge Expedition to the Torres Straits Islands, 1898–9, and has since constantly remained in touch with him.

The different essays illustrate and document the width of Seligman's own interests and contributions to the Science of Man. The range of diverse subjects—whether physical anthropology, the study of races and racial problems, psychology and psycho-analysis or the study of dreams, the organization of primitive societies or technology—demonstrates the interests of men and women who have been inspired by the work of the savant to whom they pay their tribute.

The scope in the purely physical sense, the regional extent of the essays, marks also the width of the work done by Seligman. Africa, Oceania, and Asia are especially well represented. These are also the areas covered by the field-work of the author of *The Melanesians of British New Guinea*. No writer who studies the South Seas will overlook that work. No anthropologist interested in primitive humanity, in the beginnings of culture and the simplest modes of human behaviour, ever fails to turn to *The Veddas*. No administrator or theoretical worker on the cultures of Africa could do without the *Pagan Tribes of the Nilotic Sudan*. Nor will anyone easily forget that the last two books were written in collaboration with his constant companion, Mrs. Brenda Z. Seligman. The three volumes are the charter of Seligman's claim to be *primus inter pares* among the best field-workers of our times.

As his pupils, the editors wish to express their profound indebtedness to Professor Seligman for the intellectual stimulus and personal kindness which he gives to all those who work with him. In this we are certain that our sentiments are shared by all the contributors whether these be Seligman's pupils, friends, or colleagues.

Unfortunately owing to unforeseen circumstances several friends of Professor Seligman, including Sir James Frazer, Professor G. Elliot Smith, Professor Marcel Mauss, Captain T. A. Joyce, Dr. W. J. Perry, and Dr. J. H. Driberg, were unable to contribute to this volume as they had wished.

E. E. EVANS-PRITCHARD.
RAYMOND FIRTH.
BRONISLAW MALINOWSKI.
ISAAC SCHAPERA.

APPRECIATION

By A. C. Haddon

Early in 1898, after I had selected the personnel of the Cambridge Anthropological Expedition to Torres Straits, Dr. C. G. Seligman, who was an old friend of Dr. C. S. Myers, asked to be allowed to join. I had already as many colleagues as I cared to arrange for and was at first by no means disposed to accept Seligman in addition, but he was so keen that I was practically forced to accede to his persistence. Seligman at that time was a qualified medical man and was more particularly interested in pathology, to which science he had already made contributions of value. He was also interested in psychology, but he had no training in anthropology nor any special leanings in that direction. When he joined the expedition at Thursday Island in April, 1898, he brought as a handsel an account of the seclusion of girls of the Yaraikanna and Otati tribes of the Cape York peninsula, which was subsequently published in the *Reports*, v, 1904, 205–7. This was his first effort in ethnology. During the stay of the expedition in Torres Straits and New Guinea, Seligman paid particular attention to native medicine and surgery and made clinical observations on the diseases of natives. He also discovered and described the women's puberty customs in the western islands of Torres Straits. When in New Guinea he undertook some interesting investigations in the Mekeo and Rigo districts, including experiments on the tactile sensibility, keenness of eyesight, colour vision and the like of various tribes. Thus it will be seen that the observations he then made were more or less associated with his earlier interests.

It was during this expedition that Dr. Rivers first became interested in ethnology, as previously his work had been done in laboratories on the physiology of the senses, rather than in pure psychology. He was the first to apply the genealogical method in ethnological field-work and to demonstrate its value in sociological inquiry. Seligman was thus a witness of the evolution of this important new technique, of which he afterwards made considerable use. Indeed, it is not claiming too much to assert that at this time Seligman was learning how to make ethnological investigations by seeing other students engaged in field-work and by co-operating with them and joining in the discussions of problems as they arose. I do not know to what extent Seligman at that time had the very varied interests

he showed subsequently, but at all events the potentialities
were there and they rapidly showed themselves as the opportunities arose.

Seligman went with us to Sarawak and thus had a new
experience. He now came into contact with different types of
people, having a varied range of cultures, who were in every
respect very unlike the Papuans and Papuo-Melanesians with
whom he had previously become acquainted.

This was the first stage of Seligman's ethnographical career
and it was from the experiences that he had thus acquired that
his subsequent independent work was based.

In the summer of 1903 Seligman took a fishing holiday in
Hampshire, for he is a keen fisherman when the opportunity
presents itself. He casually met Major Cooke Daniels and as
they became friendly Seligman naturally spoke about his
experiences in New Guinea, and thereby his American friend
was stimulated to finance an expedition to New Guinea and,
fortunately, remembered an overlooked balance in one of his
banks. The scientific direction of the expedition of 1904 was
entrusted to Seligman, Cooke Daniels undertook the administration and the study of the material culture of the natives, and
Dr. W. Mersh Strong volunteered as assistant. For reasons
that are not worth recalling, no general account of the expedition
was published nor were the observations on material culture.
It may be here noted that Dr. Strong remained in New Guinea
and took service under the Government of Papua, and also that
practically the whole of the ethnological specimens were presented
to the British Museum by Major Cooke Daniels.

The information obtained on this expedition was published
some years later by Seligman in his fine book *The Melanesians
of British New Guinea*, Cambridge, 1910. Malinowski, Armstrong,
Fortune, and others have built upon the foundations of the social
organization of the Papuo-Melanesians so well and truly laid
by Seligman, and by more intensive and prolonged study of
limited areas have greatly increased our knowledge. When one
remembers the short time Seligman could give on this expedition
to any one locality or to any particular sociological problem, it
is amazing what varied and accurate information he amassed.
It demonstrated his indefatigable zeal and general knowledge
of anthropology, and his ability to seize upon those features
that really matter, which have characterized him ever since.
By his field-work and the marshalling of his investigations into
book form, Seligman passed from his apprenticeship into the
rank of a recognized master.

The most important event in Seligman's career was his
marriage with Brenda Z. Salaman in 1905. She had a training
in Zoology at Bedford College, which helped her in her later work.

All of Seligman's friends of that time can appreciate what this marriage has meant for him personally and for the fuller opportunities it afforded him for ethnological research.

Seligman maintained his interest in pathology and prosecuted his researches therein, and he obtained a gold medal for his London M.D. thesis on his pathological work in New Guinea. He was pathologist to the Zoological Society from 1905–7, but it had become clear by about the latter year that this science must be dropped by him as an active pursuit.

It was about this time that Seligman became interested in Chinese ceramics; he naturally began collecting in a small and tentative manner and his æsthetic appreciation was reinforced by historical and ethnological study. Slowly he and Mrs. Seligman accumulated a collection of Chinese ceramics, which, I am told, is much appreciated by connoisseurs. It was love of Chinese art that led to a long-desired visit to the Far East in 1929–1930, during which he accumulated much material of ethno-psychological interest.

I had long been desirous that some of the most backward peoples, such as the Andamanese, Vedda, Bushmen of South Africa, and the like, should be studied intensively by trained observers. Being in close touch with the Hon. John Ferguson (a relative by marriage and editor of the *Ceylon Observer*, who always had made the welfare of Ceylon his prime concern), I enlisted his aid and he with the help of Dr. Arthur Willey induced the Legislative Council to make a grant to enable the Seligmans to investigate the Vedda in 1907–8. We all know the great value of their work, not only in description, but for the light it shed on wider problems. It is evident that many of the observations made on these shy and jealous people could not have been obtained had not Mrs. Seligman been present, and had she not actively participated in the investigations. This was her first effort in field-work, and thereafter she has been her husband's companion in the expeditions to the Sudan and also has made herself an authority on kinship and social organization. As *The Melanesians of British New Guinea* marked the opening of Seligman's career, so *The Veddas* emphasizes the scientific partnership of the Seligmans.

Then followed the memorable investigations of the ethnology of the Sudan. A few years after the re-occupation, the late David Hogarth advised the Sudan Government to provide funds for a small ethnographical survey and this was entrusted to the Seligmans. The first joint expedition took place in the winter of 1909–1910 and this was followed by expeditions in 1911–12 and 1921–2. A glance at the Bibliography will indicate the wide scope of the researches then made : archæology, physical anthropology, material culture, social structure and function, psychology, religion, racial problems were all investigated and discussed, but every now and again Seligman found time to renew his old interest in New Guinea, as the titles of various papers testify.

The Fellowship of the Royal Society was conferred on him in 1919 in acknowledgment of his eminence in anthropology.

Seligman's interest in psychology, though always active, was enormously stimulated by his War service in a " shell-shock " hospital. It was his experience gained at Maghull, as much as his anthropological field-work, that led him to compose his Presidential Address to the Royal Anthropological Institute in 1924, entitled " Anthropology and Psychology : a study of some points of contact ", in which he delivered his soul on " a portion of that little-known borderland where social anthropology, psychology and genetics meet in common biological kinship ". In this Address he discussed the extravert and introvert types among civilized people and savages, and the dreams of non-European races, and since then he has published several papers on psychology.

No anthropologist has had a wider experience in the field or has studied so many aspects of human life. He has found interest in the most simple objects, in the relation of man to man, and in human ideas and ideals, and in all he has appreciated the broader implications. Fortunately, this is not an obituary notice and so I cannot be expected to enter into more personal matters or to do more than express the admiration and affection we all feel for " Sligs ".

THE *TANDU* INDUSTRY IN NORTHERN NIGERIA AND ITS AFFINITIES ELSEWHERE

By Henry Balfour

One of the objectives of a tour which I made in Nigeria in 1930, was to see for myself the process, as practised by the Hausawa, of making flasks, boxes, and other receptacles from animal membranes, by layering and moulding the membrane over clay shapes, or cores, which are subsequently broken up inside the completed vessels, when the latter have dried sufficiently to retain the shape imparted by the cores. Among the Hausa this industry is known as the *tandu* industry, and is widely practised, very large numbers of objects made by this technique being still manufactured. As far as I am aware no detailed description of the technique has been published hitherto, and it seemed to me that the process was worthy of study, since it not only has an intrinsic interest as a specialized technique, but also a comparative interest arising from its geographical dispersal.

So, when I was spending a few days in Katsina, on the northernmost border of Northern Nigeria, I asked the Emir to arrange for me to see the *tandu* manufacturing process as thoroughly as possible in the brief time at my disposal. He very kindly at once issued orders to this effect. When I was about to start for the scene of operations, the Emir remarked, " By the way, I have myself never watched this industry in operation, so I will accompany you." This was particularly fortunate for me, as he, realizing my objective, was able to insist upon the various stages being exhibited clearly before me, and to secure for me the specimens required for illustrating the sequence of processes involved and the appliances used in the industry.

We found a *tandu* worker's shop in one of the very narrow, winding back-streets of the town. The workshop consisted of a very small, unfurnished, mud-floored room opening directly on to the street. The Hausa craftsman was squatting upon the ground close to the doorway, where there was sufficient light to work by, the rest of the room being but sombrely lit. Before him lay a freshly-flensed cow-skin, upon which he had already started working. The skin had not been tanned, and the distinctly trying atmosphere in its neighbourhood did not suggest that it had been treated with any kind of preservative, though it may, possibly, have been steeped in salt water.

5

The first stage in the proceeding consisted in splitting the hide into three layers. For this, the skin was spread, a portion at a time, over a smooth, flat slab of very hard stone, perhaps 18 by

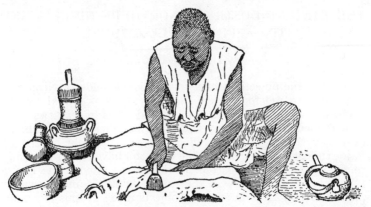

FIG. 1.—*Tandu* craftsman slitting a fresh cow-skin into three layers. Katsina, Northern Nigeria, 1930.

15 inches in superficial area. The man then very neatly and skilfully separated the hair-bearing dermal layer from the less compact, adipose subcutaneous layer of connective tissue, using

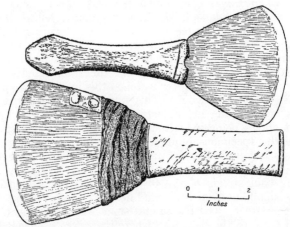

FIG. 2.—Wide-edged, spatulate knives used for slitting the skin and for cutting out and trimming the pieces of membrane for layering on to the clay cores. Katsina. One-third actual size.

a peculiar spade-like knife with wide, very sharp terminal cutting-edge (Text-figs. 1 and 2). The hairy layer was laid aside, when separated, as being concerned with the later stages of the process.

Next, the underlying connective-tissue layer was similarly split into two thin sheets, both of which were to serve as the principal material used in building up the skin vessels. The sectional diagram (Text-fig. 3) will serve to show the splitting of the rawhide into three layers, A being the separated portion of the hairy cuticular skin, B and C the two parts of the divided subcutaneous layer of connective-tissue, and D the slab of stone. At intervals throughout the process, the knife-edge was resharpened by rubbing it upon the stone slab.

A number of air-dried clay cores of various shapes had previously been prepared and were standing on the floor ready for use (Pl. I, Figs. 1, 2, and 3). One of these was selected, having the shape of a flask or vase with bulging body and high, sub-cylindrical neck. This was to serve as a core upon which the skin vessel was to be built up. The operator then cut out a piece of one of the layers of divided subcutaneous tissue (B and C in the diagram), shaping it so that it would lap round a considerable portion of

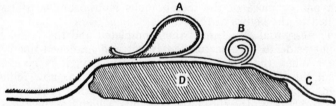

Fig. 3.—Diagrammatic section showing the slitting of the cow-skin into three layers. A = the hairy cuticle ; B and C = the two layers of the divided subcutaneous membrane ; D = the stone slab upon which the cutting is performed. Katsina.

the core. It must require considerable experience to cut out the pieces in shapes best adapted to covering the core in the most effective, uniform, and economical manner. The edges of this piece of membrane were pared down very thin. The membrane was then applied to the surface of the core and was pressed on to it, forming a thin covering of tissue. Other pieces of the membrane, similarly prepared, were applied in the same manner, until the whole of the core was closely enveloped in membrane (Pl. I, Fig. 4). Wherever the pieces of membranous tissue meet and overlap, they adhere tenaciously to each other, by virtue of the inherent glutinous nature of the material, and the thinned edges, when well pressed home, cause the joins to become invisible, as though completely " fused ". The membranous covering thus forms a seamless, continuous coating of the exact shape of the core, and, when dry, will retain the shape permanently. A second layer of membrane may be super-posed on the first, if it is desired to render the walls of the vessel thicker and stronger, for making vessels of larger size.

Before they are put aside to dry and harden on the cores, certain details may be added to complete some of the types of vessels. Looped handles are added to many of the vase-shaped examples (Pl. I, Fig. 5). Each of these is formed by cutting out a strip of the membrane, an inch or more in width, and folding this longitudinally, so as to form a three- or four-layer-thick band, which is compacted by squeezing, the ends being left flat and expanded. The band is then bent into hoop-form and the expanded ends are pressed against the membrane covering the core, to which they firmly adhere. Two, three, or four of these loops may be affixed to the body of the vessel, for the attachment of suspending cords.

A lid, in the form of a cap, fitting closely over the rim of the vase, is usually added (Pl. I, Fig. 5). This may be made either by covering the top of the core with another sheet of the membrane which overlaps the upper part of the skin vessel (after the latter has been dried), or it may be shaped upon a separate core of the appropriate shape. These lids are frequently embellished with one or more of the membranous loops, similar to those applied to the bodies of the vessels.

The essential structure is thus completed and the vessel can be put aside to become completely set and hardened upon the core. When the membrane is sufficiently dry, it is necessary to get rid of the clay-supporting core, which has now fulfilled its function. The skin vessel is hammered with a stick or bone so as to break up the core into fragments, which are then shaken out, leaving the completed skin shape as a light but firm, thin-walled vessel, more or less translucent (Pl. I, Fig. 6). It is tough and unbreakable, without seams or visible joins, and is capable of holding liquids. These vessels are an excellent substitute for pottery, being well adapted to transport, by reason of their light weight and their non-fragile quality. They are naturally much favoured by horsemen and camel-riders.

Flask-shaped vessels made by the *tandu* technique in Northern Nigeria vary in size from tiny flasks for containing antimony or galena, some barely 2 inches high (Pl. II, Figs. 17–22), up to huge milk-churns more than 2 feet high (Pl. I, Fig. 10). The largest example which I obtained in Katsina is 24¾ inches (62 cm.) in height, measured without its lid (Pl. I, Fig. 10). The smallest flasks are usually made upon a core in which the globular body is of clay, while the neck is a piece of reed stuck into the clay (Text-fig. 4, *a* and *b*) : the latter is removed when the clay is broken up. Somewhat larger flasks are made for containing snuff (Pl. II, Figs. 23–9) ; others, still larger, are receptacles for milk and other liquids (Pl. I, Figs. 7–9). Small circular and rectangular skin boxes (Pl. III, Figs. 35–9) with lids fitting closely over them are also made upon clay cores of the appropriate shapes (Pl. III,

Figs. 31–4) and are used for holding kola-nuts and other small objects ; larger circular boxes with close-fitting conical lids are another product of the *tandu* technique (Pl. I, Figs. 13, 14), and are used as food-boxes by nomads. But the shaping of the receptacles for use, while it is the primary object of this industry, does not necessarily complete the work. Usually the flasks and boxes are decorated more or less elaborately, and this is where the hairy cuticle of the hide comes into use. Pieces of this are cut out into plain or dentated strips or into ornamentally shaped panels, and these are applied to the surface of the membrane vessel, while the latter is still upon the core and before it has dried. The pieces are affixed with the hair outwards and they adhere tenaciously to the surface. A patterned effect is thus produced, and, by selecting pieces of the cuticle having white,

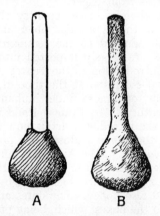

A   B

Fig. 4.—Making a small *tandu* flask, for containing antimony or galena. A = the core with clay base and reed 'neck'; B = a similar core encased in membrane. Katsina.

black, or brown hair, the *appliqués* designs are given colour values. The effect so produced is often very striking and attractive (Pl. I, Figs. 7–10). Other decorative methods are frequently adopted, for the embellishment especially of the smaller objects. Strips of red or green leather may be applied to the surface, or the whole surface may be coated with thin leather (Pl. II, Fig. 29). Snuff-flasks and boxes are often decorated with patterns of incised lines and may be stained in patterns as well (Pl. II, Figs. 25, 26). Ornamental bead-work coverings are also seen (Pl. II, Fig. 22). The largest decorated vessels, such as that shown in Pl. I, Fig. 10, are, I was told, much favoured as betrothal gifts bestowed by young men upon their fiancées, a delicate hint, perhaps, that the latter will be expected to work at the churn after marriage. A somewhat unusual article made by a *tandu*

craftsman is the toy gun (Pl. II, Fig. 30) which was moulded in
membrane over a clay core and is decorated with strips and patches
of black- and white-haired cow-skin and with strips of green leather.

Considering the time and skill required for making these
tandu articles, their selling-price appears remarkably low.
Antimony- and snuff-flasks, for example, are sold in the markets
for prices varying from twopence to sixpence each, and this for
decorated examples !

One sees the products of this industry on sale in nearly all
the native markets in Northern Nigeria and to a considerable
extent in Southern Nigeria, too. I do not at present know to
what extent the technique may be practised in other parts of
West Africa (the Gold Coast, Dahomey, Togoland, Camerun,
etc.), but there seems to exist a considerable export of *tandu*
articles to these areas from Nigeria.

To the north of Nigeria, in the country of the Tuareg, skin
flasks and boxes of the types described are in considerable
demand, being well adapted to the requirements of a nomad
life. These articles are largely imported into the region from
Nigeria, and their introduction to the Tuareg may be due to the
incursion of Songhai colonists, at the time of, or as a result of,
the Songhai conquest of Agades under Muhammad Askia, early
in the sixteenth century. Mr. Francis Rodd is of this opinion,
but he adds that the introduced art is now indigenous among
the Tuareg, and the *tandu* industry is practised by them,
especially by the women, in the Air district, though not by the
truly nomad element among the Tuareg. Boxes of the type
shown in Pl. I, Figs. 13 and 14, are chiefly used by them for carrying
butter or dates and also honey. The dates are boiled and then
pressed tightly into the boxes, which, being practically air-tight,
enable the contents to retain their moisture. Flask-shaped vessels
are used for liquids or honey, and the smaller flasks for holding
snuff or saltpetre (for mixing with tobacco, to bring out the
flavour) ; the latter are ornamented with incised designs and
staining, in the same way as the boxes, a form of decoration
which Mr. Rodd attributes to the Songhai.

In Damergu, which lies between Air and the northern border
of Nigeria, honey is carried about in very large containers " shaped
like the Roman glass lacrymatories ", Mr. Rodd informs me,
which are rendered air-tight by a thong tied round the neck
and with a piece of wet hide over the mouth. These receptacles
may be up to $2\frac{1}{2}$ feet in height, and, although they are
not decorated, are presumably of the type represented here in
Pl. I, Fig. 6. I do not know whether these are manufactured in
the district or imported from the south.

Other parts of the African continent can claim this technique,
though the dispersal appears at present somewhat sporadic

and disconnected.   A very interesting specimen, given by Sir
Flinders Petrie to the Pitt Rivers Museum in 1897, is shown
in Pl. V, Fig. 59.   It was excavated by him in the Ramesseum
at Thebes, and is dateable between the nineteenth and twenty-
second dynasties (i.e. between about 1200 and 750 B.C.).   It
was described as a " pilgrim-bottle " of leather[1]; but I feel
convinced that this is erroneous and that it must have been made
by a process similar to that followed in the *tandu* industry.
Although much weathered and indurated into a brittle state, the
membranous material appears to be similar to that employed
in the Nigerian manufacture, viz. the subcutaneous adipose
tissue from a freshly-flensed hide ; there are no seams, though
around the periphery of the flask a thickening appears to indicate
where the edge of one of the two circular pieces of membrane
of which the body is made slightly overlaps the other.   As the
edges of the overlapping piece were not shaved thin (as in the
Hausa examples) the join is rendered visible since the overlapping
edge terminates abruptly.   The walls of the flask are fairly thick
and evidently built up by superposing one layer of membrane
over another.   The weathering process has caused the layers
partly to separate and scale away from each other.   This vessel
can only, I think, have been made by layering the membrane
over a core, which was broken up and removed after the membrane
had dried, and, therefore, it is probable that the core was of
unbaked clay, easily broken.   The neck was formed similarly of
pieces of membrane wrapped round the neck of the core, and the
pair of looped handles (one of which remains) are of membrane
applied in the Hausa manner.   A further link with the Nigerian
tandu is suggested by the decoration of the vessel with patterns
of incised lines, a style of ornamentation very prevalent upon
the Hausa *tandu* articles.

So far I have seen no other example of the kind from ancient
Egypt, but, doubtless, others exist and would repay examination.
The practice of this technique in ancient times in Egypt suggests
that here we have the source whence the Nigerian industry was
derived.   As far as I am aware, the manufacture of articles in
this manner has ceased to be practised in Egypt, but the ancient
industry may very probably be represented still in the modern
craft of West Africa.

Elsewhere in Africa we find the technique being followed
in a region very far distant from the other two areas mentioned.
South of the Zambesi the same method of moulding membraneous
material over clay cores, for making such objects as snuff-flasks,
is still being practised by some of the Bantu tribes.

---

[1] J. E. Quibell, *The Ramesseum*, 1898, p. 13, "A ' pilgrim bottle ' in leather
was found with a scratched pattern exactly like that of the same shape in pottery,
suggesting a leather origin for this form."

The account given by the Rev. J. G. Wood (*Natural History—Man*, 1874, i, 174) is the most detailed which I have as yet found. He describes a method adopted by the Kafir for making snuff-flasks. " The Kaffir begins by making a clay model of some animal, and putting it in the sun to dry. . . . When a cow is killed, the Kaffir removes the hide, and lays it on the ground with the hair downwards. With the sharp blade of his assagai he then scrapes the interior of the hide, so as to clean off the coagulated blood which adheres to it, and collects it all in one place. With this blood he mixes some powdered earth, and works the blood and the powder into a paste. Of course, a small quantity of animal fibre is scraped from the hide and mixed with the paste, and aids to bind it more closely together. The paste being ready, the Kaffir rubs it over the clay model, taking care to lay it on of a uniform thickness A few minutes in the burning sunshine suffice to harden it tolerably, and then a second coat is added. The Kaffir repeats this process until he has obtained a coating about the twelfth of an inch in thickness. Just before it has become quite hard, he takes his needle or a very finely pointed assagai, and raises a kind of coarse nap on the surface, so as to bear a rude resemblance to hair. When it is quite dry, the Kaffir cuts a round hole in the top of the head, and with his needle, aided by sundry implements made of thorns, picks out the whole of the clay model, leaving only the dry coating of paste. By this time the plastic paste has hardened to a peculiar consistency. It is very heavy in proportion to its bulk, partly on account of the earthy matter incorporated with it, and partly on account of its extremely compact nature. It is wonderfully strong, resisting considerable violence without suffering any damage. It is so hard that contact with sharp stones, spear-heads, or a knife-blade is perfectly innocuous, and so elastic, that if it were dropped from the clouds upon the earth, it would scarcely sustain any injury." Wood figures one of these snuff-flasks in the form of an elephant, and refers to other animal forms similarly rendered— ox, rhinoceros, hartebeest. He also figures a small gourd-shaped snuff-box made in the same way and covered with bead-work.

I give here (Pl. III, Figs. 40–4) illustrations of five examples of this craft. Two are in the form of oxen, and three of the gourd-shaped type. The centre one has a bone spoon, with which the snuff is taken, attached to it. It was collected in 1827 by Capt. H. F. de Lisle. These testify to the accuracy of Wood's description of the mode of manufacture.

In the Catalogue of the Natal contributions to the Colonial and Indian Exhibition, held at South Kensington in 1886, the following item appears on p. 59 : " *Ifongwana la manyama*, snuff-boxes moulded from scrapings of an ox-hide." These were of the character of those described above.

Ratzel, in *Völkerkunde*, 1895, ii, 75, figures two of the gourd-shaped Kafir snuff-flasks, and describes them as made from blood, connective tissues, and clay. And on the coloured plate opposite to p. 64, one of the animal-shaped examples is shown and described as made from animal's bladder and resin.

Dudley Kidd (*The Essential Kafir*, 1904, p. 331) says: " I have frequently seen the Pondo children making small clay oxen to play with. Sometimes they bake the clay images of oxen and stretch a piece of the intestine of an animal over them, allowing the membrane to dry ; then, the clay casts broken, the oxen stand forth in a semi-transparent gelatinous form, having been previously teased into little dots and ridges by a sharp piece of bone." The correctness of this description seems to be doubtful, as the baking of the clay cores would appear unnecessary and, indeed, would render their removal far more difficult than if the clay were merely sun-dried. Also the membrane referred to (intestine) would seem less well suited to the purpose than the connective tissue and blood mentioned by other writers. The specimen shown in Pl. III, Fig. 42, moreover, obtained from the nearly related Amampondomisi, is clearly made from the latter much denser material.

It is, however, quite clear that the technique practised by certain Bantu tribes of the Zulu-Xosa group is essentially the same as the *tandu* technique of the Sudanic-Negroes in Nigeria, although the two areas are geographically far apart and, as far as I am aware, this technique is not now seen in the intervening regions. The possibility of a common origin, traceable to an Hamitic source, occurs to one, but it is, perhaps, unwise to speculate too freely as to the dispersal routes of this industry, and better to await further evidence regarding its distribution in Africa. The interesting problem remains of linking up the three recognized homes of the technique in Africa, viz. Ancient Egypt, Northern Nigeria, and South Africa, each of which is separated from the other two by an immense distance.

Leaving the African continent, we may now turn to another important home of this industry. An identical method of manufacturing vessels of membranous tissues is widely pursued in India, particularly in the more northerly areas. The technique has been more elaborated in some of the Indian areas than in Africa, and has reached a high pitch of development. The most detailed account which I have found of the method of procedure in India is that given by W. Hoey in *A Monograph on Trade and Manufactures in Northern India*, published in Lucknow in 1880. The description applies to the industry as practised in Lucknow. I quote his account in abridged form. " Kuppesaz —Maker of leather jars. The large kuppas in which ghi and oil are carried in the East are familiar to everyone who has once

passed through an Indian bazaar ; but the tiny leather phials
(called *phuleli*) made like kuppas and used to hold scented oils
are a much more remarkable product of the skilful hand of the
kuppesaz.   These may be seen hung in lines in the *gandhis'*
shop and are often of but one tola capacity.   The kuppesaz
buys up the clippings (*katran*) of undressed hides and skins . . .
and . . . *gudar* or *chilan* (i.e. scrapings) of half-finished skins.
These clippings and parings he brings home, scrapes them and
thins them and steeps them in water till they become soft and
pulpy. He prepares hollow mould of unbaked earth of the size
and shape required and on this he spreads the pieces of soft leather
which adhere and unite so as to present the appearance of one
piece. He covers this mould with from 5 to 8 layers.   He
then takes a ring of earth and lays it on the neck and works over
it the edges of the layers from the body of the mould. He dries
the kuppa in the sun : taps it with a stick till the mould breaks
and then inverts the kuppa and the earth tumbles out. The ring
which has been completely covered with leather is preserved
unbroken to give shape and solidity to the mouth of the kuppa.
. . . These clippings have to be steeped, cleaned, thinned with
a *rámpi* (scraper), and steeped again.   Each successive layer
has to be dried on the mould before another is applied. In addition
to the *katran* . . . *gudar* will be required. This is mixed with
khali, steeped in water, pounded into pulp and applied to the
middle of the kuppa in the girth after the second layer of *katran*
to give firmness and is also applied over joinings. . . . *Phulelis*
are made of only one layer. . . . They are sold by the kuppesaz
at 1½ as. per score to *gandhis*. They are very rapidly made and
the *katran* of one hide suffice to make a score."

The above quotation from Hoey gives a number of interesting
details, though the use of the term " leather " is misleading,
since the clippings and parings are obtained from undressed hides
in their natural state and untanned. Apart from minor differences,
the technique is the same as that of the Nigerian Hausa.

Through the kindness of Dr. J. H. Hutton and the Deputy-
Commissioner of Lucknow, I received several medium-sized
and small *kupis* manufactured in Lucknow. These range from
2½ to 7 inches in height and are flask-shaped with short
necks. They are thin-walled and easily dinted, giving readily
to the touch. A sun-dried, very friable, clay core, upon which the
membranous material would be layered, was also sent
(Text-fig. 5a). It is hollow throughout and thin-walled ; a hole
about ⅛ inch across is left in the centre of the base. One of the
completed membrane flasks is represented in Fig. 5b, showing a
thickened lip made from an *appliqué* roll of the membrane. The
base is flattened, where the membrane covered the hole at the
bottom of the core.

I am not at present fully informed as to the distribution of this craft in India, but I have collected evidence pointing to a wide dispersal in Northern India. From the southern area I have no information.

From Mirzapur, N.W. Provinces, two specimens of oil-flasks were sent to me in 1893 (Pl. IV, Figs. 46–8) and described by Mr. H. E. Drake Brockman as "made of strips of the longer stomach of a cow or buffalo, moulded on a clay core, the membrane having been soaked for 24 hours in salt and water. The core is then broken up and carefully removed." One of these I bisected vertically, in order to show the hollow core of unbaked clay *in situ* (Fig. 48). These examples are roughly made for ordinary use, and the walls are quite thin and pliable.

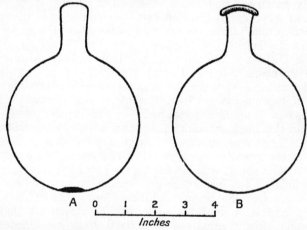

FIG. 5.—*Kupa* making in Lucknow. A = the hollow core of air-dried clay ; B = oil-flask of thin membrane with thickened lip, formed over a core. One-third actual size.

A small oil-flask of similar rough make, from Patna, Bengal, is shown in Pl. IV, Fig. 45.

Some highly finished examples of *kuppas* and *kupis*, made in Beawar, in the Ajmere-Mewara Province of Rajputana, were sent by Mrs. Leslie Saunders to the Indian Institute in Oxford. Two of these are figured here (Pl. IV, Figs. 56, 57). Both are in the form of flattened, wide-shouldered jars, the shoulders and narrow sides being slightly concave. The walls are thick and extremely strong, and the whole surface is very smooth and even. Patterns cut out in paper are *appliqués* to the surface, and the smaller flask is painted blue and red. A coat of varnish of some kind has been applied over the whole surface.

From Bikanir, Rajputana, I figure an oil-vessel, *tel kappa* (Pl. IV, Fig. 55), "made by covering a clay core with hide scrapings, etc.," sent to me by Major R. C. Temple in 1892. A thick flange runs up either side of the body and these give attachment to a pair of loop handles of cane-work. A spout of turned wood, surmounted by a tin nozzle, is fitted into the neck, for pouring. This flask is very stoutly built with thick walls. In the *Journal of Indian Arts*, vol. iv, January, 1891 [No. 33], is a coloured illustration of an oil-vessel of the same form and, apparently, a product of this same technique, but highly decorated in lacquer with gilt floral designs in low relief. This also is a product of Bikanir State, where elaborate lacquer work is a speciality, and, probably, the most elaborately ornate examples of the craft of the *kuppesaz* hail from this State.

An example, highly decorated in low-relief, gilt, which I recently purchased in London, is shown in Pl. V, Fig. 58, and is a typical specimen of the elaborated technique from Bikanir.

In the Punjab there are several centres where this handicraft is pursued—Gugaira, Montgomery District ; Khairpur, Muzaffargahr District ; Multan, and, no doubt, many other places in the Province. In his *Punjab Manufactures*, p. 130, Baden Powell writes : " The *kuppa* is made of a leathern material, which is, in some cases, I believe, made of hide—camel hide and others—but more often, especially in the smaller sizes, of a glutinous skin made by boiling the intestinal integument of horses, cows, etc., into a gluey mass. A large clay block of the size and shape of the intended vessel is taken and the softened material plastered all over it, well beaten together and left to dry. After this is finished the interior clay is broken up and picked out." In this account the terms " leathern " and " hide " are misleading, and it is desirable to verify the statement that the membrane chiefly employed is derived from the " intestinal integument ".

A massively built-up jar, described as from the Punjab, is shown in Pl. IV, Fig. 50. Its walls are thick and very strong, and it is decorated all over with cut-out paper patterns, *appliqués*, and then covered with a thin, transparent coating or wash of glutinous material. Two examples of similar type, but undecorated, a *kuppa* and a *kuppi*, are figured in the *Journal of Indian Art*, vii, pl. 9, as from the Punjab. In the same volume is a coloured plate showing several elaborate examples of jars and flasks made by this technique from Khairpur, Muzaffargahr District, Punjab. Some of the shapes are fanciful, decorative effect having been aimed at. These are ornamented with the *appliqués* designs cut out of paper. Similar types are exhibited in the Indian Museum, South Kensington, which were obtained in Multan, Punjab, and two of the types I figure here (Pl. IV, Figs. 51, 52) from specimens in the Pitt Rivers Museum, together with a tumbler (Fig. 53) of similar technique and decorated with paper patterns. The three latter specimens are believed to have come from Multan. One flask-shaped example (Pl. IV, Fig. 52) has been formed upon a core having five large holes passing through the body; the holes were lined with the membrane, which is continuous from front to back; the completed flask, after elimination of the core, has the body, as it were, " tunnelled " through in five places.

A flask for oil (Pl. IV, Fig. 54), described merely as from N. India, has its sides gadrooned, with broad, vertical ribs. It is elliptical transversely and is broadest at the flat base.

Mr. K. de B. Codrington tells me that small *kupis*, for holding toilet-oils and scents, are sold in Hyderabad, Deccan, for half an anna to one anna.

Finally, mention must be made of an oil-flask, *sireshom* (Pl. IV, Fig. 49), which was obtained in Afghanistan. It is a small example, roughly made and thin-walled. It resembles in make examples from Mirzapur, but is fitted with a loop-handle. I have no information as to whether it was made in Afghanistan or imported into the region; but in either case it gives evidence of the use of these vessels of membrane in this northern area.

Further evidence, extending the dispersal of this interesting and specialized technique, will, no doubt, be forthcoming, and it seems important that its complete distribution should be ascertained, with a view to determining the original home of the invention and the routes along which the technique was dispersed. Detailed information regarding this industry in Persia, Iraq, and Arabia would be of interest, in view of the possibility, or, as Mr. K. de B. Codrington urges, probability of its having spread into India as an accompaniment of Islamic diffusion. The same influence may, perhaps, have carried the technique into Western Africa. But, if I have rightly diagnosed the early example from the Ramesseum, it is clear that this industrial process in Africa long antedates the rise of Mahommedanism, and, therefore, its diffusion also may have taken place in pre-Islamic times.

For kindly help received while compiling the above notes on this specialized industry, I wish to express my cordial thanks to the Emir of Katsina, Mr. F. de F. Daniel, Lieut.-Commander A. G. G. Webb, and Mr. Francis R. Rodd, for information regarding West Africa; and to Dr. J. H. Hutton, the Deputy Commissioner of Lucknow, and Mr. K. de B. Codrington, for details relating to India.

18 HENRY BALFOUR

LIST OF PLATES

(All the specimens figured are in the Pitt-Rivers Museum at Oxford.)

PLATE

I. 1, 2, and 3 = Cores of air-dried clay ; 4 = core completely covered with membrane ; 5 = core covered with membrane to which loop-handles and a close-fitting cap have been added ; 6 = *tandu* vessel of membrane from which the clay core has been removed ; 7, 8, and 9 = completed *tandu* jars with handles and lids, decorated with *appliqués* strips of hairy cuticle ; 10 = *tandu* jar of the largest size, ornamented with panels and strips of hairy cuticle, black, white, and brown, and with decorated lid. The above were all collected in Katsina, 1930. 11 = lidded jar of membrane, for oil and food, collected in Katsina by F. Rodd, 1922 ; 12 = double food vessel, with upper and lower compartments, obtained in Algiers by J. W. Flower, about 50 years ago ; 13 = circular food box with close-fitting lid, decorated with stained patterns, Tuareg, Sahara, collected by D. Randall Maciver ; 14 = a similar food-box collected by F. Rodd from the Tuareg of Agades, Aïr, 1922 ; 15 = small circular box with close-fitting lid, Tuareg, Sahara, from Sir A. Evans's collection ; 16 = a similar box from Timbuctoo, from R. P. Wild's collection.

II. 17 = Small antimony-flask with tubular cover, decorated with strips of hairy cuticle, Katsina, 1930 ; 18 = double ditto of similar type, collected by A. G. G. Webb in Zaria, N. Nigeria ; 19 = antimony-flask decorated with strips of hairy cuticle and dyed leather, Katsina, 1930 ; 20 = ditto encased in decorative leather-work and with leathern fringe, Zaria, 1930 ; 21 = a similar example, Nigeria ; 22 = antimony-flask covered entirely with bead-work, obtained by P. F. Herbert from a Yoruba in Ibadan, S. Nigeria ; 23 = snuff-flask, undecorated, with cylindrical cover, Zaria, 1930 ; 24 = ditto, ditto, Gold Coast, collected by R. P. Wild ; 25 = ditto with engraved patterns over the surface, Katsina, 1930 ; 26 = similarly decorated example, Zaria, 1930 ; 27 = snuff-flask, covered with hairy cuticle, alternately black and white, N. Nigeria, collected by Miss Badcock ; 28 = smaller ditto, Zaria, 1930 ; 29 = snuff-flask encased in a decorative covering of dyed leather, obtained by R. P. Wild from a Hausa trader in the Gold Coast ; 30 = a toy model of a gun of moulded membrane covered with black and white strips of hairy cuticle and with narrow strips of dyed leather, Nigeria, from Sir R. C. Temple's collection.

II. 31 = Clay core for moulding a small *tandu* box, sub-rectangular shape ; 32 = ditto, circular shape ; 33 = circular core for moulding a box, with the base covered with membrane, the lid not yet formed ; 34 = subrectangular core with base and top coated with membrane in two pieces, to form the box and its close-fitting cover. The above were collected in Katsina, 1930. 35 to 39 = boxes for kola nuts, etc., of membrane moulded over clay cores. The close-fitting lids are decorated with engraved lines and by staining. Nigeria. 40 = a snuff-flask made by layering hide-scrapings, blood, and powdered earth over a clay core ; a bone snuff-spoon is attached to it by a thong, Kaffir, South Africa, collected by Captain H. F. de Lisle in 1827 ; 41 = another similar, Kaffirs of the Transkei, collected by Dr. Kingston ; 42 = another similar, obtained by Dr. F. Corner from the Amampondomisi, Tsolo district, Kaffraria ; 43 = snuff-flask moulded in similar manner in the form of an ox, S. Africa, from Miss Acland's collection ; 44 = another, slightly different, collected by Archdeacon Woodroofe in South Africa.

IV. 45 = A small oil-flask, made by layering membranous material over a clay core, Patna, Bengal, from Sir R. C. Temple's collection ; 46 to 48 = two similar oil-flasks, of which number 46 is in the finished state, while 47 shows the exterior and 48 the interior of a specimen which I bisected in order to reveal the hollow clay core *in situ*, collected by H. E. Drake-Brockman in Mirzapur, N.-W. Provinces, in 1893 ; 49 = an oil-vessel, *sireshom*, made by coating a clay core with skin-scrapings, Afghanistan, from Mrs. Courtenay Bell's collection ; 50 = a thick-walled oil-jar, *kupa*, decorated with cut-out paper patterns *appliqués* to the surface, Punjâb, from General Pitt Rivers' collection ; 51 = an ornamentally shaped jar with cover, similarly ornamented, Multan, Punjâb, collected by A. Brown, *c.* 1895 ; 52 = an ornamental flask the body of which is pierced by five " tunnels ", covered with paper patterns, Multan ; 53 = a drinking-mug with similar decoration, Multan. The two last were formerly in the Plymouth Museum. 54 = an oil-jar with gadrooned surface, N. India, from General Pitt Rivers' collection ; 55 = an oil-jar, *tel kuppa*, of moulded membrane, with flanges to which are attached loop-handles of cane, fitted with a duct of wood and tin for pouring the oil, Bikanir State, Rajputana, from Sir R. C. Temple's collection, 1892 ; 56 = a very finely made *kupa*, stoutly built and very strong, decorated with a small panel of cut-out paper, the whole surface being varnished over, collected by Mrs. Leslie Saunders in Beawar, Ajmere-Mewara Province, Rajputana ; 57 = a smaller similar flask, *kupi*, painted and varnished, same data as the last.

V. 58 = A very elaborately decorated *kupa*, with gilt flora ldesigns in low relief, Bikanir State, Rajputana. 59 = a flask made, apparently, by moulding membranous material over a clay core, the surface is decorated with incised lines, excavated by Sir Flinders Petrie in the Ramesseum at Thebes, Egypt, in 1897, with objects ranging from the XIXth to the XXIInd dynasties.

PLATE I

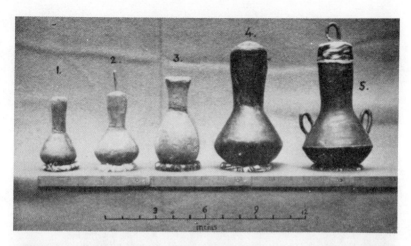

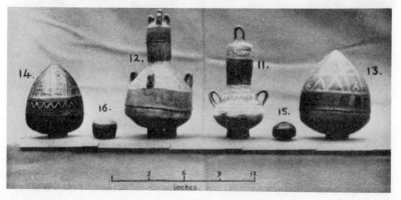

CLAY CORES AND VESSELS OF MEMBRANE, WEST AFRICA

PLATE II

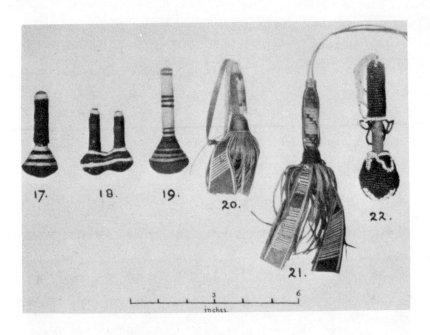

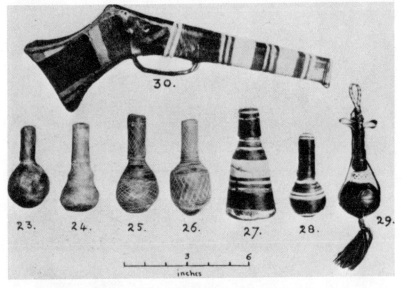

FLASKS OF MEMBRANE, WEST AFRICA

PLATE III

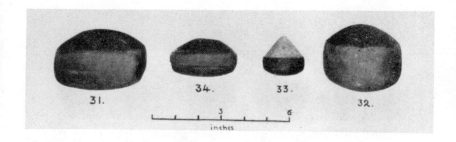

CLAY CORES AND SMALL BOXES OF MEMBRANE, WEST AFRICA

SNUFF-FLASKS OF BLOOD, MEMBRANE AND CLAY, SOUTH AFRICA

[face p. 18

PLATE IV

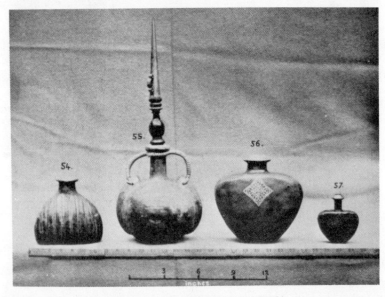

VESSELS OF MEMBRANE, INDIA

PLATE V

HIGHLY DECORATED VESSEL OF MEMBRANE, BIKANIR, RAJPUTANA

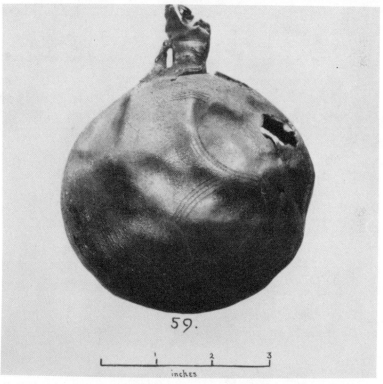

FLASK OF MEMBRANE, ANCIENT EGYPTIAN

PSYCHANALYSE ET ETHNOGRAPHIE

Par Marie Bonaparte

Je n'ai pas besoin de rappeler aux lecteurs de ce recueil l'œuvre si considérable du Professeur C. G. Seligman. D'autres que moi sauront exposer, de façon plus compétente, ses importantes contributions à l'éthnographie, cette science si jeune encore, et dont le véritable essor ne date pas de beaucoup plus d'un demi-siècle. Ses observations au contact direct des indigènes, au cours de ses expéditions en Afrique, travail dans lequel Mme Seligman lui apporta une si efficace collaboration, son œuvre d'élucidation des faits observés, lui ont donné la place qu'il mérite parmi les ethnographes de notre temps.

Mais ce à quoi, comme psychanalyste, je veux particulièrement rendre ici hommage, dans l'œuvre de Seligman, c'est à la largeur de vues, à l'intuition psychologique qui lui ont fait si bien comprendre l'importance de la psychanalyse pour l'ethnographie, ainsi qu'en témoignent les essais qu'il a consacrés à cette matière.[1]

La méthode psychanalytique, instrument d'investigation de l'inconscient

La psychanalyse, mèthode édifiée voici trente à quarante ans par Sigmund Freud au chevet des névrosés, et qui lui a permis de saisir le mécanisme psychique des psychonévroses, est devenue peu à peu la science même du psychisme humain. Non seulement les troubles de l'appareil psychique, mais son fonctionnement normal sont soumis aux lois régissant le penser inconscient. Les lois de condensation, de déplacement, de souci de figuration etc. se vérifient quotidiennement chez chacun de nous, dans l'élaboration des rêves de nos nuits : le rêve, pour qui sait le comprendre, est " la voie royale " menant vers l'inconscient.

Mais non seulement nos rêves, chacune de nos pensées, de nos actions, sont le produit de cet obscur travail qui préside, au plus profond de nous, à l'élaboration inconsciente de notre pensée et de notre activité dites conscientes. Quelques rares philosophes avaient bien, avant Freud, pressenti et même

---

[1] C. G. Seligman:" The Unconscious in Relation to Anthropology," *Brit. Journ. Psychol.*, xviii, 1928, 376; " Temperament Conflict and Psychosis in a Stone Age Population," *Brit. Journ. Med. Psychol.*, ix, 1926, 196; " Anthropological Perspective and Psychological Theory," *The Huxley Memorial Lecture for* 1932), *JRAI.*, lxii, 1932.

affirmé l'existence et l'importance de l'inconscient. Mais ils l'avaient fait un peu comme on parlait du centre de l'Afrique avant Livingstone et Stanley. Freud est l'explorateur qui y pénétra le premier.

LE DOUBLE CONTENU DE L'INCONSCIENT

Ainsi Freud est le premier qui sut voir ce qui peuple vraiment l'inconscient. D'abord nos instincts, ces instincts éternels de vie et d'agression qui constituent le fonds biologique indestructible de tout inconscient humain, quelqu'idéales, intellectuelles, esthétiques que puissent être parfois au-dessus, dans nos civilisations, les superstructures. Puis le résidu des événements de notre toute première enfance, lesquels modèlent, différemment dans chaque cas, cette matière première de nos primitifs instincts. C'est ici que l'importance de l'entourage de l'enfant éclate, importance qui nous autorise à définir l'homme " un animal familial ". Car, contrairement à ce que certaines écoles sociologiques affirment, la psychanalyse, s'appuyant sur l'observation directe du matériel humain, nous enseigne que tout homme, avant d'appartenir au " groupe ", appartint à la " famille " et que la famille primitive, la petite horde menée par un mâle — telle celles des grands anthropoïdes de nos jours encore — dut préexister aux vastes collectivités.

C'est dans ses relations au père, à la mère, aux frères, que l'homme apprend à cette heure et dut apprendre à l'aurore des temps, les premières lois de la morale, cet ensemble des prescriptions permettant aux hommes la vie en commun.

LE COMPLEXE D'ŒDIPE

On sait en effet que Freud a trouvé, au centre du psychisme inconscient de tout homme, de toute femme, névrosés ou dits bien portants, les traces indélébiles de ce qu'il a appelé le complexe d'Œdipe. L'enfant, en dépit des préjugés encore trop souvent en cours, n'est nullement un " innocent " ; sa sexualité s'éveille avec la vie. Certes une sexualité différente de celle de l'adulte, mais une sexualité aspirant, sur son mode épars, inachevé, aux satisfactions sensuelles. Ainsi le petit garçon convoite pour lui toute la tendresse, toutes les caresses maternelles, avec désir d'élimination du père, rival gênant ; ainsi la fille, après une première période d'attachement à la mère, reproduit, en inversant les rôles, la même double attitude envers le père aimé et la mère rivale.

Or, voici que Freud, étendant sa vision au delà du chevet de ses analysés, a su voir que le complexe d'Œdipe est l'héritage commun de toute l'humanité. Cas particulier du conflit entre mâles qui domine la vie sexuelle de tous les mammifères, cas dans lequel le père, en tant que mâle le plus proche, est pris d'abord pour rival, comme la mère pour premier objet d'amour, le complexe humain put sans doute, par l'homme, être " surmonté ", en vertu justement de la longue enfance dévolue par la nature à l'animal humain.

La sexualité humaine évolue en effet en deux temps : la première floraison, qui s'épanouit vers la cinquième ou sixième année, avec le complexe d'Œdipe, est bientôt suivie de la *période de latence*, pendant laquelle la sexualité de l'enfant s'endort, tandis que se constituent en lui, sous la pression éducative de son entourage, et sans doute aussi de son atavisme qui l'y rend réceptif, les réflexes de la pudeur, du dégoût, de l'esthétique, de la morale. À la puberté seulement, lorsque mûriront les glandes sexuelles, la libido se réveillera, avec une vigueur accrue, ré-activant les restes du complexe d'Œdipe. La résultante des inhibitions créées pendant la période de latence, où la libido infantile se laissait encore endiguer, avec la poussée pubère de la libido qui s'oppose après coup plus ou moins victorieusement à ces inhibitions, constitue enfin la sexualité individuelle adulte de chaque être humain.

Le totémisme et l'exogamie

L'éthnographie, par les faits qu'elle nous apporte, nous permet de vérifier la validité universelle des lois présidant à cette évolution.

Les sociétés primitives connaissent en effet deux grandes institutions dont l'origine a longtemps défié la sagacité des chercheurs : le totémisme et l'exogamie. Maintes hypothèses en ont été proposées, mais nous, psychanalystes, pensons que seule la psychanalyse a éclairé d'un jour vraiment pénétrant la genèse de ces deux institutions primitives fondamentales.

Freud, en effet, s'appuyant sur l'immense documentation contenue dans les ouvrages de Sir James Frazer, a montré que les prescriptions de l'exogamie comme celles du totémisme correspondent aux deux grandes interdictions culturelles qui s'opposent à la réalisation du complexe d'Œdipe. Si le primitif soumis à l'exogamie n'a pas le droit d'avoir des rapports sexuels avec les femmes de son clan, c'est que ces femmes sont toutes, par " déplacement ", contagion si l'on peut dire, des femmes de sa famille, des " mères " ou des " sœurs ". C'est un inceste élargi qu'il commettrait en s'accouplant à elles.

De même, dans le totémisme, la vénération de l'animal totem, la protection que l'on croit qu'il accorde à ceux de son clan, et l'interdiction de le tuer, et bien d'autres indices encore, font voir que le totem (lequel est expressément qualifié par les primitifs d'ancêtre de leur clan) est pour eux un substitut du " père ". C'est l'antique défense œdipienne du parricide qui s'est " déplacée " sur l'animal totem.

Le " retour infantile du totémisme " peut d'ailleurs s'observer dans les phobies d'animaux de tant de nos enfants. Le loup, le cheval, le chien, et autres animaux, sont, pour l'enfant qu'ils terrifient, autant de substituts du père à la fois aimé et redouté. L'enfant reproduit d'ailleurs en général, au cours de son évolution, les attitudes du primitif. La loi biogénétique se vérifie au psychique comme au physique ; l'ontogénie y reproduit la phylogénie. L'importance de ce phénomène est très grande, car rien ne s'effaçant de l'inconscient au cours de la vie, chacun de nous est comparable à un document où se serait inscrite, certes en abrégé, toute l'histoire et la préhistoire de l'humanité. C'est ce qui permet au psychanalyste, au cours de son long, minutieux et difficile travail, de retrouver, au fond de l'inconscient du plus civilisé des hommes, ces vestiges des temps disparus, les modes de réaction archaïques de ses ancêtres primitifs.

Ces vestiges, une fois mis au jour, rien n'est plus instructif que de les comparer à ce que nous pouvons observer des primitifs réels peuplant encore la terre, et c'est ici que l'ethnographie et la psychanalyse, comme nous l'avons déjà indiqué, peuvent réciproquement s'éclairer.

La morale et la magie

On voit alors que l'expérience clinique psychanalytique et l'observation ethnographique se complètent, et démontrent, par la concordance de leurs résultats, l'unité fondamentale du psychisme humain, l'universalité des lois qui le régissent.

Après l'exemple fourni par le totémisme, celui apporté par l'étude génétique de la morale le montrera.

L'ethnographie avait apporté, sans en comprendre encore toute la portée, une contribution importante à l'étude de l'origine de la morale. Elle nous avait en effet appris à connaître le *tabou* des primitifs. Mais la psychanalyse a, à son tour, apporté à l'ethnographie une contribution inestimable en montrant la parenté, que dis-je ? l'identité du *tabou* des primitifs avec les commandements et les interdictions de la névrose obsessionnelle, et de là, avec *l'impératif catégorique* de toute conscience morale.

L'école sociologique avait eu le mérite de poser le caractère exclusivement social de toute morale ; la psychanalyse a tenté de mettre au jour la genèse de celle-ci. Reprenant l'hypothèse de Darwin sur la horde primitive, Freud a exposé comment le parricide primitif avait dû engendrer, dans la horde des frères triomphants, d'abord le remords, puis, par résurrection

du père disparu dans l'animal totem que l'on ne *doit* plus tuer
et par l'exogamie que l'on doit respecter, la première morale.

. . . .

Les contributions respectives de l'ethnographie et de la
psychanalyse en ce qui touche à l'animisme et à la magie nous
fourniront encore un nouvel exemple de leur féconde collaboration.
On sait l'étonnement et le mépris qu'inspirent à tant de
civilisés les croyances de l'animisme, les pratiques de la magie
chez les sauvages — en dépit de ce fait, d'ailleurs, que tant de
croyance animiste subsiste parmi nous dans les diverses superstitions populaires.

Or, des ethnographes avaient bien su voir que la magie, chez
les sauvages, poursuit l'obtention de la nourriture, a pour but
la multiplication ou la prise de possession de celle-ci, par la
pêche ou la chasse ; ils avaient bien vu encore qu'elle vise souvent
la conquête des femmes, l'augmentation et la préservation de
la puissance virile, ou bien, par les charmes hostiles, l'élimination
des ennemis et des rivaux, et par les charmes conjuratoires
l'éloignement des démons dont l'animisme peuple le monde ;
des explorateurs avaient aussi décrit par le menu les diverses
pratiques magiques des diverses tribus, mais toutes ces observations et constatations restaient en deçà de la compréhension de
l'essence de la magie en soi.

Pour définir un couteau, il ne suffit en effet pas de le décrire
en disant : le couteau est un instrument qui sert à couper le
pain, le fromage, etc. ; il convient aussi de savoir si le couteau
est en silex ou en acier.

Or, c'est de la matière dont est constituée la magie que la
psychanalyse s'est occupée. Par la comparaison avec les
phénomènes de la névrose obsessionnelle, où l'obsédé attribue
à ses moindres désirs, à ses moindres idées un pouvoir souverain,
la psychanalyse a la première compris que la magie, " technique
de l'animisme ", est basée sur la " toute-puissance des pensées "
que s'attribuait l'homme au stade infantile, archaïque, du
narcissisme.

Le nourrisson, alors, quand il avait faim, ne voyait-il pas
accourir sa mère ? La mère, au début, ne satisfaisait-elle pas, et
sans qu'il eut besoin même de parler, ses premiers désirs ?
L'homme alors grandi continuera parfois à attribuer à l'univers,
mère élargie, la même condescendance, et à lui-même le même
souverain pouvoir. L'éducation à la réalité a beau apprendre à
l'enfant grandissant la limitation de sa puissance, le principe
de plaisir, qui régit l'inconscient, y demeure, et tend à maintenir
au fond de l'homme, sous l'influence du désir, la croyance à
son propre pouvoir souverain. La différence entre le primitif
et le civilisé consiste alors en ceci que ce qui est resté assez apparent
chez le premier est bien plus caché, refoulé, chez le second.

Je me rends compte de la difficulté qu'il y a à exposer en quelques pages des questions d'une telle complexité, surtout à des lecteurs dont sans doute une grande partie n'a jamais pu étudier une névrose obsessionnelle, cette névrose qui nous restitue mieux qu'aucune autre manifestation psychique les modes de penser archaïque de l'enfant et du primitif. Je dois cependant me borner. Qu'il me suffise d'indiquer encore le jour dont la psychanalyse a éclairé les trois grandes ères qu'a traversées l'humanité : l'animiste, la religieuse et la scientifique.

L'ère de l'animisme, où le monde apparaît à l'homme anthropomorphiquement peuplé de démons que la magie apprend à conjurer, correspond d'après elle à ce stade infantile du narcissisme, où l'enfant s'attribuait encore la toute-puissance sur l'univers, et dont nous venons de parler. Puis l'humanité semble être entrée, le père réel, humain, ressurgissant sous le totem primitif, au règne des grands dieux à figure redevenue humaine : Osiris, Zeus ou Jéhovah. Alors l'homme, ayant dû reconnaître la limitation de son propre pouvoir narcissique, remplaça la technique de l'animisme, qui était la magie, par la prière, technique de la religion, employée par l'homme qui ne saurait donc renoncer à obtenir la réalisation de ses désirs. Le père est ici prié de réaliser les désirs du fils.

Mais les dieux eux-mêmes s'effacent de l'horizon humain, comme le père vieilli disparaît de celui de l'enfant devenu homme. L'humanité commence à entrer — par une élite seulement d'ailleurs — au stade scientifique. Et l'homme renonce alors à obtenir la réalisation de ses désirs par la prière, par la faveur d'un père exalté imaginaire : il ne l'obtiendra plus que de lui-même, non plus par la technique de la magie, mais par celle, par exemple, de l'ingénieur. Cependant les grands maux inévitables conférés par le destin, la vieillesse, la mort, il ne lui reste plus alors qu'à les subir avec le sentiment stoïque d'accepter les lois de la nature. Cela est dur. Aussi l'homme, le savant lui-même, garde-t-il toujours, enfouis en quelque recoin obscur de lui-même, des vestiges du mode de penser religieux et même animiste.

LA PSYCHANALYSE ET LES ETHNOGRAPHES

Je sais que la psychanalyse est loin d'être en faveur auprès de la plupart des ethnographes. Aux " diffusionnistes ", elle apparaît au moins superflue. A certains " évolutionnistes ", éloignés ou ignorants de ses disciplines, elle semble trop hypothétique. Les adeptes de l'école " fonctionnelle " la trouvent souvent aussi hypothétique, mais surtout trop " évolutionniste ".

De plus, les ethnographes sont des hommes, et par là restent soumis aux lois du psychisme humain. Ils ne sont pas indemnes des résistances que rencontre un peu partout la psychanalyse, et qui sont dues, comme Freud l'a si bien montré, à la blessure profonde qu'elle constitue au narcissisme humain. Celui-ci ne peut lui pardonner d'avoir montré, par la découverte du déterminisme rigoureux émané de l'inconscient, que l'homme n'est pas maître en sa propre maison. Il ne peut davantage lui passer d'avoir révélé le contenu de cet inconscient, tout imprégné de sexualité ; l'importance du sexuel dans la vie de ce noble animal qu'est l'homme heurte de front l'idée que l'homme se fait de sa propre "dignité". La vérité est que, pour pouvoir juger sciemment de la véridicité générale de la psychanalyse, et par suite de sa validité particulière pour les sciences ethnographiques, il faut la connaître, et pour la connaître il ne suffit pas d'avoir feuilleté ou même lu des ouvrages de psychanalyse. Car il n'est qu'un seul livre où se puisse vraiment apprendre la psychanalyse : son propre psychisme personnel. Il faut soi-même avoir été analysé pour pouvoir juger de la valeur de la psychanalyse.

Mais, quoique certains en pensent, la psychanalyse a apporté à la science de la vie primitive une contribution qui ne saurait être négligée. Il y a en effet deux grandes faces sur lesquelles peut s'étudier toute société humaine, voire tout être humain : la face économique et la psychologique.

On sait que l'école " matérialiste " considère que les idéologies d'une société donnée, comme d'un homme donné, sont strictement déterminées par les conditions matérielles où cette société ou cet homme doivent vivre. On ne saurait certes nier l'importance de ce facteur, mais à côté des instincts *anaux* en rapport avec la matière, il y a dans l'homme les instincts libidinaux proprement sexuels, qui semblent plus indépendants des conditions économiques.

Une double étude des conditions de vie des sociétés comme des hommes s'impose ainsi à tout ethnographe. L'importance de la sexualité dans la vie humaine fait qu'aucune étude de l'homme ne saurait aller bien loin qui néglige en lui les manifestations multiformes, des plus crues aux plus modifiées, de cet instinct. Or, pour étudier la sexualité d'un être humain, la connaissance de la psychanalyse est irremplaçable. De même que tout psychanalyste devrait être quelque peu ethnographe, de même tout ethnographe devrait être au moins quelque peu psychanalyste.

Et le temps nous presse, par ailleurs. D'ici peut-être cent ans, mais peut-être même avant, les primitifs que porte encore la terre seront ou éliminés, ou plus au moins entamés par nos civilisations. Ceux qui restent encore sont les précieux et fugitifs témoins d'un temps disparu. Certes, ils diffèrent tous de nos ancêtres du temps des cavernes, ils ont subi à leur façon une évolution aussi longue que la nôtre à partir de ce temps, mais enfin ils le reflètent un peu plus fidèlement que nous, citoyens de Londres ou de Paris.

Il faut se hâter d'étudier ces vestiges survivants de l'humanité primitive. Et il faut, sans préjugés moraux, religieux ou esthétiques, sans pudibondesie, tâcher d'observer et comprendre l'intégralité de la vie primitive. C'est ce qu'ont déjà tenté de faire, chacun à sa façon, un Seligman, un Malinowski, un Róheim. C'est ce que feront, il faut l'espérer, leurs continuateurs.

Dans cette investigation qui nous apprend, à la lumière de la vie d'autres hommes, d'une vie aux formes différentes et semblables pourtant, a mieux nous connaître nous-mêmes, la psychanalyse seule peut porter le flambeau dans les plus obscures profondeurs.

HEHE CROSS-COUSIN MARRIAGE [1]

By G. GORDON BROWN

The institution of cross-cousin marriage is of considerable importance in the Hehe social structure. Numerically, it accounts for one-quarter of all marriages, a proportion far in excess of what might be expected from chance,[2] and the attempt to discover the determinants of such marriages involves an examination of some of the most fundamental facts of Hehe social organization.[3]

Of the cross-cousin marriages recorded, about four-fifths are between men and the daughters of their maternal uncles, the remaining fifth between men and the daughters of their paternal aunts. Not all these marriages are between " first " cross-cousins, they include marriages between cousins once or further removed, and even between people who are only classified as cousins, but who are not related by blood at all. It is, nevertheless, possible to treat them as one kind of marriage, because they all show certain characteristics distinguishing cross-cousin marriages from marriages between people not kindred.

This large proportion of marriages between cross-cousins justifies the statement that this is a preferred marriage. It is well, however, to assign a precise meaning to the word " preferred ". In reading accounts of several other tribes, the impression carried away is that cross-cousin marriage is preferred in that every man tries to marry a cross-cousin, and only marries a woman who is not a kinswoman when he fails to get a cross-cousin. This is not the case with the Hehe. The cross-cousin

[1] Grateful acknowledgements are made to the Rockefeller Foundation, through whose generosity two field-expeditions to the Hehe were made possible, and to the International Institute of African Languages and Cultures, who gave additional assistance to the second expedition. Acknowledgments are due to Professor B. Malinowski, Professor A. R. Radcliffe-Brown, and Brenda Z. Seligman. Their writings and teachings have contributed greatly to the present analysis of cross-cousin marriage. It is regretted that absence of an adequate library in the field renders more specific references impossible.

[2] This proportion and the others given below were arrived at by an analysis of about 160 marriages. An analysis of marriages in another area of the tribe gives nearly the same result. It should be added that clan descent is patrilineal.

[3] The Hehe are a Bantu tribe occupying the Iringa district of Iringa Province, Tanganyika Territory. Their numbers are given provisionally as 50,000 to 60,000. Accounts of their social organization have been given by E. Nigmann, *Die Wahehe*, Berlin, 1908 ; by O. Dempwolff, " Beiträge zur Volksbeschreibung der Hehe," *Baessler-Archiv*, Band IV, Heft 3, 1913 ; and by G. Gordon Brown, " Bride-wealth among the Hehe," *Africa*, vol. v, No. 2, 1932, and " Legitimacy and Paternity among the Hehe ", *American Journal of Sociology*, vol. xxxviii, No. 2, September, 1932.

marriage is preferred only in that, proportionate to the possible marriages within the community, more marriages take place between cross-cousins than between people not kindred, or between people related in a different manner. It is the purpose of this paper to show under what circumstances such marriages take place, why they are preferred, and the manner in which they are related to the total social organization.

It is convenient to begin by giving native opinion on the matter. We collected the opinions of many informants; the following text states the native point of view most comprehensively.[1]

A free translation is as follows: "Some people marry their cross-cousins because they realize that they are not of the group with whom marriage is forbidden. A child of an uncle (i.e. a nephew) says, ' I shall go and court my cousin, the child of my uncle, because we are related; they will give her to me, they will not refuse me, if my cousin loves me; my uncle will give her to me out of the kindness of his heart [literally " from a white liver "] because I am the child of his sister.'

" Again, if there is the child of a paternal aunt, the boy goes, he says, ' I shall court my cousin, the child of my aunt, for I am the child of her brother, I know we shall agree well, she, as the girl's mother will not refuse me, for I am as her child, and we are members of the same clan.' Thus the cousins become betrothed.

" Other people think thus: ' Let the children marry cross-cousins, so that the relationship will not be lost, so that it will continue.'

" But there are others who forbid their children to marry cross-cousins, they think it is not good. They say, ' If you marry a cross-cousin the relationship will become lost; for if the children fight they will go to law about it, the girl will get a divorce and leave her husband, who is her cousin. Then the parents will hate each other; the mother of the boy will hate her brother, the father of the girl, and the father of the girl will hate his sister, the mother of the boy. For she will say, " You, you taught your daughter to leave my child," and the father of the girl will say, " And you, you taught him to beat my child." If they quarrel thus they will hate each other and the members of the family will become estranged.'

" Thus some forbid their children to marry a cousin, again others like their children to marry cousins, they believe it to be good."

It is not suggested that a native explanation is always sociologically satisfactory, but I believe that this text, properly

[1] The native text has been omitted for reasons of space, as a complete translation of it is given.

expanded, is an adequate explanation of cross-cousin marriage among the Hehe.

To begin with there is the suggestion of the difficulty of getting a wife; "my uncle will not refuse me", "my aunt will not refuse me." It is an article of Hehe belief that wives are hard to get, and in fact courtship is a difficult matter. There is first the fact, among a polygynous people, that most young girls when they attain maturity have many men seeking to marry them; the competition is always keen. Secondly, young girls quickly appreciate their position and become difficult, Finally, a suitor is generally opposed by the bulk of the girl's family, and even when it is decided to accept the suitor ceremonial opposition and delays continue. Of all three factors making marriage difficult, the real and ceremonial opposition of the family is the most important and deserves more detailed examination.

When a man decides he wants to marry a certain girl, he must first get her consent.[1] This is sometimes easily obtained, but oftener than not it takes some time and trouble. This gained, his troubles only begin. He must next win over the parents, first the mother, then the father. This is done both informally and ceremonially. Informally he tries to break down the real opposition of the parents; ceremonially he must send an intermediary with a hoe, who pays court for him in stereotyped phrases, and who is ceremonially refused, until, and if, the real opposition subsides. The suitor must also break down other opposition. A grandparent of the girl, an elder sister or brother, even possibly an uncle or aunt, may be exerting influence where they have no authority. In brief, the presumption is always against the suitor who offers himself, and while some suits meet with only ceremonial opposition, many must overcome real obstacles. Courtship is considered so hazardous by the men that there are special medicines to aid it. These medicines are not love philtres; they are, it is true, given to the girl herself, without her knowledge, but the aim of them is to overcome the complex obstacles that confront every courtship. The high price paid for them is an index of their felt need. Ordinary courtship-medicine costs a bull; a particularly powerful medicine of which we know costs a cow and a bull; and the user must also commit incest with a sister to make it efficacious.

The formal and ceremonial obstacles to marriage are nearly as bad as the real and personal ones. The intermediary who carries the hoe is returned time after time over a period of at

[1] Before European occupation, our informants tell us, the consent of the girl was not needed, her father disposed of her as he would. There is no way of checking this statement by observed fact. It seems at least probable that the girl had less freedom of choice than now.

least a month, occasionally for several months. When the girl's parents decide to give way the intermediary is told to come on a certain day, when the betrothal ceremony is to be held. The suitor sends a party of intermediaries, three or four people. They come as suppliants. They are asked their business, and the genealogy and character of the suitor are discussed frankly. Any cause of quarrel between the family of the suitor and that of the girl must be settled ; the girl's male relatives sit in judgment and any compensation for injury must be paid by the suitor's family. This part of the ceremony is not mere formality. We have never seen a suitor rejected at this stage. But at one betrothal he was judged to have failed in courtesy and was at first refused ; the party broke up, and it was only reassembled because the father of the girl feared the censure of the neighbourhood. After these affairs are threshed out, the girl picks up the hoe as the sign of consent to the betrothal, bride-wealth (*mafungu*) is stated, and the rejoicing begins. *Kulumba* is " to agree upon the *mafungu* " ; *valumbite*, " they have settled the bride-wealth," implies that the first formal stage towards marriage has been passed.

After the betrothal the suitor has certain rights over the girl ; he can, for example, exact compensation for adultery if anyone lies with her ; but he is not yet married, and he is still in the position of a suppliant. At the marriage ceremony (*luwungo*) his family must again submit to judgment upon their misdeeds to the bride's family. If the *mafungu* has not all been collected, his intermediaries must beg for terms. Various small payments must be made to the mother, to the father, and to the bride her-self. He knows no peace until the father finally consents to let the girl go away, although there have been rejoicings for several hours. His final position as husband is gained with great difficulty and only after repeated supplications.

These obstacles to marriage are obviously not intended to make marriage impossible. At the same time they are not empty ceremonial. They are personal and social expressions of a real reluctance to part with a member of the family, and are specifically directed to the person who is actually taking the daughter away. Of course, the daughter is not taken away absolutely or for ever. She does not cease to be a member of her own family ; she frequently visits her parents ; she is still addressed by the name of her clan ; and she can always in emergency receive help and shelter from her father or brother. At the same time, she leaves the home ; her society, her economic services, her obedience, are now due to her husband. In a limited but very real sense she passes into the possession of a stranger ; and the family, although they must eventually give way to one man or another, resist her loss. Hehe marriage is, therefore, a socially

regulated act of hostility,[1] and many of the real and imagined
difficulties of getting a wife arise from that fact.

In about three-quarters of Hehe marriages, these difficulties
are overcome, and marriage takes place between people not
related by kinship, or related so distantly that the kinship bond
is of little importance. The other quarter comprises marriages
between cross-cousins ; as our text shows, in such marriages the
man reckons on the support of at least one parent of the child, a
maternal uncle or a paternal aunt. Why these particular relatives
are chosen requires a partial account of Hehe kinship.

The Hehe enter into effective relationship with a large circle
of kindred, but we are here concerned with only a comparatively
small group. This group includes a man's parents, his father's
brothers and sisters, and his mother's brothers and sisters, in
the ascendant generation, and, in his own generation, the children
of all these people. It will be noted later that cross-cousin
marriage sometimes means marriage between people somewhat
distantly related, for example, between what we should call
second or even more distant cousins. But the nature of cross-
cousin marriage is determined by the relationships existing
within the more limited group. Hence an analysis of these
relationships will serve the present purpose.

A Hehe man grows up knowing, and recognizing as members
of his close kindred, a group of girls and women any one of whom
he refers to and addresses as *muhatsa vangu*, "my sister". They
refer to and address him by the same term. These women are,
first and closest, the daughters of his father (*dada*) and mother
(*yuva*) [2] ; these are pre-eminently his *vahatsa*. The members of
the next group consist of the daughters of his father, but of a
different mother ; they are nearly, but not quite, as close to him
as the daughters of his own mother. The next members of the
group consist of what we should call his female first cousins, and
they divide into four sub-groups. There are the daughters of his
father's brothers (he addresses each of these men as *dada*,
"my father"). All of this group he will know well, unless his own
father has moved far from his original home ; and even then he
will probably have visited them. The Hehe reckon descent
patrilineally, so that these women bear his own clan-name, and his
own praise-name, and avoid eating the same animal.[3] Equally
close to him, in fact, though there is not the bond of a common

---

[1] Acknowledgments are due to Professor Radcliffe-Brown for the development of this point of view.
[2] The term *dada* undergoes certain changes ; thus *dada* is "my father",
udado "your father", *udade* "his father", *udadetu* "our father", *udadenyu*
"your (pl.) father", *udadawo* "their father". *Yuva* "my mother", *yaya*
"my maternal uncle", and *yuva hengi* "my paternal aunt" are treated
similarly. For the sake of convenience I have used the simplest forms throughout.
[3] Cf. G. G. Brown, "Paternity and Legitimacy among the Hehe," *Amer.
Journ. Sociol.* September, 1932, pp. 187–8.

clan, are the daughters of his mother's sisters (whom he also calls *yuva*, " my mother "). These he will also know well; his mother will often visit her mother, will meet her sisters there, with their children; and the child himself will frequently stay with his maternal grandmother for months at a time, playing with his mother's sisters' children, who are also visiting her, as though they were his own brothers and sisters. Similarly, at the residence of his grandmother, he will meet the children of his maternal uncle, *yaya*, and in childhood and in early youth will refer to and address the girls as *muhatsa vangu*. The children of his paternal aunt, *yuvahengi*, he may or may not know well, according to circumstances ; she may have married a distance away, and between her children and himself there is not the bond of a common clan, nor of common childhood memories ; but he will have paid her, at least, visits of ceremony, and her daughters will also be *vahatsa*. Besides these closer relatives there will be women of the same generation whom he must also recognize as *vahatsa* ; members of his clan, descendants from a common great-grand-parent ; and people related to him only by marriage. But the bond implied by the term *muhatsa* wears very thin with distance of kinship, and it is his sisters and his first cousins of whom he thinks primarily when he uses the term *muhatsa vangu*.

The bond implied by the term *muhatsa* is thus one of close kinship between members of the opposite sex, close intimacy, an attitude of protection as man and woman grow older. The mutual obligations are primarily obligations of full brother and sister, but they are extended to first cousins. The bond between those calling each other *muhatsa* creates another relationship, that eventually divides the first cousins into two groups. At a comparatively early age the incest bar colours the relationship of the boy to some of his *vahatsa*.

Practically all children indulge in sexual play, probably from the age of eight or nine years old, but by that time both boys and girls have learned that there are some members of the opposite sex with whom such play is forbidden. It is *mwiko* (forbidden, with the suggestion of an undefined supernatural punishment) to commit any act, or say any word that has a sugges-tion of sexual significance about it. Certain persons are *vakwi* (for-bidden sexually), and the boy must quickly learn who they are, not only to avoid the supernatural curse, but to avoid the much more real parental punishment. Of his *vahatsa* he learns that some are *vakwi*, others are not. And it soon comes to him that the *vahatsa* who are *vakwi* are really and always his *vahatsa* ; those *vahatsa* who are not *vakwi* may also be referred to as *vahitsi* (sing. *muhitsi*). Thus the distinction is gradually made, that his father's and his father's brothers' daughters, members of his own clan, are *vakwi* (forbidden sexually), and also his mother's sisters' daughters.

On the other hand his mother's brothers' daughters and his father's sisters' daughters are not *vakwi* ; he may indulge in sexual play and sexual badinage with them.

It has been necessary to show these differences in detail because of the two important implications of the term *muhatsa*. Primarily, it connotes close kinship between members of the opposite sex and of the same generation ; secondarily, it signifies the existence of the incest bar. In its first meaning, it is used as a term of affectionate reference and address to all women who are kindred as described ; in its second meaning, it is applied only to actual sisters and parallel cousins. Thus in referring to, but not addressing, a female cross-cousin, a Hehe man will use the term *muhitsi vangu*, when the occasion demands exact definition.[1]

These observations on the use of the two terms are generalizations of a host of complex social activities and do not give the full truth. The Hehe domestic groups live under such a variety of conditions that any generalization is a falsification of many individual cases ; for example, in some families the difference between *muhatsa* and *muhitsi* as terms of reference is made from the beginning, but in general the foregoing observations are true.

It is thus clear that a Hehe man seeking a wife *may* marry a woman within the close circle of kinship. As a boy he may have played sexual games with her ; as a youth he may have had an intrigue with her ; in his early maturity the existence of intimate personal bonds may have ripened into a mutual desire for marriage. Indeed, it is in many cases just this reason and no other that causes cross-cousin marriage. Attraction is based upon long-standing acquaintance ; cross-cousin marriage is the first marriage sought by both parties, and no further explanation is needed.

But this does not account for a large number of cross-cousin marriages. And it is these other marriages that cause cross-cousin marriages to be " preferred " in the sense described. A youth receives several rebuffs in seeking a wife He cannot gain the affection of a girl ; if he gets that far he may not overcome the opposition of parents or other relatives ; marriage-medicines, if used, fail. In discouragement, sometimes at the invitation of the maternal uncle or the paternal aunt, he courts the daughter ; the way is made easy for him, and he at last gets a wife.

As already noted, four-fifths of cross-cousin marriages are between men and their maternal uncles' daughters. This may be regarded as the typical Hehe cross-cousin marriage. The question thus arises, What are the particular determining factors ? The negative one, the absence of an incest bar, has already been dealt with. A positive one, the presence of a sympathetic parent

---

[1] *Muhitsi* is also applied to a male cross-cousin.

in place of a hostile one, has been mentioned. Beyond all this, there is something in the nature of the relationship between a man and his maternal uncle that adds a further factor.

Our text says, " my uncle will give her to me out of the kindness of his heart, because I am the son of his sister." The maternal uncle is thus expected to show particular kindness to his sister's son. This attitude grows from the elementary family circle. When young, brother and sister live in the closest intimacy, only one field of interest, that of sex, being barred. When the woman grows up and marries, she still looks to her own family for ultimate protection. First, she depends upon her father ; when he becomes aged or dies his son, her brother, becomes head of the family, assuming all property and legal obligations to his sister. These obligations to a sister often involve considerable expenditure of time and money. If a woman leaves her husband, she goes to her brother for protection, and may live for months in his household. If she gets a divorce, her brother must repay the bride-wealth (*mafungu*) received from her husband on her marriage. If she gets into a legal dispute, the brother supports her in court. In short, he assumes all obligations to protect and support her, and thus to the child, at such times, the mother's brother is head of the family.

There is a difference between a man's attitude to his father and his father's brothers on the one hand, and to his maternal uncle on the other hand, and it is based upon the difference between the functions of the two sexes. In a patrilineal tribe like the Hehe, the father and his family represent authority. There is usually tenderness as well, but fundamentally the father gives the child his social position, and generally directs his activities to a great degree before maturity, to a less degree afterwards. The mother represents tenderness and protection. She has no direct authority over the child after his earlier years (though she has very great influence), but he turns to her and in a less degree to her sisters (whom he also calls *yuva*, " my mother ") when paternal pressure becomes too hard, or when in disagreement with his father. The mother's brother, the maternal uncle, represents thus two things. First, he is a man of the ascendant generation, and according to Hehe standards entitled to great respect ; and secondly, he is a member of the mother's line, and therefore fundamentally represents protection. As a male, the maternal uncle gets respect ; but since he has no authority over the child the Hehe solve the problem by making this respect very ceremonious ; a host of minor polite observances are due the maternal uncle. In the general run of Hehe life this anomalous position, and the ceremony surrounding the relationship of uncle (*yaya*) to nephew (*mwipwa*), prevent any direct interference with the actions of the nephew. But in an emergency the uncle may be appealed to by the nephew, or may intervene, unasked, on the nephew's behalf. Such emergencies are rare, and will not occur in the life of everybody, but we have recorded several. One case was that of a young boy, who was living with his father, and who received harsh treatment from his stepmother, his own mother being divorced. He ran away from his father, and went to the home of his maternal uncle. The uncle not only sheltered him, but supported him during the legal disputes that followed. In another case a woman was beaten to death by her husband. Her horrified relatives immediately took her children away, and they were brought up in the household of their mother's brother. Thus the maternal uncle, as head of the mother's family, can, and does, intervene on behalf of his sister's children, overriding paternal authority in cases of emergency.

Such an emergency arises when a man reaches the age of marriage and is unable to find a wife. His father's brothers cannot help him, because their daughters belong to his own clan, and it is not their specific function. His maternal uncle can, and often will help him. Hence the appeal to the maternal uncle, or his voluntary intervention when he sees his nephew's plight, is a very frequent solution of the marriage difficulty.

With the paternal aunt (*yuvahengi*) the relationship is somewhat different. She is a female of the paternal line ; that is, she is a person without authority herself, but belongs to the authority-owning group. The result is much the same in formal observance as with the maternal uncle ; she is treated with ceremonious respect, to an even greater degree than the uncle. At the same time, she maintains a very great interest in her brothers' children. She is among the first to visit them ceremonially after birth, and she expects them to visit her when she is ill. When they become mature she may render them various services. In one case, for example, a paternal aunt undertook all the exacting business of negotiating a marriage, and arranging all the ceremonial courtship. But, generally speaking, she has not the same rights of intervention that a maternal uncle has. An appeal to her is, therefore, based somewhat differently ; she is appealed to as a close relative, and as possessing the additional bond of membership in the same clan. According to Hehe kinship-values these grounds are, on the whole, weaker than those upon which the appeal to the uncle is based. Moreover, she has not a man's authority over her daughter ; however strong her influence, her husband has the final word in the disposal of their daughter, and he may have nephews of his own whom he wishes to favour. Thus the marriage of a man with the daughter of his father's sister only occurs one-quarter as often as that of a man with the daughter of his mother's brother.

Up till now there has been no discussion as to what particular kind of maternal uncle or paternal aunt is appealed to. Obviously, when one's mother has so many men she calls *muhatsa*, the child knows many men as *yaya*. It has been noted that the relationship between a man and his maternal uncle grows out of the original family group; the brother is the protector of his sister. When a woman's father dies, the man she looks to first for protection is her full brother, son of her own father and mother, and if there are more than one, she looks to the eldest. The mother's eldest brother is thus the primary *yaya*. But younger full brothers must equally lend their support, though the first appeal is made to the elder brother; they are thus *vayaya* to the same degree without the same onus of responsibility. But an examination of marriages into the family of the maternal uncle show that nearly half involve maternal uncles more distantly related; mother's half-brothers, mother's parallel cousins, and even in a few cases men who are only maternal uncles by classification, not by blood. An example of the latter is that of a man who married a daughter of a brother of his mother's co-wife. He called the co-wife " mother " (*yuva*) but she was not related to him by blood; he called the woman's brother *yaya*, an extreme extension of the term. When describing his relation to his wife he said she was " like a cross-cousin " (*ndauli muhitsi vangu*).

Excluding this last case for the moment, it is seen that the appeal for a wife may be made to varying degrees of kin. Although the functions of maternal uncle are assumed in their entirety only by full brothers of one's mother, yet the extension of the term indicates an extension of the function, though the obligations are less in accordance with the remoteness of the kinship bond. Thus, an appeal to any person called *yaya* has some chance of success simply because all male members of one's mother's family in her generation assume to some degree the right to intervene or the obligation to respond to a request. In the same way, a paternal aunt who is not the full sister of a father may be induced to assist a man she calls " nephew " (*mwipwa*).

So far, two motives for cross-cousin marriage have been discussed; reciprocal affection between the cousins themselves, based upon long acquaintance; and the avoidance of all the conflict involved in marriage into a strange family. Our text next indicates another motive; the deliberate arrangement of a marriage between cross-cousins so that the relationship shall not be lost. This requires expansion to be intelligible.

Mention has already been made of some differences in the relationship of a man to his father's family and to his mother's family. Other differences now need to be added. A man is as much attached to his mother's family as to his father's, often even more attached. But at the same time his relationships to his father's family are more widespread than to the family of his mother. For membership in his father's family also implies membership in his father's clan. Clan membership is never lost, at least in Hehe theory. All direct patrilineal descendants of one male ancestor in the remote past constitute a group ; a group, it is true, of unknown extent, but still a group a member of which enjoys certain rights of and assumes certain obligations towards all other members of the group. Relationship to the father's family thus continues infinitely. On the other hand, one's relationship to one's mother's family is a matter of two generations only, or three at most ; at the same time it is something precious, and marriage into the mother's family will reaffirm the bond for another generation at least.

Looking at the matter from the point of view of the uncle, similar motives are in play. The children of his sister belong to another clan ; his sister is his closest relative ; and to her children he has a peculiar but intimate relationship. If they marry strangers the bond will become diluted in another generation. The arrangement of a marriage will reaffirm that bond. That this motive is sometimes strong may be shown by several family histories ; cross-cousin marriage has persisted for two or three generations, a son of each cross-cousin marriage marrying back into his mother's family. It may schematically be represented thus :—

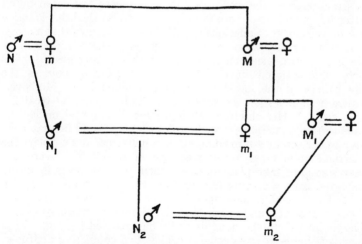

m and M, sister and brother, each marry ; m has a son, taking his father's clan name N_1 ; M has a daughter and a son, m_1 and M_1. N_1 marries his cross-cousin m_1. Of this marriage a son is born taking his father's name N_2. M_1 has a daughter m_2. N_2 marries m_2, his cross-cousin. In each case the marriage reaffirms the bond with the mother's family *m*, and the relationship continues.

Paradoxically, but quite comprehensibly, the value attached to the relationship to the mother's family is shown by a refusal to marry into it. Our text summarizes the danger so well that little need be added. Marriage is a risk, and if a marriage results in conflict both groups of parents are drawn into the quarrel with estrangement resulting. By some people, therefore, the bond is valued too much to be risked ; the relationship may die out in the future, but a very valued relationship exists in the present, and the following generations may look after themselves.

Some of the details of cross-cousin marriage throw light upon its nature. These have been touched upon in a previous paper.[1] First, the *mafungu* (bride-wealth) is less. Ordinarily a man transfers 2 cows, 1 bull, 20 shillings, 2 sheep or goats, and 3 hoes to his wife's family. In cross-cousin marriage, this is reduced ; 1 cow and 1 bull, 8 or 10 shillings, 2 sheep, and 3 hoes are generally demanded ; often even less. The reason lies in the fact that the *mafungu* is exacted to bind the marriage ; the greater the *mafungu*, the greater the bond. But in cross-cousin marriage a bond already exists ; therefore less property need be transferred to make the marriage endure.

The other important difference is that the groom must bring to the wedding a special ox, which is not part of the *mafungu* but is slaughtered at the wedding, cut up in pieces and eaten by all attending members of both families. This ox is called the *ndumula lukolo* (the cutter of relationship). It has been shown that a cross-cousin is in many ways treated as a sister ; she is addressed by the same term, she belongs to the intimate family group, she is only differentiated in the eyes of the growing boy as the importance of the incest bar is pressed upon him. Moreover, unless he marries her, he continues to address her and treat her as a sister. Her children call him *yaya*, " maternal uncle," he calls the child *mwipwa*, " nephew " or " niece," and he may even give to her son one of his daughters in marriage, and consider the marriage as a cross-cousin marriage in turn. Moreover, if a marriage does take place between their children he is in future debarred from marrying her, or from committing adultery with her. His daughters look upon her, and address her as *yuvahengi* " paternal aunt," and in addition she becomes " mother-in-law " (*mukwi vangu*) to the daughter who has married her son. Thus marriage between cross-cousins evokes two conflicting attitudes. On the one hand it is considered desirable, for the variety of reasons shown. On the other hand the relationship so resembles that between brother and sister that there is at least a suggestion of incest in such a union. Therefore the relationship must be

[1] G. Gordon Brown, " Bride-wealth among the Hehe," *Africa*, vol. v, No. 2.

ceremonially " cut ", or severed. This is done by the deliberate slaughter and consumption of an ox devoted to that purpose.

It remains to describe the relationship that exists between a man and his maternal uncle when that maternal uncle becomes also his father-in-law. In speech both terms *yaya* " uncle " and *mukwi vangu* " my father-in-law " may be used to refer to him, ordinarily he will be addressed as *yaya*. In action the ceremonious respect must merely be increased. The problem, in fact, is not difficult. Both to an uncle and to a father-in-law ceremonious respect is due ; to the father-in-law rather more than to the uncle ; thus to treat the latter as a father-in-law also fulfils one's social obligations of respect to an uncle. Without going into detail, the same is true of a paternal aunt who has become one's mother-in-law.

To summarize, Hehe cross-cousin marriage is based upon two related facts in Hehe social organization ; upon the value set upon kinship bonds, and the potential hostility to those not so related. Fundamentally it arises from the close relationship between brother and sister. This relationship has its effect upon the attitude of each one towards the other's children. The man extends his protective attitude towards his sister to her children, and when the hostility of other kinship groups cannot be overcome, and the nephew cannot get a wife, he intervenes on his nephew's behalf and offers his own daughters. The deliberate arrangement of marriage so that the relationship may continue is merely another manifestation of the same close bond between brother and sister ; her children belong to the family and clan of a stranger, and his family and hers will drift apart in the course of time unless it is reunited. The marriage of their children will be such a reunion. These motives exemplify the strength of Hehe kinship and the value set upon it. Kinship is not the only social bond, but it is the one they value most, and upon which they most depend in the ordinary course of life and its emergencies. Other bonds may be set aside or disregarded, but to the Hehe certain fundamental kinship obligations are unalterable and only close with death.

MODERN SURVIVALS OF THE SUMERIAN
CHATELAINE

By Louis C. G. Clarke

The discovery by Mr. Woolley at Ur of a gold chatelaine consisting of tweezers, apparently for depilation, an ear-pick, and a pointed instrument, probably a toothpick, with a case in which they were kept (Fig. 1), puts back the known date of the invention of this combination of implements by at least 2,000 years. Hitherto none were known of a date earlier than the Hallstatt period.

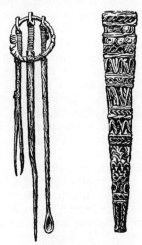

Fig. 1.—Ur.

In *Antiquity*, vol. v, 1931, fig. 15, 337, a similar chatelaine in copper from Susa is published in R. de Mecquenem's paper on " Excavations at Susa in 1930 ". This set also has a case. These two specimens of chatelaines on rings are the only two I know of any date which have cases ; individual items are found in a case, or étui, but not when they are held together by a ring. The type must have originated in Mesopotamia, as it is unknown in Egypt, where ear-picks do not appear until Roman times, although tweezers are found amongst the earliest metal objects, occurring in early tombs of Abydos, El Amrah, etc. (see J. de Morgan, *Récherches sur les origines de l'Égypte*, Paris, 1896, p. 200 and fig. 534). It is highly improbable that the combination should have been invented more than once and we can safely presume that all such chatelaines are derived from the Mesopotamian prototype.

I cannot find any specimens of these groups in Europe until the Early Iron Age, although tweezers alone, usually of bronze but occasionally of gold, are known from many districts. There are tweezers from Mycenæ, and Mr. Wace tells me that he has found them at Kalkani with a burial dating between the fifteenth and twelth centuries B.C. Déchelette, in his monumental work *Manuel d'archéologie préhistorique celtique et gallo-romaine*, vol. ii, pt. i, " The Bronze Age," pp. 340–1 and fig. 136, says that they are found among the grave-furniture of both sexes in tumuli in Bavaria and Bohemia, that they are found in the Lake Dwellings of Switzerland, and that as early as Bronze Age II they spread from Southern Europe to Scandinavia.

According to Déchelette it was during the Hallstatt II period that " une petite trousse composée ordinairement d'une pince, d'un cure-oreilles et d'un grattoir passés dans un anneau " appeared in Central Europe (Déchelette, loc. cit., vol. ii, pt. 2, 880 and fig. 370). He figures specimens of simple form from Bavaria, Bohemia, and Hallstatt itself, and more ornate sets from the Jura and from Northern Italy. In the latter district they were apparently not uncommon ; several are figured by Randall MacIver, *The Iron Age in Italy*. One bronze set hung from a bronze fibula of late leech type studded with coral, from Palestro, and another of gold and silver, from Rebbio, he assigns to the late Comacine period, about sixth–fourth centuries B.C. He figures also a single ear-pick with elaborately modelled head and a forked object with head in the form of a female figure, from a cemetery of the eighth–sixth centuries at Novilara. The little forked object, probably a toothpick, which Déchelette calls a " grattoir ", is, I think, the prototype of the implement which I call a sickle-shaped object and which I believe to have made its first appearance in Roman times.

In his vol. ii, pt. 3, 1271–4, Déchelette says that the use of the " pincette à épiler et des instruments de toilette en bronze ou en fer, séparés ou réunis en trousse, subsiste à l'époque de la Tène (figs. 547–8) ; toutefois, les trousses que nous connaissons ne se composent ordinairement que de deux ustensiles, la pincette et le grattoir. La curette auriculaire est rare ". He figures, however, a fine set with all three implements, from Aussonce, Ardennes (fig. 548, no. 1).

In Roman times they were very common, and some elaborately ornamented ones are found in Britain, such as the enamelled specimens in the Canterbury Museum.[1] I have fragmentary ones from London in my own collection. It was during Roman times

---

[1] I am indebted to Mlle. Henry for drawing my attention to these.

apparently that various other combinations arose, such as a single implement with tweezers at one end and an ear-pick at the other ; and now appeared for the first time a new implement with a sickle-shaped blade which was perhaps also a toothpick. I have a fine bronze one found in London with this curved blade at one end and an ear-pick at the other (Fig. 2). This sickle-shaped addition seems to have spread early to the East, as it appears in a very fine combination implement in bronze, believed to be of Tang date (Fig. 3). It is still to be found in the East ; I have a fine long silver chatelaine set with turquoise and coral, from the Lepchas on the Tibetan borders, in which this implement appears

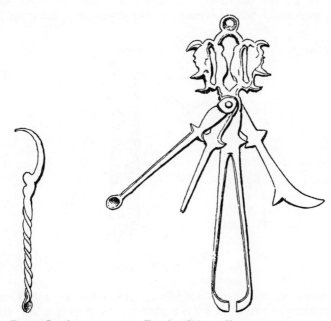

FIG. 2.—Roman London.   FIG. 3.—China : Tang dynasty.

together with the ordinary pointed toothpick, tweezers, an ear-pick, and a small brush. This type, I believe, is found in Kazzan graves of ninth century A.D.

The use of the chatelaine in Asia is very common. A specimen which Mr. Oscar Raphael bought from a Huwaitat Arab of Hejaz Kingdom (Fig. 4), and gave me, is very similar to the one found at Ur. In India the ear-picks and tweezers are very common, and they were in common use in China and Korea from at least as early as Tang times. A common form at that period was the combined ear-pick at one end and tweezers at the other such as we have already seen were in use in Roman times. Sometimes the ear-pick folded into the tweezers ; this type appears also in the Eastern Roman Empire. If nowadays the typical variety hanging on a ring has been superseded to a large extent in China by a form of chatelaine with various implements hanging from chains, the original type lingers in Korea ; Professor Seligman brought me back from Seoul a chatelaine degenerate from the type, having two ear-picks and two small hanging ornaments at the sides, doubtless the remains of toothpick and tweezers. Ear-picks frequently occur on the top of hairpins in China and Japan, and I have elaborate ones from each country.

In Africa, except in Roman times, the toilet implements are rare except in Abyssinia, where a silver or brass ear-pick, occasionally with tweezers, is frequently seen hanging on the

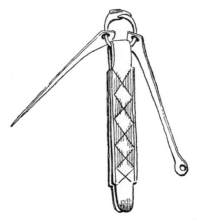

FIG. 4.—Arab.

chests of the men. Sometimes iron tweezers and a pointed implement are worn by the poorer class of people and are used to extract thorns from the feet. There is in the Museum für Völkerkunde at Hamburg a set of implements including the sickle-shaped toothpick and an earpick from the Pangwe tribe in the Cameroons. This is probably a late introduction from European or Arab culture.[1]

In America, tweezers are found in Mexico and Peru. In the latter country they are generally shaped like a small bivalve, and are frequently ornamented with an animal on top. From Peru alone I have seen ear-picks, and these are the most elaborate and beautiful that I know. They are made of gold, silver, or copper. The tops are fashioned with animals, birds, or human

[1] I am indebted to Baron B. von Richthofen for information about this set.

beings, of exquisite workmanship. Fig. 5 shows two specimens from Cuzco and Nasca. They appear to be chiefly of Inca date. Bingham found them at Machu Picchu—an entirely Inca site ; he had apparently never seen any before, as in his article " The Story of Machu Picchu ", in *The National Geographic Magazine*, February, 1915, he illustrates two and says, " They were probably intended for use in supplying the small quantity of lime needed in connection with chewing coca leaves." An interesting point about these Peruvian ear-picks is that they always have a minute perforation at the top for suspension, as have the tweezers, so they were probably worn round the neck as the Abyssinians wear them to this day ; but until scientific excavation has been done in cemeteries of the Inca period we cannot be sure of this. In any case, although the Peruvian copper tweezers might have

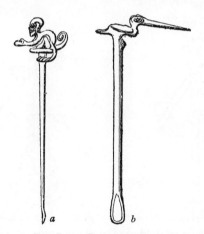

FIG. 5.—*a*, Cuzco ; *b*, Nasca.

been derived locally from bivalves, it is difficult to believe that the ear-picks could be other than an introduction from the Old World.

The use of the chatelaine with its usual trinity of objects was continued into post-Roman times. They are found in Merovingian (Déchelette, vol. ii, pt. 3, fig. 549) and Anglo-Saxon graves. The Museum of Archæology and Ethnology at Cambridge contains several Anglo-Saxon sets, but these usually include only two of the three implements. Three graves from the cemeteries at Barrington, Cambs., contained sets of a bronze ear-pick and two toothpicks hung on an adjustable ring ; a group from Burwell, Cambs., consists of two toothpicks and an ear-pick with perforated bowl, all of silver ; at Girton, Cambs., three sets each consisting of an ear-pick and a pair of tweezers were found in urns, and a similar set came from an urn in the cemetery in St. John's College cricket field, Cambridge ; all these probably belong to the sixth century A.D.

After the Dark Ages the combination is rare, but I have silver ear-picks of late sixteenth- or early seventeenth-century date, two of which have oblong slits in the stem and were perhaps used as bodkins as well as ear-picks. I have a very fine French gold set attached to a pink enamelled heart, with the sickle-shaped and pointed toothpicks and an ear-pick without tweezers (Fig.6), of seventeenth-century date ; perhaps the use of the latter had died out in polite society owing to the custom of depilation being no longer practised. The use of small ear-picks and tweezers combined, as found in the Roman Empire, in China, and in Korea, was common in the eighteenth century, and most étuis of the period contain them. I have even a twentieth-century one bought in London just before the War.

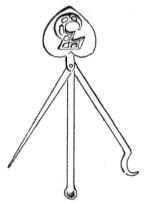 

FIG. 6.—French: Seventeenth Century.   FIG. 7.—Dutch: Eighteenth century.

I have also a small gold case of about the year 1800 containing a small gold ear-pick with the other end pointed evidently for use as a toothpick. A gold toothpick in a very similar case, which belonged to Charles I when he was Prince of Wales, was sold in London for a large sum some time before the War.

It was not only in the East that ear-picks appeared on the tops of pins for the hair, as I have a charming Dutch silver one—probably used for keeping a cap on the head.

It was apparently in Holland in the eighteenth century that a remarkable development occurred in the use of these sets. Fig. 7 shows a silver folding set with an ear-pick and a toothpick closing up like the blades of a pocket-knife, with a seal with a coat of arms hinged on below. Fig. 8 has still an ear-pick, a pointed toothpick, and a very debased form of the sickle-shaped toothpick, but has as well a stop for pushing down the tobacco in the pipe and a hook-shaped implement for cleaning out the pipe ; the

seal with coat of arms remains. In a perfectly modern implement
(Fig. 9) may be seen the remains of the chatelaine ; the ear-pick's
bowl has been enlarged into a sharp-sided spoon for scraping out the
pipe—the pointed toothpick blunted at the tip for pushing down into
the stem of the pipe, and the stop as in the Dutch silver specimen.

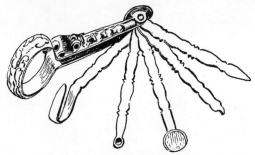

Fig. 8.—Dutch : Eighteenth century.

The combination of tweezers and pipe-cleaners is found
amongst the Lamuts in Kamchatka. Dr. Bergman says : " Every
pipe has a cleaner, which usually hangs on to the tobacco-pouch by
a strap. This is often inlaid with copper and, like the pipe, made
by the Lamuts themselves. Side by side with this pipe-cleaner
is often attached to the men's tobacco-pouch a little pincer-like

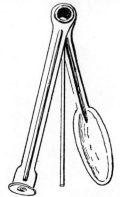

Fig. 9.—Austria : Twentieth century.

apparatus, which also is inlaid. This is used with which to pull out
hairs " (*Through Kamchatka by Dog-Sled and Skis*, Bergman, 1927).
Since writing the above I have received; through the kindness
of Dr. T. J. Arne, of Stockholm, a beautiful modern silver chatelaine,
elaborately chased and set with turquoises, from Yazd, in Persia ; it
includes tweezers, earpick, toothpick, and two implements of
uncertain use.

ZANDE THERAPEUTICS

By E. E. EVANS-PRITCHARD

The Azande attribute sickness and misfortune, whatever may be its nature, to witchcraft and sorcery. This does not mean that they entirely disregard secondary causes but, in so far as they recognize these, they generally think of them as associated with witchcraft and magic. Nor does their reference of sickness to supernatural causes lead them to neglect treatment of symptoms. On the contrary they possess an enormous pharmacopœia, and in ordinary circumstances they trust to drugs to cure their ailments and only take steps to remove the primary and supernatural causes when the disease is of a serious nature or takes an alarming turn. Nevertheless, we must remember in describing the Zande classification of diseases and their treatment that witchcraft may always be a participant in their origin, and that if the Azande do not always and immediately consult their oracles to find out the witch that is responsible, it is because they consider the sickness to be of a minor character and not worth the trouble and expense of oracle-consultations. I have elsewhere [1] described what they do to frustrate the action of witchcraft, and in serious illness the Azande undoubtedly regard this as the main objective. The character of the disease is closely bound up with notions of etiology and treatment. Whether they have any correct conception of the physiology of man and the effect of their drugs on the organism or whether they think that they somehow react on the supernatural agencies which cause sickness, is a question which we may leave open at present, but I have no hesitation in saying at the outset that their notions of physiology are very hazy, that their drugs almost entirely lack therapeutic value, and that their ideas about disease, its cause and cure, are usually without any foundation. It would be very surprising if this were otherwise.

Azande know diseases by their major symptoms. Hence when symptoms develop they are able to diagnose them as a certain disease and to tell you its name. An analysis of Father De Graer's list of Zande diseases with their etymological derivations shows us that they may be roughly classified under the following headings [2] :—

(1) Diseases named simply after the part affected.

---

[1] " Witchcraft (*mangu*) among the Azande," *Sudan Notes and Records*, 1929.
[2] R.P.A. M. De Graer, " L'art de guérir chez les Azande," *Congo*, 1929, pp. 220–254 and 361–408. All numbers in parentheses refer to his account.

(2) Diseases named after the sensations they produce or their effects on the organism.

(3) Diseases named after something in nature to which they bear a resemblance.

(4) Diseases named after their causes.

(5) Diseases named after their cures.

On the whole the purely homeopathic character of much of Zande treatment is evident at a glance. It is manifest that abstention from a certain fish on the part of pregnant mothers will not prevent convulsions in their infants ; that ashes of the burnt skull of a red bush monkey will not cure epilepsy ; and that ulcers will not heal by the sick man drinking powdered tooth of crocodile in water. In the same way it is no remedy for bronchitis " to reduce to cinders a dog's tongue or the roots of *bakazagbwate* and to eat them without touching them with the hand. They are placed on a woman's stool called ' *bata* ' and thus licked by the sick person " (244). If massage is of value in treating a small child suffering from *denge*, swelling of the sides of the thorax, it is surely a useless injunction which says that the masseur must be a homicide or a mother of twins (243). The cure for elephantiasis of the scrotum is an application to the scrotum of the pulp of the fruit of the sausage tree, or eating a plant called *sungbwa* cooked with termites called *amatindi*. One may presume that the fruit of the sausage tree and the mound home of the *amatindi* termites bear a resemblance in Zande eyes to elephantiasis of the scrotum. I was told that the best treatment for epilepsy was to pour some liquid drug under the patient's finger-nails. For a malady of the eyelids the Azande know no other remedy than to bend over the mound of the tomb and lightly rub the sick eyelid on the earth (253). Indeed some of the diseases as well as their cures seem fictitious. Thus *hima ngorongba* is a sickness which can have no real existence. The *ngorongba* or the *paka*, as it is also called, is a small pimple hidden " aux endroits pilifères du corps " of a man or of a woman and visible only to specialists. The presence of this pimple in either parent causes the death of their child when it has reached one or two years of age. Thus all their children will die in succession if the pimple has not been removed. The parents are conducted by members of the family on to a stony outcrop on which they lie down completely naked, and while the leech looks for the pimples in their hairs, members of the family make a great clamour and hurl the most abusive expressions at the heads of the father and mother. The procedure is supposed to facilitate the work of the leech by making the pimples more visible. Once located they are removed from the skin by a knife (249–250).

In view of Father De Graer's painstaking study of Zande nomenclature of disease and of their therapeutic practices—he lists almost a hundred different maladies and between three hundred and four hundred drugs—it is the more surprising to my mind that he can put any faith in the therapeutic value of Zande drugs (220, 226, 227). His faith would appear to rest on the assumption that Azande would hardly have continued to use drugs for centuries if they possessed no curative values, a faith which is unhappily contradicted by the history of European medicine and by the history of magic everywhere and at all times. The enormous number of drugs which the Azande employ and the complete repertoire of herbal products they bring to bear on a single disease at once demonstrate their lack of therapeutic value, when we reflect what scientific pharmacology really implies. One cannot say with absolute certainty that Zande drugs for syphilis, consumption, dysentery, gonorrhœa, etc., are totally ineffective as curative agents, but in the light of the history of our own treatment of these diseases it is as near certainty as non-experimental argument can be. Lack of space forbids an account of Zande treatment for them, but the reader may consult Father De Graer's paper on the subject.

Nevertheless, the very fact of naming diseases and differentiating them from one another by their symptoms shows a great deal of empirical knowledge. They are often very skilled in the detection of early symptoms and our own doctors have told me that they seldom err in diagnosing early leprosy. They are naturally much less sure in diagnosing disease affecting internal organs such as the intestines, the liver, and the spleen. Also they know beforehand the normal course of a disease as soon as its symptoms are pronounced. They often know what the later symptoms will be and whether the patient is likely to live or die and how long he is likely to survive. Besides their ability to give a prognosis they can also tell you the etiology of disease, and though their notions of causes are generally far from objective reality, the fact that they recognize different causes for different illnesses is a tribute to their powers of observation and logical reasoning. The cause to which they attribute maladies often cannot help being the true one as in cuts, scalds, burns, bites, and they are aware of such facts as that the occurrence of syphilitic symptoms is necessarily preceded by sexual intercourse with an infected person. Moreover, almost every disease is not only diagnosed and its probable course foretold and its relation to a cause defined, but also each disease has its own individual treatment, which in some cases has evidently been built up on experience and in others, though probably quite ineffectual, shows a logico-experimental element. A few examples of empirical therapeutics will illustrate this statement.

Some Zande treatments undoubtedly have therapeutic value. On one occasion a kettle of boiling water was accidentally knocked over a sleeping boy in my kitchen and he was terribly scalded down the whole length of one side of his body. He was treated as for burns and the scalded parts were protected from the air by honey, on which was sprinkled the flowers of the *önvute* plant, which are fluffy like dandelion flowers. This is done in order to give consistency to the honey, and hairs of a wild cat may be used for the same purpose. If no honey is available when a person is burnt they coat the affected part with flour. They also anoint the sores with an ointment made of burnt *memegbara* mixed with oil.

Their treatment for headache is possibly efficacious. They bind the temples tightly with cord, though it is realized that this is less a cure than an alleviation of pain through a lessening of the pressure of blood. They also cause counter-irritation by drawing blood by suction through a gazelle's horn. This is placed on the temples just in front of the top of the ear. The narrow end of the horn is coated with a lump of wax and, when the operator has created a vacuum by sucking through the horn, he closes the aperture by biting on the wax with his teeth, drawing it over the mouth of the horn. The horn fills with blood from the incisions which have been made on the temple, and when it is full they pierce the wax with a little stick and hold a leaf beneath to catch the blood. This wet cupping treatment is said to cure headache if it is not occasioned by witchcraft, for if this is the case it will continue in spite of cupping. Another cure is to make slight incisions on the sides of the temples and to rub into them red pepper pods. They also pull out a few hairs from the head of the sick man and burn them and hold them to his nostrils. In a similar manner they place some smouldering barkcloth in a little cup made of leaves and hold it under the sick person's nose. For the same purpose they use crushed leaves of the *vötöli* plant, which emits a sharp scent. They are as small as laurel leaves but in shape are not unlike oak leaves. Father De Graer mentions a number of other plants which are useful for smelling or for making lotion to pour up the nostrils or for rubbing into incisions made on the forehead (253-4).

They make use of an enema in dysentery and severe diarrhœa. This consists of a gourd with a long thin mouth filled with water which has been boiled with a number of herbs (385). Possibly also their treatment of neuralgia is effective : they bind a slightly warmed compress above the affected member and then massage it from the compress to the extremity of the member. The compress is to prevent the *akilima*, the small grubs which are supposed to cause the disease, from going towards the body and compel them to go towards the extremity (371-2).

For a swelling of the forearm, hand and running towards the wrist, called *ndiwa* or *baguru*, they cause counter-irritation by putting the arm into a nest of *agogodogo* ants, which slightly pinch the skin (383).

Anyone who has lived in Zandeland will moreover have noticed how careful Azande are to wash sores and wounds with hot water, and they do not desist from this task however agonizing the cries of a child patient. They are equally careful to protect wounds from exposure to the air by covering them with leaves or wood-dust or bast or animals' fur. Doubtless the nicotine they place on sores acts as an antiseptic, and it is possible that some of the many decoctions, lotions, liniments, unguents, ashes of burnt herbs, powders, infusions, clay plaster, etc., may have therapeutic value, but I can express no opinion on this matter. The same may be said of massage and hot compresses for various ailments.

Azande know emetics which take quick effect, but I do not think that they are acquainted with any genuine aperients. In the old days when people sometimes drank a poison test of strychnine their relatives tried to restore them by administering a drug made from scraped *badangi* creeper mixed with scraped inner bark of the *kpoiyo* tree. The patient swallowed these slimy substances and was invariably and violently sick. The only cure for constipation I have recorded is to take some leaves of a wild plant called *tande*, which Azande use as a vegetable, and rub them together between the hands into a ball. This ball is pushed a little way up the anus by a finger so that it forms a tight wad. This treatment is said to loosen the bowels shortly afterwards. Possibly also their cure for diarrhœa has some value. They take an unripe banana of the *bira* species and cut it into slices and dip them into salt and eat them. Also they take a hen's egg and, breaking it, empty its contents on to an old potsherd and heat them over a fire after adding some palm-oil. Then they drink this mixture. Father De Graer says that they introduce into the anus a young bruised leaf of tobacco as a cure for diarrhœa, especially for infantile diarrhœa (389).

My own experience has been that Zande remedies are of an almost completely magical order : thus a typical Zande cure is that for pneumonia (*bôtuma*)—also called *zelekondo* and *kaza nganzira*, though this last seems to be a name lately introduced. The prescription runs as follows : Take roots of *mbegi* and mix with malt in boiling water and give to the patient to drink. Take a root of *bavurugbwate* and scrape it and place scrapings with cold water in a leaf-wrapping and squeeze some of the mixture up the sick man's nostrils out of the sight of people. Bind cord tightly round the chest. Such prescriptions are usually accompanied by spells. I have seen a good number of drugs being prepared and have accounts of a far greater number. I will not reproduce these here but will only remark that I have never been able to observe any difference between their preparations and the preparation of *materia medica* in magical rites of all kinds. A typical example of Zande treatment is that for early morning biliousness, which produces acute shivering fits and nausea. As I sometimes suffered from this malady (called in Zande *kelegbundu*) myself I had an incentive to inquire into the remedy, though I have never had the curiosity to try its therapeutic properties. The patient's sister's son places him at the side of the threshold of his hut and places an open-woven basket over his head. The sister's son then lights a handful of straw and runs several times round the patient, finally extinguishing the straw in front of him. He then takes cold water and sprinkles it over his maternal uncle, which causes him to shiver violently. Then he removes the basket, and taking the patient by the hand raises him and shakes his arms by raising them and bringing them down forcibly. Later they make an infusion from a certain creeper and wash the patient with it in the middle of a path.

It must not be supposed, moreover, that because part of a treatment is of real therapeutic value it is necessarily the part which Azande stress as really vital to the cure. I had a good example of the manner in which magical and empirical treatment are employed at the same time when a boy who formed a member of my household was bitten by a snake which was said to be very poisonous. One of our neighbours, who was known to have a vast knowledge of drugs, was immediately sent for and said that he knew exactly what was required. He had brought with him a knife and some drugs (a piece of bark and some kind of grass). He first of all ate some of the bark and gave the remainder to the boy to eat. Both chewed it and after swallowing the juice spat out the wood. They did the same with the grass. The leech told me afterwards that he partook of the medicine himself so that were the boy to have died he could not well have been accused of having administered bad medicine to him. He also told me that he had addressed the bark, saying that if the boy were to recover let him belch and that if he were to die let him refrain from belching, so that the drug had an oracular action. Having administered these drugs he then took out his knife and made an incision on the boy's foot where he had been bitten by raising the skin between his fingers and drawing the blade of his knife across it with several light strokes. As soon as blood began to ooze out of the cuts he took the boy's foot in his hands and raising it to his mouth sucked at the incisions forcibly and for some time. He then said that the boy was to be kept perfectly quiet and admonished him not to move about. After a while he began to belch on account of the drugs he had eaten, and on seeing this happy augury the leech had no longer any doubt that he would speedily recover, although he warned him that the pain would spread up the leg and that he would feel it keenly in the region of the heart.

In what then lies the difference between the magical and the empirical elements in Zande therapeutics ? In attempting to answer this question we must first frame it in accordance with Zande terminology, and ask what is the difference between the magical and empirical elements in *ngwa* when it is used therapeutically. This raises a linguistic question into which I do not wish to enter here, but we may understand that such actions as sucking a snake-bite and placing honey on a scald are not properly speaking *ngwa*, and that this term refers in normal usage to drugs. At any rate I shall use it in this sense here and defer a full discussion of the matter to a final account of Zande magic. I mention the point in this place because it is evident that the Zande sees a behaviouristic difference between preparing and administering drugs and the coating of a scald with honey. At the same time I have no reason to suppose that the man who sucked the snake-bite and gave the bitten boy drugs to eat distinguished between the efficacy of the one and the efficacy of the other treatment. A man who places a basket over his maternal uncle's head and pours cold water on him to cure early morning nausea does not distinguish the therapeutic effect of his actions from those of a man who smears honey on to a scald. If witchcraft does not interfere both treatments will be efficacious.

We can only distinguish between the magical and the empirical elements by their objective results, the one in no way effecting a cure and the other having a curative or alleviating action on the patient. It is not necessary for Azande to understand the physiological and chemical processes by which a cure is effected for us to class it as empirical rather than magical, but it is necessary that the treatment should, in fact, have therapeutic value. The greatest care is, therefore, necessary in classifying treatment as magical or empirical, because usually it is an extremely complex mixture of both. Thus the action of a drug may be in accordance with its purpose while the treatment may not, e.g. a drug given to cure syphilis by vomiting may cause vomiting and to this extent is empirical, but vomiting may in no way cure syphilis and to this extent it is magical. Or a treatment may be empirical in some respects but magical in others, e.g. massage may be of use in treating swelling of the thorax in children, or for fracture, but it is clearly a magical injunction which insists on it being carried out by a homicide or mother of twins in the first instance, and by a member of the Amazungu clan in the second instance.

It does not seem to me to be possible to make any differentia-
tion between the two by distinguishing between affective states.
The Zande leech certainly acts with confidence, but he is equally
confident whether his treatment be of therapeutic value or not.
As I have already pointed out, Azande prepare their drugs to
heal the sick and administer these in just the same way as when
they are preparing *materia medica* to give them powers of song
or to practise as a witch-doctor or to protect their homes and
families from witchcraft.   They boil and stir the ingredients in
precisely the same manner and utter similar spells over them.
Thus in consumption (*dinge*) they take a root of *ngorodimo*
and a root of *ngaranda* and scrape them into a gourdful of water
and let them soak there, adding salt and uttering a spell over
them.   Then they decant the mixture and pour it into the
patient's mouth.   The deep intramuscular abscess called *abagita*
is said to start with blood alone and without pus.   At this stage
they apply a cupping-horn near the mouth of the abscess.   When
pus has formed the place is lanced, and the patient swallows a
number of drugs and rubs others on to the abscess.   One of these
drugs is a little fish of the whiskered variety, probably a cat-
fish, which is applied alive to the abscess and is addressed, " Little
fish are you—I place you on the abscess, let the abscess disappear."
In treating syphilis, which they know is caught from contact
with an infected woman, they take a root of *bafuafu* or *bamolu*
and scrape and cook it with sweet potatoes.   They mash the
sweet potatoes with the scrapings and the patient drinks an
infusion from this mixture after it has had a long spell uttered
over it.   The medicine will then cause violent sickness and clear
the liver, which is the place where syphilis and, indeed, most other
diseases are considered to be localized.   In his account of leprosy
Father De Graer shows the action of spells in the preparation
of drugs (377).
It is true that when performing so simple an action as washing
a sore with warm water they do not utter a spell, but the same
is often true of preparation of drugs and other actions of leech-
craft which have no therapeutic value.   The spell is not an
essential element in the performance of magic among the Azande,
and we cannot argue from its presence or absence how the
performer participates emotionally in a rite.   That there is often
an emotional condition to be observed in the performer (or more
often his employer) is true, but I cannot tell whether this is
a constant element in all performances or not.   In any case the
fact that they are more disturbed in treating pneumonia than in
treating cough, in treating mortal abscesses than in treating
simple lesions, does not determine the efficacy of their treatment. The danger to life is the cause of anxiety and is extraneous
to the specialist ritual of a leech.

Here I can only touch on the theoretical problems which arise from a study of Zande therapeutics, for they go too deep for a short exposition. They concern the whole relationship of empirical to mystical thought and behaviour in human society and their complicated interaction, which is, perhaps, more clearly shown in the history of medicine than elsewhere. I can only attempt a condensed analysis of one aspect, the ideological one.

In Zande notions about disease we find that ideas of witch-craft and sorcery may be present, and that, in their notions about drugs, there may be present the idea of mystical force in the drugs, the *mbisimo ngwa* " the spirit of the drug ". But these notions are not always of the same intensity. In some cases the disease and the mystical cause form an ideological unity ; in others this unity is broken up and we find a belief in dual causation by two distinct forces, the disease itself and the witchcraft which conditions its occurrence and continuance in the organism. Lastly we find in many cases the belief in witch-craft as a causative agent in disease sinking into the background, and what we call natural causation dominant. This separation tends to take place when the disease is of a slight nature or its cause is evident to the senses (slight in its organic effects rather than in relation between organic effects and therapeutic treat-ment, since this last is so undeveloped). Nevertheless, the treat-ment may be just as magical, in our sense of the word, in a slight as in a serious illness. But here again Zande belief is not con-sistent and identical. In internal diseases they trust to the mystical properties of drugs to cure a patient. But even here there can be little doubt that when the action of the drug is of a precise and local nature, as in an emetic for instance, the Zande regards its action very much in the same way as a layman in our own society regards similar drugs, not mystically but also not pharmacologically. Furthermore, we get treatment in which the mystical action of drugs has fallen apart from the treatment in which drugs are not used—in which there is a local as well as a general treatment—e.g. the sucking of a snake-bite and internal administration of a drug, or in which there is local treatment alone, as in smearing honey on burns. There is a vast variety of behaviour and opinion which defies rigid classification because they shade into one another in a complicated pattern of interconnections. I can only show the general lines along which I believe that the subject can be treated by arranging single examples typologically. I conclude by doing this for Zande notions of causation in sickness.

I was some twenty months in Zandeland and was constantly associated with every kind of sickness. At one time I spent about two hours every morning dressing sores, but eventually I gave up this practice when I found that it took too much of my time. When, therefore, I generalize about Zande notions of causation I do so on a fairly wide experience. I have invariably found that when a Zande is struck down by general and acute sickness, with sudden and severe symptoms and rapid course, as in certain types of fever, pneumonia, cerebro-spinal meningitis, influenza, etc. (as far as my diagnosis goes), that his relatives and neighbours straight away connect his collapse with the primary cause of witchcraft or bad magic, almost always in cases of sudden collapse with sorcery. They do not say that the sick man is suffering from such-and-such an illness and that this illness is due to sorcery. The illness itself is diagnosed as bad magic—they say straight away when they see the symptoms " It is *kitikiti ngwa* ", " It is sorcery." They will immediately apply to a man who knows the *ziga*, the antidote, to the bad magic and ask him to administer it to the sick person. In the same manner it sometimes happens that a man thinks he has seen evil-bringing *adandala* cats in the bush, and if he falls suddenly sick within the next two or three weeks he will know that his sickness is due to their influence and ultimately to the woman who placed them in his path. The sickness, in fact, proves that he really did see *adandala* and that he did not imagine that he had seen them or mistaken some other cats for them. His relatives will therefore send for a specialist who knows the antidote to *adandala* if they do not know it themselves. Here again they may not name the sickness at all, but simply say " It is *adandala* ". Certain social situations will in the same manner produce a direct and sole reference to the primary mystical cause. Thus, if a man dies when he is wearing the string worn by those who have taken on themselves the responsibility of vengeance-magic, it is at once said that he has broken a taboo and that the magic has turned on him and killed him. If such a man is ill his relatives will pay the specialist who has made vengeance-magic on his behalf to destroy its potency by placing it in the cool waters of a marsh. Or again, if an adulterer or thief falls ill they know the reason of his illness at once, and seek out the offended husband or owner of property and try to persuade him to withdraw his magic. This is the only cure. In all these cases we have a simple pattern of thought and single line of behaviour :—

Mystical Cause- - - - - - - - - - - -Acute Illness- - - - - - - - - - - -Treatment (directed
          (sorcery   against mystical
          taboo, etc.)   cause and disease
                                                                          together).

But less serious sickness, chronic sickness which comes on slowly and is protracted and not accompanied by violent symptoms, or local sickness, Azande generally attribute to the action of witchcraft rather than to sorcery, and in this case there is no question of immediately applying an antidote because there are no drugs against witchcraft.[1] Moreover, here they distinguish much more clearly between the disease itself which is responsible for the ill-health and the witchcraft without which the disease would not have seized this particular man. Here the pattern of thought is more complicated since it admits dual causation, the disease itself and the witchcraft acting with it not so much as the cause of it but as a necessary condition of its occurrence and continued existence in the body of its victim.

This duality runs right through Zande thought in its relation to witchcraft. A man is wounded by an animal and the Zande attributes his misfortune to the animal and to witchcraft together. Taking a hunting metaphor he says that the animal was "first spear" and witchcraft "second spear", since both played a part in his death. We must be careful not to present Zande thought too logically by saying that the animal was the agent of witchcraft, for I do not think that Azande work out a chain of causation in this manner but that they look on both causes as operating at the same time. Thus in disease also they conceive of the disease and witchcraft as separate interacting causes. A man suffers from a deep intramuscular abscess, and although they think of the abscess as a cause and existing in its own right, they believe that it would not have attacked this particular man or at least would not have developed or continued to molest him if it were not for the co-operation of witchcraft (or possibly of good magic if the man had committed some crime). In the same manner Azande do not imagine that any other thing than boiling water has caused a scald, if we mean that any other thing has been a sensible occasion of the scald, but he knows nevertheless, that the accident would not have occurred but for the presence of witchcraft. This complexity of thought, this recognition of dual causation, is shown also in Zande treatment which is carried out along two lines, by the administration of drugs which deal with the disease and by the mechanism of oracles which divulge the name of the witch who is responsible so that it is then possible to induce him to remove his influence :—

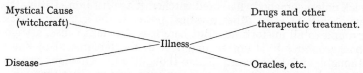

Mystical Cause (witchcraft) — Illness — Drugs and other therapeutic treatment.
Disease — Illness — Oracles, etc.

In such cases the disease has to be diagnosed and named and the specific remedy applied. This very naming and identification of the disease objectifies it and gives it a reality of its own

[1] For the difference between witchcraft and sorcery in Zande culture see my paper, " Sorcery and Public Opinion in Primitive Society," *Africa*, 1931.

independent of witchcraft, just as the animal which has wounded
a man has an independent existence of its own and only comes
into co-operation with witchcraft under certain conditions in
situations of sickness or death, or just as boiling water is something *sui generis* and witchcraft is something *sui generis*, but their
combination is necessary to cause scalding. Even in internal
sickness the Zande often makes its independent and objective
reality clearer by attributing it to grubs and worms or some other
concrete cause, and in this case we may say that they distinguish
between the cause of ill-health and its symptoms. In diseases
which are attributed at the same time to the activity of the
disease itself and to witchcraft it is always the presence or absence
of witchcraft which is the determining factor in the patient's
death or recovery. Hence the more serious the disease becomes
the less they trouble about administering drugs and the more
they consult oracles and make counter-magic. At death their
thoughts are directed only towards witchcraft and revenge,
to purely mystical causation, while in minor ailments or at the
early symptoms of an illness from which a man may be expected
to recover without difficulty they think less of witchcraft and
more of the disease itself and of curing it by the use of drugs.
This is seen in those small ailments in which they are able to
give a fairly sure and optimistic prognosis, for they often do not
refer them to any supernatural agency at all but simply name
them and treat them. Thus when a man cuts his foot either they
do nothing or wash it and bind it with leaves, and it is only when
it begins to fester that they commence to trouble about witchcraft. In the same manner ulcers may be attributed to themselves
and no one troubles to consult oracles or take any other steps
to counteract supernatural agencies :—

Disease- - - - - - - - - - - - - -Illness- - - - - - - - - - - - -Treatment against Illness.

But even here when supernatural causation ceases to be
explicit, i.e. referred in social behaviour to the action of witchcraft or magic or the spirits of the dead, if you were to question
a Zande he would certainly insist that he would not have been
sick unless somebody had used witchcraft against him. Ultimately
witchcraft or some other mystical power is the cause and background to all misfortune. But here it is a distant cause, a vague
background. It is not so manifest in the foreground of Zande
thought and behaviour. Their thought and behaviour are not
directed towards it as a sole or even major objective. This
objective is the disease itself. But let the illness continue or
show alarming symptoms, then the concept of witchcraft comes
into the foreground of their consciousness and obscures the
independent action of the disease. Supernatural causes are never
excluded entirely from Zande thought about sickness, but they

are sometimes more, sometimes less, prominent. A theoretical treatment of Zande therapeutics could go very much farther than I have taken it but the lines along which it could be developed are, I think, clear from what has been said so far. We found that Zande thought about disease is essentially mystical, in Lévy-Bruhl's sense of belief in supernatural causation, but that the degree of mysticism is not always the same and is not always absolute so that it allows the notion of disease as an independent causative factor to be present also.   It is, therefore, possible for them to separate the two and deal with them separately. Treatment therefore takes two lines : one deals with the mystical cause and one deals with the disease.   But even in the treatment of the disease itself we find an empirical element, particularly in treatment of local and external symptoms, side by side with a mystical element in the internal absorption of drugs endowed with magical potency by rite and spell.   Were we to proceed further in our analysis we should find empirical behaviour and thought also in the very core of witchcraft, sorcery, oracles, and *materia medica* of all sorts.

THE MEANING OF DREAMS IN TIKOPIA

By Raymond Firth

The investigation of the nature of dreams, their importance and their significance in the life of primitive peoples, is a subject in which interest has grown in recent years. This is due particularly to the stimulus given by Dr. Seligman, who has collected much information relating to a number of " typical dreams " in various parts of the world and provided valuable suggestions for their study. It is perhaps then appropriate that an essay in a volume dedicated to him should be concerned with one of his favourite topics. Though to my regret it was not convenient for me in my field-work in Tikopia to follow in entirety the methods of procedure indicated by Seligman, which would have added greatly to the interest of this account—the method of analysis by frcc association was not used—I have been able to bring together illustrative material which corroborates to a considerable degree some of the results he has obtained. This article through the exigencies of space consists mainly in a statement of the general character of dreams and dream interpretation in Tikopia ; the adduction of full texts and detailed discussion has had to be postponed till a later occasion.

The folk of Tikopia, a small, isolated, crater peak standing well out in the ocean to the south-east of the Solomon Islands, are a branch of the great Polynesian stock.[1] On first acquaintance with these natives one would be inclined to think that dreams would not play any great part in their life. They impress the observer by their practicality, their concentration on the material side of things, their indifference to matters which do not serve some directly useful end for them. They are by no means devoid of artistic feeling, but they normally waste little time in enhancement of their possessions ; their bark-cloth is abundant, but coarse and plain ; their woodwork skilful and effective, but rough. A thing passes muster, however uncouth, so long as it is efficient. The European who thinks to create an impression, in traditional style, by the display of some trick or piece of mechanical ingenuity as " white man's magic " finds himself put out of countenance. These natives are not taken in by supernatural explanations : the thing is clever, they admit, they cannot do the like, but it is made by men's hands ; how then

[1] A brief description of some aspects of their culture is given in articles in *Oceania*, i, 1930–1931 ; *Journal Royal Anthropological Institute*, lx, 1930.

does it work, and what is its use ? " Tough-minded " savages,
in fact !

There is some excuse, then, for wondering if such flimsy stuff
as dreams is of any interest to them, and whether they ever
allow their conduct to be influenced by such immaterial considerations. Casual observation in this direction is not encouraging,
but closer acquaintance reveals that beneath the crust of
materialism and practicality lies an active belief in a world
of spirits and immaterial forces, potent for good or evil, a firm
conviction of their interference in the affairs of humanity, and
a sensitiveness to any phenomena, however trivial and bizarre,
which might portend action from the other side of the veil.
The Tikopia dream, and they regard their dreams as significant
of supernormal influences, though they do not attach equal
weight to them in all circumstances.

Our study of the matter may be begun by indicating the type
of replies elicited by concrete questioning when the subject is
first opened. The question is put, " Does a person when sleeping
look on other persons, meet them, have speech with them, go
fishing or to the woods, and on waking find that he still lies on
his bed mat ? "

It is admitted by the natives that such a thing happens : it
is called *te miti*.

" Do *miti* occur often ? "

" To some people, yes ; to others, no ! "

" These *miti*, are they true ? "

" Some are true, others are false, others are dreams only "
(*te miti fuere*)—without significance, that is. As the inquiry
proceeds further a mass of information is revealed which indicates
that considerable attention is often paid to dreams, and the
diagnosis of them is thought to throw light on the affairs of the
normal waking life. Nevertheless, dreams in Tikopia do not
obtrude themselves on the ethnographer. Unless he makes
specific inquiry it is possible for him to be for a considerable time
in close contact with the people without hearing a dream told
to a group of listeners or advanced as a reason for following
some line of conduct. There is no taboo against making known
one's dreams ; they are told willingly and openly on request,
in good narrative style, with the native attention to detail and
command of dialogue, sometimes with a strong affective reaction.
But no systematic scheme of telling them exists, no formal
technique of interpretation has been elaborated. Dreams when
related are told casually, on waking or at odd moments of leisure
during the day. Many of them, though vividly remembered, are
not reported in public at all. Some dreams, too, have no significance assigned to them. It may be said, indeed, that the weight
attached to a dream varies as the emotional intensity of the

personal situation at the time, that a dream receives attention and credence largely in so far as it can be related to some question immediately at issue within the social horizon of the dreamer. It is this correlation of dream interpretation with the situation of the moment that explains the inconsistency frequently to be found in assigning a meaning to such experiences.

The Tikopia explanation of the cause of dreams varies according to the precise nature of the experience, but rests at bottom on the general theory of the mobile soul. Every person has a *mauri* or *ora*, an intangible entity normally invisible to the waking eye, which may for convenience be designated the spirit or life principle—the native terms being generally used synonymously—and this is capable of leaving the body during sleep and wandering abroad. *" Tou mauri ku poi tatafau "* " Thy spirit has gone strolling " was an explanation made by one informant. In this condition the *mauri* has experiences which are transmitted to its mortal owner and constitute the stuff of his dreams. The natives have no clear theory as to the relation between spirit and body at this time ; they are separate, yet the adventures of the spirit part become the responsible agent, the property of the whole, and a person in narrating his dream uses the pronoun " I ". Both spirit and body, in fact, are treated as the Ego. Other persons seen in dreams are *prima facie* the *mauri* of such persons, though here an important qualification has to be made, as will be seen below.

Dreams of visits to distant places are readily explained by the mobility of the *mauri*, which can flash about at will, annihilating space, while the same power also allows it to journey to Rangi, the Heavens, and have contact with persons long dead. These are represented by their own spirits known as *mauri* in their lifetime, but now as *atua*. The recognition of another person either living or dead in a dream encounter, however, is not necessarily taken to mean that it is his own spirit entity which is present. Many dream experiences are the result of the inter-position of *atua* of another kind, spiritual beings who have never belonged to human kind and lived upon earth, but who for their own purposes, generally malicious, counterfeit familiar forms in order to deceive the dreamer. We shall return to this point again.

The problem of mobility of the spirit of the dreamer in time does not arise for the Tikopia, since any experience which might be considered as an incursion into the past or future is sufficiently explained by the thesis of spirits of the dead living in the present in Rangi, or the powers of counterfeit possessed by non-human *atua*.

A question of primary interest is the nature of the dreams which natives have, what constitute the " typical dreams "

F

of the culture under review. I did not conduct an elaborate inquiry on these lines, but such investigations as I made show that many of the same types of dream context are found among the Tikopia as among ourselves. In this my material agrees with the general conclusions of Professor Seligman.[1]

Dreams of physical oppression of the nightmare variety occur, and are believed to be due to unidentified *atua* of the non-human category. Such a spirit comes to a man as he lies asleep, steals up and presses him down, sitting on his chest or on his belly. The presence of the *atua* is made known to the sleeper by a heavy feeling on his body, as of a great weight laid thereon, and to onlookers by his uneasy movements. He turns uneasily, grunts, and may even call out in his sleep. If his movements are violent his neighbours waken him and question him. Such experiences are regarded as definitely unpleasant, and may be remembered for years afterwards. Thus one informant, a young married man, the son of a chief, told me of such an adventure he had when he was a child. He went to Maunga Faea, a locality much frequented by spirits—*e tapu*—and there he chewed betel, chewed betel in great quantities. Then he slept and an *atua* came to him and sat on his chest. He shrieked in terror, the spirit disappeared, and a few moments afterwards he woke. He was surrounded by people who, as it turned out, had awakened him, and to them he cursed vigorously, objurgating his ghostly visitant. In this case the physiological prelude to his experience was probably the amount of betel consumed, but such a reaction is not recognized by the natives. The betel may have caused the sleep —or stupor, as it apparently was—but the spirit-haunted spot was the cause of the nightmare. To the Tikopia a dream experience is a reality—not identical with the reality of waking life ; contrary to some anthropological opinion, there is no confusion between them—but an adventure of the spirit. It may be deemed true or false as a portrayal of events, the figures of the dream may be considered to be masquerading for purposes of deception, but their spiritual character is never doubted.

In fact the experiences of people in dreams are regarded as proof of the existence of spirits, and much of the information regarding the method of locomotion of these, their appearance, speech, and habits, retailed as common knowledge, is derived from the dreams in which they play a part. In discussing the movements of *atua*, Pa Fenuatara, a particularly intelligent informant, said, " Persons in this land see them in a dream, in sleep at night." Dreams are valuable circumstantial evidence for the reality of the spirit world.

A spirit afflicts a man in sleep for various reasons, pure spite being the commonest, but one explanation given is more

[1] *Man*, 1923, 120.

charitable. The spirit comes to the sleeper because, it is alleged, it finds itself on a strange path in its wanderings, it does not see any light thereon, and says to itself, "The way is dark, I will return to men." Then it approaches a person and touches him.

An outcome of the belief that a person is always liable to molestation by strange spirits is the habit of the Tikopia of not sleeping with an axe or knife by his side. An *atua* may come to him and deceive him, pretending that it is a man coming to fight him. Then the sleeper, alarmed, seizes the weapon and blindly slashes with it, to the danger of property or life. He may cut a house-post, or even injure someone. The absence of intent in such a case is well recognized by others. " He strikes blindly only, and indeed that person is foolish, he is sleeping."

Dreams of personal activity of a violent order, with an unpleasant affective reaction, are not infrequent among the Tikopia. The dream of running with clogged feet, impelled to flee yet held back by invisible restraint while some being, either man or spirit, is in pursuit, is well known. The Ariki Taumako, a chief of vigorous and somewhat dour personality, who formerly had several experiences of this type, assigned the cause of the clogged feet to the subject's sleeping with knees drawn up—*e me peru*. If a man sleeps with his legs straight out—*e fora*—and is chased by a ghost in a dream, then he is free to run, but if he is in a bent position, his flight must be impeded. This logical explanation, it will be noted, does not appeal to physiological factors as the cause of the dream but only as a factor of limitation within it ; the dream itself, the spirit encounter, is an independent matter already assumed.

The remark of the Ariki that he *formerly* experienced the dream of clogged feet is significant. According to his own statement he no longer has this. The same is true of the dream of jumping from a cliff. As a commoner (*taŋata vare*) not yet elected to the chieftainship, he often experienced this sensation in sleep ; nowadays he is not subject to it " because I have become chief ". The differential liability of commoners and chiefs to dreams of nightmarish type or to bad dreams as a whole is acknowledged to be general. It rests upon the responsibility which the chiefs feel for the lives and prosperity of their people. Unpleasant dreams they regard as portents of evil, and a chief having had a vivid experience of this kind is considerably disturbed, and speculates as as to its meaning.   " Sleeps the chief, dreams badly, wakes with a start then, and thinks what it may be, a man will die, or a hurricane will strike ? "   The precise form of the misfortune is uncertain but some disaster is indicated. There is no doubt that the chiefs take their responsibilities seriously in this as in other respects. With common people, however—as with a future chief before his election—there are no cares of such magnitude, and a bad dream

is not regarded as necessarily ominous, and is treated more
lightly. This difference in the weight attached to the dreams of
chiefs and commoners is in line with distinctions made in many
other social spheres. Whether chiefs actually do practically
cease to have such unpleasant dreams—which would indicate
a high degree of co-ordination of their mental and social norms—
I am not prepared to say. I have only statements made privately
as above.

Dreams of violent action of a kind common to other cultures,
including our own, are general in Tikopia. A person is walking
up in the hills, and either jumps or falls over a cliff, and wakes
with a start ; he is afraid and runs ; he goes for a walk and sees
people fighting, or he himself has a struggle and kills a man.
The significance given to such dreams varies with individual
preoccupation, and they may be entirely neglected.

The dream of losing a tooth has no stock meaning. " A man
may dream that a tooth has dropped out, he wakes up, but no !
the tooth is still there. There is no meaning to it."

Certain types of dreams are, however, regarded as being of
more importance than others, and definite interpretation may
be assigned them. These are concerned particularly with the
pursuit of fishing, and the sphere of birth, sickness, and death
—all, it may be noted, aspects of human life peculiarly liable
to chance, and therefore apparently where some degree of
assurance in advance is welcomed.

Birth dreams embody a certain kind of personal activity,
of a neutral order. A woman dreams that she goes to the stream,
fills her water-bottles, and puts them in a kit on her back. It
is believed that this indicates she will conceive and bear a girl-
child. Or if she goes out fishing with a *kuti*, a small scoop-net
used on the reef by women, then the same interpretation is
attached. Dreams of a similar type associated with pursuits of
sea-fishing portend the conception of a man-child.

" She who sits there, will sit in pregnancy, will bear a male."
This dream has the same result, whether the woman has previously
conceived or not. Any one of the *kano o paito*, the relatives, is
competent to give an indication of this kind ; a person in the
family dreams, of so-and-so, and announces the next morning
that she will bear a child. The husband of the woman is also
an eligible subject for such dreams.

Dreams of death also occur. Seremata, a young bachelor
and expert fisherman, for example, dreams on occasions that
he sees a canoe approaching shore with some of his relatives in
it. The canoe runs in on a breaker, then swings and overturns
—an accident which happens in real life. This he accepts as an
indication that someone of his relatives will die, and waits
accordingly for the news.

Death dreams in Tikopia have, as one might expect, a tragic, gloomy, or disturbing context. They are not of the irrelevant type found in some native communities. There is usually a fairly close correlation between the affective character of the dream and that of the real experience supposed to be foreshadowed by it. Dreams of personal action, as of being chased by a spirit or of falling from a cliff, do not usually share this character of portents. They are regarded as events completed at the moment, not to be resolved in the future—perhaps since the final issue of the dream is really successful. Unpleasant scenes witnessed in a dream foretell undesirable events.

Another variant of the canoe dream is one in which the omen is given by the nature of the fish caught. Seremata says : " A man sleeping sees a canoe coming in with fish. He is looking at a good thing if it has brought hither fish in plenty, but if it is concerned with a shark, a shark the body of which has fallen in, is emaciated, is like a sick man, then the dream is bad, a man of his family group, or he himself will die." The association here between the gaunt appearance of the fish—" with ribs showing " is the idea conveyed by the term *maki* in the original ; the same word is also used as a substantive, denoting epidemic disease—and the appearance of a sick man is very clear, especially when reinforced by this simile used by the narrator himself. Again our informant remarks :—

" I will be asleep, and will see my father, who is dead, enter. I look at him, and his body is good, that is he comes well-intentioned ; but he comes and his body is bad, it is unsightly, as it were, like that of a person who is ill, that means he is angry, he is on the point of coming to afflict the family group. If I decide to narrate this to my relatives I do so ; but if not, I sit then and observe the signs." Here the omens are derived from the physical appearance of the spirit dreamed of : the native term *para* here translated as " unsightly " denotes such conditions as wrinkled, rough, scaly skin, a disintegration of the flesh, an unpleasant condition of the body, which is held to be a reflex of the state of mind of the *atua*. For some insult or neglect, real or fancied—it would hardly be pure malice, from one's own father —he intends to visit disease or death on some member of the family circle.

As already indicated, however, dreams of evil are not always significant of illness or death ; here as in other dream interpretations there is considerable variation. Thus, quoting Seremata again : " I will be sleeping in Ravenga here, my relatives are dwelling in Faea. I sleep, the funeral of one of them takes place, when it is light the following day I go then to him, I go, go, he is sitting there, no ! a deception merely." Such dreams may be a correct forecast or may correspond to no reality. As he says,

" There is no sign for it that I know " (*Siei se fakamailoŋa mona kau iroa*).

There is one notable exception to the general rule that dreams of unpleasant events are to be construed as pointing to misfortune. This is in regard to fishing, particularly from a canoe at sea. The convention is that contact with human excrement in a dream is the sign of a good catch on the following day. Pu Rangifau, white-haired and frail, but once a famous ocean-rover and deep-sea fisherman, speaks of such a dream in his quaint style :—

" The canoe is pulled, pulled then on to a bad place. A person sleeps, looks at the fish of the canoe being obtained. It came to rest then at the place which is bad. The person wakes and says, ' Talk of the land about my dream ! I slept then of the canoe which will slip ashore hither.' We speak to him, ' That there, a fish dream is that thing.' Goes to sea, brings hither the fish, is correct the person who sleeping had his dream. The canoe is set in a filthy place, that is a fish dream ; we know that a fish dream is that thing."

This statement, though cryptic, describes the dream of a person in regard to his family canoe. He dreams that he sees it at sea, fishing, then, paddled inshore, and having shot the breakers, hauled up on land where it comes to rest on a spot defiled by excrement (" a bad place "). Waking, he narrates his dream to the household, who identify it as a token of a good catch, an interpretation which later events justify.

To dream that one's hand is smeared with ordure is also a fish dream indicating that one will haul up a shark at the next trip of the canoe to sea. The interpretation of unpleasant material, excrement, as signifying success, and abundance of fish is a curious piece of symbolism and difficult to explain, though the psychoanalyst might be able to provide a solution. The suggestion of association with ordure is unpleasant to the Tikopia in ordinary life, as is shown by the commonest form of curse, " May your father eat filth." In esoteric formulae, however, the higher gods are requested to excrete upon the land and into the sea, this being explained by the natives themselves as a deprecatory metaphor for the granting of fruits and fish as food supply. The identification of fish with excrement in this case may give point to the dream interpretation, though I have no confirmation of this from natives, for whom this association is an unexplained convention. One may wonder to what extent the knowledge of this convention actually produces the appropriate dream, and how far such dreams occur to fishermen in contrast with other members of the community. On this point I have no precise information, but the impression I received was that this was the dream of *tautai*, sea-experts, who had it more frequently than others. It was mostly with such men that these dreams were discussed.

The degree of rigidity in attaching a stock meaning to dreams is of importance. With fish dreams, as elsewhere, there is no absolute interpretation which is automatically adopted by the dreamer. Out in a canoe on the lake in the early morning I once heard Pa Fenuatara tell of a dream which he had had the night before, in which he had trodden into excrement and defiled his foot. This was at the time of the sacred fishing expedition in which all the clans engage in competitive spirit, striving as to who shall bring home the first shark. But Pa Fenuatara was in doubt as to the meaning of his dream. "A fish dream, for certain," said one of the paddlers. "I don't know!" said Pa Fenuatara reflectively, and continued to ponder over it for some time.

Each dreamer is liable to be uncertain as to the significance of his experience, until events have proved the correctness or otherwise of his surmise. He submits his dream to the opinions of others but accepts their judgments tentatively, holding his own verdict in suspense to await results. Dreams may be true or false, and as Seremata says, there are no signs by which we may know them—until they have been confirmed or refuted by the passage of time.

Inquiry into the reason for the falsity of dreams brings us back once again to the Tikopia theory of the motive power of dream experiences in general. They are the result of spiritual manifestations, of one's own spirit entity the *mauri* in contact with the external world, the *mauri* of other persons, or *atua*, the spirits of the dead, or beings outside the human range altogether. Some *atua* are well-disposed and truthful, as those of one's fishing-canoe, who are allied with the family and send fish-dreams to replenish the family larder. Others are mischievous or ill-natured, such as the spirits of the woods, of the earth, and of the ocean-floor, beings who, never having borne the vesture of humanity, have no social affiliations with men, and desire to wreak on them an injury where possible. Hence they are responsible for dreams which do not mirror the future from a true angle, they misrepresent the situation, and deceive mortals. It behoves a man always to be on his guard, lest by accepting the conventional interpretation of a dream too readily he be tricked and led into a snare. It is for this reason that persons, however ready to attach a definite meaning to the dreams of others, are usually cautious regarding the explanation of their own, until such time as events seem to justify a conclusion.

At the same time the doctrine of truth and falsity of dreams allows the belief in the virtue of dreams as omens to remain intact. Any dream the immediate sequel to which violates the general convention of interpretation is at once diagnosed as a lying dream, one sent by ill-disposed spirits to deceive the dreamer and confuse his course of action.

This brings us to the consideration of dreams of sexual intercourse, from which general category dreams of incest need not be here distinguished. Such experiences are not infrequent, among married men as among bachelors, and among women also. The object of the dream may be an unknown person, a fellow villager or a member of the immediate household. The explanation advanced by the Tikopia is the same in each case. If it were possible to discuss them in detail, it could be shown how dream experiences of a sexual type are held to be inspired by malignant spirits who take on the form of a person of the opposite sex, even of a near relative, and invite to connection. The mind of the dreamer is swayed to compliance, and on awakening the deed is realized.

This principle of dealing with such dreams on the basis of spirit-impersonation has two important functions. In the first place it tends to avoid any serious emotional disturbance occasioned by the thought of having violated a taboo—a man knows that he has not had relations, even in the spirit, with his mother, his clan-sister, or the wife of a friend, but with a stranger, an impersonator of these. There is no moral judgment involved, no feeling of guilt or shame. The dreamer has committed no offence, not even in thought ; he has been duped and constrained by false spirits in familiar shape. His reaction is one of anger, he curses. He does not remain silent and sad. In this he is in a more satisfactory position than the dreamer of the Trobriand Islands, as described by Professor Malinowski.[1] The Trobriander believes in the reality of the dream-form and is severely disturbed. He is fain to explain its incestuous presence by the hypothesis of magic accidentally misapplied, but cannot escape the emotional consequences of his dream act. The Tikopia is more free : while the Trobriander excuses the fact, he denies it. The Tikopia knows nothing of magic which works through dreams. It may be noted in passing that if a young man dreams of having had connection with a girl he does not regard that as an index of real desire on either part. If he approached her in the flesh with such a tale he would be laughed at as a clumsy liar. Fancy trying to attract a girl by pretending that he has had relations with her in a dream ! What a story ! She would tell all her friends and he would be laughed to scorn. Even if his tale were true it would be a female spirit from abroad, not that of the girl herself who came to him. Such is the opinion of my native friends on this point.

The theory of spirit-impersonation removes one from the necessity of accepting seriously dream encounters which are

[1] *Sex and Repression*, 1927, p. 96 ; *Sexual Life of Savages*, 1929, pp. 331–4.

undesirable. On the other hand it goes deeper into the layers of the cultural strata than does the point of view of many native peoples. Sexual intercourse in a dream is intercourse with an *atua*, who is possessed of considerable powers, and the result is a loss of vitality on the part of the dreamer. The consequence is not inevitable, and the event itself decides, but illness may easily follow a dream of sexual congress, incestuous or otherwise, owing to the malignancy of the impersonating spirit. In practice, such a dream is usually produced to assist the diagnosis of an existing case of illness. It is even probable that such dream experiences are invented or transmuted *ad hoc*, as when a close relative of a chief a few days *after* the beginning of his illness relates an ominous dream alleged to have taken place the night *before* the first signs of sickness were observed. The mechanism of this dream diagnosis and the cure cannot be discussed here. It is sufficient to indicate that dreams of sexual intercourse, including those of incest, take their place along with other manifestations of spirit activity in providing an explanation for illness, and by consequence a point of departure for healing activities. By spirits can spirits be fought, and the whole technique of the treatment of disease begins from this general basis. The sexual dream has thus a significance far beyond that of a mere experience in sleep ; it is an important link in an institutional chain.

As a point of general interest it may be noted that the idea of the Tikopia that a dream may be a false reflection of events owing to deception practised by spirits bears against the criticism which Durkheim has advanced against Tylor's theory of animism. Durkheim argues that the savage could speedily find out that dream experiences were untrue, an illusion of the imagination, by comparing notes when awake with the person thought to be encountered in sleep. The inconsistency would soon prove to him that his dreams were not to be relied on as evidence, and any idea that he might form as to the existence of a separable soul, a double of himself, could receive no corroboration therefrom.[1] The doctrine of the Tikopia anticipates this criticism by postulating the existence of further spirits of a mischievous order, on whom may be laid the onus of dreams which are not in accord with fact. The spirit of the dreamer himself takes part in these experiences—this is basic—but the behaviour of other participants in the dream can never be checked because though identified as friends and relatives it is possible for them to be mere impersonations. The dream as an adventure of one's spirit double can never be invalidated by other testimony and the native faith in the existence and power of the human spirit to wander outside the body remains unshaken.

[1] *Elementary Forms of the Religious Life*, 1926, p. 57.

In conclusion a further word may be given on the native interpretation of dreams of the portent type. In discussing the place of dreams as omens in a primitive community a stock meaning for each is often given by the ethnographer, the suggestion being that these meanings are constant for all dreams of the same type. There is no such rigidity in Tikopia society. Similar dreams may be rendered in different ways on different occasions, according to the problems of the moment, the standpoint of the dreamer, and the course of action he desires. In other words, there is considerable elasticity of interpretation, stock attributions of meaning are few, and the value that is set on a dream tends to be a function of the immediate practical situation of the dreamer and his relatives. This flexibility of the dream interpretation is one of the factors in preserving the belief in dreams. If a dream makes an impression it is told to the family circle and its meaning sought. At any given time there is a certain background of social interests against which it may be set ; a fishing expedition, the future of a newly-married pair, and a quarrel over the boundary of an orchard, for example. The dream is discussed in this general context, and its bearings as an omen decided. But its interpretation is dependent on human fallibility : members of the family circle may disagree regarding it. Hence when its promise as originally understood is not fulfilled, the reason is found in a false attribution. The anticipated result did not follow, it is said, because the dream really referred to another situation.

When a dream is not borne out in fact the dreamer may say it has lied, whereas other people repudiate this suggestion, saying that the dreamer has merely construed it wrongly. To reinforce their contention they can usually point to different interpretations of their own, slighted at the time, but now vindicated.

By admitting the fallibility of human understanding of the message vouchsafed by spirits, credence in the genuineness of that message may be retained unimpaired. Thus an institution or a belief persists in society, turning its very failures as weapons against the human agents who might be tempted to call its validity in question.

FREUDIAN MECHANISMS IN PRIMITIVE NEGRO PSYCHOLOGY

By MELVILLE J. HERSKOVITS

The analysis of the drives which actuate the behaviour of primitive folk presents one of the most difficult problems confronting the cultural anthropologist, since it necessitates a comprehension of traditional values entirely foreign to the observer's own background. Among the non-literate Negro peoples of West Africa and the New World, this same problem is heightened in interest by the widely spread distribution of patterns of behaviour that reflect a characteristic psychological " set ". An example, taken at random from the travel literature of the West Indies, will serve to illustrate the point. The account tells of a " Danse Congo " held on a small island off the coast of Haiti. This dance was given by the richest man on the island, one Polynice, and host and guests were having a fine time of it ; yet one of the songs sung by a guest was :—

" Polynice is the tax-collector. He comes riding at night on his white horse to rob us ; we will drive him away with stones, and a misfortune will happen to him."

The observer, commenting on this song, states that Polynice " accepted it without malice ", and " doubtless would have felt hurt and neglected if they hadn't sung it ".[1]

Investigators, seeking understanding of the significance of occurrences such as this, have turned to the concepts of the various schools of psychology for aid, and anthropological literature does contain numerous psychological interpretations. However, analyses of primitive behaviour based on the Freudian postulates are seldom encountered. The reasons for this are not difficult to see. The method of the Freudians themselves has been one of clinical analysis, and when the psychoanalysts have stepped out of their clinics to apply their theories to society as a whole, and particularly to primitive man, their disregard of anthropological methodology has carried its own conviction of insufficiency. Like all other disciplines, anthropology has special techniques to cope with its problems. Those unacquainted with cultures other than their own, except through an outdated literature that persists in the concept of the primitive man as a child, are easily captivated by the speciously convincing

[1] W. B. Seabrook, *The Magic Island*, pp. 225–6.

character of deductions as to " origins " drawn by the use of a methodology that is now discredited.   As a result, one witnesses such scientifically unacceptable conclusions as those presented by Freud in *Totem and Taboo*, to cite one of the earliest examples or, to cite one of the latest instances, the arguments of Rank in his volume *Art and Artist*.[1]

It is not necessary to do more than to state these facts, however, since both the dangers to the anthropologist in too fervent a devotion to the Freudian system, and the gains which should accrue from a realization of its significance as a technique to be used with other methods, have recently been fully assessed.[2] As has been suggested, anthropological recognition of the availability of psychoanalysis as a tool to be tested, and, if valid, applied in the study of primitive social behaviour, together with the recognition by at least one psychoanalyst of the necessity of studying primitive cultures at first-hand through field investigation,[3] gives hope that the question of its degree of applicability to the problems of anthropology may soon be resolved.

In this paper it is proposed merely to indicate certain aspects of the psychology of primitive Negro cultural behaviour which may be the better understood when some of the broader, simpler concepts of psychoanalysis are applied to their interpretation.   It is not intended to do more than to present and point out the definite material contained here.   Thus, we will not be concerned with the question whether or not the fact that the dream-interpretation of the Dutch Guiana Negroes, " if a person dreams he sees snakes, that means he has enemies," is of significance for the Freudian theory of dream-symbolism ;   whether or not " when you dream of monkeys, it is Obia Winti [4] that is seeking to come to you " derives from sex-symbolism or from the historic fact that, in West Africa, it is the supernatural monkey-like " little people " of the bush who are believed to have given magic to men.   Nor will we concern ourselves with the validity of conclusions such as expressed by the student who, having drunk

[1] For example, on p. 170 of the English translation Rank provides us with the following, which is only one of the many statements of its kind that might be quoted :   " The primitive precursor of this head-gathered pillar-man of Greece may be found in the wooden house-pillar of art in the South Seas . . ."

[2] C. G. Seligman, " Anthropological Perspective and Psychological Theory," *Journal of the Royal Anthropological Institute*, vol. lxii (1932), pp. 193–228.

[3] Geza Róheim, " Psychoanalytic Technique and Field Anthropology," *International Journal of Psychoanalysis*, vol. xiii (1932), pp. 6–22.   However, the exaggerated field-technique of Róheim, as revealed in this and other papers, and his unquestioning acceptance of Freudian terminology, coupled with his undisguisedly emotional strictures on the acceptability of Malinowski's study of the Oedipus complex among the Trobriand Islanders, make one fear that this grain of acceptable material will be so far overshadowed by the faults of the work that its chief result will be further to prejudice anthropologists against psychoanalysis as a working technique.

[4] An Obia spirit.

deeply at the Freudian fountain, remarked that the slouching gait of American Negroes is due to a castration complex, for it was obvious that he had not observed the motor behaviour of Africans, or for that matter, of New World Negroes, carrying head-burdens. What is to be reported here are field data, with native interpretations of them which suggest the availability of psychoanalytic concepts as an aid to understanding primitive psychology.

Among the most widely employed concepts of psychoanalysis are those of repression and compensation. Together with the associated concept of the unconscious, it may be said that the mechanisms implied by these two words are basic to psychoanalytic theory. It is, therefore, not without interest that we find numerous examples of these mechanisms in Negro cultures ; not only this, but that there exists both a recognition of the nature of the neuroses as induced by repression, and of the therapeutic value of bringing a repressed thought into the open, though the explanation of the phenomenon is usually given in terms of the working of supernatural forces. It seems valid to assume that this sanctioned release of inhibited feelings was at the basis of the Haitian performance recounted at the beginning of this paper, and this conclusion becomes inescapable when knowledge of the historical derivation of the practice of singing songs which state grievances against those in power is available to reinforce the psychological explanation. For socially institutionalized release constitutes an outstanding characteristic of the Negro cultures of West Africa and of the New World. That this is the case among the Ashanti is testified by Captain Rattray. Thus, during the *apo* and similar ceremonies, to revile those in power or about to assume power is not only permitted but urged, the reason being given that this is done so that the soul of the one who rules will not be sickened by the evil thoughts held against him by those whom he may have angered.[1] Similarly, in explaining the broadness of the action in many Ashanti folk-tales, Captain Rattray gives the native explanation of how it is held to be " good " for people to discuss and laugh at things otherwise forbidden. He concludes that " West Africans had discovered for themselves the truth of the psycho-analysts' theory of ' repression ', and that in these ways they sought an outlet for what might otherwise have become a dangerous complex ".[2]

In Dahomey, the institution of the *avogan*, the dance in the market-place, is similarly recognized by the natives as affording release for suppressed emotions. At stated periods the people

[1] R. S. Rattray, *Ashanti*, pp. 151–171. See especially the songs quoted on pp. 156–7.
[2] R. S. Rattray, *Akan-Ashanti Folk-Tales*, pp. ix–xii.

of each of the quarters of the city of Abomey have in turn their opportunity to stage such a dance. Crowds come to see the display and to watch the dancing, but, most of all, to listen to the songs and to laugh at the ridicule to which are held those who have offended members of the quarter giving the dance. Names are ordinarily not mentioned, for then fighting may result. In any event, the African relishes innuendo and circumlocution too well to be satisfied with bald, direct statement. However, everyone who is present already knows to whom reference is being made. Thus the song might be :

> " Woman, thy soul is misshapen.
> In haste was it made, in haste.
> So fleshless a face speaks, telling
> Thy soul was formed without care.
> The ancestral clay for thy making
> Was moulded in haste, in haste.
> A thing of no beauty art thou,
> Thy face unsuited to be a face,
> Thy feet unsuited for feet." [1]

A name may be used, but usually it is one given for the occasion, and employed as a symbol of baseness or treachery :

> " Call Adjevu to me, I would insult her . . ."

This same release through song is accorded co-wives. Nothing could have offered more striking testimony of the manner in which songs of this kind have a welcome place in domestic Dahomean life than the reaction of the wives of a chief who were asked to sing some of them. The first response was shocked amazement that anyone not a Dahomean suspected the existence of such songs ; when, however, they were convinced that this was more than a shot in the dark, their amazement gave way to peals of laughter before and after the singing. In the following song, which may serve as an example, the recrimination of one co-wife against another—a princess—is masked by the reference to her as a " man of rank " ; the singing takes place while the women work together in a court-yard of their husband's compound :—

> " O son of King Hwegbadja
> To you I bring news
> With you I leave word
> That a man of rank who kills and then steals is here.
> Something has been lost in this house
> And the owner has not found it.
> The man of rank who kills and then steals
> Has been here."

[1] I am indebted to Mrs. Herskovits for this translation.

Even the play of fancy in a language unknown to outsiders is not scorned by the West Africans to get release from repressed grievances, and this is especially true where their impotence against European control is concerned. The experience of companies who have recorded West African songs sung by Africans in European ports which, when offered for sale in West Africa, were found to have their popularity rest especially on the fact that many of them made sport of the Whites, is a case in point.

As in West Africa, so in the New World this channelling of emotional release takes characteristic forms. Among the most picturesque of these is the *lobi singi* of the Negroes of the coastal region of Dutch Guiana, especially of Paramaribo. This socially recognized form of ridicule is most often directed against a woman who has taken a man away from another. Less ritualized, the *lobi singi* may take place between two women who have quarrelled if, while the two are both working in a compound-yard, one of them sings songs which, though traditional in words and melody, have a reference that everyone present recognizes as applicable to the other. In the ritualized form, however, the ceremony of recrimination is one which takes preparation and must be carefully staged. A musical accompaniment is provided, and the friends of the aggrieved woman, dressed in their best, come to assist her in shaming her rival. The locale of the performance is the yard of the compound where the offender lives, and this woman, at the appointed time, barricades herself in her cabin and gives no sign. The occasion has been well advertised, and many spectators are present when the injured woman arrives with her friends and the music.

The players arrange themselves before the tightly-shut house ; the music to one side, the audience making a cleared space for the dancing. The songs are all of leader-and-chorus type, and the phrase ending the chorus is sung with a few dancing steps, accompanied by a disdainful lifting in back of the voluminous skirts of the traditional dress of the Paramaribo Negro women. As the steps are executed, the exclamation " Ha ! Ha ! " is heard. The words of the songs are to-day no longer as pointed as they were before recourse to the Dutch courts on charges of slander made watchfulness necessary. But the songs sung at the present are still adequately suggestive, as examples demonstrate :—

> " What can an ant do
> With a cow's head ?
> Ha ! Ha !
> She must eat the meat,
> And leave the bones.
> Ha ! Ha ! "

Again the injured woman may sing :—

> " You are handsomer than I
> You are fatter than I
> But I am sweeter than you.
> Ha ! Ha !
> That is why, my treasure,
> My treasure, cannot bear,
> To leave a sweet rose
> To come to the house of a crab.
> Ha ! Ha ! "

Or, she may tell how the man who has jilted her was worthless until she took him up :—

> " When I bought my cow, my cow,
> When I bought my cow,
> When I bought my cow, my cow,
> My cow did not even have horns ! "

It must be recognized that the Negro sees in the *lobi singi* a twofold purpose—to make the woman who has been wronged " feel better " and also to castigate the offender with ridicule. And those who have worked with Negroes know that ordinarily they prefer a blow to ridicule.

There is, however, still another type of *lobi singi*, which affords the release that comes through public confession and public proclamation of the intention to turn to a new and better way of life. A girl who has been promiscuous and who later desires a respected place in the community, herself leads the singing, and the songs dwell on her past mode of life ; the young men she has led astray, the women she has wronged, her intention to reform. Whatever the lines, the members of the chorus do not fail to end with the dancing steps and the exclamation " Ha ! Ha ! ". The following is an example of the songs sung at a *lobi singi* given by a young woman for herself :—

> " If I were a rich man
> I would buy a large farm.
> And what would I plant in it ?
> And what would I plant in it ?
> I would plant experience in it
> So that when I went out
> Experience would be a perfume for my body.
> Ha ! Ha ! "

That repression is a cause of neurosis is an elementary tenet of psychoanalysis ; the fact, explained in different terms, has been recognized by Negroes in even more explicit fashion than in the instances which have been quoted. Often the explanation of the importance of release takes the form of assuming supernatural vengeance as a cause of the ills that follow on repression. Instances from the beliefs of both African and New World Negroes which demonstrate this are to be found ; however, it will suffice to restrict examples to certain institutions studied in Guiana. The most explicit statement, one that would be instantly recognized as valid by any psychologist, has to do with the cause of insanity. The Paramaribo Negroes see it as bound up with the *winti*, as the African spirits worshipped by the coastal Negroes of Guiana are named. These spirits, which are inherited, are thought to come to an individual at about the age of puberty, after which active worship in the form of dancing to drums takes place. Everywhere in the New World, before and after emancipation of the slaves, pressure has been used by European officials to discourage the worship of these pagan deities. This has driven the worship of African gods—in this instance the *winti*—more and more into secret ritual. Yet the forbidden dances do take place. In Paramaribo dancing is permitted several times during the year, and then the adherents of the *winti* worship them openly. But there are some *winti* who drive their followers to more frequent worship with an urgency that cannot be denied ; and at such times a basin, over-turned in a larger container of water, is struck to simulate the drums ordinarily employed and the devotees dance. Were they to inhibit the call of the gods to dance and persist in their refusal over an extended period of time, the Negroes say they would go insane. Indeed, the *winti*-worshippers insist that the insanity found among the Christian Negroes of Paramaribo is due to this cause. It is believed that these persons have inherited spirits, and because their new religion prohibits dancing for them, the resistance to doing the bidding of the inherited gods robs them of their reason—that is, the spirits which " possess " them drive them mad.

An even clearer appreciation of the consequences of repressing emotions—in this case, anger, bitterness, or hatred—is seen in the Guiana concept of *fiofio*. Historically, this can be related to that same *apo* ceremony which Rattray has described among the Ashanti, that period of release from the ordinary social controls that marked the time when a man might make free with anyone, even the King himself. In Suriname, however, the form of the belief is different from the institu-tionalized license that marks the African periods of freedom from restraint. *Fiofio* is primarily the name of an insect. However, it is also conceived as a spirit which, taking the form of this insect, enters the body, causing illness and even death. This deadly presence is brought on when a quarrel between intimates has not been followed by a reconciliation, and when some gesture of affection occurs between such participants to a quarrel at a later date ; in a phrase, when hypocrisy, conscious or unconscious, is practised, the souls of those concerned are resentful, and their owners sicken and die.   An example will make clear the concept and the behaviour resulting from it.   We may suppose that two close friends, or two relatives, or two persons who are members of the same household have quarrelled, and no reconciliation has been effected.   Time passes, the incident loses its importance, and gradually the two may no longer even consciously remember that it had taken place, so that a normal friendly relationship is resumed.   Then one of them accepts something from the other.   Since the inner hurt has never been healed, ill-luck—bad crops, illness, children stillborn—befalls one or the other of them, or both.   Diviners are consulted, and if it is the long-standing difference that is shown to be the cause of the trouble, the ceremonial retraction known as *puru mofo*—literally, " withdraw from the mouth "—takes place.   The one who has wronged the other calls on the soul of the wronged one, saying :

" *Akra Kwami*,[1] I did not mean to offend you.   I was hasty. Do not avenge yourself on me, or on my wife, or our children. I beg you, overlook what I said and do not bear me any ill-will."

He takes water in his mouth, and spurts it over his doorway three times, repeating the formula each time.   The retraction is preceded and followed by ceremonial washing—" to wash *fiofio* " is the native phrase—when the parties to the quarrel pronounce this formula :—

" Just as this broom sweeps heaviness away, so, too, must your heaviness go away.   Just as the mother hen carries her child until it breaks the egg,[2] so everything that you carry must break and come into the open."

Should the ceremonial retraction not take place, it is believed death will ensue.   To have honest dislikes is natural enough and, says the native, these do a man no harm ; it is only when quarrels are masked in surface friendliness and an ancient grudge is harboured that it is dangerous to make an exchange of belongings or accept any gesture of affection.

The discussion thus far has had to do with socially sanctioned mechanisms which permit of release from inhibitions and conflicts of various sorts.   What has been shown is that among the primitive Negroes, both in Africa and the New World, patterned types of psychic purges are recognized as valid ; what is important for a psychoanalytic approach to the understanding of these

---

[1] That is, " Saturday soul."

[2] The imagery here is somewhat confusing ; the meaning is " Just as the chick emerges from the egg-shell, so the sickness must leave the person who is ill ".

social data is the fact that, in every case, the native explanation of the particular type of behaviour, though ordinarily couched in terms of the supernatural, can be restated in terms of the unconscious.

Less sharply pointed toward Freudian mechanisms, but nevertheless intelligible in terms of compensation through rationalization, are the following attitudes from Dahomey.   Among a people where the worship of gods and ancestors plays as prominent a rôle as it does there, it is necessary to explain national mishaps on grounds other than the powerlessness of these beings who rule the destiny of the living, for it is clear that doubt in their power would rob the Dahomean of the security he feels in the structure of his world. Rationalizations of such mishaps, therefore, are not lacking. A small-pox scourge or a locust plague is a punishment meted out for the misdeeds of the living, for a breach against supernatural decrees. Defeat in a battle comes as punishment for violating the edict of an ancient ancestor that there be peace ; the conquest by the French is accounted for by the fact that King Glele, the father of that Behanzin who was the reigning monarch when the French took Dahomey, had advised his son against war, and especially against war with the Whites who were the makers of implements of war—guns and gunpowder. Because, therefore, Behanzin followed his own headstrong course, the ancestors would not support him, and Dahomey fell. Since it is not always convenient to comply with the non-worldly edicts of the ancestors—for some of them were short-sighted humans, and the Dahomean laughs as he tells of these rulings—it is the letter of the law which is often obeyed to cope with such taboos, but not the spirit. Thus for the ancestor who enjoined peace, a village has been selected and ordered to remain forever at peace.   When King Tegbesu found it tiresome to have the marks of the leopard's claws cicatrized on his forehead, as the ancestors commanded, and in consequence remain inaccessible to all other humans, he designated a man to act as his substitute for the observance of this, and himself took all the prerogatives of kingship, and the freedom to enjoy them as well. Since it was felt that there were spiritual dangers in warring against other kingdoms who had powerful gods of their own, it was not the King of Dahomey who declared war, who directed the campaign, and who took the slaves. The Minister of War did the first two, and the soldiers did the last. During a war the King's tall stool was occupied by the commanding general, and the King himself sat on a low stool, and nominally he was under this officer. When slaves were captured, each soldier received from the King's hand a few cowries—admittedly a ceremonial gesture—and thus " sold " each of the captives to the King, on whom no vengeance could then fall, for he was only engaging in barter. It is significant that this payment was called " washing the hands ".

Another instance of behaviour immediately available for Freudian analysis may be given. This trait differs somewhat from those heretofore discussed, and is taken from the customs of the Bush-Negroes of Suriname, a people whose isolation in the bush has largely protected their African culture from European influence. The example to be cited contributes material for the consideration of the extent to which the Oedipus complex may be variously shaped in different cultures. Malinowski has shown that among the strongly matrilineal people of the Trobriand Islands, the Oedipus complex in its classic form is not found, but that the unconscious hatreds are transferred to the maternal uncle, the incest-wish to the sister.[1] The social organization of the Bush-Negroes is legally matrilineal, spiritually patrilineal, resembling in its double exogamic features the principal outlines of the Gold Coast type from which it derives.[2] What, then, is the form this " nuclear complex " takes in such a society ?

It was not in an investigation of Bush-Negro psychological processes, but during an attempt to obtain as much detail as possible regarding death-customs, that the answer came in terms of an Oedipus reaction as " correct " psychoanalytically as though it had been stated by Freud himself. The question which had been asked was, " When a man dies, do they destroy his house ? " And the reply : " Not unless he has done black magic. If it is an ordinary man, his widow lives there with his daughters." " What happens to his sons ? " " They are sent away for a long time." " Why ? " " Because the soul of a man loves his daughters but hates his sons, and if they remained in his house, his ghost would kill them." " And if a woman dies ? " " Then the husband continues to live there with his sons, for if it is a woman's ghost, she will destroy her daughters. But her sons, she loves them and watches over them."

[1] Cf. *Sex and Repression in Savage Society, passim.*
[2] Cf. M. J. Herskovits, " The Social Organization of the Bush-Negroes of Suriname," *Proceedings of the XXIII International Congress of Americanists,* 1928 (New York, 1930), pp. 713–727.

Northwestern University,
Evanston,
Illinois.

DECADENCE IN INDIA

By A. M. Hocart

The work of Sir John Marshall exempts me from the task
of proving that art in India from the first century B.C. follows
the same curve, exhibits in succession the same symptoms as
the art of Greece or of the Middle Ages.[1] He leaves me only
to sum up the results.

Like the archaic art of Greece and the work of the medieval
Primitive Painters, the Indian art of before Christ is distinguished
by good and leisurely craftsmanship, but faulty technique.
It has not yet mastered its materials. Its ambitions are not
high, yet the performance is good. It does not strive, but is
easily contented. It is interested in things, not ideas. It likes
above all things to tell a story. The gates of Sanchi, one of
which has been cast for the Indian Section of the Victoria and
Albert Museum, are covered with Buddhist legends told in a
simple spirit. So were the somewhat later monuments of
Amaravati, the spoils of which adorn the staircase of the British
Museum.

Narrative gradually fades away, and sculpture devotes
itself increasingly to the portrayal of ideal figures. It enters
on what we may call the classical phase which culminates in
the fourth and fifth centuries of our era, the period known as
the Gupta era. It has all the characteristics which mark classical
art elsewhere : mastery of technique, perfection of form,
aspirations that do not transcend the means of expression, self-
restraint, the complete adaptation of the means to the end.
Among its finest productions is to be numbered the Sanchi
torso at the Victoria and Albert Museum.

Gupta art, like all art, passes its zenith and declines into a
florid and elegant, but nerveless accomplishment. Then comes
the revolt against form without content, against the excessive
restraint imposed by classical standards of perfection. It is
the romantic period of Indian art. The emotions rise up against
the tyranny of intellect, and in the pursuit of intensity destroy
form. The revolt is in full swing in the seventh century. Even
those who do not like its violence and defiance, its exaggeration
and cult of the monstrous, must allow a certain greatness to

[1] *Sketch of Indian Antiquities*, Calcutta (Government Press). For Egypt,
Greece, Europe, see Sir W. Flinders Petrie's *Revolutions of Civilization*, London,
1922.

that art : at all events it is better than the inanities of late
Gupta, just as our romantics, with all their faults, are better
than their artificial and hackneyed predecessors.   It may be
unhealthy, but it is powerful.[1] Being a revolt against the period
immediately preceding it, it harks back to archaic models.
(Decadence is always archaistic.) Old types and old subjects
are revived ; but no expert will ever mistake an archaistic for
an archaic piece of work.   The spirit is entirely different, and
the spirit always peeps through the surface of imitation.   The
romantic art of India delights in the presentation of old myths
which had suffered the eclipse of Buddhism ; but it is not the
story that really interests the artist, but the opportunity for
emotional expression and for flaunting an aggressive creed.
The moral bias is typical of decadence.

The revolt wears itself out : the energy departs ; the
monstrous ceases to be vigorous and is merely tame, and nothing
is left but that standardized and uninspired art which is the only
Indian art known to most Europeans.

It is the final phase of Indian art which Prof. C. G. Seligman
had in view when he classed the Indians as an introvert people.
He was thinking of the classical period of the Greeks when he
put them down as extraverts.   The characteristics which he
has ranged under those two psychological terms are not so much
the mark of race as of phase.[2]   To speak in less technical
language we might say that to take an interest in things and
rejoice in activity for its own sake is archaic, to be interested in
ideas and act from ulterior motives is decadent.

Concerning the progress of art in India we have abundant
evidence, because much of the art is recorded in durable materials
such as stone and bronze, and so has survived.   Students also
abound, for the study of art is a pleasant hobby.   But art is
not the only activity of man, not even the most important.
We cannot hope successfully to diagnose the malady of decadence
unless we study its symptoms as manifested in man's other
activities.   This is not easy because the materials are scanty
and the students few.   I will not venture, therefore, to study
them in the vastness of India, but will draw chiefly on the
familiar, if meagre, evidence that has come to my notice during
my archæological researches in Ceylon.[3]

Ceylon is linked to Northern India, from the first century B.C.
to the sixth A.D.   Then something happened.   We do not
know what ; but we find Ceylon switched off from Northern to
Southern India.   Its normal progress is arrested ; there is, as

[1] See my " Many-armed gods " in *Acta Orientalia*, vii (1929), 91.
[2] See his " Anthropology and Psychology," *Journ. Roy. Anthropological Inst.*, 1924, p. 13.
[3] The evidence is scattered through my " Archæological Summaries " in the *Ceylon Journal of Science*, section G, vols. i and ii.

far as one can venture an opinion on an obscure period, a drop in artistic achievement ; then the ascent is renewed. The peak is reached after India is well advanced in decline ; the classical period lies in the ninth or tenth century. That shows that the phases are not quite as regular as they appear in Sir Flinders Petrie's book. No doubt there are strict laws, but their operations are disguised by disturbing factors. The disturbing factor in this case seems to be a wave from Dravidian India.

As usual, archaizing tendencies appear with the beginning of the decline. They begin to show themselves in the tenth century. Types of sculpture are revived which had gone out of fashion in the fourth century. This archaizing appears in religion. The Buddha had been cremated and his remains deposited in topes, hemispherical structures, brick or stone versions of our own round barrow. The tope had thus become the chief Buddhist shrine. Up to the fourth century A.D. it was the centre of worship. Kings vied with each other who should build the largest, as the pyramid builders had tried to surpass one another, and the dimensions reached rivalled those of the pyramids. The maximum was reached in the fourth century. Then it dropped to small dimensions, and became an appendage to a monastery containing other shrines on an equal footing. In the twelfth century the colossal tope reappeared, and the largest ever built belongs to that century. It was a last flicker before the extinction. The colossal tope does not appear to have been attempted after the thirteenth century.

We know from the Pali chronicle that the history of the tope reflects the history of doctrine. Ceylon was converted to Buddhism when it was still in that fairly pure form later known as the Little Vehicle. Ritual and mystical tendencies, however, soon spread from India to Ceylon under the name of the Great Vehicle, that form of Buddhism which still prevails from Tibet to Japan. By the fourth century it was disputing the ascendancy, and may have won it.[1] In the twelfth the Church was purged of heresy and Ceylon returned to the Little Vehicle in which it remains to the present day.

The chronicle is concerned solely with pious benefactions and religious rivalries, and tells us nothing about such fundamental things as population, food, finance. We have to piece together the evidence of ancient works to supply this blank.

Since towns have come into existence they contain most of the history of civilization. It is the towns that make and mar it to a great extent. They grow and grow, at first promoting intellectual life and political organization, then passing the point of their greatest utility and upsetting the whole balance of society and of mind. The towns of Ceylon were built of mud and thatch

[1] S. Paranavitana, " Mahayanism in Ceylon," *Ceylon Journal of Science*, G, ii, 35.

so that we cannot trace their growth on the ground. Their monasteries were built of brick and stone, when they were wealthy enough. Their numbers give us some idea of the wealth and population. In the eighth, ninth, and especially the tenth century they multiply rapidly. They blossom forth most just before the decadence.

The irrigation system is even a better index. That part of Ceylon which took the lead down to the fourteenth century, the North and the South-East, receives scarcely any rain from May to October, and in consequence gets dried up. Such a country cannot maintain more than a scanty population without the aid of irrigation. Quite early, we do not know how early, streams were dammed to fill up in the rainy season and water the fields during the dry. Up to about 250 B.C. a small artificial lake 255 acres in extent was sufficient to supply the needs of Anuradhapura, the capital. Then another was added covering about 396 acres. By the second century A.D. a third was in existence with an area of two or three thousand acres. In the fifth century the original reservoirs had to be fed by a new one some 20 miles distant, covering 39,000 acres. These " tanks ", as they are called in Ceylon, not only supplied the city, but also irrigated the fields. They bear witness not only to the growth of the towns, but to the steady increase of the land under rice cultivation. Numerous other large irrigation works all over the country tell the same tale. Then comes a period of chaos ; the irrigation works are neglected, and at the same time there is a dearth of monastic buildings. Evidently the country is getting depopulated. In the twelfth century an effort is made to stem the ebb. Dams are repaired, and new ones made on a colossal scale, like everything at this time. The largest of all was made next to the new capital : it had a dam about 9 miles long. Ceylon thus bears out Sir Flinders' generalization that the greatest engineering feats come towards the end of the effective life of a nation, when art is getting exhausted. These efforts at reviving agriculture were followed by a worse relapse. The Sinhalese resumed their retreat southwards into the wet zone, where cultivation can dispense with great irrigation works. The dry zone was abandoned to the jungle, which still holds it against the attacks of the white man.

Incidentally, I have illustrated a typical symptom of approaching decadence, megalomania. The craze for size appears in all ages : whenever anything comes into vogue each one tries to go one better than the other, until a limit is reached and interest decays with the power of doing better. This passion for size is especially virulent before final collapse of a people. The Communes of Northern Europe built their loftiest cathedrals on the eve of their extinction. The Roman Empire

reached its greatest expanse under Trajan, eighty years before
Gibbon begins his story of the decline. Athens was most brilliant
and far-ruling when the Peloponesian war began. Ceylon was
no exception. Small as the buildings of the tenth century may
appear to us they were large for Ceylon and show an increase
over the preceding centuries. Huge stones were often employed
in their construction some 15 tons in weight. It is more in
the extent of the monasteries than in the size of individual
buildings that the striving after greatness is apparent. This
striving is reflected in the language of the inscriptions. Down
to the first century B.C. there are numerous inscriptions which
run somewhat like this : " The cave of the Lord Tissa, son of
the Lord Abhaya, is given to the church of the four quarters."
By the third century it has become, " The great king, Malu
tisa, caused to be built a sitting hall," and so on. In the tenth
the style is, " The great king, Abhaya . . . lord by lineal descent
from the great lords of the soil of the Island of Ceylon ; who
promoted the religion, having comforted his people with showers
of boundless all-embracing, gentle and pure qualities . . . " and
so on in interminable periods into one of which you could easily
pack several of Dr. Johnson's. This grandiloquence masks
decay. Anarchy follows, then the Indian summer of the reign
of Parakrama Bahu the Great. That vigorous and unscrupulous
monarch in the twelfth century united the distracted country
and set himself to surpass all his predecessors. He built the
largest tope, the largest temple, the largest palace, and the
largest reservoir. His foreign policy was equally aspiring. He
carried his arms into South India and even into Burma.

All this splendour was hollow. The largest reservoir has not
stood the test of time as well as some of the others, and it was
made up of several older ones. The largest tope is mistaken
for a hill by the unobservant visitor, whereas topes twelve hundred
years earlier still retain their facing. The most ambitious
temples of the twelfth century were largely built of brickbats
taken from earlier monuments. Stone is sparely used, poorly
cut, and often pilfered from the works of predecessors. We
have here lighted upon another symptom of decadence :
resources have not kept pace with ambitions ; to do things
greatly it is necessary to do them cheaply. The additions
made in the thirteenth century by Parakrama's successors are
distinctly shoddy.

The national finances were evidently as specious as the
building. Only a few years after the great Parakrama's death,
King Nissanka Malla announced in an inscription that the
land " had been distressed by the inordinate exactions of former
kings ".[1] Heavy taxation has always been the penalty of

[1] *Epigraphia Zeylanica*, ii, 133.

decline. India suffered from it like the Roman Empire. The Moghuls took one-fifth of the produce of their subjects, nearly as much as our income-tax.

Nissanka Malla in the inscription I have quoted claims to have remitted taxes for five years, and to have abolished the tax on the cultivation of clearings in the forest. All his inscriptions show a painful desire to capture the suffrages of the people by financial leniency. But the money had to come from somewhere, because the social services had to be kept going ; in fact Nissanka lays great stress upon them as a claim to the gratitude of his people. The copper coinage tells us how the problem was solved. Copper coins of the great Parakrama are not common.[1] Under Nissanka they begin to get common ; but the record belongs to one Sahasa Malla, whose output in two years about equals that of the great Parakrama and his other twelve successors in over fifty years. There is only one possible inference, and that is that the government dared not increase taxation and fell back on inflation. In spite of that changes of government were frequent, the average reign being little more than a year. Then came a king who reigned twenty years but of whom I have never found a coin.

The social services, as I said, went on as usual under Nissanka. In his numerous and bombastic inscriptions he likes to dwell on the alms-houses he built, the grants he made, the exemptions he allowed to those in straitened circumstances, and the largesses he made, " pearls, precious stones, corals, and such other jewellery in abundance." " He quenched the fire of indigence with plenteous showers of wealth consisting of *kahavanu* coins, copper, bell metal, gold, silver, pearls, clothes, and jewellery. He appointed ministers and other officials and provided them with livings. . . . He repaired the great tanks, channels, and embankments. And thinking that robbers commit robbery on account of a desire for wealth he gave them whatever they liked and in this way removed the fear of thieves. . . . He provided the members of the Church who led pure lives with the four requisites. . . . He promoted religion and science by providing suitable means of subsistence for those versed in the doctrine and in the branches of knowledge."

The dole had always existed in Ceylon, as everywhere else, because there always are people who cannot maintain themselves and others who won't. What is symptomatic of decline is its inordinate development. The inscriptions of a single king are not sufficient proof that this evil was chronic. We require statistical evidence, and this is hard to get, and we can only

[1] A copper coin inscribed Parakrama Bahu is fairly common, but Mr. H. W. Codrington has come to the conclusion that they belong, not to the first, but to the second king of that name, and he is undoubtedly right.

hope that further researches will throw light on the matter. In the meantime we can note that the archæological evidence points to a steady increase in alms-houses. Remains of them earlier than the ninth or tenth centuries are rare, just like the monasteries to which they are attached. It may be that before that time they were usually built of perishable materials ; but even so a change to stone indicates a greater expenditure under that head. It is only in these centuries that we know of huge stone canoes that were filled with rice for distribution. Inscriptions show also a great multiplication of grants to monasteries. Nissanka Malla went further in the direction of public largesses than any according to his own evidence. A new and significant feature, too, is his anxious catering for popular favour. We learn the reason from one of his inscriptions : the throne was not secure, and there was a party that wanted to set up another king not of royal caste. The constant changes of kings also bear witness to the unrest.

Mendicancy has remained to the present day the blight of India and Ceylon. There are parts of London which now do not fall short of India in this respect, but in India it permeates the whole country. It means that a large part of the population has taken to parasitic habits because it is unable to subsist otherwise. India has never developed a system of administration comparable to that of Greece, Rome, and Modern Europe, and therefore an organized system of national relief could not develop. There Church and State are indistinguishable, and therefore relief takes the form of religious benefactions, and the monasteries are the centres of relief.

Travellers in Ceylon have been impressed by the multitude of ancient monasteries around the ancient capitals, and they have commented on the rampant parasitism they imply. It is not quite fair, however, to regard these swarms of monks as consisting entirely of drones. A great many were doubtless nothing more ; but a great many took the place of our school-masters, professors, parsons, hospital staffs, and charitable organizations. But there is a limit to the number of such persons which society can usefully employ. Exceed that limit and the surplus differ from drones only in that they are busy. A country which had to maintain as many intellectuals as Ceylon had to in the tenth century is top-heavy. The excess of intellectuals is not only superfluous, but mischievous ; for men whose brains have been trained to activity, but have not been given a useful outlet, are sure to find one in pure destructiveness. Finally, the multiplication of intellectuals must result in the decline of intellectual achievement, for it is necessary to go deeper and deeper in order to recruit, and so the average is lowered, and those born to think are swamped by those for whom thinking is merely

a claim to be exempted from the rough work of life. The latter
history of Sinhalese literature is one of mechanical copying.
The monastic order sank lower and lower, so that when it was
reorganized in the eighteenth century, the king had to send to
Burma and Siam in order to renew the apostolic succession.

All this time the Tamils from India were pressing hard;
but the common foe could not unite the Sinhalese except for a
short time under Parakrama Bahu. After him the Sinhalese
gradually withdrew southwards. Then the Portuguese seized
their coasts. These invasions were the consequence, not the
cause of their decline. The South Indians had been invading
Ceylon since the first century B.C., but the battle swayed
backwards and forwards till the eleventh century. It was not
till then that the Sinhalese began to yield ground for good and
all, and took refuge in the mountain fastnesses, the last resort
of the weak.

I have outlined the rise and decadence of India and Ceylon
from the first century B.C., but the history of India does not
begin then. What came before that ? Was India steadily
rising from the time of our earliest records, the Vedas, about
1000 B.C. ? Does the first century represent a continuation,
not a beginning ? As we go backwards in time from the earliest
art we meet with facts that are at first disconcerting. First,
in the third century B.C. the most extensive empire that ever
spread over India before the British, and empires are symptomatic
of the end rather than of the beginning. Then in the sixth
century we assist at the birth of a religion which is a characteristic product of decadence. Buddhism is pessimism : existence,
it says, is evil, it means pain and sorrow ; escape from it lies
only in extinction. Those are not the sentiments of a people
with the future before them, but of a nation that has lived.
Pessimists there always are in every age, but it is only in periods
of decline that they find a ready ear with the majority. We are
living in such a period, and so we are in a good position to understand Buddhism. The author of Ecclesiastes represents that
phase among the Jews. This disgust with life would have been
unintelligible to the early Greeks and Romans ; but it was a
favourite theme of the Fathers of the Church. The only conclusion possible is that in the sixth century B.C. India was in a
state of decadence.

Let us analyse the Buddhist doctrine to see if we can discover
the cause of its pessimism. Contact, it says, causes sensation,
sensation desire, and desire pain. It would seem then that the
people to whom the Buddha addressed himself so successfully
were suffering from an excess of desire ; for moderate desires
are not painful, but pleasurable, if they can be satisfied. They
must have wanted more than they could win or enjoy, and so

they suffered.   We are familiar with that state of mind in spoilt
children, and in spoilt adults for that matter : they have their
way so invariably that they fret more to be denied it, than they
rejoice to have it.   When life has been made too easy it is apt to
become painful.   The legend of the Buddha shows that the
Indians had already then made this psychological discovery.
It depicts him as living in luxury, never allowed to come into
contact with the ugly side of life.   He becomes satiated with
pleasures, and over-sensitive to the unpleasant.   The crisis
comes one night after the usual pleasures : his wife and his
dancing girls are asleep, and the sight fills him with disgust.
He escapes from the palace, and wanders forth into solitude.   At
first he rushes to the other extreme, and almost starves himself
to death.   Finding no balm in extreme asceticism he returns
to a middle way, a life of renunciation without severity.   He
suppresses all desire and retires from the world of senses into
one of ideas.   He seeks peace within.

It matters little whether the legend is true or not.   Fiction
is often truer than history, for fiction tells us what the people
feel, and evidently they felt that the need of their times was not
the conqueror of empires, but the man, who having conquered
the tyranny of desire, showed others the way to do the same.

This situation recurs whenever man's success over his
environment has been such that all his desires are satisfied,
and he is obliged to create new ones.   The pursuit of novelty
for a time diverts his mind, but that fails sooner or later like
all drugs.   Desire becomes painful because it is so intense and
can no longer be satisfied.   Horace has described the flight
from black care in one of his best known odes.   It was about the
same time that Poseidonius, a late Stoic, declared, like the
Buddha, that " pain arose out of passion and desire ",[1] for at
that time Rome was beginning to suffer the pains of decadence.
A Bishop recently went deeper, I think, into the causes of our
present troubles than all our economists, when he put the blame
on our habit of putting our happiness too much in externals,
and hoped the crisis would do us good by forcing us to discard
the unessential to which we clung.   A lady specialist in social
study recently declared that " it was not so much organic
diseases from which the nation was suffering, but from . . .
all sorts of nervous complaints which meant a nerve-wracked
population.   Everywhere the tendency was to strive after a
social condition which was just a little higher than the one in
which we happened to be at the moment.   We were striving
after gods that were not worth striving for ".   Men at the present
day are merely restating in more modern, and sometimes more
scientific terms, the discovery which had been made by the

[1] Ritter und Preller, *Historia Philosophiæ Græcæ*, p. 436.

Buddhists and contemporary sects some 2,400 years ago, and remade later by Stoics and Christians. The great development of mental therapy within the last few years shows that the same mental disease is forcing us to seek much the same kind of treatment.

One curious effect of the disease is that whenever a patient finds, or thinks he has found, a remedy he must at once impart it, or even impose it. Buddhism sent out missionaries beyond the confines of India, even to Syria. Proselytism always tends to intolerance, and the history of Buddhist councils is not more edifying than that of Christian ones. Intolerance is not peculiar to an age of decadence ; what is peculiar is its recrudescence after an age of tolerance, for the classical age is usually one of intellectual emancipation. Decadence sets back the yoke.

One result of this propagandist spirit is to accentuate that uniformity or standardization which seems to be the result of an abnormal growth of the population. Perhaps it is the natural reaction to a need for mechanizing everything in a society that has grown so big that the individual is lost in it, and the personal touch becomes impossible. Every one must think alike, because every one must act alike, and there are too many to discuss and compromise. All character is levelled out of Buddhist scriptures : it is not men that pass across their stage, not even types, but standardized machines devoid of feeling. There is no interest in the individual.

Standardization goes hand in hand with centralization. The individual does not count : all authority is at the centre. Buddhism is contemporary with the extinction of the old principalities of the Sakyas, the Kolis, the Licchavis, by empires such as that of Kosala. These empires were in turn absorbed by the biggest of them all, that of Asoka, who has been called the Constantine of Buddhism. Some at least of these empires were ruled by upstarts despised by the old aristocracies which they destroyed.[1]

It would lead too far afield to make an exhaustive catalogue of all those characteristics that mark Buddhism as a reaction to decadent conditions. Only one more need be mentioned. No religion has ever carried pacifism to such extremes as Buddhism. Non-resistance is one of its key-notes. To take the life, even of an animal, is sinful, and this sin must be avoided at the cost of one's own life.

If Buddhism is the product of a decadent age it must have been preceded by a classical period, and the classical by an archaic one. Our earliest records are the Vedas, about 1000 B.C. It is no longer possible to regard them, with the earlier Vedic scholars, as the spontaneous effusions of primitive man just awakening

[1] *Jataka*, iv, 146.

to the beauties of the world and bursting into song like birds at a spring dawn. Mankind was already very old in 1000 B.C. ; and the Vedas had centuries of poetic technique and ritual behind them. The error of the discoverers of the Vedas does, however, bear witness to the freshness and manly vigour which marks those hymns and which contrasts with the weariness and soft prolixity of Buddhist writings. The moral contrast is equally remarkable. Buddhist hymns and prose subordinate everything to morality and idealism. Morality, in the narrow sense of being " good ", " saintly ", does not worry the Vedic singer : his dominant interest is increase of progeny, cattle, wealth, health, and security. He has no wish to proselytize, because that would mean sharing with others, even enemies, the secret of material prosperity. He is innocent of pacifism ; it is part of his religion to smite the heathen.

The next stage is represented about 800 B.C. by a voluminous prose literature on the ritual. There is no longer the same freshness. Cold reasoning prevails. There is as yet, however, no sign of idealism ; the end is still purely practical : the ritual aims at nothing more than material prosperity. We hear much of evil, but it is not moral evil, not sin, but only the hostile powers that blight man and cattle, and abet his enemies.

In the later ritual books a kind of mysticism begins to make its appearance. Much stress is laid upon knowledge as a substitute for ritual. This tendency grows. Asceticism comes more and more to the front. From an early time it was prescribed as a preparation for the sacraments, but by degrees it overspread the whole lives of religious men. As world weariness increased it became a favourite escape from the world. And thus we come down again to Buddhism.

Thus between 1000 B.C. and the present day India has passed through two cycles of rise and decadence. There is nothing surprising in this. Minoan Greece declined, and then emerged again as the Greece we know. On the ruins of the Roman Empire a new civilization has been built. Sir Flinders Petrie thinks Egypt was revived several times.

We can now understand what has seemed a paradox to students of Indian art. Buddhism is pessimistic : it is not for the happy ; it scorns the senses and seeks to escape from them. Yet early Buddhist art is happy and softly sensual : it delights in alluring female figures and in worldly pleasures. In the classical period the frescoes are still happy and sensual. The paradox is only apparent : early Buddhist art belongs to an entirely different phase from the original Buddhist gospel. The art has inherited the doctrines of the gospel, but the spirit has passed away. The bas-reliefs of Barhut and Sanchi stand in the same relation to the Buddhist canon as the medieval art of Europe to the New Testament and the Fathers. Primitive Buddhist artists, like the Italian and Flemish Primitives, took their subjects from the preceding decadence, but not their outlook. The pious legends were merely good stories to tell in pictures.

Just as our Renaissance dropped Christian for Pagan subjects, so the Indian Renaissance, which began in the fourth century, harked back from Buddhist hagiology to the old Vedic gods. There was this difference, however, that we have only used the Pagan gods as a poetic fiction. The Vedic gods had never died out, and were revived in earnest.

I have dwelt much on Buddhism because it reveals the nature of decadence better than anything else in Indian history, perhaps than in any history. The gospels may grapple with the same disease, but it is by way of exhortation : they offer no diagnosis. Buddhism is more methodical and comes nearer to our modern psychology, not in its conclusions, but in its manner of proceeding. It marks an important stage in the history of mental pathology. The Greek philosophers may have far surpassed the Indians in their analysis of mental processes, but India has made considerable contributions to the study of functional disorders, in a manner typically Indian, not from a purely speculative interest, as the Greeks would have done, but from practical motives, to remove suffering. One reason why the Indians have always been so interested in the disease is that they have suffered from it so acutely. For decadence is a functional disease of society made up of all the functional troubles of the individuals that compose it.

THE ANTHROPOLOGICAL VALUE OF THE SKULL

By ALEŠ HRDLIČKA

The anthropological value of the skull has been recognized since Herodotus, who points for the first time, so far as known, to racial differences in the skull ; but more particularly since Peter Camper and Blumenbach, who definitely initiate craniological studies and measurements for racial comparison. With the subsequent works of Soemmering, Morton, Anders Retzius, de Baer, Broca, Quatrefages and Hamy, Barnard Davis, Flower, Kollmann, Sergi, R. Virchow, Topinard, Schwalbe, and many others—to mention only those who are already gone—the study and measurements of the skull assumed such an importance and extent that they overshadowed all other research in anthropology. This state of affairs has been further strengthened, since 1856, through the extremely detailed and interesting studies on the crania of early man, and since the 'sixties by those on the head of the living. The methods of study and measurement grew in complexity ; the data were converted into " indices " and treated mathematically ; the man-made indices and the misunderstood mathematical results became gradually so many fetishes of classification ; the plasticity and changeability of parts as well as of the whole cranium were almost forgotten ; and the skull became enthroned as the paramount arbiter of matters racial.

During this great *skull-reign* the whole of mankind was subdivided by the rapidly petrifying indices ; ethnic derivations, however improbable otherwise, were handily determined by the same ; enthusiastic evolutionists lost completely the sense of evolution ; and nature in general was made to conform to the mechanized new discipline. Publication after publication appeared analysing by a few indices of the skull the populations of different countries and their origins ; negroids were shown in Scandinavia, Cro-Magnons or Nordics wherever there was anything worth while ; the nineteenth century Eskimo were identified with a 12,000 (or so) B.C. Frenchman ; Australians and Melanesians appeared marvellously in America ; all the brachycephals were " mongoloids " and came from Central Asia ; and there was a general carnival of unconstrained determinations. The cure-all, the solve-it-all-and-be-done-with-hard-work — a panacea so many have always been and are still seeking wherever hard endeavour is involved—had been found at last for Anthropology.

H

But the exhilaration somehow could never reach above the half-hearted, for annoyingly there remained something subconscious, the subdued voice of which kept on warning against the all-sufficiency of the new acquisition. And an earnest, sober, irritating worker here and there, instead of following the crowd, stayed contrarily behind and now and then even issued a chilling warning.

Besides which there kept on cropping up pestering conditions. It thus came about that, no matter how " pure " the group of human and even other living beings, each of the cranial or head measurements and indices showed a very material range of variation. This variation was seen to amount to from over 10 to 20 per cent of each individual measurement or index. Thus a series of skulls, if sufficiently large, even where there could be the least question of admixture—as with the Old Egyptians, some of the American aborigines, the true negroes, and others— would give cephalic, facial, and nasal measurements and indices that, regardlessly, transgressed on both the lower and the higher established subdivisions of these indices, which by rights belonged to other ethnic groups ; and once in so many specimens there would be a case where more than one of the exceptional conditions were united in one and the same head or cranium. Such cases were branded as " exceptional " or, even more commonly, came to be viewed with a deep shadow of doubt as to their legitimate descent ; yet they persisted in keeping within the " normal " curve of distribution of their series and to recur, under differing guises, when there was more material.

Thus, in the end, evidence accumulated that a skull or a head, especially a skull or a head near one or the other extreme of the normal variation series, might be sufficiently unlike the mean of its kind to fall within another subdivision of the established classifications. In other words, a few members of even the most critically selected ethnic group, the standard skull or head of which was, for example, mesocephalic, would show on one side dolicho- and on the other subbrachy- or even brachycephaly, without there being in evidence any substantial facts that would justify their elimination. Moreover, this phenomenon was found to be not an exception but the invariable rule in all cases, both in man and other living beings, where the series of samples were large enough for the determination of somewhere near their full range of variation.

This inevitably implied a new view of conditions : that of not only the presence of broad normal variability, but also of an absence of discontinuity of skull characters, within the human and, as was learned later, any given species, regardless of the number of its apparent " races " or segregations.

It thus became plain that racial groups of human skulls or

heads, or of any other parts, organs, or characters of the body, are never discontinued racial entities, but connect throughout the human groups in the extremes of their normal variation. Nor is this, it was found, a mere interdigitation, it is an actual connection. And this is a very consequential realization.

However, the above is not all that has been learned, though there is, oddly, still but a very imperfect general consciousness of these realizations.

The evidence of Early Man, and that of many phyla of animals and plants, has absolutely convinced every anthropologist of the fact of anthropo- and biogenesis, or, as commonly termed, organic evolution. This great recognition, reduced to its simplest expression, means that in the course of time, under the action of a multitude of natural agencies, every part of every organism, man included, has changed in a regressive or progressive manner. One of the most fundamental properties of all living matter is its plasticity. Organic plasticity means changeability or, as usually expressed, morphological adaptability under changing conditions.

The remains of Early Man show that very great changes in the human skull and all its parts have taken place within the last five-, three-, and even less than one hundred thousand years ; and there is ample ground for the conviction that the human body in all its parts, including the skull, is still plastic, still adaptable, still mutable. Thus, Matiegka has shown that the skulls in the limited region of Mielnik, Bohemia, where there had been no immigration, have changed in form since the eleventh century ; von Luschan has indicated a similar change in Styria, and Sir Arthur Keith has pointed repeatedly to changes in the skull, the facial parts, and the teeth within historic times in England. Stature has been changing markedly within 150 years in the U.S.A. and is changing now in North-Western Europe, Japan, and in other countries. The masticatory apparatus, and with it the nose and the whole face, with the progress of civilization have everywhere undergone and are still undergoing important modifications. The American Indian under changed conditions of life has rapidly acquired obesity and changed in many cases so that he has become almost worthless for type study. There are remarkable changes progressing before our very eyes in the Eskimo. And the entire system of training and education of modern man is subconsciously based on and made possible only by his continued plasticity.

All of which implies that the human head, skull and body are not immutable but are capable of sustained modification, and the evidence shows that they do change lastingly under effective conditions. Thus we come to the second fundamental property of the human cranium. The first was its extensive inherent variability, the second is that of its continued evolutionary modifiability.

The third basic quality of the human skull is its temporary responsiveness to environmental conditions. Such temporary effects are those that are capable of altering an individual head or skull but are not propagated.

By environmental conditions are understood all those factors that are not inherent in a person. These factors fall into three main categories, namely, the pathological, the functional, and the direct mechanical. These different factors are capable of causing an endless line of cranial alterations.

The *pathological* changes in the brain-case were dealt with by Rudolf Virchow and many other authors, while those of the face have been shown especially by dental students. Those of the vault range from scarcely perceptible to monstrous. They have been and are now being commonly overlooked in anthropometry, in the less pronounced cases, by those who lack pathological training and due experience. For example, an otherwise excellent student has described a rickety scapho-cephalic human skull as normal; and there is no telling how many more or less affected heads and skulls have come to be included in the different anthropological series that constitute the published anthropological materials. As to the lesser alterations in the facial parts, due to pathological conditions of the teeth and jaws, there is no larger series of measurements extant, either on the living or on the skeletal parts, that has not been more or less affected through such conditions.

The possibilities of *functional* alterations in the skull cannot be questioned. The entire skull or head is, in fact, if we go deep enough, a more or less fixed result of such alterations. The brain-case enlarges and modifies with the growth of the brain. Its shape cannot but be affected by the mechanical pressure and stresses of the muscles attached to it—recall the interesting experiments of Arthur Thomson in this connection. The orbits are doubtless altered directly or indirectly through functional causes, and this is even more true of the nose, as shown by Thomson and Buxton, as demonstrated by the differences in the nasal structures of the Eskimo in different parts of his territory, and as indicated by other evidence. And great alterations may be produced in the jaws and the whole face through either the over- or under-development of the functions of mastication.

As to the *mechanical* deformations of the head and skull, their range is great, and many a specimen suffering from a milder defect of this nature has been included by the inexperienced among the " normal ". There are incidental deformations in life, above all those due to cradle pressure, as common in Germany and Central Europe, among some of the Asia Minor people, and in some of the American Indians. There are deformations post-mortem, by the pressure of the earth upon the softened skull. And there are the very numerous intentional deformations, some crania with which are known to have been taken for " normal " at one time or another and helped to sustain various conclusions. All of which is not to detract from the real value of the study of the skull or head, which is precious indeed to Anthropology, but to help to place this study in its proper perspective and scope ; to urge the necessity in every worker of proper preparation for such studies ; and to point out that the exercise of constant erudite and critical care is needed in such studies, and in the deductions drawn from the materials.

The more or less empirical and mechanical craniology of the past is rapidly nearing its end. There should and will be, if this branch of science is to progress properly, no more cranio-logical instructions to " travellers ", no more entrusting of important anthropometric work to raw undergraduates, no more disguising of the rankness of procedure or inadequacy of numbers by petty mathematical reasoning.

Modern craniology calls for broad professional preparation, for experience, constant care, critical sense, and a full conscious-ness of the limitations of the subject. These conditions must be realized if craniology is to be saved from falling into a very undeserved disregard or even disrepute.

THE ORIGINS OF SACRIFICE AS ILLUSTRATED BY A PRIMITIVE PEOPLE

By GUNNAR LANDTMAN

These lines are written to convey a tribute of affection and esteem to Professor Seligman. As a medium for my homage I appeal to his great interest in that far-away country, British New Guinea, in regard to the anthropology of which he is one of the foremost authorities. The object of this article is to lay down certain principles of primitive cult which are founded on observations made among one of the native tribes of British New Guinea.

The extensive theoretical literature which exists regarding the origin and growth of religion is in the main devoted to throwing light upon the psychological aspects of the relation of man with a supposed preternatural world. We are confronted with a branch of research in which the human mind has exerted perhaps more ardent efforts to reach the true understanding of things than in any other field of learning. Ingenious theories have been created concerning the early forms of religious cult as represented by primitive peoples.

The latest developments of modern anthropology, however, give good promise of succeeding in founding the history of religious evolution on a firmer basis than has hitherto been the case.

Religion, in a wide, ethnological sense of the word is, I believe, regarded by all leading modern representatives of that science as universal throughout the human race. But we must remember that it is not long since men like Herbert Spencer and Lord Avebury considered themselves entitled to deny the universal existence of religious ideas. This change of opinion to a great extent depends on the fact that our present information regarding the mental and ritual life of many uncivilized peoples is much more thorough than it was a few decades ago. But apart from theories recently held regarding the non-existence of religion among the lowest known types of people, our actual knowledge of many so-called primitive races leaves but little doubt that religion among some of them is at a very rudimentary stage— that it cannot have advanced far from the very beginnings of mythology and cult.

Instead of contenting ourselves with speculative theories regarding the problems connected with the earliest aspects of

religious development, would it be too audacious simply to
establish, by careful investigation, which forms these various
beginnings of religion assume in real life ? I am of opinion that
we might find it possible to pursue a method of descriptive study
regarding the manifestations of native mental life, based on
similar principles to those applied to the study of native economic
and industrial life. By ascertaining in full all we require to know
regarding supernatural ideas and practices among individual
tribes, and collecting a sufficient amount of material of this
kind from all available sources, we ought to be able to obtain
a descriptive account of all the actual data which would tend to
make the history of religion an exact branch of study. An
adequate series of monographic researches, establishing the
varieties of religious thought and worship in the primitive stage,
would in any case provide us with a reliable basis for comparative
study without our having to resort to general theories and using
individual instances more or less as illustrations only. A general
theory can never claim to cover the whole scope of religious
rites and customs because of its inability to take different stages
of evolution into sufficient consideration, nor is it possible to
explain a multitude of heterogeneous functions from one and
the same point of view.

A descriptive history of religion thus outlined would throw
light upon many problems connected with the origin and early
development of religious life. We need only mention the much
discussed question regarding the character of the earliest supernatural beings believed in and worshipped, in other words the
relation between ancestor-worship and nature-worship, further,
the sentiments predominating in the attitude of the worshippers
towards the worshipped, the origin of religious images, the
beginnings of prayer and other elements of cult, etc.

Of these various problems I must, on this occasion, restrict
myself to a single one. My purpose is to set forth a few observations regarding the beginnings of the offering. We will try to see
what may be learned regarding the history of cult from the study
of a people whose religious stage must be looked upon as very
little developed. The reader will find it natural, too, that for
this purpose, I choose an aboriginal people of whom I possess
first-hand knowledge, the Kiwai Papuans, of British New Guinea,
among whom I have spent two years studying their anthropology.
I hardly need to point out that what I am going to say is only
intended to serve as an illustration of the method just mentioned.
In order to arrive at anything approaching actual results we should
have to avail ourselves of more extensive material than we could
here consider, extending over a great many different peoples.

As is well known, there exist many divergent theories regarding
the earliest forms of offering and the fundamental ideas expressing

the intentions of the offerer. E. B. Tylor, acting as a pioneer in this field, is the creator of the hypothesis that sacrifice was originally a gift offered to supernatural beings to secure their favour and minimize their hostility. As this purpose gradually became transformed in the mind of the sacrificers, the dominant note became that of homage, which again passed into that of renunciation. In conformity with his theory of ancestor-worship as the sole source of religion, Herbert Spencer thought the origin of sacrifice was to be found in the custom of leaving food and drink at the graves of the dead. As the ancestral spirits rose to divine rank the refreshments placed for the dead developed into sacrifices. Much interest and appreciation were bestowed on Robertson Smith's theory, according to which all sacrifice was originally a sacramental communion between the worshipper and the worshipped, whether in the sense of a communal meal to which the gods were invited as guests, receiving their share in the food and drink, or of the possibly still older belief, that the divinity was incarnate in the sacrificed man or animal (the former a member of the totem clan, the latter a totem animal) and that by eating the flesh and blood of the victim the sacrificers renewed the bond with the supernatural being and became participants in his divine life. Offerings without communion, according to him, are a later religious product. The main features of Robertson Smith's theory have been professedly adopted by F. B. Jevons, Salomon Reinach, and others. E. Durkheim maintained that both the essential forms of evolved sacrifice—the act of oblation and the act of communion—are found in terminal form in the Australian Intichiuma rites. Sir James Frazer's theory is that primitive man, in order to avoid the anger of the spirits of Nature and to conciliate them, resorts to the same means which he employs towards human beings on whose goodwill he happens to depend : he addresses requests to them and he makes them presents. On the other hand, the assumptions on which the worship of the dead is founded are mainly that the dead retain their consciousness and personality and that they can powerfully influence the fortune of the living for good or evil : this is the key-stone of the propitiation or worship of the dead. According to Westermarck the idea that supernatural beings have human appetites and human wants led to the practice of sacrificial gifts being offered to them. If such offerings fail them they may even suffer want and become feeble and powerless. Thus in early religion the most common motive is undoubtedly a desire to avert evil. The practice of human sacrifice, according to this writer, is based on the idea of the substitution of a victim for other individuals whose lives are in danger, which in course of time led to the offering of animals instead of men.

May I now bring before the reader my friends the Kiwai Papuans, asking them to let us know what they think and do when approaching a supernatural being by means of an offering ?

First let me state the general character of the religious ideas entertained by the Kiwais. Among these natives we find none of the attributes of a more highly developed religious life ; thus they lack any conception of a supreme god. They have no systematized ideas as to a supernatural world in which everybody believes, and no priests. No public cult exists : no prayers are said or offerings made in which a larger or smaller group of the population participates. Individual worshippers will practise one and the same rite as long as it seems to be of any avail, then they will try some other form of appeal or magic.

The Kiwais entertain very pronounced ideas regarding the continued existence of the soul after death, the appearance of the ghosts, and the abode of the dead. In addition, the natives believe in a vast number of mythical beings. Of some of these little is known beyond the name, but others exhibit a marked individuality. All are firmly believed in, and must receive every consideration when people come into contact with them in their various undertakings and occupations. In general no actual communication takes place between men and these beings, but some of them are in the habit of visiting one person or another in dreams and are remembered with occasional gifts of food. The various beings enter into a great number of folk-tales and myths. Among the Kiwais the initial period of religious development is exceedingly rich, comprehending the folk-lore stage of the conception of a supernatural world, whereas of cult and ritual only the very beginnings can be traced.

In what manner are offerings made among the Kiwai Papuans ?

Let us first see how they are practised in the case of the dead. A spirit does not always start on its way to the land of the dead at once, but often for some days haunts the vicinity of its former home. For a few nights after a death all the doors are kept carefully barred, and no one ventures out in the dark. Some food is regularly put by the ladder of the house for the spirit. Sometimes the people indoors will hear a whistle from outside or a tapping or scraping on the wall, by which the spirit signals its arrival and, awe-struck, they all begin to wail. They also throw out some food to the spirit, asking it to go away. If the spirit is not given anything, it will wander round the house until daybreak, looking for food.

On the whole the natives stand in great dread of the spirits of the dead, whoever the people may have been in their lifetime. Ghosts are known to carry away the souls of living people and also to cause illness, and must therefore be carefully kept away. In order to send a spirit away, some man will perform certain rites, asking the ghost to go to the land of the dead, " You devil (spirit) now ; you no come back this place ; what road belong you— you go ; woman (and) piccaninny belong you he stop house, that road you shut him ; me fellow look moon he light, sun he go up ; you go Adiri (the land of the dead) now—all same sun he go down." I am, here and in the following, using pidgin-English for translating native utterances, as it seems to answer to the native mode of expression better than ordinary English.

Grave-offerings invariably accompany the burial of the dead. On the grave a small hut is erected, a few personal belongings of the deceased are hung up there, also gifts of food ; and, in addition, a fire is lighted at the foot of the grave for the benefit of the dead. These tributes are maintained for a longer or shorter period and are afterwards renewed on certain occasions, particularly at the time of the performance of certain of the great ceremonies, or the dead will manifest their displeasure to their survivors.

How important it is not to neglect these duties is shown by certain incidents related in the traditions of the people. On the occasion of the great so-called Turtle-ceremony the Mawata tribe, as usual, attended to the graves of their dead. They cleared and decorated the ground, put down food, and finally poured out coconut milk on each grave, saying, " You look out turtle, give me fellow ; I give you plenty kaikai, make place nice." The grave of one man only, named Bidja, was neglected by his kins-folk. Everybody speared many turtle except Bidja's clansmen, who did not get a single one. In the night his spirit appeared to them and reprimanded them for having slighted him. It was not his fault that they had not caught any turtle ; they should have looked after his grave properly. On arriving home the men went straight to Bidja's grave and performed all the ritual duties there. Their next harpooning expedition was very successful. After that they taught the young men what they had learnt, impressing upon them not to forget the graves during the turtle-fishing period.

Simple as they are, similar gifts represent almost the only kinds of offering met with among the Kiwais of which a few more instances may be given. Once when spearing a dugong (*Halicore australis*) a Mawata man, Maiva, got entangled in the rope and was drowned. For some time afterwards the people did not dare to go out to the reefs. At last a few men went. From their platforms the harpooners saw in the moonlight the drowned man swimming towards them like a huge frog. Seaweed covered him, his head was very big, and behind him trailed the rope in which he had been entangled. They all put down their harpoons in terror. The ghost came near, passed by close to the platforms, and vanished on the other side. After the phantom a great shoal of dugong followed, but the men did not succeed in spearing any and decided to go back, being afraid of those dugong. Later on the people again went to the reef. This time they threw food into the water for the drowned man, and they speared many dugong. Thenceforward the harpooners always threw food for Maiva into the water and said, " All right, you bring dugong; you no come along me fellow; you go right up what place you belong. You no cut him rope, you no take him out *kúior* (harpoon-head). Kaikai belong you here, you take him." Nowadays no more offerings are made to Maiva, and the people no longer see him. Offerings of this kind do not seem ever to have been made regularly for any considerable length of time, but occasional presents offered to spirits are frequent.

The spirits of people who have been drowned or killed by a crocodile or a snake, and also those of suicides, are greatly feared because they will try to lure friends to a like death. In order to lay the ghost of a man taken by a crocodile the people build a small hut, like that erected on a grave, at the place where the man met his death, and put food inside. They want the spirit to remain there and say to it, " You no come where people he stop ; you devil (spirit) now ; house belong you here ; you stop here." If this is not done, the ghost, who does not want to be alone, will fetch one of his friends to suffer a like fate.

If a hunter has perished in the bush, the people always leave there some of the game killed by him. " Ghost belong him," they will think, " you me (we) no savy, him he kaikai. Poor fellow, he been hard work; no good (that) people take him pig altogether. Ghost belong him he look round, by and by got nothing, by and by hard up." The same rule is followed with respect to harpooners lost at sea ; in fact, people do not dare to keep a dugong, etc., speared by anyone who has subsequently perished. But even apart from deaths occurring on hunting or harpooning trips, a little of their spoil is generally left for dead relatives : " No good I kaikai good kaikai ; I no savy poor mother father belong me—I no savy devil (spirit) belong him he there alongside that time I spear."

If the people fear that somebody has been lost at sea, they try to find it out in the following way. Some food is tied to a string, which is fastened to a stick like a fishing-rod. One night some men go to the beach, walk a short distance into the water and dangle the food over the surface. One of them calls to the missing man and says, " Suppose you proper lose (lost) you take that kaikai." The arm of somebody drowned will be seen reaching out of the water and snatching the food away. If the arm is covered with sea-weed, the people conclude that it belongs to some " long-time-devil ", but if it is quite smooth, they will know that the man they are looking for has really been drowned and that it is his arm. Should no one take the food, this is a proof that the man has escaped to some other place and may be expected to return when the wind becomes favourable.

In a folk-tale a number of sisters in succession were secretly killed by a wicked man, until only one of them remained. Feeling uneasy about the fate of the others, she went to the grave of her parents, cleared away all the bushes, placed a great heap of food there, and said, " My mother, my father, I give you fellow good kaikai. You fellow come speak me good talk that time I sleep, what place all my sister he stop, where he go, what he do. Suppose you come speak me to-night, all right ; suppose you no come speak me, I dig him out head (skull) belong you two fellow, chuck him away along bush." In the night the parents came to the girl in a dream and told her all about her sisters.

In order to obtain advice from his dead parents a man will sometimes dig up their skulls from the grave, wash them clean, rub them with sweet-scented medicines, and sleep close to them (with one skull in each armpit, it seems). Not infrequently when doing so he will provide himself with a stick and threaten to break the skulls if the parents do not appear promptly. In one tale the parents excused themselves for being late by pleading their old age which prevented them from moving very quickly.

As has been stated, a great multitude of spiritual beings inhabiting nature are found in the mythology of the Kiwais, and to some of them offerings are made of exactly the same description as those to the dead.

Almost every conspicuous place in the landscape is thought to be the abode of some mythical being. In certain cases the existence of such local beings seems to be taken as a matter of course, although hardly anything can be told of them except the name, which is generally that of the place with the word *abéra* (father) or *nogére* (old man) affixed. Certain of these local spirits are akin to human beings, others are mythical animals, and occasionally we even meet with trees endowed with miraculous properties.

At Haemuba, a point on the coast, lives a being named Tube. He is particularly associated with a certain Mawata man, teaching him in dreams the use of garden medicines, which knowledge the man imparts to other people. Sometimes Tube appears to him in his garden in the shape of a snake or iguana, but he knows who it is from signs which the animal makes with its head. Once he saw Tube in the bush looking like an iguana, and it had in its mouth a little branch of a tree, which was a medicine. He obtained this by gently patting the animal on its head. The first taro pulled out of the ground is shared by the man and Tube.

Another being, Sivagu, is the " master " of Augaromuba,

a point between Mawata and Mabudavane. He appears in the
shape of a man, a snake, or a hawk. As far back as the people
can remember, there has been a large hawk's nest in one of the
trees which no one would destroy. By hovering over the canoes
the bird shows the people the right course. Particularly when
on a fighting expedition, the people carefully watch the movements of the hawk. If it swoops from the top of the tree towards
the water and there wheels once, flapping its wings, the people
had better return for they will be defeated. But if it floats
smoothly in the air, this signifies that the way to victory is clear.
Sivagu, too, imparts useful information to certain men in dreams,
and sometimes to obtain it people go and sleep at Augaromuba.
On arriving there a hunter will chew and spit out a certain
medicine, asking Sivagu to help him in finding game, and on leaving
the place he will put down a small piece of meat for the spirit.

On Abaura Island underneath the ground there lives a being
called Wiobadara. At night he has been seen in human shape,
in the day as a snake. He pushes up the sand into hills, and
sometimes he transforms the ground, so that the women cannot
find the crab-holes. Then they put down food for Wiobadara,
asking him to give them crabs.

The Gimini sandbank formerly belonged to two brothers of
Mawata, Gubo and Moiso, who have been regarded ever since
as the guardians of it. When the Mawata people went to look for
turtle-eggs there, Moiso's descendants used to put down for
him food and two water-bottles (because he had two wives),
and Gubo's people put down food and one water-bottle (he had
one wife only). At the same time they asked the beings to show
them turtle-eggs.

On Marukara Island there used to live a being of the kind
called *mamagárena*. The island belonged to a Mawata man, Odai,
and when he came there to look for turtle-eggs he used to pour
some fresh water on the sand and ask the *mamagárena* to help
him. When Odai died, the people used to appeal to him as well
as to the *mamagárena*, when asking for turtle-eggs, and when doing
so they poured out water and put down a little food. One night
a man, when sleeping there alone, saw the *mamagárena* moving
about in its human form, and being afraid, he shot an arrow at
it. The next morning he found the same arrow sticking through
the body of a snake, and that was the *mamagárena*. Since then
it is very rarely that the people find turtle-eggs in Marukara.
The being used to speak to certain people in dreams.

Pamoa, living in the Oriomu River, resembles a man, but is
akin to the water-beings called *óboúbi*. He once made friends
with a man called Ivogu, who used to paddle his canoe up the
river, shooting game. Ivogu always gave Pamoa a share in the
spoil, and the latter made a tally of the bones by tying them to

a rope. Ivogu's younger brother also used to hunt up the river, but he treated Pamoa badly. One day Ivogu, who had climbed a coconut tree, was attacked by an evil spirit, but Pamoa threw him the tally-rope, which was very long, and he climbed down by it. On a subsequent journey the younger brother was killed by the same evil being, for his tally-rope was too short, so Pamo could not save him.

Three groups of water-beings called *nágimarkái*, *kíbumarkái*, and *usárabi* are associated by the Mawata people with the harpooning of dugong. They are appealed to by harpooners and let the people know beforehand how a harpooning expedition will succeed, give advice in dreams, and were formerly presented with offerings of dugong bones.

A rather interesting group of sylvan beings, the *étengena*, live in large trees, wells, or in the ground. They are particularly associated with agriculture and help the owners of the gardens in whose vicinity they live. They appear in the daytime as snakes, pigs, or wallabies, at night in human form. The owner of the garden will ask the *étengena* to look after the plantation and to pass his water there (from which the growth prospers) ; the being can also protect the man from being bitten by a snake or getting hurt when cutting down a tree. The *étengena* gets a share in every first-fruit obtained from the garden. Sometimes the being becomes quite attached to the owner of the ground, and when the latter dies and the people are wailing in the village, the *étengena*, too, can be heard crying in the bush.

Many supernatural beings are considered to be particularly wild and dangerous, and to these the people do not make any offerings at all, as it is considered useless to try to appease them. One group of such beings, the *órigorúso*, have obtained their name from their habit of eating everything raw. They have enormous claws and tusks and swallow their prey whole without chewing. The ears are so immense that when sleeping at night the being uses the one to lie upon and the other for a covering. Another highly malignant being is the *útumu*, the spirit of a man who has been killed in a fight and whose head has been cut off. The blood which has spurted from his neck shines in the night like fire. Many people, mistaking this light for an ordinary fire, have walked right into the clutches of the monster.

I have here given only a few examples of the offerings which the Kiwai Papuans present to some of the supernatural beings in which they believe. But I feel confident that whatever instances could be added would prove to be of exactly the same kind without throwing any fresh light upon the subject in hand.

What conclusions can we draw as regards the early practice of making offerings, so far as the Kiwai Papuans are concerned ?

All their offerings are typically *gift-offerings*, among which the grave-offerings, too, must be reckoned. The Kiwais on the whole have very vague notions regarding the character of the various spiritual powers. As far as they form an idea of these existences, they picture them according to their own conception of themselves and other men. As a matter of fact, where else would they find the prototype of beings endowed with spiritual life ? There is an intensely human note in their endeavours to make the beings favourably inclined towards themselves. No other means are employed than such as would be used in the case of an ordinary human fellow-creature. In order to win the good-will of a fellow-man they would approach him with some sort of gift, and let him know what they wanted of him ; exactly the same procedure is put into practice respecting those mysterious beings which are regarded as akin to man and at the same time different. Among themselves the people are in the habit of sharing a considerable part of their spoil and harvest, and in certain respects they include their supernatural associates in the distribution of such gifts. Every offering, however, aims at some benefit to themselves, and even when it bears the aspect of an act of gratitude, we may assume that it purports to secure some boon in the future. So characteristically human is the attitude of the people towards the spirits that it sometimes takes the form of threatening, just as in intercourse between men. The purely human wants and appetites of the spirits are clearly manifested.

In opposition to the theory of Robertson Smith regarding the earliest forms of offering, we cannot find among the Kiwais any trace of a sacramental communion between the worshippers and the worshipped, only an approach with the ordinary tokens of friendship. The idea of increasing the vitality of the people forms the object of one of their great ceremonies, but this aim is followed by means of powerful magical medicines, not by obtaining strength from any supernatural beings in the form of a communal sacrificial meal or otherwise. It cannot be lack of imagination either, which accounts for the non-existence of the more complicated forms of offering and sacrifice among the Kiwais, for these Papuans, like many other aboriginal peoples, fail least of all in creative imagination as is shown by the richness of their folk-lore and their ceremonial rites ; it must, therefore, be due simply to the undeveloped stage of their cult. We cannot but think that the more intricate descriptions of offering, such as sacramental, expiatory, vicarious, purificatory sacrifices, and others, are to be looked upon as attributes of a more advanced stage of religious evolution.

Helsingfors,
Finland.

THE JOURNEY OF THE DEAD

FROM THE SMALL ISLANDS OF NORTH-EASTERN MALEKULA

By John Layard

Summary

Sketch-map to illustrate the Journey of the Dead, p. 115.

Introduction, p. 114—
"Sea Folk."
Old social organization, founded by Tagar, modified through introduction of a newer form of culture.
Dolmen-Maki and monolith-Maki.
Types of burial.
Other beliefs concerning the dead.
Three accounts of Journey of the Dead.
Not death, but ritual, confers future life.

Vao Version, p. 118—
Burial at sundown. Pig killed.
Enters "Cave of the Dead". Is opposed by Guardian Spirit called Le-hev̄-hev̄, but Tagar-Lawo intercedes.
Proceeds on uneventful journey to Tsingon Bong-na-un.
Lights beacon. Is ferried to Ambrim and mounts volcano.
Nightly dance of the dead. Reception by them. Mal-kalaut.
The dead dance all night and sleep all day.

Atchin Version, p. 120—
Burial at sundown. Pig killed. Wand placed in grave. Mourners sound the Departing Signal on the gongs.
Ascends Mountain and eats fruit of Magic Tree. Walks round "Whistling-stone".
Walks through "Cave of the Dead". Proceeds to Pan-womu and strikes canoe with wand.
Goes to Bong-na-un. Meets Guardian Spirit called Le-saw-saw.
Lights beacon on small island and is ferried over on canoe of driftwood to "place of the ghosts" near Ambrim.

Wala Version, p. 122—
Burial. Proceeds with wand and fowl to "Cave of the Dead".
Gnaws trunk of Magic Tree.
Walks round "Whistling-stone".
Walks through Cave.
Strikes river with wand, and the waters part.
Encounters "Nose-devouring Stone".
Removes burial-mats at Pinalum.
Arrives at Wenush (Bong-na-un). Meets Guardian Spirit who is a stone and a shark and associated with a crescent moon, pentacles, and a bird.
Lights beacon. Ferryman named Shules paddles over to see who he is, and reports to Ambrim. Dead man's kinsmen ferry him over.
Nightly dance of the Dead. Head and bones fall asunder at dawn. Newcomer's head first falls off on seventh night.
Dead man plants banana on Ambrim.
Journey accomplished immediately after death.

INTRODUCTION

It is proposed in this article to give an account of the Journey of the Dead as recorded from the three northernmost of the " Small Islands " situated off the north-east coast of Malekula, in the New Hebrides. Since the three versions differ in essential details, an attempt will then be made to analyse them into their component parts, and estimate in some measure how the stories came to be built up.

It is first necessary, however, to give the briefest outline of the cultural context in which they are set.

" Sea Folk "

The Islands in question are Vao, Atchin, and Wala. These form part of a group, extending to Uripiv in the south, the natives of which give themselves the common title of Sea Folk (in Atchin *mwere n'das*) in contradistinction to the canoeless mainlanders of north-eastern Malekula. In spite of the fact that each island speaks a language peculiar to itself, they all share in the main a common culture with, however, considerable local variation not only as between the respective islands, but even between the different villages on one island.

*Old social organization, founded by Tagar, modified through intro-
duction of a newer form of culture*

It is probable that all these islands at one time shared a
common organization similar to that still existing on Vao, which
island is divided into three twin villages with patrilineal, patri-
local descent and local exogamy. As in all the other islands of
the group, there is a further asymmetrical division into two
nameless " Sides ", with two twin-villages on one side of the
island and one twin-village on the other.   The twin-villages
forming the smaller (western) side of Vao are Petehul and
Toghvanu, each of which has a central village lodge, while
Petehul is further subdivided into four Quarters, each split again

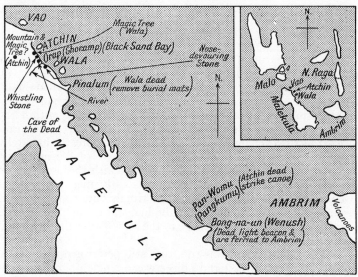

Sketch-map illustrating the Journey of the Dead.   Inset, the Northern New
Hebrides, showing islands mentioned in discussion.

into two great-families, each Quarter and great-family having
its own private lodge.   In Toghvanu this organization, said to
have been introduced by Tagar (Banks Islands Tagaro, Polynesian Tangaloa) shows already signs of decay, since here there
are but three Quarters instead of four.   In Wala and Atchin
(probably also in the eastern villages of Vao, though my information does not extend to these) it is now in ruins owing to the
introduction of a newer form of culture necessitating the division of
each village into ten as opposed to the former eight great-families.

This newer form of culture had its local origin in two
villages, now extinct, but situated formerly on the Malekulan
mainland opposite the island of Wala, close to the best anchorage

in all that portion of the coast. What stimulated its development is not yet known. Its influence, however, has been profound, and is still radiating up and down the coast.

So far as the islands at present under consideration are concerned, the chief repository of this newer culture now is Wala, whence its various features are even now in process of spreading gradually northward, one by one, through the slow processes of ceremonial purchase. The main body of beliefs and practices has already been adopted by the south-eastern villages of Atchin, whence they are passing gradually to the north-western villages on that island. These in turn have passed on certain features to the eastern villages on Vao, those least affected on this island being the two western villages, Petehul and Toghvanu, which have been already mentioned.

Dolmen-Maki and monolith-Maki

The main feature of this newer culture is the enormous change and elaboration introduced into (a) the mortuary ritual; (b) initiation; and (c) the public degree-taking rite called Maki. This is a rite, based on mortuary, that is to say resurrection, ritual performed by alternate generations of males within the villages at intervals of roughly thirty years. Through the performance of this rite each individual takes his place among the hierarchy of the living dead, and so acquires the power of life hereafter. Originally connected in all probability also with the propagation and well-being of the human race, this early meaning appears to be now lost in the elaboration of ritual, but it still remains essential to the welfare of each individual and to the position and even the existence of each village in the social order that it should be for ever re-enacted.

In the older form of this rite, that still performed at Petehul, on Vao, the central material object was a single dolmen of considerable proportions at which each officiating member killed a tusked boar and changed his name. As a result, however, of the newer culture, on Wala, Atchin, and the eastern villages of Vao, ten shrines are now built, one by each of the ten great-families into which the village is divided, and the central feature of each shrine is a monolith coupled with a diminutive dolmen,[1] with a wooden image placed immediately in front. Plain monolith and image combined represent the far-off ancestor of the lodge, while other, solitary monoliths, as well as natural coral blocks, are said to be the petrified remains of individual ancestors and culture heroes.

The two forms of the rite I shall refer to as the dolmen-Maki,

[1] Cf. Dr. Perry's " dissolith ", first so named in his *Megalithic Culture of Indonesia*, 1918, p. 16.

and the monolith-Maki, the former characteristic of the older and the latter of the newer form of culture.

Types of burial

There is no space here to enter into the details of this most elaborate rite, though the increased insistence on the monolith both on Wala and on Atchin will be seen to have a bearing on the subject of this article. Associated with the older dolmen-Maki culture we find the burial of old men (i.e. those who have performed the full Maki rite) in the squatting position, as is still the case on Vao. Associated with the newer monolith-Maki old men are buried in the extended position now in use on Wala and the south-eastern villages of Atchin, while a yet nobler form of burial on Wala and on the Malekulan mainland consists in inhumation in a sitting posture, together with the subsequent removal and special treatment of the head.

Other beliefs concerning the dead

All these features will be seen to have a close connection with the Journey of the Dead. Before describing this, however, it is as well to bear in mind that the usual beliefs concerning the power of the dead over the living to be found in other parts of Melanesia are also present here. The ghost lives also in or near the grave, where offerings are made, is present in his house and lodge, watches over the lives and ceremonial observances of his descendants, and accompanies them on sea-faring expeditions. It may also enter the body of a descendant, causing sickness as a punishment for some neglected duty ; in divining rites it may enter the body of the medium causing an epileptoid seizure, or else into a bamboo which raps out answers in reply to questions put to it. According to one set of beliefs rather loosely held on Atchin, the spirit also rises to the sky to join the supreme being Tahar (Vao Tagar), who is at once a man and sun and moon, and came in a canoe to found society and provide the necessaries of life.

Three accounts of Journey of the Dead

In all this medley of co-existent beliefs we shall, however, confine ourselves here to what is believed concerning the way the dead live their own lives, unhampered by the affairs of those they leave behind.

According to this belief, the dead of all three islands are said to continue their existence on one of the volcanoes on Ambrim, a large island some 50 miles away, where they dance all night, and, according to the different accounts, either sleep or become disintegrated during the day.

The three accounts deal mainly with events occurring on their journey thither down the coast of Malekula, from a promontory on which they are invisibly ferried over to their future home. These accounts were not mere isolated contributions, but form part of an intensive inquiry into the mortuary rites of all three islands which has not yet been published. My original intention was to tabulate and compare the results of all three inquiries on the spot, discuss discrepancies and fill up gaps where these occurred. This, however, proved impossible owing to lack of time and the accumulation of material, and my intention of returning to the field has not yet been fulfilled.

It is due to this that of the Journey of the Dead I have at present but a single account from each of the three islands, and therefore cannot guarantee against omissions. This means that though these accounts may be relied upon as representing positive belief on the respective islands, negative evidence must be taken with caution except where it is expressly stated by the natives that a given belief held in one island is not held in another.

Not death, but ritual, confers future life

Although a man earns a future life by ritual observances during lifetime, and once on Ambrim apparently continues his existence without hindrance from those left behind, the successful accomplishment of his journey thither is entirely dependent on the ritual attendant on his burial. For were the boars not sacrificed, with whose ghosts he must appease the Spirits which oppose him, he could not get through. Nor, without the wand which in two versions is buried with him, could he part the rivers on his way. It is not death, but ritual which opens up the way to future life. The moment when the ghost sets out upon its way is not the moment when the body dies, but that at which it is committed to the ground with due observances. For this reason, while it is immaterial what time of day young men, who do not make this journey, are buried, the burial of old men of high degree occurs of necessity at sundown, when the nightly dance of all the previously dead begins on the volcano and the new ghost receives official welcome.

With this brief introduction, we can now turn to the details of the three versions of the story.

VAO VERSION

Burial at sundown. Pig killed

As already stated, burial in the squatting position occurs at sundown. The body is arrayed in all the finery and insignia due to the dead man for the rank which he has taken in the Maki rites. Immediately before inhumation a communion feast is held in which a morsel of the food is placed actually in the mouth of the dead man. This is the first of many subsequent communion rites which do not concern us here. The body, wrapped in fine mats, is placed within the grave and a pig is killed for payment by the dead man to the Guardian Spirit.

Enters " Cave of the Dead ". Is opposed by Guardian Spirit, called Le-heṽ-heṽ, but Tagar-lawo intercedes

The dead man first makes his way to the long black-sand beach called Ghoramp (in Atchin, Orap) situated on the mainland between the islands of Atchin and Wala. Here he enters a cave called *barang na ta-mat* " Cave of the Dead ". As he goes in, his way is blocked by a Guardian Spirit called Le-heṽ-heṽ. It is not known whether this Spirit is a man or a woman. All that is known about its nature is that it is "irresponsible and in all things defiant".[1]

As the ghost of the dead man tries to enter the cave Le-heṽ-heṽ pulls him back. But there is another Spirit, called Tagar-lawo, who takes the side of the new-comer and says to Le-heṽ-heṽ, " Leave him alone. Let him come and join all his friends over there " (indicating the inside of the cave). Le-heṽ-heṽ then leaves hold of the new ghost, who presents the Spirit with the ghost of the pig killed at burial. If he had not such a pig, Le-heṽ-heṽ would devour him (*Le-heṽ-heṽ e ghani*). The new-comer also pays a pig to Tagar-lawo [2] for having pleaded for him, and then goes inside into the cave, to " join his dead friends who are gathered there ".

Proceeds on uneventful journey to Tsingon Bong-na-un

He does not stay, however, but continues on his lonely way for 40 odd miles down the coast until he comes at sundown to the promontory called Tsingon Bong-na-un on the coast facing Ambrim. It is important here to note that in this version nothing happens to him on the way. It was expressly stated on Vao that the people on this island know only the barest outlines of the journey, and are ignorant of the far more detailed knowledge possessed by the peoples both of Atchin and of Wala.

Lights beacon. Is ferried to Ambrim and mounts volcano

It is, however, known that, arrived at Tsingon Bong-na-un, the dead man makes fire for a beacon to attract the attention of

[1] Thus, a recent historical figure who was forced by family honour to commit what would otherwise have been the awful crime of slaying his own sister's son was called Le-heṽ-heṽ.

[2] In my account of the mortuary rites, no mention is made of the killing of a second pig for payment to Tagar-lawo. This is probably a case of omission.

the ghostly ferryman on Ambrim, and also breaks off a piece of seaweed called *ro-go-rọmbol*, and beckons with it.   At this the ferryman, named Lingi, sets out from Ambrim in his ghost's canoe. Such ghostly craft are not canoes in anything but name, but simply any kind of flotsam floating on the water. The name of this canoe was first given me as *wuwun* " banana-skin ", but later it appeared that any piece of banyan bark or other minute object would serve the ghostly purpose just as well. Lingi, the name given to the ferryman, is a descriptive word, used in ordinary conversation as a verb meaning to take or to conduct, particularly in a canoe. This ferryman now paddles over in his flotsam craft and takes the new-comer back with him to Ambrim, where he is escorted up to the big volcano called Bot-gharambi " Source (base or origin) of the fire ".

Nightly dance of the dead. Reception by them. Mal-kalaut

The crossing takes no time at all, for it is still dusk when he arrives, just as the nightly dance of all the dead begins. The new-comer is placed in their midst and all the others dance around him till a famous ghost named Mal-kalaut [1] calls out " *Lause* ", the customary way in which the leader ends a dance in actual life. Then all the others answer " *Lause* ", and the dance is over.

The dance is repeated throughout the night by the dead of all the villages of Vao in turn, in the rotation prescribed for ceremonial occasions during life, and, as in life, these are succeeded by those from the six Atchin villages, and, more vaguely, by those from the remoter islands of the group.

The dead dance all night and sleep all day

Nothing more seems to be known on Vao about the life led by the dead, excepting that they dance all night and sleep all day. The Wala story, to be told below, that the dead dance as skeletons and that their bones fall asunder and their heads fall off at dawn is vehemently denied.

ATCHIN VERSION

This version stops short at the arrival of the dead man in the " place of ghosts ", near Ambrim, and gives no account of his reception there. It was obtained in the south-eastern village of Ruruar, where extended burial is the rule.

---

[1] Mal-kalaut was a man of La-mbarang, one of the four Quarters of Petehul, and is famous as the inventor of the use of human bones as arrow-tips. He is possibly to be identified with Navagaru-kalat, the founder of the Quarter and introducer of warfare.

Burial at sundown. Pig killed. Wand placed in grave. Mourners sound the departing signal on the gongs

Much more is known on Atchin than on Vao about the details of the dead man's journey. This is reflected in the mortuary rites. As on Vao, the body is arrayed with all the finery and insignia due to the dead man for the degree which he has taken in the Maki rite. A first communion rite is held (though I have no record of the dead man actually being fed as is the case on Vao) immediately before its burial, wrapped in fine mats, at sundown. A pig is killed for presentation by the dead man to the Guardian Spirit, here called Le-saw-saw, whose position in this story will be seen to be no longer in the cave, but on the promontory facing Ambrim. With the body in the grave is also placed a cane which in the Wala version will be seen to be a wand, cut to the length of the dead man's body, with which, in that version, he parts the waters of rivers encountered on his way.

The mourners, among other rites which do not concern us here, now sound a special signal on the gongs, representing the footsteps of the dead man as he walks away. This signal is unknown on Vao. Only the mother-gong [1] is sounded (the rest of the gong-orchestra remaining silent) with a series of separate beats, at first loud and slowly, then faster and faster and ever more softly as the footsteps recede, till towards the end the beats are almost inaudible. Finally, after a long pause, one last booming blow represents his arrival at the home of the dead. This is the only signal known to me in which the mother-gong is used alone. It is impressive in its simplicity, and is called *e tu-tu-tu-loni e wiel* (the syllable *tu* being repeated *ad lib.*), meaning, " It accompanies him as he goes."

Ascends Mountain and eats fruit of Magic Tree. Walks round " Whistling-stone "

Thus speeded, the dead man first ascends a mountain on the mainland, the name of which is Tawŏ-leter-rum-rum, a feature absent from the other accounts. Here he climbs a tree called *wi-n'men-men*, and eats the fruit. He then goes down to the shore, to a stone called *ni-wet wen-wen* " whistling-stone ", which he walks round, drawing in his breath with a whistling sound.

Walks through " Cave of the Dead ". Proceeds to Pan-womu and strikes canoe with wand

Then he walks through a cave called *pwereng ta-mats* " Cave of the Dead ". No Guardian Spirit, however, meets him here,

---

[1] The mother-gong is the leader of a gong-orchestra consisting, in addition, of at least two further pairs of large upright slit-gongs and numerous portable horizontally-played gonglets.

nor is there any gathering of the former dead. So he walks out on to the black-sand beach called Orap, going on down the coast till he comes to a place called Pan-womu (Pangkumu on the Admiralty Chart), where there is a village of living people. As he passes along the beach in front of the village the dead man strikes one of their canoes with his wand, and the people, hearing it, say, " A man of Atchin (*to-so*) has died." [1]

Goes to Bong-na-un. Meets Guardian Spirit called Le-saw-saw

Then he proceeds down the coast till he comes to Bong-na-un, the promontory facing Ambrim, where he meets the Guardian Spirit, here called Le-saw-saw,[2] and, presenting her with the pig, is allowed to proceed on to the white-sand beach.

Lights beacon on small island and is ferried over on canoe of driftwood to " place of the ghosts ", near Ambrim

In front of this beach is a small island called *Noror sin ta-mats*, and the dead man wades over to it and lights a beacon with sticks of the *rapol* [3] tree in order to attract the attention of the ghosts (there is no mention of a ferryman). These then come over in canoes, which are not real canoes, but pieces of driftwood called *ulu nuamp*, and take him with them to a place near Ambrim called *ngambu sin ta-mats* " place of ghosts ", to which the dead are said to go.

WALA VERSION

Burial. Proceeds with wand and fowl to the " Cave of the Dead "

Men of high degree in Wala are wrapped in fine mats and buried either sitting or extended. In either case they are arrayed previously, as on Vao and Atchin, with the insignia due to the degree they have attained in Maki ritual. I have no record of the dead man actually being fed, though many communion feasts are held.

[1] There is no mention in this version of this wand being used to part the waters, as in the Wala account, but this is clearly a case of omission.

[2] In the mythology of Atchin, Le-saw-saw is definitely represented as a woman, the mother of ten petromorphic brothers closely associated with the creator Tahar. These brothers are now represented by ten natural coral blocks on the coast of Atchin, while Le-saw-saw herself and her mother, Le-rapol, are present in two humanly-erected monoliths by the wayside leading down to the ten brothers.

[3] In the Vao version we are not told with what wood the dead man lights his beacon, but are informed that he " also breaks off a piece of seaweed called *ro-go-rombol*, and beckons with it ". *Rombol* is the Vao equivalent of the Atchin *rapol*. Here, then, we have the same word used to designate two quite different materials, but with the common object of attracting the attention of the ferryman. Clearly it is of ritual and not material significance. What this signifies I do not know, but it is interesting to note that the mother of Le-saw-saw is also called Le-rapol.

The time of burial was not recorded. As in Atchin, a cane
(*ne-mairi*), here called by the special name *ne-row*, translated
" measuring-stick ", is cut to the exact length of the dead man's
body and placed beside him in the grave. This will be seen to be
a wand with which he parts the waters of the rivers encountered
on his way. At the same time, a fowl is killed. This is subsequently eaten by the four men who buried him. But it is
its ghostly part that matters, for the dead man now takes the
wand and, slinging this over his shoulder with the ghost-fowl
hanging from the hinder end, makes his way on foot to the " Cave
of the Dead " (*pwereng sin temets*) on the beach at Orap.

Gnaws the trunk of magic tree

Outside the Cave is growing a fruit tree of the kind called
navi,[1] which here goes by the special name of *nu-wi men-men*,
and the first act of the dead man on arrival there is to gnaw the
trunk of this tree with his mouth.[2] Somehow the mourners at
the graveside know when he has done this—for it occurs
immediately after burial—and now they feel relieved, cease
weeping, and laugh, saying, " He has gone right away now, for
he has gnawed the *nu-wi men-men*."

Walks round " Whistling-stone "

Outside the cave there is also a stone, called *ni-wet wen-wen*
" the whistling-stone ". Having gnawed the tree, the dead man
now shoulders the wand with the fowl slung on to the end of it,[3]
and walks twice round the stone, whistling softly.

Walks through Cave

The dead man now enters the cave. No Guardian Spirit
bars his way ; nor have I any record here of meeting with the
former dead. He walks right through the cave and, coming
out at the other end, proceeds southward along the black-sand
beach of Orap.

Strikes river with wand, and the waters part

Half-way down the beach there is a river.[4] When the dead
man comes to it he strikes it with his wand and the waters

---

[1] This appears to be the same as the *na-avri* tree in the South-West Bay
story of the " forbidden fruit " (J. W. Layard, " Degree-taking rites in South-
West Bay, Malekula," *JRAI.*, 1928, lviii, 216). The fruit of this tree is round
and red, like a small apple. Babies whose mothers have no milk are reared on it.

[2] In the Atchin story he eats the fruit.

[3] This mode of carrying an object, slung on to a stick placed over the shoulders,
which is so familiar to ourselves, is one which as a matter of fact is never employed
by these natives in real life. The position seemed so peculiar to my informant
that he drew a special picture of it for me in the sand.

[4] This river is shown on the Admiralty Chart.

part, retreating on either side to let him pass through and closing up again behind him when he has gone.

Encounters " Nose-devouring Stone "

He continues southward until, at the southern end of the beach, he comes to a place called *Wetu* " Stone ", where there is a solitary upright stone called *ni-wet or gnüsh* " Nose-devouring Stone ". This stands alone in the sea, and is a *te-mets* (ghost of a dead man). There is a story, related below, of a Vao man whose ghost was followed on its journey by two living Atchin women, who saw this Stone rise up and hit the nose of the dead man with its finger, not in order to break it, but to make it flat. It is for this reason that the dead man now quickly presents the Stone with the ghost of the fowl which he has been carrying with him, in order to save his nose from suffering a like calamity. If he delayed in presenting it, his nose would be flattened. If he had no fowl to give at all the Stone would eat him.[1]

Removes burial mats at Pinalum

The exact route followed now is not known, the next fixed point being the promontory of Pinalum, where he takes off the mats in which he was wrapped at burial. The people of this place frequently find the tassels of these mats lying about and say, " A dead man passed by last night." It is only the tassels, *tsum weren bwen* " tassels of the mats ", that are found, and never the plaited part, and the reference may simply be to some marine or coastal growth.

Arrives at Wenush (Bong-na-un). Meets Guardian Spirit who is a stone and a shark and associated with a crescent moon, pentacles, and a bird

Next, he comes to a place called Wenush, close to a promontory called *Gunsin te-mets* " Dead Man's Nose ".[2] This is the Bong-na-un of the other versions. Here he meets a petromorphic Spirit not mentioned to me in the course of this narrative, but of which I learnt from the accounts of mortuary ritual. This Spirit dwells in a stone standing in the sea. This stone is also said to be a shark (an attribute of petromorphic heroes not unknown in North-Eastern Malekula), and on it is perched a bird which in some way attracts the passing ghost. If the dead man

---

[1] This Stone is mentioned only in this version, and is the only object besides the Guardian Spirit to which any kind of payment is made. From its position in the middle of the journey and from the fact that only a fowl, and not a pig, is paid to it, its importance would seem to be subsidiary to that of the Guardian Spirit. The undesirability of the nose being flattened would appear to indicate the fact that prominent noses were characteristic of those responsible for the introduction of this portion of the story.

[2] For comment on this name, see final paragraph of note 1, page 125.

comes upon this stone he is devoured by it and drowned. This calamity would doubtless, as in the other versions, be averted by payment of a pig, for the dead man does in fact attain his destination. Unfortunately, the name of this Spirit was not given, but there is no doubt from its position in the story that it is Le-saw-saw, the Guardian Spirit, of the Atchin version. In mortuary ritual this Spirit is represented by a giant mask called *sam-sam* or *sambe-sambe* (in Atchin *sap-sap*), dialectical variants, without the feminine prefix, of the word Le-saw-saw.[1]

Lights beacon. Ferryman named Shules paddles over to see who he is, and reports to Ambrim. Dead man's kinsmen ferry him over

At Wenush, where the dead man has now arrived, there is a village of living people. Here he steals a brand from one of their fires when they are not looking, and with it lights a beacon on the reef. Shules,[2] the ferryman on Ambrim, sees the fire and paddles over in his canoe to see from what place the dead man hails. He does not take him over, but returns alone to Ambrim to tell the former members of the dead man's village (? family) that one of their number is waiting on the other side. Then they all go over in their flotsam canoes, and take him back with them to the land of the dead.

Nightly dance of the Dead. Head and bones fall asunder at dawn. New-comer's head first falls off on seventh night

On Ambrim the dead dance every night and all night long till the appearance of the Morning Star (*ne-mutso naterin*), when

[1] On the eve of the Hundredth Day after death, the day on which the mortuary officials cease their vigil in the dead man's lodge, and they and certain other relatives break their fast and bring their mourning to an end, this giant mask, about 20 feet in height, is publicly displayed and shot at by the men, while the assembled women weep. This portion of the rite occurs at sundown, presumably in memory of the hour of the dead man's trial. The mask consists of a human face geometrically designed, surmounted by a tall, narrow, tapering super-structure on which are represented a conventionalized shark, a bird, crescent moon, three pentacles (symbols which occur elsewhere in Malekulan ritual), and other indecipherable designs. Similar giant masks, called by the same name and also referred to definitely as " ghosts " (an indication that the Being represented is considered as having once been alive), are similarly displayed and shot at on the Hundredth Day after the great Maki sacrifice, and on the Thirtieth Day of initiation, when the new initiates issue from seclusion after their ritual death in the initiation lodge, sure indication of the mortuary origin of both these rites. All three displays form part of the innovations brought in by the newer culture, and do not occur on Vao.
From the name of the promontory, "Dead Man's Nose," on which this petromorphic Spirit stands, it might be thought that it is but another version of the Nose-devouring Stone already met with. This may, of course, be so, but does not follow from the name, since the word *Gunsin* " Nose " is used for " promontory " in Malekula in much the same way as we use our word " Ness ".
[2] This name may be connected with the Atchin word *Shul-shulen*, used to designate the feast of communion with the dead.

their heads fall off and their bones fall asunder till they join together again the following evening. The newly-arrived ghost dances with them, but his head does not fall off till the seventh night after his arrival, which is also supposed to be the night when the body finally rots in the grave, and is that on which those at home blacken their faces and begin their fast.

Dead man plants banana on Ambrim

I have an isolated note that the dead man plants a banana in the land of the dead on Ambrim, but under what circumstance I do not know.

Journey accomplished immediately after death

The whole journey is accomplished almost in a flash, since the spirit lights the beacon as a signal to the ferryman almost immediately after burial.

TALE CONCERNING THE JOURNEY OF THE DEAD

Account of two Atchin women who followed a dead man journeying from Vao to Ambrim

A story is told on Wala explaining how it is that the facts about the journey of the dead and the life of ghosts are known. It is interesting that the ghost which was followed should be that of a man from Vao, where less is known concerning these things than in any of the other Small Islands. The natives of each island, however, are convinced that their own version of the tale is true for all the other islands in the group.

An old man on Vao died, was adorned as usual for burial with his arm badges, fowl's feathers, and other insignia, and set out on his journey to Ambrim.

When he came to a place called Woremet, he was seen by two Atchin women, who were so taken by his finery that they wished to marry him. So they followed him to the " Cave of the Dead ", where they saw him gnawing the *navi* tree. And they followed through the cave, and on to where he struck the waters of the river with his wand, and passed through. And then they came to Wetu, where the dead man delayed in presenting his fowl, and the stone rose up and with its finger struck the dead man's nose so as to make it flat. Then one of the women said to the other, " Now we see that this man is no good. He is no man but a ghost." But they followed to Pinalum, where the dead man took off the mats in which he was wrapped. Then they came to the place called Gunsin temets, and all three lit fires on the reef.

Shules, the ferryman, saw the fires and paddled over. And when he saw that it was a Vao man, he paddled back to Ambrim and told all the dead from Vao to come over and fetch the newcomer. This they did, and the two Atchin women went with them to Ambrim. When they arrived there, one of the women was frightened, and said to the other, " I've begged you all the time to go back, but you would not, and now you really do see that this is not a man, but a ghost ; and here we are among nothing but the dead."

And they stayed there seven nights. And every evening, when the crickets (*bong-le-muisi*) began to sing they saw the bones of the dead join together and become alive, and they watched them dance till their heads fell off at the rising of the morning star. And at dawn after the seventh night the head of the man they had accompanied fell off also.

But now the unusual happened. For the Atchin women must return home, but could not find their way alone. So this man became alive, and said, " I will take you back to Atchin." And he still had his wand. So, having ferried them over to Gunsin temets, he walked northward with them along the coast, and whenever they came to a river he struck the waters with his wand, so that they parted and the three walked through on dry ground. And he went with them till they came to the Cave of the Dead, where he left them, saying " *ko reldrel e matur, ko reldrel e mairi* " [1] and himself returned to Ambrim.

The two women returned alone to Atchin, but straightway died. But the Atchin people brought them back to life by kneeling on their chests and suddenly releasing the pressure, so that the breath came back into their bodies. This method of artificial respiration is called *mu wushi luani*.

When they came back to life they related all that they had seen. And that is how it is known that the dead go to Ambrim and that after seven days their heads fall off, and why care is taken to kill a fowl at death and to place the wand with the body in the grave.[2]

---

[1] The translation of this is doubtful. It may mean " he dances sleeping, he dances waking ", or possibly, " he dances from the time of lying down to sleep to the time of rising " ; the use of the word *mairi* may contain a punning reference to the cane from which the wand is made.

[2] I recorded the beginning of another tale concerning a man named Burial, of Lawor, one of the extinct mainland villages from which the newer culture emanated, who did not believe in the story of the Guardian Spirit, saying : " Even if it is true that Le-saw-saw stands in the way, I won't present her with a pig, but will go down to the sea by another road, and avoid her." So when he died, he took with him thirty pigs, and went by another way to the sea, and when he came to the beach he waded across to the island and lit a fire of *rapol* wood. Unfortunately at this point my informant was interrupted, and I never heard the sequel.

JOHN LAYARD

DISCUSSION

Let us now attempt to analyse the story, beginning with a comparative table of the three versions.

Comparative Table

	VAO	ATCHIN	WALA
	Takes pig.	Takes (wand and) pig.	Takes wand and (pig and) fowl.
Mountain.		Ascends mountain called *Tawo-leter-rum-rum*. Climbs tree called *wi-n'men-men* and eats fruit.	
ORAP.		┊ ··········	Gnaws trunk of tree called *nu-wi-men-men*.
		Walks round *Whistling-stone* (*ni-wet men-men*) drawing in breath with whistling sound.	Walks twice round *Whistling-stone* (*ni-wet men-men*) whistling softly.
	Enters *Cave of the Dead*. Meets *Le-hev̄-hev̄* and *Ta-gar-lawo*. Gives each a pig.	Walks through *Cave of the Dead*.	Walks through *Cave of the Dead*.
			Parts waters of river with wand. Encounters *Nose-devouring Stone*. Presents fowl.
PINALUM			Takes off burial mats.
PAN-WOMU		Strikes canoe with wand.	
BONG-NA-UN	┊ ········	Meets *Le-saw-saw*. Presents pig.	(According to mortuary ritual) meets Stone Being associated with shark and hawk.
		Crosses to small island called *No-ror sin ta-mats*.	Arrives at place called Wenush, close to promontory called Gunsin Te-mets.
	Lights beacon and beckons with sea-weed called *ro-go-rǫmbol*.	Lights beacon with sticks of *rapol* wood.	Lights beacon on reef with brand stolen from living people.
Ferry and Ferryman.	Ferried over by man called Lingi in canoe of banana-skin (*wuwun*).	Ferried over on piece of driftwood.	Ferryman named Shules comes to see who he is, and fetches his dead kinsmen who ferry him over.

	VAO	ATCHIN	WALA
Land of the Dead.	Ambrim; volcano called *Bot-gha-rambi.*	"Place of ghosts" near Ambrim.	Ambrim.
Arrival there.	Arrives at dusk as nightly dance of the dead begins. Is placed in the middle, while the dead dance round him. Dance led by ghost named Mal-kal-aut.	(No further information from Atchin.)	
The Dead dance all night.	The Dead dance all night and sleep all day. The Dead dance by villages on successive nights as during life.		The Dead dance all night till rising of morning star.
Heads fall off at dawn.			Heads fall off at dawn and bones fall asunder, till joined together the following evening.
Seventh night.	(Belief in falling off of heads vehemently denied.)		Newly arrived spirit dances with them, but head does not fall off till seventh night.

These facts may be analysed as follows :—

Analysis of the Preceding Table

COMMON TO ALL	VAO ONLY	COMMON TO WALA AND ATCHIN, BUT NOT TO VAO	ATCHIN ONLY	WALA ONLY
Cave of the Dead.	Ghosts of the previously departed dead within the Cave.			
Guardian Spirit	called Le-heṽ-heṽ.		called Le-saw-saw.	(name not recorded).
		represented in mortuary ritual by giant mask.	called *sap-sap.*	called *sam-sam* or *sambe-sambe.*
	A malicious Being.	A Stone.	also a woman.	also a shark assisted by a bird (mortuary ritual).
	met at Cave. Accompanied by Tagar-lawo, who intercedes for new-comer.	met at Bong-na-un.		

K

COMMON TO ALL	VAO ONLY	COMMON TO WALA AND ATCHIN, BUT NOT TO VAO	ATCHIN ONLY	WALA ONLY
Payment to Guardian Spirit	a pig.		a pig.	(a pig.)
	Pig also paid to Tagar-lawo.			
	(Nothing further known of journey till arrival at Bong-na-un.)			Nose - devouring Stone at Orap, placated with a fowl.
			Ascends mountain with female name.	
		Magic tree.	on mountain.	outside cave.
			climbs and eats fruit.	gnaws trunk.
		"Whistling-stone."		
		Magic wand.		
			strikes canoe.	parts waters of river.
				Takes off burial mats at Pinalum.
Arrival at Bong-na-un.				
			wades over to small island.	goes to place called Wenush.
Lights beacon	and beckons with seaweed called ro-go-rombol.		with sticks of rapol wood.	with brand stolen from living people.
Met by Ferryman				
	called Lingi (= conductor).			called Shules, who returns to fetch the dead man's former kinsmen.
Diminutive flotsam canoe				
	of banana-skin, banyan, bark, etc.		of driftwood.	occupied by the dead.
Home of the Dead on Ambrim	volcano.		"place of ghosts."	

(From here onwards my information is confined to Vao and Wala.)

COMMON TO VAO AND WALA	VAO ONLY	WALA ONLY
The dead dance all night.		
New-comer dances with them.	Description of dance, led by famous spirit named Mal-kalaut.	
	(Falling off of heads vehemently denied.)	Heads and bones fall asunder at dawn. Head of new arrival does not fall off till end of seventh night.

Older and newer forms of culture

In attempting an analysis of these stories it is essential to remember that the older form of culture, with burial in the squatting position and the dolmen-Maki which are now found in the village of Petehul, on Vao, was at one time common to all three islands, but has since been profoundly modified by the introduction from the Malekulan mainland of a newer form of culture characterized by the monolith-Maki and extended burial. This culture has its present seat on Wala, whence it has spread in almost complete form to the Atchin twin-village of Ruruar (in which this island's version was recorded), while on Vao, though it has already exercised considerable influence, this influence is not nearly so profound.

Beliefs held on Wala and Atchin only, but not on Vao, may then be safely taken to belong to the newer form of culture, while those held exclusively on Vao belong to the older. We shall expect also in all the islands to find evidence of a compromise between the two.

Features peculiar to Vao

Let us examine first those features of the tale which are peculiar to Vao. In the first place we find :—

(*a*) The existence of the previously dead within the cave. This is at complete variance with the conception of a home of the dead on Ambrim.

(*b*) The presence of the Guardian Spirit in the cave, instead of barring the way to Ambrim at Bong-na-un as in the other versions.

(*c*) The presence, unknown in the other versions, of a second Spirit, Tagar-Lawo, who persuades the unwilling Guardian Spirit to let the dead man pass, and is himself rewarded with a pig.

Cave, and not volcano, once the dead man's goal

These features all suggest that at one time in the development of the story the cave itself, and not the volcano, must have been the dead man's goal.

Guardian Spirit and Tagar-lawo. Sukwe and Tagaro. Raga version

Now the names of the Guardian Spirit, in Vao Le-hev̄-hev̄ and in Atchin Le-saw-saw, can be shown, through the operation of phonetic laws, to be philologically equivalent. The word Le-saw-saw, shorn of its feminine prefix *Le-*, is also equivalent to *sap-sap*, the name of the giant mask representing this Being on Atchin, and also with the Northern New Hebrides culture-hero Supwe, spelt by Rivers Sukwe and by Codrington, according to the convention of the Melanesian Mission, Suqe. Tagar-lawo is also equivalent to the Northern New Hebrides Tagaro on the one hand, and to the Atchin Tahar, creator of all things, on the other.[1]

In Raga (Pentecost), from which one Vao village claims its origin, Tagaro is said to have a brother " Suqe, who accompanies and thwarts him. Tagaro came down from heaven, made men and other things, and went back again to heaven. Suqe belonged to the earth ; his head was forked, therefore he had two thoughts in it. Whatever Tagaro did or made was right, Suqe was always wrong. . . . Tagaro sent him to a place where there is a bottomless chasm, somewhere inland in Araga (Raga), where he rules over the ghosts of the dead ".[2]

On Vao it is said of the Guardian Spirit, who has been shown to be equivalent to Suqe, that it is " irresponsible and in all things defiant ". This Spirit is associated with the good-tempered Tagar-lawo in precisely the same way as the erratic Suqe with the good Tagaro in Raga, and in both cases this Being is said to be the Guardian of the Dead. There is no doubt, then, that the stories correspond. In Raga, the tale ends in the cave ; there is no further journey. Here in the cave, in Vao also, the tale must once have ended.

Malo. Supwe. Home of the dead in the Cave associated with dolmen-Maki

Now in Malo, the next large island immediately north of Vao, belonging to the same matrilineal area as Raga, there is a form of dolmen-Maki actually called the Supwe (Suqe). Moreover, old men, that is to say those of high standing in the Maki rite, are called in Atchin *sup* and in Vao *humbe*, which are the same word according to the sound-changes already indicated. Vao is the present seat of the dolmen-Maki, while in Atchin it has only recently been superseded. In Wala, the stronghold of

---

[1] In Wala and Atchin the sounds *v* or *w* (i.e. bilabial *v*), *b*, *mb*, *m*, and *p* are all more or less interchangeable, so that Le-saw-saw frequently sounds more like Le-sav-sav, while the mask representing her is called in Atchin *sap-sap*, in Wala *sam-sam* or *sambe-sambe*. Here the shorter clipped form *sam-sam* represents the usual pronunciation by the younger men, while the older men retain the longer and more dignified *sambe-sambe*. These all represent what may be regarded as the normal phonetics of the Small Islands of Malekula. In Vao, however, and at places like Matan-vat on the northern coast of Malekula, a peculiar phenomenon is present. In all labial and nasal consonants the tongue is protruded slightly beyond the lips, so that pairs of consonants so pronounced, such as *d* and *b*, *m* and *n*, p and *t*, are at first almost indistinguishable without comparative philological knowledge. One effect of this is that *v* and *w* assume a sound almost exactly corresponding to the English voiced *th*. Thus my first spelling of Le-heṽ-heṽ (the Vao version of Le-saw-saw) was Le-heth-heth. Since finding this invariable phonetic rule, however, I have adopted the practice of writing down these consonants according to their philological equivalents but at the same time placing a long stroke over them indicating this protrusion, of the tongue. Further invariable sound-changes include the softening of Atchin *s* into Vao *h*, and the reduction of Vao *g* or *gh* to Atchin *h*.

[2] R. H. Codrington, *The Melanesians*, Oxford, 1891, p. 169.

the monolith-Maki, the word for "old man" is quite different. It is then clear that Supwe, together with the words for "old man" derived from it, is primarily associated with the dolmen-rather than the monolith-Maki. Since this Supwe is also primarily associated with the cave, it becomes clear that the conception of a home of the dead within the cave, together with a non-petromorphic Guardian Spirit and the accompanying Tagar-lawo, belong to the older level of culture associated with the dolmen-Maki.

Wala and Atchin version. Cave here also once the final goal

Let us now turn to the Wala and Atchin versions of the story. That the cave was here also the final goal would seem to be suggested (a) by its very presence in the story, quite meaningless in its relation to a home on Ambrim, and (b) by the position of the "Whistling-stone". From the account given in the Atchin version that the dead man walks round this stone "drawing in his breath with a whistling sound" and from the report of one of the mortuary officials at a recent burial that he heard the dead man whistling round his grave "drawing his breath in and out just as he did before he died", it is clear that this whistling represents something in the nature of a death rattle. The position of the stone outside the entrance to the cave is a clear indication that this feature of the journey represents the final act of the dead man before he enters the unknown.

Ambrim story an addition, only partially accepted on Vao

To this belief in a home of the dead within the cave has then been added at some later date the new conception of a home of the dead on a volcano situated on Ambrim, where the dead dance all night till dawn, when their heads fall off and their bones fall asunder, together with a series of events occurring on their journey thither.

This new belief, held, with slight variations, both on Wala and on Atchin, has been accepted in part indeed on Vao, but with such slight conviction that—

(a) the dead still hover, with their attendant Guardian Spirit, in the cave ;

(b) there is expressly stated ignorance of what happens to the dead man on his journey from the cave to the promontory at Bong-na-un ;

(c) there is no gong-signal to accompany him on his way, and

(d) the Wala story of the disintegration of the head and bones of the dead after their nightly dance on Ambrim is vehemently denied.

Clash between two beliefs. Ritual copyright. Only those new features are accepted which do not interfere with existing ritual or belief

Why should this new belief, if held at all on Vao, be held so grudgingly and in such mutilated state ?

The explanation lies, I think, in the extent to which the various elements of the new belief clash with already existing mortuary and Maki ritual. Here we meet with a fundamental aspect of Small Island culture. No new rite or ceremony, no new mode of inhumation, no new method of house-building, decoration, song or dance, nothing in any aspect of material or ceremonial culture from the most important down to the most trivial, may be adopted by one individual, family, or village from another without payment to a previous owner or practitioner. Such payments for important rites are extremely heavy. Each separate item must be paid for, always to the last owner. In the case of public rites, such copyright transactions occur almost invariably between contiguous villages. When we remember, for instance, that the Maki ritual in all its complexity takes roughly thirty years to perform, that it is made up of countless smaller rites, each of which must be separately bought, that this can be done only when the rite is actually performed, that there are six villages on one island, and that we are here dealing with three such islands, then some conception will be gained of the number of generations it will take under existing conditions in the Small Islands for any given rite to circulate.

Beliefs unconnected with ritual have, on the other hand, no bar to circulation.

Dead on Ambrim, beacon, ferryman, flotsam, canoe, nightly dance of the dead

Thus the plain conception of a home of the dead on Ambrim meets with no ritual objection. Burial at sundown may well coincide with former practice, and in any case time is not purchasable. The only other ritual observance is the minor one, also not purchasable, of sacrificing a pig at burial so as to be on the safe side " in case the dead man should start quickly on his journey ".

In the same way, beliefs concerning the lighting of a beacon at Bong-na-un, the ferryman and the passage over in a diminutive flotsam canoe are ritually innocuous. It may be noted in passing, however, that while the name given to the ferryman on Vao is purely descriptive, that recorded on Wala has almost certainly ritual significance connected with the feast of communion with the dead. This feast, however, is common to both forms of mortuary rite, both that in which burial is in the squatting position, as on Vao, and that in which it is in the extended or sitting position as is the case on Wala, so that the dropping of the name on Vao merely shows less familiarity with the story.

All-night dancing by successive villages in set rotation, as reported of the dead on Ambrim, is a feature common to all mortuary and both Maki rites on Vao as on the other islands, while the special Vao account of Mal-kalaut leading the dance is a faithful representation of what actually takes place on these occasions, using a local ancestor as the leading figure.

This exhausts those features of the tale which are common to all three islands, as well as those which are peculiar to Vao.

Features peculiar to Wala and Atchin

Let us now turn to those peculiar to Wala and to Atchin, and inquire as nearly as we can why this should be the case.

Transference of Guardian Spirit to Bong-na-un. Disappearance of Tagar-lawo

In the first place we find the new conception of a home of the dead on Ambrim to be held so strongly as to have caused the transference of the Guardian Spirit from the threshold of the cave, where she is met with in the Vao version, to the reef at Bong-na-un, which, according to the new belief, is the final point of departure of the dead from Malekula for their new home on Ambrim. A secondary effect of this transference is the complete loss of the companion Spirit Tagar-lawo. The cave, once populated by the dead, is now empty and but an incidental feature of the journey.

Petromorphic Beings. Association with monolith-Maki

What of the remaining features of the story as related in the Wala and the Atchin versions ? Prominent among these are upright Stones.

Not only is the Guardian Spirit transferred from the cave to Bong-na-un, but here, according to the Wala version, she becomes a Stone standing in the sea. The dead man also meets with the Nose-devouring Stone at Orap and the Whistling-stone outside the cave. Whether the Whistling-stone is or ever was endowed with life there is no evidence to tell ; the stories show, however, that the other two are definitely petromorphic Beings endowed with life and thought and power of action.

Both on the Malekulan mainland and on Wala and Atchin culture-heroes of both sexes are frequently said to have the

power of transforming themselves into stone. Many of these may
be seen represented by natural coral blocks or humanly erected
monoliths. To what extent this petromorphism obtains on Vao
I do not know. It is quite certain, however, that it has nothing
like the prominence there as on the other islands. I have, moreover, already stated that the chief innovation of the newer
culture radiating northwards from its seat on Wala is the
enormous increase in monoliths representing ancestors which are
erected in the Maki rite. This new monolith-, as opposed to
the old dolmen-Maki, has not yet reached the village Petehul,
from which the Vao version of the story was obtained, and it
was here definitely stated that knowledge of events on the portion
of the journey between the cave and Bong-na-un was peculiar
to the other islands. It would then seem that these features of
the journey are definitely connected with the newer form of
culture and the Maki monoliths.

   It is of interest here to note that these features are not denied,
but merely ignored, on Vao, since on this island there is no
definite bar to the idea of monoliths, but they are simply not of
the same absorbing interest ritually as they are on the two
other islands.

Magic Wand

   Another feature of this portion of the journey is the magic
wand cut to equal the length of the dead man's body and buried with
him in the grave. This, too, does not occur in the Vao version.
It has already been pointed out that burial in the squatting
position is associated with the older form of culture and the
dolmen-Maki still found on Vao, and that the newer culture,
together with the monolith-Maki, introduced extended burial.
A moment's thought will show that no wand cut to the length
of the living figure could possibly fit in to any grave in which
the body does not lie at its full length. The magic wand is
thus also seen to belong to the newer form of culture unacceptable on Vao owing to conflict with existing mortuary
practice.

Heads of the dead fall off. Sitting interment

   Let us now turn to the Wala version of the nightly dancing
of the dead, whose heads fall off and bones fall asunder every
dawn. In Vao this statement is not just ignored. but vehemently
denied, and it is simply said that the dead dance all night and
sleep all day. Here we are again face to face with mortuary
practice and belief. For, while on Wala and the Malekulan
mainland the heads of the dead are removed from the body
some time after burial and receive special treatment, on Vao

any such disturbance of the body after death is definitely abhorred.

This feature is then also seen to belong to the newer form of culture, but to be unacceptable on Vao because conflicting with existing practice and belief.[1]

Seven-day probation as opposed to five-day probation on Vao

In the Wala version of the story the head and bones of the newly-arrived dead man on Ambrim do not fall asunder till the seventh day. This indicates a seven-day period of probation before the dead man achieves full status in the future life. It is on this day, and not till then, that his relatives at home on Wala first blacken their faces. The number 7 is associated throughout the mortuary ritual in these islands with burial in the extended position, while that associated with burial in the squatting position is 5. It is, therefore, on the fifth day after death that the blackening of faces begins on Vao.

Now, we are told by Codrington that Suqe " would have men die only for five days ",[2] a statement indicating resurrection, or at least attainment of full status in the future life, on the fifth day after death. This belief would then appear to be associated with burial in the squatting position and the home of the dead within the cave.

In Wala a survival of this belief is seen in a rite held on the eve of the Fifth Day after death, for though the dead man is supposed to have made his way to Ambrim on the night of burial, there is yet a fear that he may still be lingering near until this day. So four men are detailed to stand, two on either side of the grave, and to perform evolutions with their hands designed to drive the ghost away, while at the same time they draw their breath in and out with a whistling sound similar to that made by the dead man at the Whistling-stone. This agrees with the supposition already arrived at that whistling (though probably not the Whistling-stone itself) is associated primarily with the older cult of the home of the dead within the cave. This survival does not, however, interfere in any way with the celebrations held in Wala on the seventh day in honour of the dead man's achievement of full status on Ambrim.

In Vao the conflict of belief takes quite a different form. Here, where old men are buried in the squatting position, and the

---

[1] It is unfortunate that I did not obtain the Atchin version of this portion of the story. One of the Wala mortuary practices that have not yet reached this island is this removal of the head. It would be of the greatest interest to know whether this culture-lag had or had not the effect of preventing the acceptance of the Wala story of the falling off of heads among the living dead on Ambrim.

[2] Codrington, ibid., p. 169.

conception of a home of the dead on Ambrim is only partially
accepted, there is for old men no celebration on the Seventh
Day at all, and faces are blackened on the Fifth Day after death.
It is clear, too, that in the older layer of belief, the dead did
not start out on their journey immediately after burial, for it
is not till the day following burial that ten boars are sacrificed
for the use of the dead man on his journey. New ideas associated
with the Ambrim journey have, however, gained sufficient
credence to have caused the slaying of a small pig by the chief
mortuary official at burial, so that *in case* the dead man should
" go away quickly " and the ten pigs killed on the morrow should
be too late, the dead man should have at least one ghost-pig
with him, with which to pay the Guardian Spirit at the outset
of his journey. Here, too, the burial of old men at sundown
is clearly timed to coincide with the reception of the dead man
on the volcano. The seven-day period of probation (though not
on the volcano) is also grudgingly accepted in one statement
made to me on Vao to the effect that, " We rest in our graves for
seven days. On the seventh day our heads fall off our bodies.
Then we start on our journey to Ambrim." [1]

Though the number 7, so far as mortuary practice is concerned, is essentially connected with extended, as opposed to
squatting, burial, it occurs so frequently in all initiation rites,
particularly as the period elapsing between ritual death and
resurrection, and also in both Maki rites, that I hesitate to assign
it exclusively to either form of north-eastern Malekulan culture,
though in its present context it would seem to be associated with
the newer.

Banana

A further doubtful feature, so far as significance and culture-
level are concerned, is the report from Wala of the planting
of a banana by the dead man on Ambrim. In the Vao mortuary
rites, the fourteenth day after death is one of great activity
and marks the end of the assistant mortuary officials' vigil in
the dead man's lodge. Among the many minor rites performed
on this day, a banana and a special kind of yam are planted
in the dancing-ground and surrounded by a circular fence.
Similar fences are erected on the thirtieth day after death on
Wala, and at an unrecorded date on Atchin, though I have no
mention in my notes of the planting of bananas in them. On
this doubtful evidence it would, on the whole, appear as if this
feature of the Ambrim story, though unrecorded, had been
adopted, with its attendant ritual, on Vao.

[1] This statement may, on the other hand, have referred exclusively to young
men, who, though buried in the extended position, do not go to Ambrim after
death (see p. 140).

Mountain and Magic Tree. Associated with the Cave (?)

Only two features of the journey now remain to be considered. The first of these, occurring only in the Atchin version, is the ascent by the dead man at the outset of his journey of a mountain called Tawô-leter-rum-rum. Tawô is the name of a tree with buttress-roots appearing frequently in ritual, but the significance of which I do not know. *Le-ter* is the title taken by an elderly woman when her son performs the Maki sacrifice. This is the case in both forms of Maki. What is the function of this mountain, and why it should receive this name, I cannot say.

The last feature is the Magic Tree. This tree is stated to be a *navi*, which has a round red fruit with an appearance not unlike that of a small apple. It is apparently the same as the *na-avri* tree, which grew the forbidden fruit in the story of that name recounted from South-West Bay. The special name given to the tree is in Atchin *wi-n'men-men*, and in Wala *nu-wi-men-men*. *Men* is probably a modification of *man*, the word for "magic"; *n'* and *nu* are articles. In real life the *navi* fruit is used, among other things, for rearing babies whose mothers' milk has failed. Whether this fact has any significance in relation to the giving of new life to the dead I cannot say.

Mountain and Magic Tree both appear to be closely associated with the cave. Why the Mountain should appear only in the Atchin version I do not know, nor can I offer any explanation why both are absent from the account obtained in Vao. These may be cases of omission, and in the absence of any further evidence it is not possible at present to determine to which culture-level they belong.

The results of this discussion are tabulated overleaf.

Newer and older cultures : terms used locally

One necessary observation remains to be made regarding what, for the purpose of this paper, I have termed the older and the newer cultures. One thing which I have purposely left out of this discussion is the fact that in Vao, though old men are buried in the squatting position and in their case no attention whatever is paid to the seventh day, young men are buried in the extended position, and though their bodies remain untouched, their heads are said to fall off on the seventh day in the grave, and on the seventh day a rite is performed by the living to celebrate this supposed event. Thus the burial of young men is clearly associated with what I have called the newer culture, and the supposed severance of the head on the seventh

Older form of culture surviving on Vao.	Newer form of culture with its present seat on Wala.		?
(Tagaro and Sukwe.)	(Tahar only.)		
Squatting interment.	Extended interment associated with sitting interment and removal of the head.		
Dolmen-Maki.	Monolith-Maki.		
	(accepted on Vao.)	(not accepted on Vao.)	
			Ascent of Mountain Magic Tree.
Home of the Dead in the Cave. Guardian Spirit and Tagar-lawo in the Cave. (? whistling.)	Home of the Dead on Ambrim.	(Special gong-signal.) Guardian Spirit at Bong-na-un. Guardian Spirit a stone and shark. Whistling-stone. Nose-devouring Stone. Magic Wand. (Dead man discards burial mat.)	
	Beacon at Bong-na- un. Ferryman. Flotsam canoe. Nightly dance of the Dead. Banana planted.		
Five-day probation period.		Seven-day probation period. Falling off of heads.	

Table showing conclusions suggested in regard to culture-level

day within the grave reflects the actual removal of the heads of old men on Wala and the Malekulan mainland. How, then, since extended burial for old men, together with the removal of heads and the importance of a seven-day probation period after death, is only now moving by slow degrees northward from Wala towards Vao, can we explain the presence of these ideas connected with young men on Vao? In the first place it must be noted that young men, not having gone through the laborious ritual necessary to the attainment of future life, do not go when they are dead to Ambrim. Therefore, the time of day at which they are committed to the ground is of no moment, and on the day after death a rite called Atean is held, expressing

THE JOURNEY OF THE DEAD 141

sorrow at their untimely end, a rite omitted in the case of an
old man, for a young man is dead and finished, whereas an old
man attains everlasting life, and those left behind rejoice.
Moreover, young men are buried in their respective dwelling
houses, whereas old men, whether squatting as on Vao or extended
as on Wala, are buried in the cemetery beside the lodge.
What complicated eddying of culture movement this denotes
I cannot at present say, but would warn the reader that in using
the terms " older " and " newer " culture I refer exclusively
to movements in progress now and in recent generations in
north-eastern Malekula, without prejudice to time-sequence of
cultures in the larger sphere of Melanesia as a whole.

Cave and Volcano in Eddystone

Some similar amalgamation of beliefs as that which I have
suggested appears to have occurred also in Eddystone of the
Solomons, from which island the dead go to a " big cave in
Mbombombelo ", where they " sleep in the daytime and go about
at night ".[1] It is an essential part of the scheme put forward
in this paper that the Vao belief that the dead " dance all night
and sleep all day ", though the scene is now laid on the volcano,
was originally associated with the cave, as opposed to the Wala
belief, associated with the volcano, in the disintegration of the
bones and the falling off of heads. The tale from Eddystone
thus corroborates this detail, but pays court to the volcano
story by placing the cave conveniently on the side of an extinct
crater.

Early Layer of Belief

Comparisons from further afield cannot be entered into here.
Cave and volcano both appear to represent approaches to a
world beneath the earth, though the cave may also indicate
the cultural memory of a tomb. Rivers thought it " probable
that the belief in an underground Hades reached through
volcanoes or volcanic vents is to be associated with the earlier
strata of the population of Melanesia ",[2] though he does not in
this connection discuss the problem of the cave.

Possible recent renaissance of north-east Malekulan culture

It is indeed quite possible that the recent blossoming, in a
peculiar form, of the culture of the north-east Malekulan mainland (of which the volcano story forms but a small part) represents
in fact a local renaissance in opposition to, perhaps even
stimulated by, an alien sea-borne culture which had made its

[1] A. M. Hocart, " The Cult of the Dead in Eddystone of the Solomons,"
JRAI., 1922, lii, 95.
[2] W. H. R, Rivers, *The History of Melanesian Society*, Cambridge, 1914, ii, 479.

home in the Small Islands, but with the decline in maritime
enterprise has lost contact with its parent cultures in the north-
eastern islands of the Group, and is now itself succumbing to
the new forms arising from the contact.

Detailed accounts of this extremely complex culture are in
course of preparation, which it is hoped will throw more light on
the whole problem.

Note on sex of Guardian Spirit

It is interesting to note that, whereas in Raga, Sukwe is a
man, in Vao it is not known whether the equivalent Le-hev̄-hev̄
is a man or a woman, while in Atchin Le-saw-saw is definitely a
woman and the mother of ten sons. At the present time in the
Small Islands the prefix *Le-* is used exclusively for women, every
woman's name beginning with it. It is remarkable, however,
that in the case of quite a number of undoubtedly male culture-
heroes their names begin with this same prefix *Le-*. In a note
on page 119 is cited the case of a man who actually took the name
Le-hev̄-hev̄. Now, in the Northern New Hebrides, including
Raga, descent is matrilineal, while in the Small Islands it is
patrilineal. Of all the islands in this group, Vao is nearest
geographically to the matrilineal area, and in its mortuary rites
shows the strongest evidence of previous matrilineal descent.
Thus we find the curious anomaly that in the matrilineal area
the Guardian of the Dead is male, whereas in the patrilineal area
it is female, whilst on the border-line between the two there is a
conflict of opinion leading to uncertainty as to what sex it is.
An explanation may conceivably be found if we suppose that
the prefix *Le-* now used exclusively for women in the patrilineal
area at one time indicated female descent, and not only female
sex, and as such could be applied to men. This would provide a
possible explanation for the application of this prefix to culture-
heroes, and also possibly for confusion in the patrilineal area,
where it is used exclusively for women, resulting, in the case of
superhuman beings, in the mistaken notion that *Le-* indicated
female sex rather than association with a former matrilineal
society.

THE SEQUENCE OF STONE-AGE CULTURES IN EAST AFRICA

By L. S. B. LEAKEY

In 1926 the first systematic investigation of the Stone-age cultures of Kenya Colony and Tanganyika Territory was begun, and although a very great deal remains to be done, it is now possible to give some sort of a picture of the sequence of cultures and their relationships to each other, and to various divisions of the Quaternary geology of the area.

Perhaps one of the most striking results of what has been achieved up to date is the very close parallel which has been established between the sequence in East Africa with that in South-Western Europe. Of many factors which make the systematic stratigraphical study of Stone-age cultures in East Africa more easy than in Europe, the more important perhaps deserve special mention.

In the first place we are fortunate that, with the important exception of small areas at high altitudes, East Africa was not affected by ice sheets at any period of the Quaternary. In Europe each successive re-advance of the glaciers tended to plough up, and otherwise disturb deposits formed at earlier stages of the Pleistocene, so that their interpretation is rendered far from straightforward. In East Africa—where for the most part world climatic changes were reflected in alternating increase and decrease in rainfall—the study of Pleistocene geological deposits is much easier.

Furthermore, the geographical structure of much of East Africa is such that lake basins without outlet, except at very high levels, are a common feature. In these the fluctuations of climate are often magnificently recorded and can usually be accurately studied. In other ways, too, the physical geography of East Africa is particularly helpful. In many places deep gorges have been cut by recent erosive action right through Pleistocene deposits, exposing magnificent sections for study, whereas in England, Pleistocene studies are all too often hampered by the inadequacy of sections exposed by man in the course of purely commercial undertakings—usually gravel-pits.

In addition to all this we have the phenomenon of the Great Rift Valley which cuts right through the area being studied, and which often exposes in its walls excellent sections of quaternary rocks extending over very many miles.

The principal areas which have been studied are the Nakuru Elmenteita basin, the Naivasha basin, the Oldoway gorge and surrounding country, the Kendu-Homa area, and the Kinangop Plateau. These areas are listed in the order in which they were studied. In point of fact the first two mainly yielded evidence concerning the Upper Pleistocene culture stages, while the next two yielded evidence of the sequence during the Lower and Middle Pleistocene. The last named region, the Kinangop, provided an exceptionally important connecting link between Middle and Upper Pleistocene, and enabled us to fill in a gap that was for a long time unbridged.

There is now abundant evidence to show that from the earliest Pleistocene times (possibly even from the Pliocene) man has been living and developing in East Africa. The earliest known culture is that which we call Oldowan. The principal tool of the Oldowan culture is of very simple form. A rolled pebble or a nodule of chert, or a rough lump of almost any kind of rock is trimmed very roughly along one edge or side, so as to produce a jagged cutting edge.

This tool, which is frequently referred to as a "pebble tool", of course persists for a very long time after new tool types had been evolved, so that its occurrence in any deposit is not proof of a high antiquity of that deposit. But in deposits which on geological and faunistic grounds are considered to be Lower Pleistocene in age, implements of this type are the only ones known, unless one includes certain very roughly trimmed or utilized flakes.

There is no doubt that the Oldowan culture persisted unchanged for a very long period, and it is not until deposits of the earliest part of the Middle Pleistocene are reached that we have been able to find evidence of the invention of any new tool types. At first all that is noticeable is a very gradual transition in the direction of crude hand-axes ; but once this transition has taken place the evolution is very much more rapid and new and more developed types of hand-axes appear, so that in the Middle Pleistocene period one sees a development from the crudest Chellean stage of culture at its base, to a very highly evolved Acheulean stage during its concluding centuries.

There is as yet no *positive* and *conclusive* evidence for the co-existence of any other culture in East Africa during the main period of the development of the Chelleo-Acheulean culture complex, but it must be mentioned that, in certain regions at least, we have indications (which await detailed study next season) that during a part of this time a culture closely allied to the Levalloisian of Europe was present also.

When we reach the closing stages of the first great pluvial period which we call the Kamasian, and which we consider to mark the end of the Middle Pleistocene, we find that four distinct cultures are co-existent. One of these, of course, is the final stage of the Acheulean ; the second is what we call Lower Kenya Mousterian; the third is the Nanyukian, which has some elements of each of the other two ; while the fourth is a very crude and undeveloped stage of the Kenya Aurignacian.

After a very short period of co-existence two of the four, the Acheulean and the Nanyukian, die out as far as we can at present ascertain, but the other two continue to develop side by side throughout the greater part of the second great pluvial period which we call Gamblian. One of the results of this long contemporaneity of the Kenya Mousterian and Kenya Aurignacian was that the former gradually developed into what we term the Kenya Stillbay, while the Kenya Aurignacian after a succession of intermediate stages reached what we term phase " c " of the Upper Kenya Aurignacian in which very crude pottery is present.

There is still a gap in our knowledge as to what developments took place after this in the Aurignacian line of culture, but there is evidence that the Kenya Stillbay gave rise to a culture stage known as the Magosian during the somewhat arid epoch which marks the end of the Gamblian pluvial period.

When the first post-pluvial wet phase (called Makalian) set in, we find that a strong culture called Elmenteitan was very widespread. It certainly has its roots in the Kenya Aurignacian although so far no connecting stage has been discovered. At the same time a culture group known as the Kenya Wilton appears on the scenes. The various industries of the Kenya Wilton strongly suggest that they are not all of the same origin. It is likely that the Kenya Wilton has a dual origin being in part a derivative of the Magosian and in part from phase " c " of the Kenya Aurignacian. Industries of strong Kenya Wilton affinities persist for a long time, and at least one of the Neolithic cultures—that known as Gumban—is descended from the Kenya Wilton.

The Neolithic cultures proper do not appear, as far as we know, until the second post-pluvial wet phase, known as the Nakuran. So far two co-existent Neolithic cultures have been recognized, the Gumban and the Njoroan. The latter is a polished-axe culture, and there are already indications that it had several subdivisions. The Gumban culture has been divided into two groups—Gumban A and Gumban B. This division is based upon marked differences in methods of burial, in the types of pottery made, and in the forms of the stone bowls used.

Beads found in direct association with Gumban industries show that trade connections with the civilizations of the period (such as the Egyptian) existed.

L

In the following table the culture stages are shown in their relation to each other and to the climatic subdivisions of the Pleistocene period.

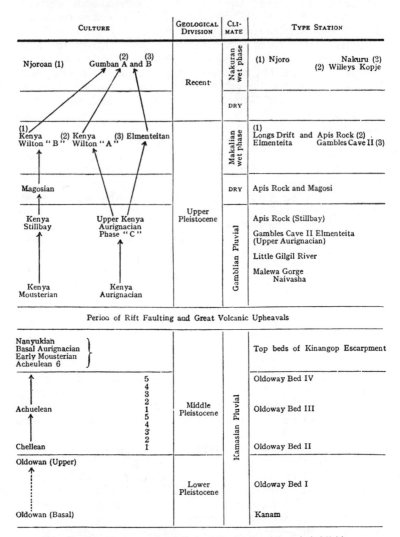

CULTURE		GEOLOGICAL DIVISION	CLI-MATE	TYPE STATION
Njoroan (1) Gumban A and B (2) (3)		Recent	Nakuran wet phase	(1) Njoro Nakuru (3) (2) Willeys Kopje
			DRY	
(1) Kenya Wilton "B" (2) Kenya Wilton "A" (3) Elmenteitan			Makalian wet phase	(1) Longs Drift and Apis Rock (2) Elmenteita Gambles Cave II (3)
Magosian			DRY	Apis Rock and Magosi
Kenya Stillbay Kenya Mousterian	Upper Kenya Aurignacian Phase "C" Kenya Aurignacian	Upper Pleistocene	Gamblian Pluvial	Apis Rock (Stillbay) Gambles Cave II Elmenteita (Upper Aurignacian) Little Gilgil River Malewa Gorge Naivasha
Perioa of Rift Faulting and Great Volcanic Upheavals				
Nanyukiah Basal Aurignacian Early Mousterian Acheulean 6				Top beds of Kinangop Escarpment
Achuelean Chellean	5 4 3 2 1 5 4 3 2 1	Middle Pleistocene	Kamasian Pluvial	Oldoway Bed IV Oldoway Bed III Oldoway Bed II
Oldowan (Upper) Oldowan (Basal)		Lower Pleistocene		Oldoway Bed I Kanam

Note.—No attempt has been made to indicate relative duration of the geological divisions.

In conclusion it must be mentioned that human remains have been found associated with certain of these culture stages, but this brief paper cannot include a discussion of them. It is sufficient to say that man of the genus *Homo* occurs at the very bottom of the sequence, and that the human remains found with a Chellean stage of culture are regarded as true but primitive examples of *Homo sapiens*.   So that at the time of writing not only the earliest true *Homo*, but also the earliest true *Homo sapiens* can be claimed for East Africa.

SPEARS WITH TWO OR MORE HEADS, PARTICULARLY IN AFRICA

By K. G. LINDBLOM

The selection of the above subject as my contribution to this volume is largely due to Seligman himself, who collected data concerning multiple-headed spears in Africa. This material he most kindly placed at my disposal, without the remotest inkling of my intention to make use of it in this way. From a scientific point of view it would undeniably have been of better advantage if *I* had handed over to Seligman my notes on these spears and suggested that *he* should work up the material. As things are, however, I am agreeably indebted to Professor Seligman and, indirectly also, to those who have supplied him with information, above all Louis Clarke, of Cambridge; Henry Balfour, of Oxford; and T. A. Joyce, of the British Museum; and, in respect of detached items of information, F. von Luschan, of Berlin; F. de Zeltner, of Paris; V. Christian, of Vienna; and Father M. Schulien, of Rome. For my own part it gives me great pleasure to express my thanks for valuable contributions to W. Schilde, of Plauen; M. Heydrich and B. Struck, of Dresden; F. Krause and P. Germann, of Leipzig; Mlle. E. Dijour, of Trocadéro Museum, Paris; J. Braunholtz, of the British Museum; Father Schulien; and H. Baumann and B. Ankermann, of Berlin. I am in particular indebted to Dr. Schilde, who most unselfishly supplied me with a voluminous and valuable bibliographical list as well as excerpts.

In these introductory remarks it should also be expressly mentioned that Seligman and I have to some extent been forestalled in that Schilde has already given attention to spears with more than one point, and, in his important essay, " Die afrikanischen Hoheitszeichen" (*Zeitschr. f. Ethnologie*, 1929), adduces a number of instances of their occurrence as well as a map of their distribution (p. 142). In this study such spears, however, only enter as a minor detail, and none are depicted.

Let me begin by giving an account, so far as is known to me, of the geographical distribution in Africa of spears with two or more points, together with what information I have regarding their employment or significance. In association with the geographical data I shall also give the available information as to staves with a forked upper end. Fish-spears, on the other hand, I have not included except in cases where concurrently

150   K. G. LINDBLOM

they are made to serve other purposes, being used as weapons, or in ritual performances, etc. With this, let us plunge *in medias res*, beginning on the West Coast of Africa and proceeding eastwards.

Schweiger-Lerchenfeld depicts a group of armed Woloff, two of whom are each carrying a two-pronged spear, but to this he does not refer in the letterpress[1]; nor have I found any references either in Bérenger-Féraud (*Les peuplades de la Séné-gambie*, Paris, 1879) or in any other works on Senegal with the exception of two of the spears depicted by Jähns,[2] on each of which there are two secondary points at the base of the main

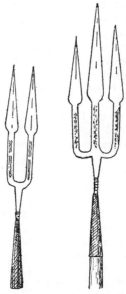

Fig. 1.—Mandigo spears. Portuguese Guinea (The Berlin Museum, Nos. III C, 5472–4).   (After Krause.)

blade. According to Jähns, these spears are in the Dresden Museum, but Dr. Heydrich tells me that search for them there has been in vain. On the other hand, both bidents and tridents are known from Portuguese Guinea. Fig. 1 shows two such implements, stated to originate from the Mandingo and used for fishing.[3]   Each point is a completely formed spear-blade and, as barbs are absent, it seems doubtful whether they are actually fish-spears. These Mandingo spears bear close resemblance to

[1] A. v. Schweiger-Lerchenfeld, *Afrika*, p. 320, Wien, 1886.
[2] M. Jähns, *Entwicklungsgeschichte d. alten Trutzwaffen*, pl. xxxi, Berlin, 1899.
[3] E. Krause, *Vorgeschichtliche Fischereigeräte*, p. 41, figs. 117, 119, Berlin, 1904. These spears are found in the Museum für Völkerkunde in Berlin, Nos. III, C. 5472–4.

PLATE VI

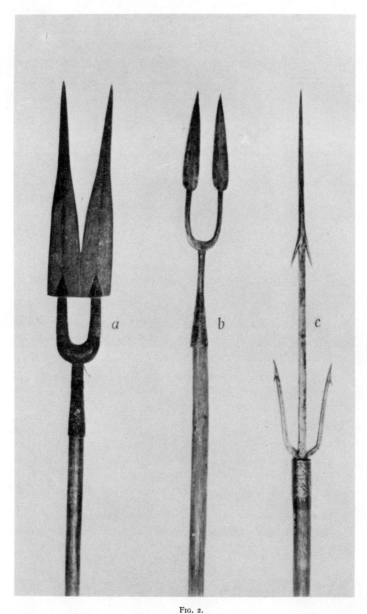

FIG. 2.

Spears. Bissagos Islands. *a*, of wood carved in one piece, and with carved ornamentation ; *b*, iron point with incised ornaments ; *c*, length of point 52.5 cm. (Riksmuseum, Stockholm, Nos. 11. 13. 18 & 20 : 09.21.238.)

the well-known Bissagos spears with one to three points, fairly common in museums, that also occur with wooden points carved in *one piece*, a few of which, forming part of the Riksmuseum collections, are here depicted (Pl. VI, Fig. 2, *a-b*; cf. Fig. 3). In the Copenhagen Museum there is a trident of wood, said to be for

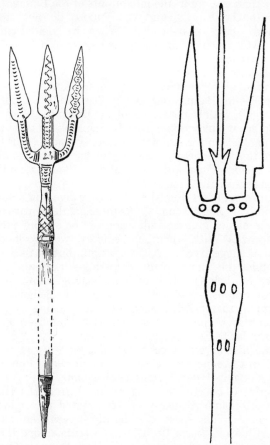

Fig. 3.—Spear, Bissagos.
(The Leipzig Museum.)

Fig. 4.—Bissagos Island spear of wood, said to be for fishing.
(The Copenhagen Museum.)

fishing, of which Seligman has sent me a sketch (Fig. 4). As, however, these Bissagos spears are barbless and, moreover, occasionally to a not inconsiderable extent ornamented (cf. Krause, Fig. 120), I doubt very much whether they should be described as " fish-spears ".[1] On the other hand, the object

[1] Schilde briefly but definitely states (op. cit., p. 94) that bidents occur as weapons in the Bissagos Islands.

seen in Pl. VI, Fig. 2, c, and the four-pointed barbed Bissago spear depicted in the British Museum *Handbook* (1910), Fig. 164, No. 21, probably belong to this category. The Dresden Museum also possesses a few spears of a similar type (Nos. 5070, 5074, 6538). According to Doelter, who, however, makes no mention of spears with more than one point, the inhabitants of the Bissagos Islands, at any rate the Bijagos and the Papels, do not themselves manufacture their spear-heads.[1] When he visited the Papel king, the latter received him carrying a spear in his hand (p. 131, though no particulars are given).

The *almany* (or *emir*) of Bondu carries a two-pronged staff as his badge of office (Schilde, p. 94). Among the Malinke about the Rivers Bafing and Bakoy (two of the chief sources of the Senegal), with the members of the Dialunfo society tridents and other spears play some part.[2] Schilde points out (p. 94) that Fulani chiefs in the region of the upper reaches of the Faleme (tributary to the Senegal) possess spears with more than one point. (Cf. *infra*, Fulani of Futa Jallon, Adamawa, and Darfur.)

Four spears in the Trocadéro Museum are stated to originate from "Guinée" (Pl. VII, Fig. 5).[3] They were given by "Schoelcher, 1885 ", and by " Roux, 1900 ". As these gentlemen are unknown to me their names give no indication of the supply provenance of the spears. With their exceedingly well-worked points, *a–c* are not suggestive of African origin but rather of Indo-China, while the more plain *d* perhaps presents a Somali appearance (cf. below). It is difficult to judge, however, merely from photographs. But in a letter to Seligman (dated 24th August, 1922), Zeltner encloses a drawing representing —so far as may be judged from the rough sketch—a spear-head of a type similar to Fig. 5, *c*, and of this he writes : " Il existe en Guinée française de ces lances : 1. chez les Soussou et chez les Mendi (Sierra Leone), 2. chez les Foulbé du Fouta-Djalon. Peut-être ne s'agit-il que d'armes de cérémonie." Pl. VII, Fig. 6, shows a spear ("covered with tiger skin "), from the Hedemann Collection, Honolulu Academy of Arts, stated to originate from Sierra Leone.[4] This spear can hardly have been used as a weapon. Chiefs in Sierra Leone, at all events among the Timne, use a long staff forked at the top.[5] Here may also be quoted

---

[1] C. Doelter, *Uber die Capverden nach d. Rio Grande u. Futah-Djallon*, p. 125, Leipzig, 1884.

[2] De Kersaint-Gilly, *Bulletin du Comité des Études historiques et scientifiques de l'Afrique occidentale française*, 1919, p. 433 (according to information supplied by Schilde, this work not being accessible to me).

[3] Mlle Dijour, who has kindly made a search at my request, has been unable to find any more in this museum.

[4] C. J. Hedemann, *Catalogue of the Collections of Weapons*, No. 411, Honolulu, 1928.

[5] N. W. Thomas, *Anthropological Report on Sierra Leone*, i, 28, London, 1916.

PLATE VII

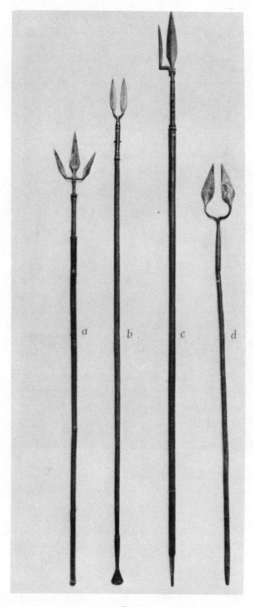

FIG. 5.

a, b, c, d. Spears. " Guinée ". (Trocadéro Museum, Paris, Nos. 51360-61 ; " Douille fer et cuivre ", Nos. 3616-17.)

FIG. 6.

Spear, " covered with tiger skin ". Sierra Leone. (Hedemann Collection, Honolulu.)

PLATE VIII

FIG. 7.

Mandingo notable with trident.   N. Liberia.   P. Germann, photo.   (The Leipzig Museum.

what has been said in a general way by Berry in his study of
the natives of Sierra Leone : " On the West Coast of Africa a
trident-shaped spear is the badge of office of a chief's prime
minister or chief man, his treasurer and man of business, and by
him carried before the chief as a symbol of his power, and forms
part of the chief's regalia." [1]

Dr. Germann has been kind enough to send me a photograph
taken by him during his expedition to Liberia in 1928–9 representing a Commendi (Mandingo) man of the Bangwalamai
village in Northern Liberia (on the route Kolahun–Fangalahun–
Bangwalamai–Pandemai), holding a trident (Pl. VIII, Fig. 7). This

FIG. 8.—Spear-head with five points. West Africa. Zeltner has seen something
similar in Sarafere on the middle Niger. (Drawing contained in a letter from
Zeltner to Seligman. 2nd August, 1922.)

spear belongs to the Germann Collection in the Leipzig Museum
(No. 34106).   This man was not a chief but one of the village
notables.   " The spear," Germann writes me, " was evidently
his badge of office, for when I was about to photograph him
he first dived into his hut and then reappeared with his spear.
Hence it is plain that he considered it highly important that he
should not be recorded on the camera plate unaccompanied by
his emblem of authority.   A chief's emblem, properly speaking,
in these parts consists—apart from the official staff—of an

[1] R. G. Berry, " The Sierra Leone Cannibals, with Notes on their History,
Religion, and Customs," *Proceed. R. Irish Academy*, xxx, B. Nos. 4, 5, p. 68,
Dublin, 1913.

elephant-tail fly-switch or else the sword worn by the chief's messengers as a warrant of their commission."

Among the Avikam, of the Ivory Coast (inhabiting an island in the lagoon at Lahou), Joseph noticed some old and rusty spears with one or two points, no longer in use. As for a long time the Avikam have been using fire-arms and do not, at any rate nowadays, work in iron, Joseph was unable to say whether the spears were of Avikam [1] manufacture.

Seligman received from Zeltner (letter of 2nd August, 1922) a sketch of a spear with five heads from West Africa (Fig. 8), which is depicted by Verneau in *Les Races Humaines* (p. 272, fig. 237).[2] This spear is not likely to have been used as a weapon.

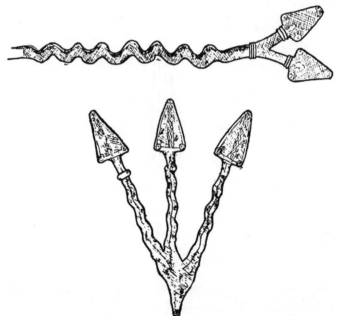

Fig. 9.—Objects of copper, found at Oyono, the Lobi region. (After Labouret.)

Zeltner adds that he has seen a similar spear at Sarafere on the middle Niger (south-west of Timbuktu), used for ceremonial purposes.

The *hogon*, the great chief of the Habe (Tombo), of the Hombori mountains in the Niger bend, who is also their high priest—" possède un bâton terminé par une fourche à trois dents, dont

---

[1] G. Joseph, " Notes sur les Avikams de la lagune de Lahous et les Didas de la région du Bas Bandama," *Bull. et Mém. de la Soc. d'Anthropologie de Paris*, i, 6, 245, Paris, 1910.
[2] I have not this work at hand.

il se sert pour séparer, en cas de rixe (brawl), les combattants "[1] (cf. Morocco, *infra*). Or, as another writer expresses it : "Dans ses promenades et dans l'exercice de ses fonctions il porte une canne en fer forgé à trois renflements ou un bâton terminé par trois branches, emblèmes du Sèrviteur de la Triade Divine."[2] Among the Bosso of the region of Lake Debo the village headman, according to Frobenius, carries as a badge of office a spear (called *ta*), not having more than one point, it is true, but with two barbs on either side of its head.[3]

In the so-called Lobi ruins in the neighbourhood of the town of Gaua—the Lobi district being situated west of the Black Volta River—objects of copper have been discovered—not spear-heads—but a bident in the form of a two-headed snake, and a trident (Fig. 9, found at Oyono, north-west of Gaua). The origin of these ruins is unknown ; the present-day inhabitants say that they found them there on their arrival. Delafosse and Labouret believe, however, that the ruins are of negro origin, and parallels to the two-headed copper snakes have been found among two other negro tribes of the same region, viz. the Nabe and the Kulango, bordering on the south of Lobi. "Yegba, sœur de Loroda, patriarche des Nabé, possédait un fétiche redoutable, nommé Marsyé ou Marsé, représenté par un serpent à deux têtes. Il avait la propriété de protéger ses fidèles et d'attirer la mort et les pires calamités sur ceux qu'on lui désignait. Le sanctuaire de ce Marsé existe encore aujourd'hui à Biguelaye (N.-O. de Bouna). Il n'est pas douteux que l'effigie découverte à Oyono ne soit celle du Marsé des Nabé." . . . "Le trident à trois têtes de serpents serait une personnification de la Terre, puissance créatrice. Les Koulango le vénèrent pour obtenir une nombreuse postérité et une moisson abondante." . . . "Ainsi donc, poteries et objets en cuivre trouvés dans les ruines du Lobi semblent provenir des Koulango."[4]

In the district of Atyuti, of Togoland, the fetish priest, who was also the chief of the country, possessed among other insignia the *odom* stick, which consisted of an ordinary stick, with short branching forks at its upper end.[5] The deity known as Jewe, worshipped by the Ewe tribe of Southern Togoland, who is the god of lightning, of snakes, of fishes, and is also a goddess, includes among the paraphernalia of its cult an iron staff

---

[1] R. Arnaud, "Notes sur les montagnards Habé des cercles de Bandiagare et de Hombori (Soudan Français)," *Revue d'Ethnographie et des Trad. Pop.*, pp. 252, 307, Paris, 1921.

[2] L. Desplagnes, *Le plateau Central Nigérien*, pp. 268, 322, Paris, 1907.

[3] L. Frobenius, *Atlantis*, vii, 72, Jena, 1924.

[4] H. Labouret, "Le mystère des ruines du Lobi," *Revue d'Ethnographie et des Trad. Pop.*, p. 195, figs. 1–2, Paris, 1920.   Labouret, *Les Tribus du Rameau Lobi*, pl. ii, Paris, 1931.

[5] v. Zech, "Vermischte Notizen über Togo u. das Togohinterland," *Mitteil. aus d. Deutsch. Schutzgeb.*, xi, 2, 109, Berlin, 1908.

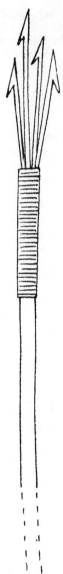

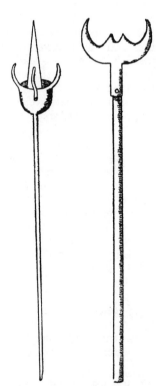

Fig. 10.—Spear for crocodiles
and large fish, also used
in war and for taking
victims for great canibal
juju. Okrika town, S.
Nigeria. (Pitt - Rivers
Museum, P. A. Talbot,
1916.)

Fig. 12.—The spear of Sarikin Rafi, and
the spear of Sarikin Masu, Hausa.
(After Tremearne.)

terminating at the upper end in two short arching branches, and known as *sofia* (god's axe).[1]

Among the innumerable deities of the Yoruba, Frobenius mentions the goddess Osun, who lives in the Osun River and is especially worshipped in Ibadan and other habitations in the neighbourhood of the river. Among the objects pertaining to her cult, weapons occupy a leading position, including spears with two or more points. At the great festivals held in honour of this goddess these weapons are stuck into the river bank.[2]

In the Pitt-Rivers Museum in Oxford there is a spear with a very long shaft and four iron points (Fig. 10, a drawing sent by H. Balfour to Seligman) from the town of Okrika, South Nigeria. It is a spear for crocodiles and large fish, but also used in war and for taking victims for some great cannibal *juju* (presented by P. A. Talbot, 1916). The Pitt-Rivers Museum possesses fish-spears, bidents, and tridents, from South Nigeria.

Among the Ibo in the Niger Delta there are "Title" Societies, composed of men who by purchase have attained to certain "titles", as they are called, i.e. ranks of honour. These titles carry different emblems, and to some of the highest ones belong, among other things, spears of special types. Among these I do not know of any with more than one point, but I take this opportunity to draw attention to a spear now found in the Riksmuseum, pertaining to the *ayari* rank and possessing a forked butt (Pl. IX, Fig. 11). This was acquired by Dr. G. Bolinder in 1931 during his West African expedition, the cost of which was defrayed by Mr. John Morehead, United States Minister to Sweden.[3]

Professor Ankermann has been kind enough to supply the information, via Dr. Baumann, that in the small village of Baba (east of Bali) in Cameroon he saw the headman carrying a two-bladed spear as a badge of office.

In the cult of Yaku ("grandmother" or "ancestor") practised by the Jukun, in the basin of the Benue, are the symbols of the cult, (1) a mud pillar with a well into which the libations are poured, and (2) a forked piece of iron planted close to the pillar and known as the "spear". Meek, who gives a detailed description of the Yaku rites, says that they "are akin to the states of dissociation and ecstacy known to the Hausa as *bori*".[4]

[1] C. Spiess, "Beitr. z. Kenntnis d. Religion u. d. Kulturformen in Süd-Togo," *Baessler Archiv.*, ii, 64, Berlin, 1912.
[2] L. Frobenius, *Atlantis*, x, 161, Jena, 1926.
[3] The forked butts of this type are otherwise "only known from Egypt", Flinders Petrie says, "where they have been found in graves with Cypriote pottery, probably therefore of northern mercenaries. . . . The use of a forked end might be either to rest on the toe, or in a loop, when riding, or to hold a cord in lancing the spear"—W. M. Flinders Petrie, *Tools and Weapons*, p. 33, pl. xl, London, 1917. Earlier these butts seem to have been regarded as bidents (see Globus, 62, 294, fig. 7, Braunschweig, 1892).
[4] C. K. Meek, *A Sudanese Kingdom*, pp. 277 sq., London, 1931.

The Jukun emigrated from Kordofan many years ago.   They are
Hamites, or semi-Hamitic, and constitute a sacerdotal hierarchy,
dominating a number of loosely organized tribes.   In the Middle
Ages they exerted considerable power over a large part of
Hausaland, but their power was destroyed by the Fulani.

The emblems of some of the spirits (*bori*) believed in by the
Hausa consist of multiple-pointed spears of a peculiar shape
(Fig. 12).   One of these spirits is Sarikin Rafi, the chief spirit

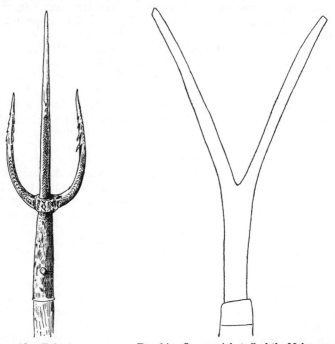

FIG.   13.—Fulani   spear.
Adamawa.   (The Leip-
zig Museum.)

FIG. 14.—Ceremonial staff of the Mahommedan
chief or sultan of Karnak Logone, S.E. of
Lake Chad.   (The Cambridge Museum.)

of the lakes and rivers.   He is the patron of the rain-makers too.
He and Sarikin Masu are originally, Tremearne says, avatars
of the same spirit.   Sarikin Masu is the name of Sarikin Rafi
when he acts as a fisher.   Similar weapons occur in Ashanti
where they are used to stick into the ground to protect the
crop sown from evil spirits.[1]

Meek has mentioned to Seligman that in Kanuri he has seen
spears with two or three blades.   So far as he knows they
were not of religious or official importance.   The chief of the town

[1] A. J. N. Tremearne, *The Ban of the Bori*, p. 416, and note p. 472, London,
1914.

PLATE IX

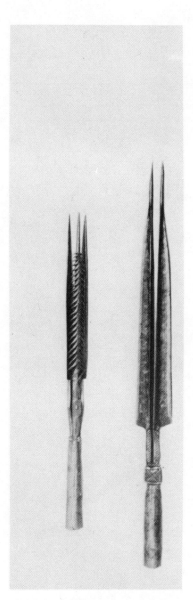

FIG. 11.

Spear with forked butt.
Carried by men of the
ayari " title ". Ibo, S.
Nigeria. (Riksmuseum,
Morehead-Bolinder Col-
lection, No. 13.13.857.)
(*See p.* 157.)

FIG. 15.

Spear-heads, bident and trident. The Fitri
Sultanate. Length of the former, 54.7 cm.
(Riksmuseum, Nos. 26.26.438-39.)

FIG. 18.

Spear, bident. Mongalla.
(The Dresden Museum.)
(*See p.* 161.)

[*face p.* 158

of Gabai, in Bornu, inhabited by a Mahommedan tribe called Ngassar—" who say they came from the town of Ngusseri, near Constantinople, some 330 years ago "—had a very good armoury, *inter alia*, long spears with four-bladed heads.[1]

The Leipzig Museum possesses a trident from the Fulani of Adamawa (Fig. 13).

Barth publishes a drawing of a fish-spear from the Musgu, an iron trident which may be supposed to have been occasionally used as a weapon.[2]

The Cambridge Museum possesses " a ceremonial staff of the Mahommedan chief or sultan of Karnak Logone " (Logone Birni) which is forked at its upper end (Fig. 14), according to a letter to Seligman from Clarke, 4th October, 1922.

From the Bagirmi there is the well-known picture in Denham and Clapperton's travels of the double-bladed spear, used for war by the cavalry who employed quilted armour.[3] From another, and earlier, work I have noted (unfortunately without specifying the author's name or the title of the work) that the sultan (*barma*) in the procession celebrating a victorious war carried a long, peculiarly shaped sacred spear. From Fitri, Lieutenant G. Moberg has acquired for the Riksmuseum two spear-heads, one with two, the other with three points, one of the latter barbed (Pl. IX, Fig. 15). Spears of this kind were carried by participants in the acrobatic exhibition of horsemanship (" fantasia ") given by the Sultan Mahmat at the time of Moberg's visit.[4]

Among the " Felata " in Darfur and Kordofan (i.e. Fulani immigrated into these countries) the sultans possess a spear with three points (Fig. 16).[5] Cf. *supra* the Fulani of Senegal, Futa Jalon, and Adamawa.

The rain-makers among the Nuba possess certain sacred spears (*oro*), and spears of this kind similarly play an important part in the Dinka great rain-making ceremony, but I do not know what these spears are like.[6]

Speaking of the southern Bari, Kotschy says : " Auch sind alle Völker mit grossen Keulen von schwarzen Ebenholtz bewaffnet und einem Dreizack mit schneidenden Klingen,

---

[1] O. Macleod, *Chiefs and Cities in Central Africa*, p. 254, London, 1912.
[2] H. Barth, " *Reisen und Entdeckungen*, in *N.- und C.-Afrika*," ii, 38, Gotha, 1860.
[3] D. Denham and H. Clapperton, *Narrative of Travels*, etc., appendix, London, 1826. The same picture in J. G. Wood, *Natural History of Man*, p. 709 (London, 1874), and F. Ratzel, *Völkerkunde*, ii, 497 (Leipzig, 1895).
[4] G. Moberg, *Rädslans land. 16,000 km. genom Sahara och Sudan*, p. 368, Stockholm, 1927.
[5] von Heuglin, in *Petermanns Mitteilungen*, Erg. H., ii, 1862, frontispiece, fig. 12, Gotha, 1863.
[6] C. G. Seligman, the articles " Nuba " and " Dinka " in *Encyclopædia of Religion and Ethics*, ix, 404, and iv, 712.

FIG. 16.—The three-bladed spear of
the sultans of the " Felata "
(Fulani). Darfur and Kordofan.
(After von Heuglin.)

FIG. 17.—Lotuko rain-spear. (From
a drawing by Seligman.)

PLATE X

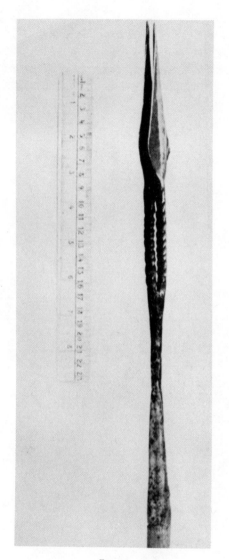

FIG. 19.
Alur spear. (Emin Pasha's Collection, Vienna
Museum.)

FIG. 20.
Spear-head. Mangbetu.
(The Dresden Museum.)

[face p. 160

welchen sie aus freier Hand gegen den Feind schleudern."[1] South-west of Gondokoro, Morlang met with a blind Bari chief (*matat*) who carried a forked staff, from the upper end of which was suspended a small bell which had been given to him by a *bunit* (medicine man) and therefore was very important.[2] According to Kaufmann—who confirms and to some extent supplements the data given by Kotschy regarding the Bari— the title of *matat* is not exclusively applied to chiefs, but " jeder grössere Besitzer führt nun diesen Titel und trägt einen zweizackigen Stock, *putet*, der wohl als Scepter gelten kann ".[3] But the Bari also possess rain-spears, and Spire makes mention of one with two points, used by Leju, the rain-maker of Shindurru, and the hereditary chief rain-maker of the Bari. Seligman has pointed out that this spear must be the equivalent of the two-bladed rain-spear of the Lotuko (see below). Seligman himself observed several spears, said to be rain-spears, among the Bari, but no two-bladed ones, although in other respects they differed from the ordinary spears of the Bari.[4]

Among the sacred rain-spears of the Lotuko, Seligman also found one which was double-bladed, and of this he has been kind enough to send me a drawing (Fig. 17).[5]

Bernatzik cites an instance from the Moru. At a game-drive with hunting-nets, in which Bernatzik took part together with a Moru " sultan ", the men carried " schwere Speere mit doppelter Spitze. Die eine ist breit und lang, die andere hat meisselförmiges Aussehen ".[6]

In the Dresden Museum there is a bident from Mongalla (Bari ?), (No. 41334). A photo of it, kindly sent me by Dr. Heydrich (Pl. IX, Fig. 18), shows two parallel points with barbs on the long proximal portion of their shafts.

According to information supplied to Seligman by V. Christian, the Vienna Museum possesses among Emin Pasha's collections a double-bladed spear from the Alur (Pl. X, Fig. 19).

Struck has pointed out to me that an Azande spear with two points (broadly lanceolate) is depicted by Brown.[7] That this spear actually originates from the Azande is evident from the fact, as Struck says in his letter to me, that the one-bladed spears that are reproduced in the same picture are typically

¹ Th. Kotschy, in *Mitteil. K. K. Geogr. Ges.*, p. 102, Wien, 1858.
² F. Morlang, in *Petermanns Mitteilungen*, p. 119, Gotha, 1862.
³ A. Kaufmann, *Das Gebiet d. Weissen Flusses u. dessen Bewohner*, p. 153, Brixen, 1861.
⁴ C. G. and B. Z. Seligman, " The Bari," *Journ. Roy. Anthr. Inst.*, 1922, pp. 466, 469, 471 ; and F. Spire, " Rain-making in Equatorial Africa," *Journ. Afr. Soc.*, 1905.
⁵ C. G. and B. Z. Seligman, " Social Organization of the Lotuko," *Sudan Notes and Records*, 1925, p. 33, pl. iii.
⁶ A. Bernatzik, *Zwischen Weissem Nil und Belgisch-Kongo*, p. 57, Wien, 1929.
⁷ R. Brown, *The Story of Africa*, ii, 33, London, 1893.

Azande spears.   The Dresden Museum possesses a bident from the Mangbetu (No. 34106, Pl. X, Fig. 20).

From the White Nile region we may proceed eastwards as well as southwards and find further instances of spears with more than one point.   To begin with, let us turn towards the east.

In Kaffa a short two-bladed spear (*shefo*, Fig. 21) formed part of the state regalia that the emperor, along with his official

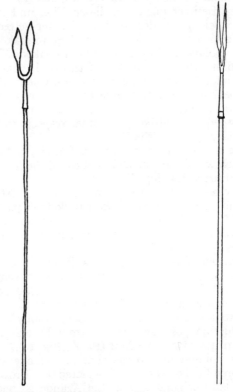

FIG. 21.—The bident (*shefo*) of the emperor of Kaffa.   (After Bieber.)

FIG. 22.—Amhara spear.   Length of shaft, 2·5 m.   (After Montandon.)

or festal garb, was invested in when exercising functions of state or on other great occasions.   The emperor carried one or two such two-headed spears in his right hand.   Except by himself— or, as a sign of him, carried by his messengers as token of their mission—no spear of this kind was permitted to be carried by any Kaficho.   The state regalia passed as heirlooms from emperor to emperor until the Abyssinians conquered Kaffa in 1897.[1]

[1] F. J. Bieber, *Kaffa*, p. 74, fig. 219, Wien, 1923.   Bieber, *Das staatliche Leben der Kaffitscho*. Globus, 1908 (Bd. 93), pp. 166 (fig.), 168.   A. Cecchi, *Fünf Jahre in Ostafrika*, p. 216, Leipzig, 1888.

PLATE XI

FIG. 23.

Abyssinian church-staves. *a*, for the common people (all wood, reinforced with a winding of iron wire) ; *b*, for nuns (with a top part of horn) ; *c*, for monks (the upper part of brass). The length of *a* is 1.37 m. (Riksmuseum, Inv. 07.42.437-40.)

FIG. 25.

Somali (?) spear. Length of the blade to the left, from point to base, 11 cm. (British Museum.)

When Cecchi saw the emperor in full court-dress, the latter carried two spears in his right hand, but Cecchi does not specify whether these were two-bladed (Cecchi, p. 427). According to Bieber, the Kaficho are descendants of fugitives from Amhara and Ennarea.

Even among the *entourage* of the Emperor of Abyssinia it appears that high officials occasionally carried a bident. Thus, it is stated in a description of the festivities held in connection with the enthronement of Abuna (archbishop) Petro : " On horse-back and flourishing a ' sonderbare gabelförmige Lanse ', Begerondi Leote (treasurer to, and favourite of, Negus Johannos) was by his personal appearance the centre of the eager spectators' admiring glances." [1]

From Amhara (with a population in the strict sense Abyssinian) Montandon depicts, among other spears, one with two blades (Fig. 22) and a shaft of unusual length (2.5 m.), though he makes no mention of its use.[2]

Of the high-priest among the Gurage, Azaïs relates that in the centre of his courtyards " ce trouve l'emblème de sa puissance : un piquet en terre avec deux branches en forme d'U ".[3] According to Montandon, the Gurage are related to the Amhara and dwell south-west of Addis Ababa, between the River Omo and Lakes Zwai (Dembel) and Horadaka.

From Abyssinia also come the staves in Pl. XI, Fig. 23. I refer to them, especially the centre one, in order to avoid arousing confusion. For it should be noted that all three of them are exclusively utilitarian, being church staves (*mokomia*) used for leaning upon (while placed in the armpit) during the long drawn-out nocturnal divine services which the congregation generally attends standing.

Let us then pass on to the Somali. In Paulitschke's monograph and other works I have been unable to find anything bearing reference to our subject, but Bricchetti depicts, without further mention, two double-bladed spears from the Northern Somali tribes, Darrod and Ishak (Fig. 24).[4] The difference in the iron sheathing at their lower ends is noticeable. It may also be mentioned that in a letter (15th September, 1922) to Seligman, Clarke categorically states that " the Somalis use a double-headed spear ". In addition I reproduce (Pl. XI, Fig. 25) a double-bladed spear in the British Museum with the inner edges sharp, the outer blunt. Braunholtz, who kindly sent me this photograph, says there are no particulars of its origin,

[1] R. Hartmann, *Abyssinien u. die übrigen Gebiete d. Ostküste Afrikas*, p. 123, Leipzig, 1883.
[2] G. Montandon, " Au Pays Ghimirra," *Bulletin Soc. Neuchateloise de Géographie*, t. xxii, fig. 111, Neuchatel, 1913.
[3] Azaïs, in *Revue d'Ethnographie et des Trad. Pop.*, vii, 22.
[4] L. R. Bricchetti, *Somalia e Benadir*, pp. 219, 223, Milano, 1899.

the piece was bought by Sir Wollaston Franks. Seligman has, however, sent me a photograph of the same spear, and in this it carries a label marked " Somaliland ". Judging from a drawing sent by Balfour to Seligman, a similar spear is found in the Pitt-Rivers Museum. This spear is merely labelled " Central Africa ", and " must have been brought about fifty years ago or so ; no details " (letter from Balfour to Seligman). On the origin of these two spears I cannot venture to pronounce an opinion. The Somali possibility should, I suppose, be taken into account, although the London spear, judging from the photograph, appears to be of rather too crude workmanship, being

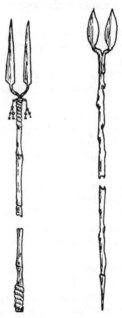

FIG. 24.—Spears from the Somali tribes Darrod and Ishak. (After Bricchetti.)

at all events substantially more clumsy than such Somali spears as I have had an opportunity of seeing. It may be that the nature of the shaft would prove indicative.

Yet another important area remains, namely, the kingdoms of the Lake Region. In Unyoro multiple-headed spears were appurtenances of the king, or at any rate of the queen (only a royal princess, i.e. a half-sister of the king, could become queen). When the king had chosen his queen and she had seated herself on her throne, she received two insignia of office. One consisted of a knife " of a particular pattern ", and the other of " a long iron spear with two sharp points like a two-pronged

fork, which was stuck in the ground, with the prongs upwards . . .
she was also given a four-headed spear, which was intended for
real use, for her new office carried with it estates and subjects
and she had the power of life and death over all her people ".[1]
From Uganda, Roscoe mentions " the regal spear ", but
he says nothing as to its appearance.[2] According to Hartmann
(op. cit., p. 123), whose source of information is unknown to me,
King Mtesa used a double-bladed spear as a kind of sceptre for
the symbol of his power.   In reply to an inquiry from Seligman,
Father Schulien has given the following information : " (1)
Double-bladed spears are insignia of supremacy.   The Kabaka
(King) of Buganda is supposed to possess supernatural power
over his enemies, and therefore in wars he is supposed to fight
as if he possessed double spears, meaning double force.   Kings
of Buganda are not supposed to really die, their spirit remains,
and double-bladed spears are placed around their graves to
enable them to overcome their enemies. (2) No legends or stories
point to their use in olden days.   (3) The high-priests of the
principal deities had double-bladed spears in their temples as
a sign of their supernatural power with which they could overcome their foes or the various ills of mankind ; in the latter case
they held the double-bladed spear in their hands as a wand,
not as a sign of magic, but to denote that they were above
ordinary creatures."   The same thing has been told me by
Father Schulien, who states that this informant is Monsignore
J. W. Campling, of Nsambya, Uganda, vicario apostolico of the
Upper Nile.   And lastly, Seligman has given me the following
description of a Baganda spear in Roscoe's collection in the
Museum of Archæology and Ethnology in Cambridge : " Iron
spear-head, with head and shaft wrought in the solid.   It has
two blades set face to face, each of which has a circular perforation
at base of blade, and there is a circular perforation through
the neck of the shaft.   Length 46·1 in.   Each blade is simply leaf-
shaped, without midrib.   From a temple."
The king of Ankole, too, possesses " sacred spears ", but those
depicted by Roscoe are exclusively one-bladed.[3]   In another
work [4] Roscoe says that the ruler of Ankole, when acting in his
capacity of judge, " usually carried the ordinary walking-stick,
a forked stick 6 or 7 feet long, called *esando*."   On the
ground of the epithet " ordinary " it seems to me, however,
uncertain whether this stick may properly be regarded as a
symbol of authority for the king.
From the " museum or armoury " of Rumanika, the king of

[1] J. Roscoe, *The Bakitara or Banyoro*, pp. 137, 146, Cambridge, 1923.
[2] Idem, *The Baganda*, pp. 194, 204, London, 1911.
[3] Idem, *The Soul of Central Africa*, pp. 70, 72, London, 1922.
[4] Idem, *The Banyankole*, p. 13, London, 1923.

Karagwe, Stanley among other things mentions double-bladed spears.[1]

Sacred spears, objects of worship, were also found in Urundi. " The great national rite is the adoration of the sacred spear of Kiranga " (a spirit accorded worship).[2] The appearance of those spears is, however, unknown to me. Furthermore, I wish to draw attention to a " Zauberspeer " (Fig. 26) from Kiziba, depicted by Rehse,[3] which shows an incipience of three points. Rehse has an illustration of it in the chapter on agriculture, but I can find no mention of it in his book. In Kiziba, the king and the ruling class consist of immigrated Bahima, and the

FIG. 26.—" Zauberspeer." Kiziba. One-third nat. size. (After Rehse.)

members of the royal family trace their descent to the first Bunyoro-ruler in Karagwe.

Sacred spears—rain-spears as well as other kinds—seem to occur among a great number of peoples of the White Nile region and farther south. Research into the types and distribution of these spears would no doubt be interesting.

For the sake of completeness I will here include an isolated instance from Tanganyika Territory, namely, among the Wataturu of the undrained area, from whom the guide-book of the Berlin Museum mentions " dreizackige Speere ".[4] In reply to my

---

[1] H. M. Stanley, *Through the Dark Continent*, i, 472, London, 1878.
[2] E. S. Hartland, in *Encycl. Rel. and Ethics*, ii, 359.
[3] H. Rehse, *Kiziba. Land und Leute*, fig. 63, Stuttgart, 1910.
[4] *Vorläufiger Führer durch das Museum f. Völkerkunde*, p. 124, Berlin, 1926.

PLATE XII

FIG. 27.

Two Kamba elders with the signs of dignity; the small three-legged stool and the
two-pronged staff. Region of Machako, 1911. (G. Lindblom, phot.)

FIG. 30.

Tumba chiefs, Bongo, Lake Leopold II district, Congo. (After
Maes.) (See p. 170.)

[face p. 166

inquiry, Dr. Baumann has informed me that the Museum possesses a spear of that kind (No. III, E. 11806), found in 1905 in a hut at Turu, and "undoubtedly of foreign origin ".[1] A drawing appended by Baumann shows its point to be roughly of the same shape as the well-known trident paddles of the upper Guinea Coast.

From the region between Lake Victoria and the Indian Ocean I only know of a solitary instance, viz. from the Akamba. Certain of their old men are called *mutumia* (pl. *atumia*). This dignity is usually reached at an age of forty to fifty. The outward sign of a *mutumia* is the little round stool, which is carried everywhere. All *atumia* are, however, not on the same level. The highest in rank are those who administer the government of the district and watch over the religion, *atumia ma nzama* and *atumia ma ithembo*. They carry a pronged staff (*maka*) as a symbol of their dignity (Pl. XII, Fig. 27). If anyone else ventures to carry such a one, he runs, at least, the risk of being ridiculed.[2]

From the Swahili I have no authenticated instance, but one from the fisher population in the village of Makunduchi in the south-east portion of Zanzibar, may be included here. At the exorcizing dance known as *nyange*—the name of a devil— a dance performed by women, "about a dozen of the women carry iron tridents affixed to long handles." [3] This devil is said to be contracted only at sea. Ingrams says that many years ago three women went down to the shore to fish and saw a devil coming towards them in a canoe holding in his hand a trident, and at the sight of him they were afflicted with madness. No one knew how to deal with this strange devil, until the remedy was revealed in a dream, and the dance *nyange* is the result. "No one can fail," Ingrams adds, "to be struck by the likeness of the sea-devil with a trident (a weapon unknown in Zanzibar and used by the people of Makunduchi only in this dance) to the story of Poseidon, and there can be little doubt that it is a relic of the worship of that deity, brought by the Greeks of old." The people of Makunduchi are Wahadimu (the original inhabitants of Zanzibar Island), but, according to Ingrams, they differ in many ways from the rest of that tribe. The villagers themselves derive the name of Makunduchi from a village of the mainland, opposite the south part of the island and called Konduchi, whence they state they came. Since (in 1907) a coin of Ptolemy X Soter (151–80 B.C.) was found at Msasani, north of Dar-es-Salaam and but a short distance from Konduchi,

---

[1] Of this spear, the Catalogue says: " Hellebardenartiger Speer, in einer Hütte in Turu gefunden, der zweifellos fremden Ursprungs ist. Holzschaft mit Messing- und Eisenband spiralig umwickelt. Eisenschuh. Lg. 1·65 m. Sammler: von Prittwitz (1905)."

[2] G. Lindblom, *The Akamba of British East Africa*, p. 144, Uppsala, 1920.

[3] W. H. Ingrams, *Zanzibar*, p. 485, London, 1931.

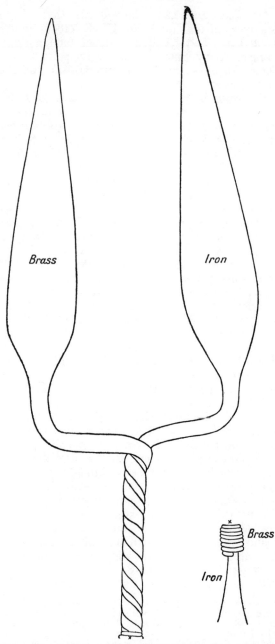

FIG. 29.—Spear from the Lower Congo. One point is of brass, the other of iron. A portion of the shaft is wound with flattened brass wire. Pointed iron ferrule, length 17·6 cm. Total length of spear 1·52 m. ; of points 25 cm. (Swedish Missionary Association Collections ; unnumbered.) (See p. 170.)

PLATE XIII

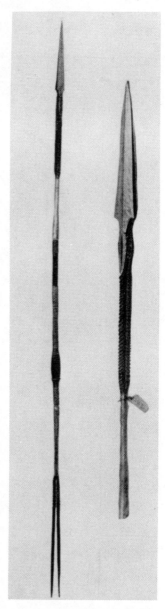

FIG. 28.
Spear with two points, set closely together.
Congo (Ubangi ?).   Length, including socket,
60 cm.   (Riksmuseum, Inv. 07.61.5.)

FIG. 31.
Spear, Lake Leopold II, Congo.
(*See p. 170.*)

there has been a tendency to identify this place with the town of Rhapta mentioned in Periplus.

I am further able to adduce a few instances from the Congo

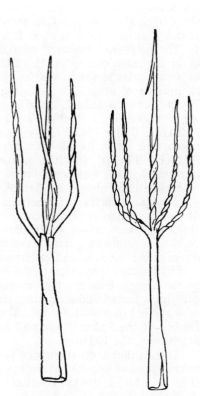

FIG. 32.—Symbol of rank for high functionaries at the court of the Paramount Chief of the Bushongo (Bakuba). (After Torday and Joyce.)

FIG. 33.—Throwing-spears. Bankutu Congo. (After Torday and Joyce.)

where, among a large number of forms, spears of two or more points are found. The Riksmuseum possesses one with two points of iron set very closely together (Pl. XIII, Fig. 28). Even the lower part is forked. The wooden shaft has a carved thickened portion, above and below which it is wound with iron, copper, and brass. Particulars as to use and locality are lacking (somewhere on the Ubangi river ?),[1] but considering its decoration it is not impossible that it belonged to a chief or was used for some ritual purpose. It was brought by Söderberg, a Swedish engineer in the service of the Congo State.

The Swedish Missionary Association possesses in its collections a double-bladed Congo spear (Fig. 29). One of its blades is of brass, the other of iron. Particulars as to locality are not given, but the spear probably comes from the lower Congo River the principal sphere of this society's activities in the Congo. It can scarcely be a weapon as it is too light and slender.

The natives of the area surrounding Lake Leopold II use— or at any rate did, when the Europeans first arrived—knives of a particular shape as well as spears with one to three points as insignia of rank. Pl. XII, Fig. 30, shows Tumba chiefs of Bongo (between Lake Leopold II and the Congo River), one of whom is carrying a double-bladed spear.[2]

Clarke (letter of 4th November, 1922) has sent Seligman a photograph of a double-bladed spear from Lake Leopold II (Pl. XIII, Fig. 31), which is of a more simple design than those mentioned in the foregoing, but of which it is distinctly stated : " objet de luxe, insigne de dignité, arme d'ostentation."

A couple of high court functionaries with the Paramount Chief of the Bushongo (Bakuba) carry among other insignia of rank (Fig. 32) " des cannes particulières taillées d'un seul morceau de bois en forme de quatre javelots réunis en faisceau ; chacune de ces cannes est garnie à son extrémité de quatre pointes de fer ".[3]

Dr. Palmaer, physician to the Swedish Missionary Association in the Congo, tells me that among the Bakete he saw a chief carrying a forked and sculptured staff or sceptre (c. 1.5 m. long) as a symbol of his authority. The Bakete are located north of Luebo on the Lulua River and have been influenced by their neighbours, the Bakuba.

The Bankutu, on the upper reaches of the Lukenye River, have a kind of peculiar throwing-spear with four to five points (Fig. 33) which is used in hunting.[4]

[1] Schmeltz and Josselin de Jong (Ethnographisch Album van het Stromgebied van den Congo, Haag, 1904–1916) depict from " Mobangi " one-bladed spears which in point of ornamentation of blades and shafts strongly resemble this spear (cf. pls. 131, 133, 148).
[2] J. Maes, " La Métallurgie chez les populations du Lac Leopold II-Lukenie," Ethnologica, iv, 94, fig. 21, Leipzig, 1930.
[3] E. Torday and T. A. Joyce, Notes ethnographiques, Bakuba, Bushongo, p. 56, fig. 45, Bruxelles, 1910.
[4] E. Torday and T. A. Joyce, Notes ethnographiques sur des populations habitant les bassins du Kasai et du Kwango oriental, p. 179, fig. 181, Bruxelles, 1922.

PLATE XIV

FIG. 34.

Spear used by sherifs with a great reputation for holiness.   Morocco (made in Fez).   Length of the point, 34 cm.;   total length, 173.5 cm.   (Riksmuseum, No. 07.41.130.)

FIG. 36.

Two-bladed spear.   Uganda   (British Museum, No. 1926.1.57.)
(See p. 172.)

[face p. 170

NORTHERN AFRICA IN ANCIENT TIMES

Newberry points out that the hieroglyph " harpoon " (bident) occurs as a ritual element on painted earthenware vessels in pre-historic graves between Cairo and Koshtamne, in Nubia, and that it has prevailed into historic time as a ritual object among the population on Lake Mareotis (Birket el Mariut, at Alexandria). The harpoon, Newberry further maintains, is the prototype of the bident and, later in time, of the trident pertaining to the Libyan god Poseidon.[1]

In this connection—perhaps merely as a curiosity—it may be mentioned that in ancient Egypt the orthodox fishing-weapon of the old kingdom was always the bident. " As this type of spear is not seen in the hands of the professional fishermen, it must be regarded either as a purely sporting weapon, or as inherited by the upper classes from an ancestry whose culture in this particular varied from that of the peasantry." [2]

Morocco.—From Morocco (Fez) the Riksmuseum possesses a multiple-pointed spear, belonging to the collection acquired for the Museum by Major A. Wester in 1907 (Pl. XIV, Fig. 34). Wester describes the spear as a "sherif-staff, carried as a symbol of rank by descendants of the Prophet". With regard to this Professor E. Westermarck was kind enough to send me the following interesting information : " When I showed the photograph of the spear to my old friend Sherif Abd-es-Salam el Bakkali he at once recognized it and told me he was the very one that bought it for Wester. Spears of this kind were used by sherifs with a great reputation for holiness—nowadays they do not, at any rate, occur in these parts of Morocco—especially at functions of acting as peace-makers between contending parties, or on other important occasions when they, the sherifs, were urgently desirous of being obeyed. The sherif then stabbed the spear violently into the ground, this being an act in the form of what the Moroccan calls *l-'ar*, which implies a conditional curse, i.e. a malediction that would smite the disobedient. Sherif Abd-es-Salam's grandfather, who was an important saint, possessed a spear of this kind which he used in the manner here described."

" Whether this spear is connected with Islam, or pertaining to some ancient Berber custom, I do not know," Westermarck adds in his letter to me. With regard to the term *'ar*, I would refer to his work *Ritual and Belief in Morocco* (i, 549–551, London, 1926). In this, he says, *inter alia*, and gives reasons for his

[1] P. E. Newberry, *Ägypten als Feld f. anthropologische Forschung. Der alte Orient*, xxvii, 20, Leipzig, 1928.
[2] O. Bates, " Ancient Egyptian Fishing," *Harvard Afr. Studies*, i, 244, Cambridge, Mass., 1917.

assertion : " There are, on the contrary, reasons to suppose that it has in a large measure an African foundation." It is interesting to note how exactly the use of this Moroccan sherif-spear corresponds with the staff of the *nogon* among the Habe people (*vide supra*).

MULTIPLE-POINTED AFRICAN SPEARS OF UNDEFINED LOCALITY

I may here add a few more spears although I am unable to localize them with certainty. The two-bladed spear (Fig. 35) was purchased by Clarke for the Cambridge Museum, and the drawing here reproduced he sent to Seligman. Clarke suggests that it might originate from Bagirmi. In the blades of the Bagirmi spears depicted by Denham, the flat planes are, however, parallel. For my part—although I have nothing but the drawing to judge from—I am rather inclined to think that it comes from the Bissagos. Firstly, because of the shape of its point, but also because the ornamentation presents considerable dissimilarities.

In the British Museum there are two double-bladed spears, with the flat planes parallel, of which Braunholtz has kindly sent me photographs (Pl. XIV, Fig. 36, and Pl. XV, Fig. 37). The first mentioned (No. 1926, 157, socketed, and wrought in one piece) belongs to the Peek Collection (purchased from Sir Wilfred Peek in 1926), and Braunholtz supposes that it originates from Uganda, which I too think very probable. The spear (Fig. 37) from the Christy Collection (No. 3915), was collected before 1880 and is labelled " East Central Africa ". Braunholtz supposes it to come from the Sudan, and for my part I would particularize this as the White Nile region.

Father Schulien has sent me photographs of spears in Pont. Museo Miss. Ethnol. Lateranense. Pl. XV, Fig. 38, shows these spears, one of which (No. 3807) is labelled " Nyasaland ", and the other (No. 3758) " Kenya " (Kenya Colony ?). They are, however, of identically the same type, and therefore must be of the same origin. Nothing similar to the ornamentation of their sockets is known to me, and it seems foreign to Negro-Africa. If these spears were in fact collected in Kenya and Nyasaland, respectively, they must have been imported into those parts or produced under foreign influence. But in such case, which ? Arabian ? Although there are no outward resemblances apparent, these spears bring to my mind the type of iron " trident "—a sort of chief's sceptre—which T. Cullen Young describes in *Man* (xxix, 189) from Northern Nyasaland.

I wish to include here a couple of spears in the Lateran Museum (Nos. AF. 4179, 38, 40, Pl. XVI, Fig. 39), although their locality

PLATE XV

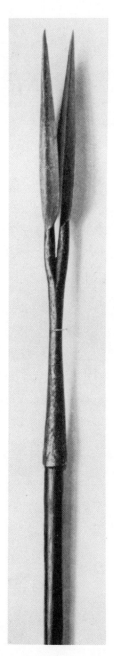

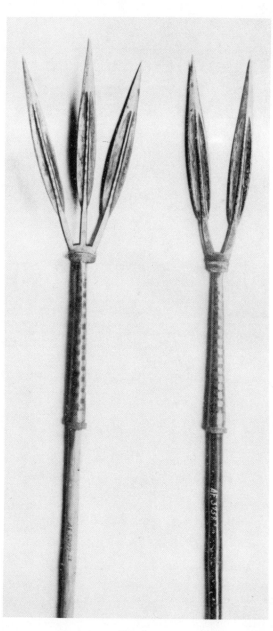

FIG. 37.
Spear. White Nile district ?
(British Museum, Christy Col-
lection, No. 3915.)

FIG. 38.
Chief's spear. " Nyasaland ", and " Kenya " (?). (Lateran Museum,
Rome.)

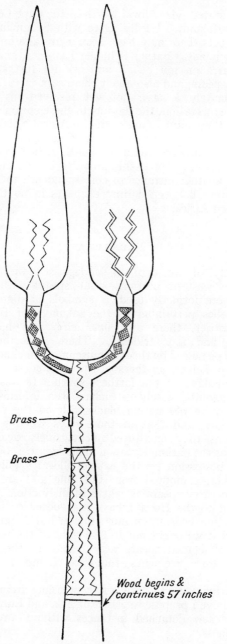

Brass

Brass

Wood begins &
continues 57 inches

FIG. 35.—Spear, etched. Bissagos ? (The Cambridge Museum.)

is definitely stated, viz. Aliwal North in the Cape Colony (south-west of Basutoland). I fully agree with Seligman who writes that he suspects there may have been a mistake in the labelling of these specimens. Father Schulien has been kind enough to write to Africa on my behalf and ask for further particulars about these spears, and also about those seen in Pl. XV, Fig. 38, but unfortunately I have not yet received his answer. If, contrary to expectation, the data as to these spears should prove correct, and they actually are native to Aliwal North, this would be very interesting, and then multiple-headed spears may probably occur in other parts of South Africa in spite of our present ignorance. Should this prove to be the case we should therein find another instance of correspondence to add to those already existent between culture elements in South Africa and North-Eastern Africa.

MADAGASCAR

And lastly, if we turn to Madagascar, we find—at any rate in the western portions—that spears with more than one point were formerly used as symbols of dignity. Among the royal relics pertaining to the Sakalava of Bueni, of the Majunga district, there are, *inter alia*, two halberds, nine " assegais ", and four tridents.[1] There is further a double-bladed spear possessed by the Riksmuseum at Stockholm (Pl. XVI, Fig. 40) from Tulear, on the south-western coast, that is to say from the Sakalava of the farthest south. It was brought by Mr. B. Ljungquist, a school-teacher, who informs me that it was made by an old native blacksmith on the pattern of an old-time model, and that in those days when spears of this type were in use they constituted an exclusively royal prerogative. The spear was the national weapon in Madagascar, but the French made their possession by the natives illegal. Village headmen were, however, exempted from this rule and are to this day permitted to carry spears as marks of distinction.

In regard to the Hova I have not succeeded in unearthing any information bearing on our subject, but I am nevertheless of opinion that we ought not to lose sight of the possibility that these multiple-bladed spears may belong to the Malayan (or Indian ?) culture elements that are found in Madagascar (*vide infra*).

Before attempting to draw any conclusions from the material collocated above I propose to glance at Asia and Europe, confining myself to a few detached instances without any pretentions of completeness.

[1] A. van Gennep, *Tabou et totémisme du Madagascar*, p. 93, Paris, 1904.

PLATE XVI

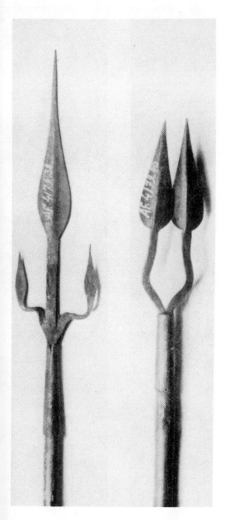

FIG. 39.
Spears, Chief's sceptre. "Aliwal North, Cape Colony " (?).
(Lateran Museum, Rome.)

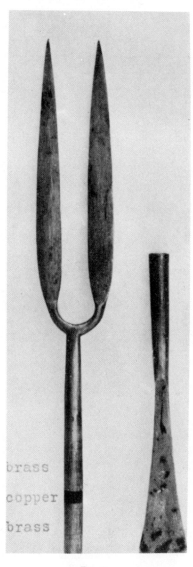

FIG. 40.
Royal spear, Sakalava. Tulear, S.W. Madagascar.
$\frac{1}{2}$ natural size. (Riksmuseum, Stockholm.)

[face p. 174

ASIA

In ancient South Arabian—Sabæan and Minæan—inscriptions bidents and tridents occur as symbols of lightning.[1] Adad, the thunder-god of the Hittites, held in one hand an axe and in the other a short-handled trident symbolizing a sheaf of thunderbolts.[2] Assyrian gods are shown with similar tridents as weapons. In the same manner we see in Babylonian art lightning represented either by a fascine of three flames or by two or three zigzag lines joined together in a stalk or handle. In Mylassa, in Caria, a coin has been recovered representing a Zeno-Poseidon, " originally, it may be supposed, the god of the ocean of the heavens but on that account also ruling the oceans of the earth." His attribute is a trident, " vielleicht erst unter griekischen Einfluss—oder ist etwa der Dreizack des Poseidon als sein Attribut nur aus dem Blitz umgedeutet ? "[3]

From the Shevaroy Hills, south-west of Madras, inhabited by the Malayali tribe, Mr. Löwenthal, the missionary, describes a temple or altar which, among other things, supports three stone celts, or cone-shaped stones, and at the side of them a *trisula* (a small iron trident, planted in the ground). Seeing that the stones are styled " thunderbolt-stones " and believed to have fallen from the skies, the trident associated with them may presumably be connected with thunder (lightning).[4] This theory is supported by the circumstance that the god Siva, in post-Vedic time the successor of the Vedic lightning-god Rudra, wields a *trisula* (Durga also often carries such a one). And this we see on coins deriving from Indo-Bactrian kings of the period immediately following the time of the birth of Christ (Blinkenburg, p. 57). It may be added that " Hindu coins and seals also bore symbols which were very numerous and diversified. Besides figures of gods and goddesses, the commonest emblems were the trident, denoting empire. . . ."[5]

Among weapons reproduced on early Indian sculptures are found tridents of various types.[6] The Artillery Museum in Paris possesses an Indian bident from the sixth century.[7] As

[1] A. Grohmann, " Göttersymbole u. Symboltiere auf Südarabischen Denkmälern," *Denkschriften K. Akademie d. Wiss. in Wien*, lviii, 1, 19 sq., Wien, 1915.
[2] E. Meyer, *Reich u. Kultur d. Chetiter*, p. 67, Berlin, 1914.
[3] E. Meyer, *Geschichte des Altertums*, 1, 716., Berlin, 1926. See also C. Blinkenberg, *Tordenvåbenet i kultus og folketro, Studier fra sprog-og-oldtidsforskning*, pp. 45 sq., Köbenhavn, 1909. The English edition of this work (*The Thunder Weapons in Religion and Folklore*, Cambridge, 1911) is not accessible to me.
[4] Blinkenberg, p. 15, fig. 1.
[5] S. Geden, in *Encycl. of Religion and Ethics.*, xii, 143b.
[6] W. Egerton, *An Illustrated Handbook of Indian Arms*, fig. 2, London, 1880.
[7] M. Jähns, *Entwicklungsgeschichte d. alten Trutzwaffen*, p. 267, pl. xxx, 15, Berlin, 1899. A. Demmin, *Die Kriegeswaffen*, p. 149, Gera, 1891.

a further instance may be added a three-pronged Indian spear (*serrate*) [1] from the Hedemann Collection in Honolulu.

As regards Persia I content myself with pointing to two veritable show pieces contained in the Moser Collection : one " runka " (*naiza*) and one trident, the head of which closely corresponds to the last-mentioned Indian specimens.[2]

In the Dutch East Indies are found spears with three to five points, and, as they seem to be very prevalent, I shall restrict myself to referring briefly to such of them as, together with notes as to their employment, are mentioned in the catalogue of the Rijksmuseum at Leiden, which contains illustrations of spears of this type with bibliographical references to particulars. The Leiden Museum possesses multiple-pointed spears from Java (" Prunklanzen ", e.g. from the Sultan of Jokyakarta, " Ceremoniallanzen "),[3] Bali (" stuck into the ground when the ruler is bathing "),[4] Borneo (" Fürstliche Lanzen ").[5] Also from Palembang, Sumatra, I know of at least one " Prunklanze " (" Hoheitszeichen "), with five points.[6] According to Krause (op. cit., p. 51), bidents and tridents occur as ceremonial weapons in Celebes, and a spear of that type is found in the Berlin Museum (No. IC, 1252). In this connection I wish to mention that Seligman has sent me a sketch of a " good Malay (double-bladed) spear with good silver mount, from Celebes ", which is to be found in the National Museum at Copenhagen. In the Riksmuseum at Stockholm there are some fine old specimens of Malay bidents, but as no particulars are given as to their employment I here pass them by. The spears just referred to—or at least a considerable proportion of them—may presumably be looked upon as related to Indian cultural influence in Indonesia.

I would also call to mind the well-known spears, including tridents, of Annam [7] and Tonkin. A number of these, from Sontai, are found in the Riksmuseum. Even more widely known may well be the corresponding class of spears from China, of which the Riksmuseum possesses a number of ancient tridents of various types (Wulff's Collection) which were used as weapons as late as in the Boxer Rebellion of 1900. " Under the names of *spetum, partisan, ranceur*, and *military fork*," Lane-Fox points out, " this class of weapons has been used in China, India, and

---

[1] Two Indian tridents of similar type with flattened points, and also two bidents, are depicted in the photographic album *Sammlung dr. Emil Riebeck*, pl. xvii, Berlin, 1884.

[2] *Orientalische Waffen u. Rüstungen. Sammlung Henri Moser.* Charlottenfels, pl. xxxv, Nos. 660–1, Leipzig, 1912.

[3] *Katalog*, xi, 209 (figs.), v, 144 (figs.), Leiden, 1909, 1916.

[4] *Katalog*, vii, 81, Leiden, 1912.

[5] *Katalog*, ii, 298 (fig.), Leiden, 1910.

[6] J. D. E. Schmeltz, " Indonesische Prunkwaffen," *Int. Arch. f. Ethnographie*, iii, 102, Leiden, 1890.

[7] See *Int. Arch. f. Ethnographie*, iii, 123, pl. viii.

Europe. They exhibit a great variety of forms, all of which are closely connected, and belong to a condition of culture corresponding to that of Europe in the Middle Ages." [1] Some of these tridents, at least, hardly appear to have been designed for use as weapons. In the catalogue of the Hedemann Collection certain Chinese spears of this class are described as "Luan Chia, processional halberds ".

Even among Japanese fighting-spears (*yaris*) there are some which may be described as three-pronged. I have also seen statues of Japanese deities provided with a sort of long, trident spear.

In Korea large iron tridents constitute the symbol of kingly power.[2]

EUROPE

As to the occurrence of bidents and tridents in Europe a few brief references will here suffice. The trident as an attribute of Poseidon-Neptune is of course well known, and was, it may be supposed, in its original form a fish-spear (or possibly also a lightning-weapon). The trident, or fish-spear, of Neptune, Flinders Petrie says, "occurs at Messana before 400 B.C., and after that often in Greece and Italy, and is a common type of coin, age of Hiero about 250 B.C. It was probably introduced by the Greeks into Egypt." [3] At the gladiatorial games in ancient Rome the lightly armed *retiarii* carried a trident (*fuscina tridens*). Tridents were employed as a charm against impotence (compare them as symbols of might and power in Asia and Africa), and on amulets they figured as a protection against the evil eye.[4]

Among war weapons of the fifteenth up to eighteenth centuries may be noted the so-called linstocks used by artillerists of the eighteenth century, which were partly weapons and partly implements, and above all the halbert, the ranceur, and the partizan. The two last-mentioned were, however, less weapons than insignia of rank (for certain officers and non-commissioned officers), and were for that reason correspondingly ornamented.[5] There is further what the Germans call "Sturmsensen" (the English "military fork"?), a sort of trident which served a practical purpose in that the two lateral blades, which were concave in their upper edges, were about midway perforated so

[1] Lane-Fox, *Catalogue of theAnthropological Collection, S. Kensington Museum*, p. 122, London, 1877.
[2] Buschan's *Völkerkunde*, ii, i, 659, Stuttgart, 1923.
[3] W. M. Flinders Petrie, *Tools and Weapons*, p. 57, London, 1917.
[4] S. Seligmann, *Der böse Blick*, i, 349, fig., Berlin, 1910.
[5] W. Boeheim, *Handbuch der Waffenkunde*, Leipzig, 1890. A. Demmin, *Die Kriegswaffen*, Gera, 1891.

N

that the weapons could be joined together by means of a pin inserted in this perforation. By this means was produced, so to speak, a single weapon, and as many soldiers as there was room for caught hold of the shafts, and with this contraption advanced against the charging foe.

Lastly, it may be recalled how from ancient times into the Middle Ages the spear carried a symbolic significance in Europe. It was the distinctive mark of a free-man, in fact such a one was simply styled a " lance ". The handing over of a spear symbolized investiture into a position of command.[1]

RÉSUMÉ

Turning our attention to the general appearance of African spears with two or more points, we find that they may be divided into two main groups, viz. :—

(1) Where the points are equal in size. As a distinct sub-group of these I here cite spears with points in parallel arrangement, having their two (more exceptionally three) blades set side by side (flat planes parallel). The material collocated above shows samples of such spears from Bagirmi, Fitri, the Fulani in Darfur and Kordofan, Mongalla (Bari ?), the Lur, the Baganda, the Lake Leopold II region, and the Congo without specification of locality. The distribution of this sub-group appears to be of a central, and comparatively concentrated, character, and I do not know of its occurrence in Africa west of Lake Chad, in the North-East, nor in Asia and Europe.

(2) With a main point and fairly large lateral points.

Passing on to the *employment* of these spears, in ten cases we have no information of any kind. Of the remainder the greater part—as also the staves—are symbols of rank for rulers, chiefs, high-priests, or other prominent personages. Others, including the " rain-spears " and other sacred spears from the White Nile region and districts south thereof, possess a religious, or at all events magical, significance. In one or two cases they are to be looked upon purely as cult objects. Multiple-pointed spears used as fighting or hunting weapons seem to occur very rarely. (The material adduced in the foregoing includes very few cases.) It may therefore be asserted that multiple-pointed spears or forked staves in Africa generally constitute symbols of rank for temporal or spiritual authority.

What, then, do these bidents and tridents symbolize ? We can find no answer to that question in the literature, or in the museum catalogues. The only information I possess is Campling's statement to Schulien regarding the double-bladed

---

[1] E. A. Gessler, *Die Trutzwaffen d. Karolingerzeit von VIII. bis XI. Jahrhundert*, Basel, 1908.

spear of the Uganda king. He is supposed to possess supernatural power, and therefore to fight as though he possessed a
double spear, meaning double force. In the same way the
high-priests in Uganda used such spears as a sign of their supernatural power. In isolated instances it may perhaps be possible
to infer that the spears or staves in question are symbols of
lightning (Jewe as the lightning-god among the Ewe of Togo),
or of the deities of the ocean, the rivers, or of fishing (Jewe as
the god of fishing ; the goddess Osun among the Yoruba ; the
spirits Sarikin Rafi and Sarikin Masu of the Hausa ; the
Makunduchi people, Zanzibar). Although somewhat hesitantly,
I may suggest another possibility, namely, that the bident
(trident) in some place or other may symbolize the tree of life.
According to Berry (op. cit., p. 67), in Sierra Leone the sign of
the Poro is the inverted Y formed in keloids down the spine
between the shoulders and branching off towards the ribs. " The
Y is the symbol of the branch or tree representing resurrection,
new birth, new life as typified by the ceremony of initiation
into the life of the tribe performed in the Poro."

Finally, there arises spontaneously the question : Is there
any connection between the different occurrences of these
multiple-bladed spears and forked staves in their character of
symbols of authority ? A question of this kind is naturally very
difficult to answer, especially as it concerns a detached culture
element which moreover consists of forms of utilitarian objects
so widely spread as spears and staves.[1] Its distribution is,
however, so nicely continuous from the Atlantic, via the Sudan,
to North-Eastern Africa (see map, Fig. 41) that one is easily
tempted to believe in the possibility of a connection. Undoubtedly
it appears to me that such connection exists at any rate within
certain portions of the distribution area : Abyssinia-Kaffa
appears to form a unit of this kind, the Bahima states another,
the large states in the Sudan, and the Bakuba together with
their neighbours, possibly a third and fourth. Although there
is no positive evidence at hand, and though I do not count
myself among those who everywhere insist on seeing a connected
whole in the spread of culture elements, I am nevertheless of
opinion that such may be the case throughout this distribution
area. As has come to pass with so many other culture elements,

---

[1] Along with multiple-headed spears and forked staves, no doubt swords and
daggers with more than one blade—or with the point terminating in lobes—ought
also to be dealt with. I do not, however, include them here, but they have
been mentioned by Schilde (p. 95), who shows that such objects occur as symbols
of authority in the Congo. Oric Bates describes a number of short, double-
bladed swords from Ashanti and Benin, " ceremonial swords used by kings and
priests for fetish purposes " (*Harvard African Studies*, ii, 187). Of significance
similar to multiple-bladed spears are undoubtedly also fasces or bundles of
one-bladed spears.

its dissemination has probably followed the high roads through the Sudan (and, if so, supposedly in an east-to-west direction), and from the White Nile region southwards.[1] If such was the case it appears to me probable that it was by Hamites (the ancient Egyptians, however, excepted) that these bident and trident spears and staves were launched as symbols of authority,

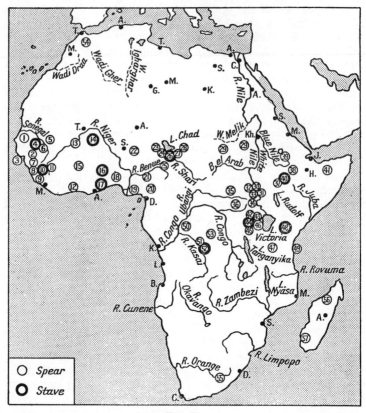

FIG. 41.

and that in the first place in the states founded by them. But at the same time one cannot altogether disregard the possibility of influence from Asia, and perhaps also, here and there, from Poseidon-Neptune.

[1] At this juncture I again wish to draw attention (in particular that of my English readers) to cultural relations pervading the Sudan as pointed out by Schilde in his treatise on African symbols of dignity (see p. 179), as well as in his study embodied in the publication to the memory of K. Weule: " Ost-westliche Kulturbeziehungen im Sudan," *In Memoriam Karl Weule*, Leipzig, 1929.

NOTES TO THE MAP

Number on map	Tribe or locality	Spear O	Stave O	Number of points	Special use
1.	Woloff	+		2	No particulars.
2.	Mandingo	+		2–3	" For fishing " (?).
3.	Bissagos	+		2–3	" For fishing " (?).
4.	Bondu		+	2	Badge of office.
5.	Malinke (Mandingo)	+		3	Signs of dignity.
6.	Fulani (Senegal)	+			Chief's spear.
7.	Fulani (Futa Jallon)	+		2–3	Ceremonial weapon ?
8.	Susu	+		2–3	Ceremonial weapon ?
9.	Mendi	+		2–3	Cermonial weapon (?).
10.	Timne		+	2	Used by chiefs.
11.	Commendi (Mandingo)	+		3	Badge of office.
12.	Avikam	+		2	Weapon (?).
13.	Saraféré	+		5	Ceremonial weapon.
14.	Habe (Tombo)		+	3	Attribute of the Hogon.
15.	Lobi, Nabe, and Kulango	+		2–3	Fetishes.
16.	Atyuti (Togo)		+		Sign of dignity.
17.	Ewe		+	2	Cult object.
18.	Joruba (Ibadan)	+		2–	Cult object.
19.	Okrika	+		4	Fish spear used for cannibal juju.
20.	Baba (Cameroon)	+		2	Badge of office.
21.	Yukun	+			Cult object.
22.	Hausa	+			Emblem of spirits.
23.	Kanuri	+		2–3	Weapon (?).
24.	Gabai (Bornu)	+		4	Weapon (?).
25.	Fulani (Adamaua)	+		3	No particulars.
26.	Karnak Logone		+	2	Chief's ceremonial staff.
27.	Bagirmi	+		2	Weapon.
28.	Fitri			2–3	Parade weapon (?).
29.	Fulani (Darfur, Kordofan)			3	Sultan's spear.
30.	Bari	+	+	2–3	Rain spear, sign of dignity, weapon.
31.	Lotuko	+		2	Rain spear.
32.	Moru	+		2	Hunting weapon.
33.	Mongala (Bari ?)	+		2	No particulars.
34.	Lur	+		2	No particulars.
35.	Azande	+		2	No particulars.
36.	Mangbetu	+		2	No particulars.
37.	Kaffa	+		2	The emperor's sign of office.
38.	Abyssinia	+		2	Carried by high officials.
39.	Amhara	+		2	No particulars.
40.	Gurage		+	2	The high priest.
41.	Somali (Northern)	+		2	No particulars.
42.	Banyoro	+		2	Royal emblem.
43.	Baganda	+		2	The king's and high priest's insignia.
44.	Banyankole		+	2	The king's judicial staff.
45.	Karagwe	+		2	Royal emblem.
46.	Kiziba	+		3	" Zauber speer."
47.	Turu	+		3	
48.	Akamba		+	2	Sign of dignity.
49.	Makunduchi (Zanzibar)	+		3	Carried in exorcising dance.
50.	Lake Leopold II district	+		2–3	Sign of dignity.
51.	Bushongo (Bakuba)	+		4	Sign of dignity.
52.	Bakete		+	2	Sign of dignity.
53.	Bankutu	+			Hunting weapon.
54.	Morocco	+			Sheriff's spear.
55.	Aliwal North ?	+		2–3	Chief's sceptre (?).
56.	Sakalava, Bueni	+		3	Sign of dignity.
57.	Sakalava, Tulear	+		2	Royal spear.

Note.—The article was handed in to the editors in April, 1932, and this accounts for the fact that some publications on the African spears, published later or which have become known to the author later, have not been included in it.—K. G. L.

Stockholm.
April, 1932.

RELIGIOUS IDEAS AND PRACTICES OF THE EURASIATIC AND NORTH AMERICAN AREAS

By ROBERT H. LOWIE

The similarities linking the cultures of Eurasia and America have been repeatedly dealt with. Tylor's essay on the patolli game, Boas', Bogoras', and Jochelson's comparison of Old and New World folk-tales ; Hatt's study of moccasins ; Thalbitzer's comments on Eurasian and American shamanism ; Glover Allen's studies of domesticated dogs ; and Hallowell's discussion of bear ceremonialism are among the better known contributions to this subject, and quite recently Laufer has dealt with the same problem. Hallowell's and Laufer's papers [1] confront us with an impressive array of economic, technological, ceremonial, and mythological resemblances, which jointly constitute a powerful argument for intensive cultural relations.

As regards mythology, I feel the cumulative evidence to be very strong ; at the same time the data seem to call for discriminatory weighing. Not all the parallels cited by the Russian authorities, for example, would convince me. We must distinguish between mythical concepts and mythical narratives ; and of the latter, again, some furnish positive proof, others at best the possibility of connection.

To illustrate this point, I am greatly intrigued by Dr. Laufer's finding the notion of the frog in the moon in Chinese as well as in South American folk-lore. While a generation or two ago we should have been content to murmur the magic phrase "psychic unity of mankind", we now realize that such unity underlies all manifestations of both diffusion and independent invention, hence is incapable of explaining any specific resemblance. Even granted that all peoples "naturally" see *something* in the moon ; why should distinct and remote tribes single out the frog from some possible dozens of animals in the regional fauna ? Strong, however, as this contention appears, it does not suffice for a satisfactory demonstration. I am impelled to seek paths of diffusion. The "frog in the moon" *motif* is not merely South American, but occurs likewise in one version of the most popular Crow hero myth and is shared by

[1] A. I. Hallowell, "Bear Ceremonialism in the Northern Hemisphere," in *American Anthropologist*, xxviii, 1–175 (esp. 156–163), 1926. B. Laufer, "Columbus and Cathay, and the Meaning of America to the Orientalist," in *Journal of American Oriental Society*, li, 87–103 (esp. 99 ff), 1931.

the Hidatsa, Mandan, Arapaho, and Gros Ventre.[1] The question now arises whether we can trace the idea so as to bridge the gap between its known occurrences in South America and the Plains ; and, on the other hand, whether a roughly continuous distribution can be established via Bering Strait, linking the Northern Plains with China. In my opinion we are here dealing with a wholly legitimate problem but not one—in contrast to the extreme diffusionists—that is solved when it is merely formulated.

For the earth-diver episode in a story of the creation or re-creation of the earth the case is stronger. With only such lacunæ as must be expected from the deficiency of our records we can trace it from the Atlantic to the Pacific Coast of North America and find it cropping up again in Central Siberia. Intercontinental dissemination is indicated. What remains a puzzle is how to account for the same incident in Assamese folk-lore.[2] In other words, can we bridge the span not only between America and Asia but between Southern and Northern Asia ? If that were possible, we could confidently continue to concentrate our attention on Bering Strait as the path for intercontinental exchanges and maintain our reserve as to direct maritime intercourse between Malayo-Polynesia and South America, although I am not disposed to deny categorically that such may have taken place.

By general consent the magic flight story ranks as a perfect example of demonstrable relations between the Old World and the New. Even Andrew Lang, normally the protagonist of independent parallelism, accepted transmission as the only tenable interpretation. The reason for this consensus of opinion is clear. The tale in question, while variously combined with other narratives, constitutes an integral whole whose parts closely correspond in significant detail. We are not confronted with a pale abstraction such as " the pursuit of the hero by an ogre ", but with a sequence of essentially similar devices by which fugitives elude a powerful enemy. Furthermore, the distribution is virtually continuous over an immense territory, so that here are combined all the criteria by which contact can be sanely inferred.

Leaving the subject of mythology as having already received considerable, though certainly not too much attention, I will turn to other phenomena.

Dr. Hallowell's researches are to my mind quite convincing as to the historical unity of Eurasiatic and American bear ceremonial and ideology. The fantastic belief that bears subsist

    [1] R. H. Lowie, " Myths and Traditions of the Crow Indians " in *Anthrop. Papers, Amer. Mus. Nat. Hist.*, xxv, 12, 52, 1918.
    [2] Idem, " Zur Verbreitung der Flutsagen," in *Anthropos*, xxi, 615 f., 1926.

throughout hibernation by sucking their paws is found in the eighteenth-century literature on the Lapps, the Kamchadal, and the Atlantic Coast Indians, and has been more recently discovered among various Algonkian groups, as well as among the Ainu. More widely spread we encounter such features as the eschewing of the generic term for " bear " in speaking of the beast, with the indispensable development of some euphemistic synonym. Kinship terms are common in this connection, e.g. the Penobscot, Yukaghir, and Yakut refer to the bear as " grandfather ". Finally, the conciliatory speeches made to the animal before killing it and the post-mortem rites— especially the disposal of the skulls—may be traced from the Atlantic coast of America to Western Siberia. The cumulative evidence adduced by Hallowell, in fact, warrants even a more positive inference as to diffusion than is suggested by his own cautious formulation.

At the same time, a subsidiary result of Hallowell's discussion may be stressed because it has not received the attention it deserves. Contrary to expectation, the most striking resemblances as to Siberian bear beliefs and usages occur not among the most westerly Americans but among the northern and north-eastern Algonkians.[1] Can it be sheer accident that in this very area flourish the typically Asiatic practices of scapulimancy and scrying ?

Leaping from one marginal region to another, I should like to suggest that some specialist on the Lapps should survey Lapp culture regarding its affinities with North America. I am, of course, aware that specific features have been dealt with by Tylor (stone-boiling),[2] Hatt (foot-gear), Thalbitzer, Hallowell, and others. What I am suggesting is a systematic collection of all relevant data, having regard also to the intervening Asiatic region. In order to stimulate such an inquiry, I will list relevant traits that have come to my notice, including for the purpose a few material traits as well as elements of social and religious life.

The resemblance of one type of Lapp tent to the conical dwelling of Northern Canada is as unmistakable as that of the Yukaghir tent to both. An old missionary describes a Lapp reindeer *battue* that immediately suggests the North American method of impounding large game.[3] Lapp women give birth standing or kneeling,[4] the latter being also customary among Assiniboine (Denig), the Crow, and Hidatsa, and presumably

[1] Hallowell, op. cit., p. 154.
[2] Tylor's quotation from Linnaeus' Lapland Tour (*Researches into the Early History of Mankind*, 1865, p. 267) credits the Finns of East Bothland with stone-boiling.
[3] Castrén, *Reiseerinnerungen aus den Jahren, 1838–1844*, pp. 44 f., St. Petersburg, 1853.
[4] E. Demant (ed.), *Das Buch des Lappen Johan Turi*, 1912, p. 22.

other American tribes. The Lapps do not take a corpse out
of the door, but lift the cover wherever the body may lie so as
to create an exit.[1] This taboo is common in America, occurring,
for example, among the Crow and Ojibwa. In Scheffer's book
there are several illustrations of Lapp tambourines that strongly
suggest the Eskimo and Eastern Algonkian style of pictography.[2]
Here, though a direct connection seems out of the question, we
should remember that realistic representation is by no means
universal among primitive peoples ; and that even crude styles
of realism may be distinctive. What I should consider possible
in this case is the persistence over a wide Arctic and sub-Arctic
area of an ancient pictographic tradition.

More striking are the Lapp taboos for women. The exclusion
of women from sacred localities, as well as their disabilities as
to touching a drum or making an offering, strongly remind us
of the Plains Indian attitude as to medicine bundles, and
Scheffer explicitly states the reason : " Die Ursache warumb sie
von diesen heiligen Oertern die Weibsbilder abtreiben, scheint
wohl keine sonsten zu seyn, als dass sie selbe zu gewissen Zeiten
unrein zu seyn schätzen." [3] Again, the ominous influence of
the female sex was recognized with reference to the chase in
a manner rather reminiscent of our Northern Athabaskans.
Thus, the rear door by which Lapp hunters brought in game
was tabooed to women, and no woman was allowed to touch
a caught game animal.[4] A menstruating woman was not
supposed to step over her husband's feet or gun, nor to go
where fishermen usually exposed their catch, nor to milk cows.[5]
In North America there is often a close parallelism between
the observances of menstruation and of child-birth. It is
therefore of interest to find that a Lapp woman in confinement
stays either in a special hut or at least a special division thereof ;
there she is only permitted to eat a little food and may drink
nothing but water.[6]

Feminine disabilities based on menstrual superstitions are
of course not peculiar to North America and Lapland. But
their intensity in Lapland, as well as some of the details cited,
are indicative of something more than mere accident.

A detail that may or may not be significant is the change of
an ailing Lapp child's name,[7] a very common Indian custom.

Overshadowing all these features because of its prominence

[1] Demant, op. cit., p. 81.
[2] Joannis Schefferi von Strassburg, Lappland . . . , Frankfurt a M. und Leipzig,
p. 140, 1675.
[3] Op. cit., pp. 115, 122, 148.   [4] Ibid., pp. 101 f., 223, 275.
[5] Knud Leems, " An Account of the Laplanders of Finmark . . . ," in John
Pinkerton's General Collection of the Best and Most Interesting Voyages and
Travels in all Parts of the World (i, 376–490), p. 483, 1808.
[6] Edgar Reuterskiöld, De nordiske Lapparnas Religion, p. 59, 1912.
[7] Ibid., p. 65. Leems, op. cit., p. 483.

in native thought is the phenomenon of shamanism. Both Thalbitzer and Laufer have called attention to significant Eurasiatic-American resemblances. The latter stresses the association of the shaman with the tambourine ; the Danish scholar points out that Lapps, Siberians, and Eskimo practise divination by lifting a weight, while Eskimo and Central Asiatic Turks share the characteristic cosmic excursion by the officiating shaman.[1] While space limitations prevent anything like a full discussion, I should like to call attention to several other traits that seem to link together our three major areas.

In Siberia the typical way of becoming a shaman is through a call by the spirits, whom the beneficiary accepts as helpers often with distinct reluctance. This is in marked contrast to the normal Plains, Woodland, and Plateau practice of deliberately seeking a supernatural protector. But, as Dr. Benedict showed long ago, the Siberian attitude appears rather markedly on or near the Pacific coast of America, and it certainly existed to some extent in Lapland, where spirits might threaten to tear a man into little bits if he spurned their proffered aid.[2] The Lapp visionary was taught a song by his visitant—often in the guise of a bird or a beast—as in many American tribes ; as among the Eskimo, the shamans used a distinctive language (*ett slags rotvälske*) ; soul-kidnapping was the dominant theory of disease, as among many Siberians as well as in American tribes of the Pacific region and in that northern and north-eastern region that seems specially linked with Siberia ; and the tricks practiced by shamans included playing freely with fire, as among such tribes as the Fox and the Menomini.[3]

If the majority of these resemblances were due to psychic unity, we should expect to find as much in common between shamanism in Lapland and the Gold Coast as between the Lapp and the North-East American phenomena, but this is contrary to fact. Indeed, the adhesion of the tambourine to shamanism, which is obviously wholly arbitrary, suffices to mark out the unitary character of Eurasiatic-North American shamanism. Combining all the traits enumerated with those listed by Dr. Hallowell in his discussion of bear ceremonialism, we may regard the area indicated as forming one gigantic unit from the angle of religious belief.

On this theory we should naturally expect more intimate relations between relative neighbours than between remote

<hr />

[1] Laufer, op. cit., pp. 99 f. ; Wm. Thalbitzer, "Die kultischen Gottheiten der Eskimos," in *Archiv für Religionswissenschaft*, xxvi, 364–430 (esp. 421, 427). Cf. Reuterskiöld, p. 53 ; Scheffer, p. 129 (on divination by lifting).

[2] Reuterskiöld, pp. 92 f.

[3] Gustaf von Düben, *Om Lappland och Lapparne, företrädesvis de Svenske ; etnografiske Studier*, pp. 271 sq., 1873. Reuterskiöld, pp. 65 f. ; Leems, p. 478 ; Scheffer, p. 136.

members of the total region defined. This corollary can, I think, be easily established. Thus, the tambourine is indeed closely connected with shamanizing throughout, but less specifically among Indian tribes than in Lapland, Siberia, or among the Eskimo. It sometimes even passes from the ceremonial into the purely secular sphere, as when I saw it beaten by Chipewyan Indians (Lake Athabaska) attending a gambling-game. Again, to mention but a few other features, a Chukchee shaman will shake his sleeping-room, loosen himself from his bonds, after being tied hand and foot, and practice ventriloquism.[1] I do not find these particular tricks recorded for the Lapps ; on the other hand, tent-shaking, Houdinism, and ventriloquism occur among the Cree, Saulteaux, and even Cheyenne.[2]

In conclusion, I should like to point to a most intriguing problem, the distribution of the vapour-bath. I am aware of the occurrence of sudatories in Hawaii and South Africa, and Baron Nordenskiöld has called attention to a South American occurrence. But the similarities between relevant North American and Finnish-Scandinavian practices are too striking to be ignored. Thus, a traveller through Northern Europe in 1681 describes apparently Finnish peasants as heating stones in the centre of a bath-house, throwing water on top, switching themselves to open their pores, and then dashing from these " fiery baths " into an extremely cold river.[3] Troels-Lund gives an equally graphic picture of sixteenth-century Scandinavians.[4] Compare this with Erman's observations among the Tlingit : some ten men were indulging in a vapour-bath in November, singing and shaking rattles ; then, with perspiration dripping from them they dashed into the icy sea nearby.[5] The Crow even switched themselves with scourges of horse-tails, buffalo tails, or sagebrush.[6] So far I have failed to find descriptions linking these occurrences in Northern Europe and North America by way of Siberia. It is clear that we must rely mainly on Russian scholars to supply the deficiency in our knowledge.

[1] W. Bogoras, " The Chukchee " (*Memoirs Amer. Mus. Nat. Hist.*, xi : *Jesup Expedition*, vii), pp. 434 sq., 439, 448, 1907.
[2] A. B. Skinner, " Notes on the Eastern Cree and Northern Saulteaux " (*Anthrop. Papers, American Museum*, ix), pp. 66 f., 153, 1911. George Bird Grinnell, *The Cheyenne Indians*, ii, 113–17.
[3] M. Regnard, " A Journey through Flanders, Holland, etc." : John Pinkerton, op. cit., i, 157, 1808.
[4] Troels-Lund, *Dagligt Liv i Norden i det* 16de *Aarhundrede ; Bönder og Kjöbstadboliger*, pp. 320–2 (Copenhagen, 1880).
[5] Aurel Krause, *Die Tlinkit-Indianer*, p. 166, 1885.
[6] R. H. Lowie, " The Religion of the Crow Indians," *Anthrop. Papers, Amer. Mus. Nat. Hist.*, xxv, 430, 1922.

University of California,
Berkeley, Cal.

STONE IMPLEMENTS IN EASTERN NEW GUINEA

By BRONISLAW MALINOWSKI

I. THE MATERIAL OF STONE IMPLEMENTS

In contributing this essay to Professor Seligman's *Festschrift*, I should like once more to express not only my personal indebtedness to his work and influence, but also the obligation of modern anthropology to his pioneering researches in Melanesia and elsewhere. I am choosing here a subject which lies to a certain extent outside my own sphere of interests, since it is mainly technological; but it is one on which Professor Seligman's researches have given us a mass of valuable information, and I trust that the few additional notes which I am able to furnish will be found to supplement this still further.

Professor Seligman was the first to determine the civilization of the Northern Massim, that is, to describe their social organization, their arts, crafts, and pursuits, and place them within the geographical area of Papuo-Melanesian cultures. At the present time there is one aspect in the material culture which has been profoundly affected under contact. These representatives of the polished stone age are no longer using implements of polished stone in their industrial pursuits. But the tradition is still very much alive, and it is possible to determine some of the main types of their implements as well as to describe their main uses. Professor Seligman has given us an account of the site from which the material used for stone implements in the Northern Massim area and over a much wider range, had been obtained.[1] From his first-hand researches he was able to establish that in the whole of eastern New Guinea there was only one place where this material was quarried, and that was at Suloga on Muruwa or Woodlark Island. "The Suloga adze blades were formerly traded from hand to hand for many hundreds of miles passing westwards at least as far as the Papuan Gulf, while on the north coast of the Possession they are found to the west of Cape Nelson." (*M.B.N.G.*, p. 15.)

Professor Seligman also pointed out the fundamental distinction made by the natives between the adze and axe blades manufactured for use on the one hand, and the ceremonial blades. "Both kinds of stones passed into trade *via* Tubetube to some

---

[1] C. G. Seligman and W. M. Strong, "Anthropological Investigations in British New Guinea," *Geographical Journal*, 1906, pp. 348 sqq. The fullest information, however, will be found in Professor Seligman's book, *The Melanesians of British New Guinea*, Cambridge, 1910, the standard work on the area. This book will be referred to in this article as *M.B.N.G.*

extent, but far the greater number of those exported from Muruwa travelled westwards to the Marshall Bennets and the Trobriands whence they were carried to the Amphlett and D'Entrecasteaux groups and so launched on their course...." (*M.B.N.G.*, pp. 530–1.) Professor Seligman's most valuable descriptions of the trade of these blades and their distribution, which will be found in chapters xl and xlix, require no further remarks. But I should here like to add a brief survey of what happens to the axe blades when they arrive in the Trobriand Islands, where the stone quarried at Suloga was the only material available for cutting, planing, scraping out, or chiselling.

Petrologically, the material has been kindly examined at my request by Dr. E. W. Skeats, Professor of Geology at the University of Melbourne, and found to be of volcanic origin. The harder and more homogeneous specimens are consolidated volcanic augite andesite ash or tuff. The bands of lighter colour are not the result of a lava-flow structure, but due to somewhat irregular bedding of the volcanic ash. Some specimens, of smaller specific gravity and less homogeneous, are from basaltic rocks (more strictly, olivine andesite) due to lava flow.

Since this stone had to be imported from a distance of over sixty miles, and since it was used up in the course of ordinary work, the objects manufactured from it were scarce and highly priced. The rarity of this material and the fact that in some specimens it exhibited the streaks of lighter colour, which appealed to the natives' artistic sense, resulted in some blades being worked out for purely æsthetic reasons and becoming nothing but objects of condensed wealth. Such stones attained the highest value among all objects of wealth, surpassing even the large arm-shells and the necklaces made of spondylus shell. But it would be difficult to express their value in terms of exchange, because unlike the other articles of value, they were not traded. The biggest stone blades in fact were considered as heirlooms (*vegutabula*) and definitely attached to one lineage. The stones, on the other hand, used for practical purposes, were often traded, and an ordinary small working stone would be readily exchanged for one or two basketfuls of *taytu*.

II. Technical Uses of Stone Implements

Let us see how the implements are made, used, and handled. First of all, the stones were roughly hewn and chipped into shape at the quarry. They were imported into the Trobriand archipelago from the east in this form, as we can see from specimens 2, 3, and 5 on Plate LXIV of *M.B.N.G.*, here reproduced. The polishing was always done in the Trobriands. There some articles received the almost complete polish, such

PLATE XVII

ROUGH AND PARTIALLY POLISHED ADZE BLADES

(*Reproduced from Plate LXIV, M.B.N.G., with the kind permission of Professor Seligman and the Cambridge Press*)

[face p. 190

as we see on specimen 4 of our Plate ; in others only the cutting edge was polished, as can be seen in the cases of 1, 6, 7, and 8.

The Trobrianders were and are daring sailors. They use for their overseas expeditions large built-up canoes, while for fishing and lagoon transport they have smaller craft. But the main part of each canoe consists of a substantial tree-trunk. In order to obtain such a dug-out, they have to fell a large tree. In the pre-iron days this was done by means of a large stone blade (*utuviya*) which was inserted into a large handle shaped like an axe ; that is, the blade was placed in the plane of striking. Specimen 2 on Plate LXIV (*M.B.N.G.*) represents such a large blade. As can be seen from it, a felling axe blade was relatively narrow ; it was thick and substantial almost to its cutting edge. Trees of a smaller size had often to be felled in order to prepare stout logs for the yam-houses, planks for yam-house flooring or for canoe gunwales, and boards used in the construction of houses. For such purposes a smaller and wider type of axe blade would be used of which Nos 1, 5, and 7 are good representatives.

After a tree was felled it was necessary to hew it all round in order to give it the required shape, whether that of a canoe, of a round log, or of a flat board. For this another type of blade was necessary, less stout, of course, and less heavy, with a straight, thin, cutting edge. Such blades, called *kasivi*, were always inserted into an adze-handle in which the cutting plane of the blade was placed at right angles to the striking plane of the implement. Specimen 6 on the Plate represents a typical *kasivi*.

Another implement was needed for the task of scraping out the inside of a dug-out. Here the blade had to be much stouter as the worker had to hew with a fair impetus ; it had also to be less broad. No. 3 represents such a blade called *kavilali*. On the Plate this is in an unfinished state ; the edge would still have to be sharpened and polished before use. With such a blade a man had to scoop out convex sides in the log, and thus to cut both transversely, as one cuts with an adze, and in the plane of cutting, as is done when cutting with an axe, and of course also at any other angle. These uses were provided for by an implement in which the blade was set in a wooden mount which in turn could be moved within the handle. It was thus an axe and adze and an intermediate striking implement combined.

Both in the making of a canoe and of a house and yam-house,[1] there arises frequently the need for cutting out holes and

---

[1] For excellent photographs of a native house in the Trobriands, a group of yam-houses and beautiful detail showing the logs in a yam-house, see Plates LXXV–VII, *M.B.N.G.* There also the various structural elements can be seen. A detailed description of the technology in the structure of the yam-house will be found in my new book on Trobriand agriculture, presently to appear under some such title as " Coral Gardens and their Magic ", where the agriculture and certain economic aspects of Trobriand civilization will be described.

grooves. For this a thin, sharp, and at the same time fairly stout, chisel implement was used called *ginesosu*. Specimen 4 in Professor Seligman's photograph represents this blade. Since such an implement had to be fixed rather firmly into its handle, it was usually polished along a wider surface than the bigger blades. For cutting away small scrub when the soil was cleared for gardens, small and thin blades with a rather long cutting edge were used. They did not greatly differ from the one described above as *kasivi* and usually consisted of planing blades worn out by long use. They were named by the generic term for blade, *kema* or *utukema*, *utu-* being the prefix for " cutting ". No. 6, if you imagine it worn out to about half its length, would be a good specimen of such a blade. They were inserted in axe-shaped or adze-shaped handles indiscriminately.

At present all these implements have been superseded by European-made steel or iron, and the change has taken place some two or three generations ago. The natives now use invariably the European-made axe-handle, but they still employ the old handles for the shafting of the adze blades (*ligogu*) and for the shafting of their planing blade (*kaylalari*). But although they have adopted European material, they use it in very much the same manner in which they must have used the old stone blades. They cut, plane, and scoop out by means of exceedingly weak and exceedingly numerous strokes, thus working very slowly—nibbling the material away. This makes it clear how they were sometimes able to work very hard wood with relatively brittle and blunt stone blades, mounted in frail handles, and secured only by binding with rattan strips. In fact, even now, their iron blades are stuck so loosely in their handles that, without difficulty, one can remove the blade from almost any implement one takes up. To use such a tool is only possible if the worker never puts too much strain upon it, and if each stroke is made with great precision and dexterity. In olden days they probably worked even more precisely and slowly than now. Again, even thus, it was often necessary to re-sharpen a blunted or broken blade, and when important work was being done, there was, for each cutter or planer, another man or two sharpening refill blades.

III. Stone Blades as Tokens of Value

As the stone material for the blades was hard to obtain and suitable for elaboration into a fine shape and beautiful polish, the implements were of great value and were, therefore, displayed and used as ornaments. This was especially the case with the adzes (*ligogu*), which were, and are, carried over the shoulder. This is done by all natives who have reached mature age, and one seldom sees a man of rank and influence, especially during feasts and ceremonies, without a *ligogu* over his shoulder. Nowadays a steel blade takes the place of the ancient greenstone.[1]

The handle of an adze is worked out with great care; it is shaped into really beautiful harmonious lines, and it is polished all over and often decorated with carvings. In olden days, men of rank would have fine, streaked, well-polished blades of the planing type (*kasivi*) inserted in their handles. Thus, even ordinary working-tools were and are used as ornaments.

This fact makes it much easier to understand the existence and *raison d'être* of the so-called ceremonial axe blades. In order to make this point still clearer, it may be advisable to make a digression and venture on a hypothesis of the probable origins of ceremonial stone blades.

As has been said, ordinary working tools are used even now, for ornamentation and display, and as a sign of dignity and social position. This state of affairs must have existed since a very remote period. Now, the natives have a pronounced tendency in all their technological achievements to go beyond the strict limits imposed by practical use. They are influenced by vanity, by the passion of display, of eclipsing one's neighbour and provoking his envy. Both producer and consumer like to make or acquire an article which is strikingly big, or strikingly well-finished, or of a strikingly fine material, even though in the process the article were to become unwieldy, breakable, and good for nothing else but display. This feature of native psychology could be paralleled by typical examples of technological hypertrophy in the manufacture of native pottery, wooden bowls, walking-sticks, ear-rings, necklaces, indeed in almost every class of article useful or ornamental ; they try to produce them of such good material, so well ornamented, so bulky, or so minute (e.g. turtle-shell ear-rings) that they become useless, even as ornaments.

In the case of stone implements, these become so well-finished, so large, so thin and streaked and well-polished, that they are too good to be used technically, too big even to be carried as everyday ornaments, though they might still be placed in specially beautiful handles and carried by a man of rank during a ceremony. Even to-day there are a few occasions, but very few indeed, on which a man may be seen carrying over his shoulder a small non-usable blade inserted into a ceremonial handle small enough to be carried. This is the case, for instance, during certain magical ceremonies in the gardens, as we can see on the Plate here reproduced.

As already mentioned only small ceremonial blades and handles

---

[1] Compare Plates XV, LXIV, LXXI, in my *Sexual Life of Savages*, 1929, and Plate XXVII of *Argonauts of the Western Pacific*, 1922.

can be used for this. But ceremonial blades of really high value for the natives cannot be worn even on public ceremonial occasions. We must imagine them again as the product of this intense craving for the *plus ultra*, for the extreme in size, quality, and finish, which governs native production and the native conception of value.

We may appear to have been making a hypothetical digression into the past but, in reality, we have simply projected into an imaginary past the results of certain psychological forces which we can still see at work perfectly well in the present time.

Let us now try to introduce some order into this apparent confusion ; some of the usable blades were made of exceptionally good material and with a specially fine finish and worn as objects of value and ornaments. I think that in olden days even they would have been very seldom actually put to practical use since they were very valuable. There was, however, a sharp line of distinction between such small ornamental blades and handles, and blades which were of a size, shape, and quality which put them entirely out of range of any practical employment. Both were *vaygu'a* (valuables). The usable ones would be called *kasivi* (planing-blade) or *ligogu* (adze blade) ; the ceremonial ones were called by one term and one term only—*beku*. The *beku* were provided purely for purposes of ornamentation with large unwieldy handles of a merely ceremonial type. Professor Seligman has reproduced on his Plates LXI and LXII the two types of ceremonial handles. The first (LXI) corresponds in its distribution mainly to the Southern Massim area, though it is found also in the Trobriands. The second (LXII) was manufactured exclusively in the Trobriands, mainly in the district of Tilataula. It is a handle of this type that we can see, on the Plate here reproduced,[1] in actual use during a garden ceremony. The very large blades were so broad at the base that they could not be inserted even in the biggest ceremonial handle in existence. Each blade had, however, a large companion handle which was regarded as its counterpart and on occasions of ceremonial display would be placed immediately against it.

The large " ceremonial " blades or, as we might call them more appositely, *tokens of value*, have then no technological use whatever ; neither can they be worn over the shoulder as ornaments. None the less, they play an extremely important part in the economic and social life of the natives. Alongside with big arm-shells and shell-made necklaces, but surpassing both these articles in value, the stone blades form the indispensable adjunct of wealth and consequently of social power. In the Trobriand Islands, social life was largely built on the power wielded and the functions exercised by the chiefs. They

---

[1] From Plate LIX, *Argonauts of the Western Pacific*.

A RITE OF GARDEN MAGIC

An offering of cooked food is exposed to the spirits for some time in the garden. The magician, with the ceremonial axe on his arm, is seen squatting to the right. In the fore-front, a big bundle of leaves which he will presently charm over

(Reproduced from Plate LIX, Argonauts of the Western Pacific)

were the leaders in war, organizers of big feasts, masters of
the gardens, leaders of overseas trading expeditions, and super-
visors of economic magic which controlled to a certain extent
public life and production. To do this, the chiefs had mainly
to rely on their wealth, which they possessed in form of stored
food and of tokens of value. On every big social occasion—
war, magical ceremony, mortuary festival, trading expedition—
the chief had to pay by distributing goods among the most
important actors. Thus wealth, and more especially wealth
in condensed form, was at the basis of the chief's power, and
thus of social order. This latter was safeguarded again by the
fear of sorcery, which, in the Trobriands was the means of
punishing crime and injustice and enforcing the chief's will,
as well as the means of less lawful transactions. But, on the
whole, as sorcery had to be paid for in tokens of value, it was
mainly at the chief's disposal and followed the chief's will.
Whether it was thus used for right or wrong in the moral sense,
it certainly was used to safeguard the existing order of things
and thus made for law and order such as they exist in a native
society.

A man who owned a big stone blade or a number of them,
acquired *ipso facto* power. Of course the chief would see to it
that no commoner acquired too many tokens of value, that is,
too much influence—the fear of sorcery or direct violence was
there to prevent any serious shifting of economic power.

There were several classes of condensed wealth or tokens of
value. But—and this is important in the present context
—the only class actually produced in the central districts of the
Trobriands, where political chieftainship was well developed, were
the large axe blades, imported from Suloga as enormous *kukumali*,
so big at times that it was difficult for one man to lift them.
They were chipped and polished in the districts of Tilataula
and Kiriwina. There were about half a dozen specialists who
would spend days, weeks, and months over one blade. The
chief was the only man allowed to import large blades, and he
was also the man who by sending regular gifts of food to the
specialist kept him going on the work. The production of
polished axe blades was in the Central Trobriands the main
process by which accumulated food was transformed into an
object of condensed wealth and thus made available for purposes
for which it would have been useless in the form of perishable
goods.

When I speak of the chief, I mean that this privilege was in the
first place vested in the Paramount Chief of Kiriwina, who
resided at Omarakana. With his consent, however, chiefs of
a lesser rank were also allowed to import and produce ceremonial
axe blades. Through the many opportunities which the chief

had of giving presents in these valuables, a great number of them found their way into the possession of lesser men. The biggest and most valuable of them remained as heirlooms in the lineage of the chief ; in that of his junior kinsmen, that is, chiefs of rank belonging to the junior lineages of the Tabalu sub-clan ; and in the hands of one or two important notables, such as the headman of Kabwaku, who was the Paramount Chief's hereditary rival.[1]

The owner would, on certain rare occasions, display the blades. Thus, once a year, everyone would exhibit the valuables he owned and offer them to the spirits of the departed, which, at that season, were supposed to visit the village. Again, when distant friends or strangers from afar came on a visit, they would be shown the tokens of wealth. During certain mortuary ceremonies the stone blades are also displayed. As a rule they are well hidden away, often buried in the ground for fear of theft.

So deep is the attachment of the natives to wealth and tokens of wealth that a dying man is covered with his valuables and his relatives comfort and strengthen him by rubbing axe blades against his chest and belly. The departed spirit then carries the spiritual essence of the tokens into the other world and offers them to the keeper of the spirits' road. (Cf. *Argonauts of the Western Pacific*, Plate LXV ; see also pp. 679 and 733 of *M.B.N.G.*)

The reader who, to refresh his memory, peruses the chapters and pages in Professor Seligman's book devoted to the subject, will recognize how completely the facts which I have observed and noted in some villages of the interior of the Trobriands fit in with his own data collected over a much wider area. In devoting this article to technology and allowing myself to indulge in a distinctly antiquarian, but I trust not merely imaginary, reconstruction, I have tried to render my tribute even more personal and discriminate.

---

[1] For a fuller statement of some of the economic conditions in the Trobriands and the relations between production, distribution, and political power, the reader is asked to consult the forthcoming book already referred to.

FOOD RITES

By R. R. MARETT

In the fifth chapter of Miss Jane Harrison's *Themis*, which
sets out to deal with the triple subject of totemism, sacrament,
and sacrifice, the central interest of the treatment is revealed
in the appended quotation, " 'What meanest thou by this word
Sacrament?' " Starting from the *omophagia*, or eating of raw
flesh, that survived in Greek ritual of the Dionysiac order,
Miss Harrison professes her physical abhorrence of such a crude
proceeding, but promises that our normal repugnance will
disappear when the gist of the rite is understood. Thereupon
she tries to prove that the *omophagia* was, in its primary intention,
neither a sacrifice pleasing to a personal god, nor a sacrament
in which communion with such a god was brought about.
Originally, she argues, the rite in question was " part of a system
of sanctities that knew no gods ", belonging as it did to a " social
organization, namely totemism, that preceded theology ". She
goes on to show, here echoing Durkheim, that totemism essentially
embodies a collective form of experience, being based on the
supposed relation between a human and some other natural
group, such as typically an animal species. This relation, as
she is able to prove from the Australian evidence, is explicitly
conceived by the totemite as a kind of identity. " That one
is just the same as me," says the kangaroo-man of his eponymous
animal. She might also have cited his even more telling phrase
that the kangaroo is " all-one-flesh " with him. Now flesh,
together with the accompanying and even more mysterious
blood, may well stand for kinship, more especially when considered
in what was presumably its earliest form, the tie between mother
and child founded on a real, and not merely symbolic, community
of flesh and blood. Miss Harrison, however, is more immediately
interested in the blood-relationship imputed to the namesake
animal or plant. Now this is clearly a symbolic or non-literal
connection, even if we make all allowance for the tendency of
the savage mind to " confuse its categories ", as the late
Professor Hobhouse puts it—or, let us say less technically, to
blur its distinctions. Paying attention chiefly to one type of
totemic rite, the so-called Intichiuma ceremony for the multiplication of the totem, she interprets it as an attempt on the part
of the human group to realize their oneness with the animal
group ; the dawning consciousness of a difference between them

being transcended in such an effort to bridge the gulf and lose themselves in a higher unity, a wider communion. Hence she terms such a rite, for all that it takes the form of a dramatic representation of the desired identity, "methectic" rather than "mimetic". In other words, instead of imitating something external and to that extent alien, they seek direct participation in a consubstantial nature that is thus not theirs and theirs at once and together. So far, then, as participation prevails over imitation—in other words, so far as undifferentiated thinking and group-emotion predominate—we may have sacrament and even sacrifices, but the net result is only a kind of magic. For Miss Harrison defines magic as "the manipulation of *mana*", which, according to her conception of it, is itself an undifferentiated kind of power or grace proceeding from sacred things in general. Religion, on the other hand, in her view implies worship, which can only be towards a power invested with a separate and distinctive being of its own—in a word, a "god". Let this brief account of Miss Harrison's general position suffice ; though the by-paths through which she wanders while finding her way to these conclusions are such as to defy summary notice.

Now what I am about to say is not meant as an attack on Miss Harrison's views, if only because in many respects I agree with her line of thought, and simply desire to suggest sundry modifications of the main argument. These are the more necessary because so much fresh evidence has accumulated since *Themis* was written—that is to say, in the course of the last twenty years. On one major issue only do I definitely disagree ; and, since it is largely a question of nomenclature, I had better clear up the matter at once, lest an unacknowledged difference of terminology lead to misunderstanding later on. I need hardly say that the stumbling-block consists in the familiar puzzle how to draw the line between magic and religion. Now Miss Harrison appears to me to be trying to run both with the hare and with the hounds. Sir James Frazer may be taken to represent the hare, while I can claim for myself a humble place in the pursuing pack. Thus on the one hand she accepts the Frazerian view that there is no religion until there is propitiation of a personality with superhuman attributes—a conception of religion that appears to me to be based on the principle, "Orthodoxy is my doxy." On the other hand, by connecting sacrament with magic, she deprives religion of one of its chosen instruments ; unless it is possible—as I do not think it is—to hold that magical bottles are suitable for preserving religious wine in all its integrity. Probably she is here following the lead, not of Sir James Frazer, but rather of Robertson Smith, the foremost pioneer in regard to all these questions ; for he was ready to class magic as just that early stage of religion when ritual seems all-sufficient because its motives remain subconscious. Indeed, Sir James Frazer was content to accept this opinion when he started to write *The Golden Bough*. Only in the second edition did he take the fatal step of dissociating magic altogether from religion on the strength of an erroneous psychology that identified the former with a kind of sham science founded on the abuse of analogy—as if the same could not be said by its detractors of the most advanced theology. Miss Harrison, however, shows no sign of postulating an age of magic separated from the age of religion by a hiatus that is logical or chronological as you please. On the contrary, her rather inconsistent language would imply that magic is religion at its pre-theological stage ; and she actually describes a system of sanctities that knows no God as " a form of religion ". If, then, it is to be Frazer or Robertson Smith, let it by all means be the latter. I protest, however, in the name of historical continuity, against the use of any such invidious distinctions. For surely it is invidious to use a term of disparagement such as " magic " to imply that the cult of the sacred is inferior in religious value in strict proportion as dogma is absent. Besides, when one looks closely into a given case, there usually turns out to be more doctrine of a kind at the back of the ritual performance than might be supposed by those who forget that thinking is a good deal older than logical thinking. I doubt indeed whether any theology would be wise to depend in the last resort on its logic. Even so it has to be freely admitted that the doctrinal background of the Intichiuma rite needs an interpreter of dreams to fathom its meaning—a meaning none the less in which a mystic might possibly find more satisfaction than in a creed reduced to Aristotelian terms. To close this part of the discussion, it is surely better to treat sacrament as a fundamental institution of religion from its first appearance in history onward to its fullest and most refined manifestations. For by so doing we shall be less likely to do an injustice either to the savage by consigning him to an isolation ward where he must play at his idle mysteries by himself, or to the votary of the most advanced religion by accusing him of following a way of life that is encumbered with dead matter.

Being prepared, then, to extend the name of religion to the kind of rite which, though godless, nevertheless belongs to the cult of the sacred, or, as Miss Harrison would say, to a " system of sanctities ", let us proceed to find a meaning for the term " sacrament " such as will be not inconsistent with such a pre-theological attitude on the part of the believer. Now it should be stated at once that neither Miss Harrison nor I would for one moment wish the food-rite—the Intichiuma ceremony and its like—to be regarded as the only kind of sacrament. She makes this quite clear by saying, " There are other means of contact, of sacramental communion, besides eating and drinking." But the commensal meal, as Robertson Smith would call it, is at least thoroughly typical of the ritual proceedings to which totemism may give rise. As for its sacramental character, this consists, in Miss Harrison's opinion, in being a means of what she calls " *mana*-communion ". Again, though less happily in my view, she speaks of sacrifice as " magical contact ", evidently using the word " contact " as equivalent to communion. In other words, a sacrament is a special means of establishing connection with what she calls a sanctity. Such in the case of the Intichiuma ceremony is the sacred totem ; the object of the rite being to enable the worshipper to participate in that sanctity—to share in a *mana*, or miraculous quality of abounding kindliness and goodwill, which has been in a way common to totem and totemite all along, but is now stirred into greater activity by inducing a fuller consciousness of its real presence. Miss Harrison's main point in laying stress on the participatory aspect of the rite is that she wishes to preclude the idea of a favour conferred from without, as by a god who of his own initiative rewards his worshippers either according to their deserts or beyond them. In the case before us, on the contrary, the *mana* is immanent in the rite itself, if we include the parties to the rite among the conditions of its realization. Thus it is like some meeting of lovers whose awareness of each other is quickened by coming into touch, so that their warmth becomes a flame. From an objective point of view, no doubt, there are two parties to such a transaction, but, subjectively, and in terms of their feelings, all difference is for the time being transcended. Such a relation, then, must be classed as sympathetic rather than contractual. In short, it is a matter of joining souls rather than of marrying a fortune. In putting it thus I am perhaps straying rather far from the letter of my text ; but I do not think that I am doing an injustice to the general purport of Miss Harrison's thought.

Such, then, by hypothesis being primitive sacrament in its root idea—namely, a rite embodying a blessing that is enjoyed rather than imputed, spontaneous rather than derived—let us go on to see how far this interpretation is borne out by the known facts about the Intichiuma ceremony. It is, however, only fair to Miss Harrison to say that she does not regard the Arunta custom as altogether characteristic of that age of primal innocence of which she is in search. I am afraid that with us anthropologists the original condition of this or that institution always tends to lie just over the horizon ; for Nature, unlike logic, abhors absolute beginnings. Now the primal group of communicants—the first

thiasos, as Miss Harrison would say—would for her undoubtedly
be the matrilineal kin already possessed of a totem wherein its
community of blood is made known to itself. Now, when such a
group eats together, it may well be supposed that a certain
festal warmth would invade and enhance their mutual relations.
Yet surely the last thing such a group would eat with comfortable
abandon would be their totem ; unless indeed Miss Harrison
is ready to accept Professor Haddon's theory that originally,
that is to say, just before observation becomes possible, the
totem was the staple food of the group ; so that the kangaroo-
eaters became known to their neighbours and eventually to
themselves as the kangaroo-men. If, however, we stick to
known facts, a totem is not so much the first as the last thing
on which a totemite would be inclined to make a hearty meal.
The totemic relation, in fact, is normally expressed rather by
fasting than by feasting. Hence one would have somehow to
argue, if the satisfying effects of a full meal are insisted on as
the emotional basis of the rite, that the kin-group has by further
evolution become so sophisticated that it has learnt to get an
additional thrill out of breaking a taboo—that a soupçon of
sin can impart zest to participation in a sanctity. For the
moment, however, it will be enough to note that the food-rite
as we find it in actual practice is pervaded with a certain shyness
or shrinking—in a word, with the taboo feeling. In short, the
postulated association between the sacramental and the festal
is not borne out by the example cited. So far is the Intichiuma
ceremony from being an *instantia crucis*, that the arm of the
crux or " sign-post " points in quite another direction.

A second objection to the use made of the Arunta food-rite
as a clue that is to lead us back to the commensal meal of a
group owning one and the same strain of mother's blood is that
these totemites are classified by the anthropologist as " cult-
societies " pure and simple. It is true that membership depends
on a sort of birth-qualification ; but so peculiar are Arunta
views on the subject of birth that one can only term the imputed
relationship metaphysical, since it rests on no physical basis
whatever. A man's mother may be of one totem and his father
of another, and yet he will belong to a third, if his mother was
entered by a reincarnating spirit when passing the stock or stone
inhabited by unborn spirits of that third denomination. Now
this may be a survival of a very primitive type of totemism, as
Sir James Frazer believes it to be ; or, as others hold, it is the
mark of a peculiar, not to say eccentric, elaboration of the older
system that associates totem with natal group in the ordinary
sense. For our present purpose, however, we need merely
note that a group of Arunta totemites is not a kin in the social
sense—in other words, is not a natal association that could have

ever been brought up together so as to rejoice in a common life and more especially in common meals. A kangaroo-man's sleeping and eating arrangements have nothing to do with his totemic status. Thus the chosen example of sacramental communion falls so far short in a second respect of answering to the supposed archetype that one almost begins to wonder whether the Arunta stand any nearer to the imaginary beginning of things than do Miss Harrison's Kouretes.

Let us see, then, whether we can get at least a little way behind the Intichiuma rite by treating it not quite so strictly as a development of totemism. After all, if there has been any decided change of opinion in anthropological circles during the last twenty years in regard to religious origins, it has been but in the direction of reducing the part played by totemism as such during that early phase which is conterminous with the hunting-and-gathering stage of society. On a closer scrutiny it has been found increasingly impossible to keep the specifically totemistic features apart from the non-totemistic in those observances, more or less common to the whole wild-feeding world, that are meant to bring about luck in procuring their daily food. I do not think that " zoolatry " is a particularly happy term to express this attitude of the hunter towards the live things hunted ; though it is better than " theriolatry " which ignores the plants altogether. But, if we do not lay undue stress on the implication of worship lurking in the termination " -latry ", it will perhaps do. Indeed, my own prejudice is in favour of stretching the word " religious " to its utmost, so as to cover practices which are of dubious validity as well as manifestations of the religious spirit at its purest and best. Thus, even when conciliation rather than control appears to be the leading motive, one is never quite sure that such a term as cajolery will not cover both intentions alike—a cajolery, however, which co-exists with, and in a way is based on, a very real respect. A wise savage might well aspire to control a vegetable or one of the milder animals, and yet would surely prefer to conciliate a dangerous beast, though none the less in the hope of getting him in the end. Mark, too, that in a very real sense the most unpleasant to tackle of all the denizens of the wild may be regarded as good ; for, as Miss Harrison proves from a number of primitive vocabularies, " good " and " eatable " may start as more or less convertible terms. Thus, although his character for beneficence is something thrust upon the dangerous beast rather than of his own seeking, his flatterers almost mean what they say when they laud his excellence to the skies ; not being too clear in their own minds whether they are referring to his succulent taste or to his kindly disposition. Besides, there is another reason why an animal or a plant—for this consideration applies

to them all—should be treated nicely lest something go wrong
with the hunting. For, no sooner is one member of the species
killed and eaten, than another is wanted in its place, so as to
be killed and eaten to-morrow. There is needed some supernatural suspension of the law that you cannot eat your goose
and have him. How precisely it is to take place is hardly Man's
concern, one would think, so long as it does take place.
Nevertheless, in expressing his desire in the collective gesture
which custom prescribes he usually manages to convey a hint
to Providence of how the thing may be done. The simplest
method is to send off each individual animal, as it is done to
death by the hunter, so that it may come alive again as soon as
it conveniently can. Thus, by leaving some part intact, the
eater gives the remaining parts a chance to reassemble ; so
that, for instance, he will consume the flesh but must abstain
from cracking the bones. It is obvious, however, that there
is much to be said for a more wholesale way of inducing a given
species to keep up its numbers. Nay, whereas replacement
one by one can merely maintain the *status quo*, there is no saying
how glorious a hunting would not ensue if the animal kind as
such could be made to devote its full energies to breeding. This
of course is exactly what the Intichiuma rite tries to do ; and the
fact that the performers have to be namesakes to the given
animal or plant is perhaps a secondary matter. For in reality
the Arunta community as a whole is ultimately responsible for
its system of rites of multiplication. But, having at its disposal
a set of animal and plant identities—not to say names—
distributed in a rather arbitrary way among its members, it
naturally chooses as its go-between those persons who are in
special touch with the various species contributory to the tribal
food-supply. Thereupon the specialists are allowed to deal
in their own way with their totems' private mode of multiplication—sometimes a very complicated affair, as in the case
of the Witchetty-grubs, of which both Spencer and Gillen
became the adopted relatives. It is certain, however, that tribal
celebrations of great importance—such as the *Engwura* or
Fire-Ceremony, that lasted some four months—are pervaded
from end to end with totemic performances, even though these
are always enacted by the separate groups who, while as it were
retaining the copyright, must yet say their piece for the
edification of all. Whatever, then, be the far-off origin of the
Intichiuma rite—a highly speculative matter at the best—its
actual function, taken at its widest, is, I contend, to further
easy finding and plentiful eating on behalf of the tribe in general.

Now, if this be so, the eating of the totem—by no means a
universal feature of these rites, and prominent only in a few—
must be subordinate in function and meaning to the motive

operating throughout. As Miss Harrison is quick to see, sacrifice and the food-sacrament go closely together. How to slay and eat nicely, so that the animals will not mind, is the problem that they have to solve between them. How, then, do the occasional parts of the Intichiuma rite that involve killing and eating help towards this solution? As regards the alleged commensality whereby the totem is entertained by his fellow-totemites at his own expense, in the first place I cannot find the slightest evidence that any such idea is present in the minds of those who perform the rite, nor can I see precisely how it would fit in with what the occasion really requires, which is surely an apology. On the other hand, I believe that, if we never lose sight of the fundamental fact that the envoys are ambassadors between the tribe and the animal or plant whose name they bear, the rest will explain itself. These ambassadors, then, are there to express on behalf of the whole Arunta people a hope and a fear.

Firstly, then, as to the hope. This hope is for food in plenty. The leader of the Witchetty-grubs rubs the stomachs of his whole party with a stone symbolizing the grub and exclaims, " You have eaten much food." This is, as Miss Harrison would say, a *dromenon*, a thing done in the sense of done ahead. It prefigures the desired abundance. If it were meant as a feast, it would be a poor substitute for the real thing, since grub inside the stomach and a stone applied to its outer surface are satisfactions that will not readily fuse. But to give utterance in the most vivid gesture-language to the common hope by means of the prefigurement of its miraculous realization—such might well be the mission of envoys who had no private and sinister interest in forwarding the petition.

Next as to the fear. When the kangaroo-men actually kill a kangaroo and each eats a morsel, and only a morsel, thereof, are not the totemites in this case taking on themselves by anticipation the brunt of that invidious action on which the tribe proposes presently to engage on the widest scale? It is the principle of handselling—of leaving the costly first step to those most competent to take it with impunity. There is direct evidence that the totemite by eating a little is held to make such eating free for the rest. Thus, so far from being of the communial type, the rite is incipiently piacular. The function of the mediator is to take upon himself the sin of the rest, so that the righteous indignation of the victimized totem may be deflected to the one group of human beings whom he would be most disposed to forgive.

Now I do not wish to exaggerate the contrast between the communial and the piacular type of ceremony, though the symbolism of sharing a blessing will naturally differ a good

deal from that of getting rid of a curse. For the fact that they
have likewise something in common is indicated by the very word
that in English has come chiefly to stand for a rite of reconciliation
presupposing the removal of a cause of trouble—in moral terms,
a forgiveness of sin. When we say "atonement" our very
pronunciation helps to conceal the etymological sense of
achieving an at-one-ness. At-one-ness, however, is by no means
the same thing as one-ness. It stands for a transcended duality
rather than for a unity that is such by nature. So, too, then,
I suggest that the so-called communial rite is from its first
inception intended to effect a miracle of at-one-ment—to build
a supernatural bridge across a natural divide. Now Miss Harrison,
I suppose, as well as Robertson Smith—whom I take her to be
following closely whenever she is not taking her lead from the
very similar speculations of Durkheim—would say that the
original kin-group has its internal squabbles to get over, so
that the common mother's blood of them would need warming
up from time to time if peace and friendliness were to reign in
the primeval home. I grant that stern taboos were presumably
needed to preserve the amenities in the earliest of fire-circles.
Thus the prohibition against intestine murder and intestine
marriage may alike have originated in the attempt to enforce
orderly and seemly relations under the sanction of the curse of
the united mothers, the high priestesses of the common blood.
There is no evidence, however, so far as I know, that their custom
of eating together—after all, a daily occurence which for this
very reason would be unlikely to acquire any special significance
and sanctity—had developed into a means of repressing
dissociative tendencies, whether in the form of a quarrel with a
kin-brother or of a liaison with a kin-sister. The only fact I know
that seems at all to the point—and it is very sketchily reported
by Howitt and may well be incorrect—is that certain totemites
ate an erring brother, apparently by way of restoring him to
their communion. As, however, endo-cannibalism can never
have been the normal mode of supplying the common table of
the archetypal kin, this solitary instance, even if its documentary
value were above suspicion, would hardly be relevant. Killing
and eating a blood-relation once in a blue moon—for a group
that needed to do this at regular intervals would not remain in
being long—could hardly serve as the starting-point of a custom
embodying the idea of commensality. In any case it clearly
involves reconciliation rather than spontaneous good-fellowship
as its basic motive. Hence I would not seek in the internal
affairs of the kin for the reason that makes eating together a
symbol of communion, but rather in its external relations with
the stranger. That, if hospitality be given and accepted, the
foreigner's potency for harm will be neutralized, is a principle

holding throughout the savage world. But from the first such
a precept implies at-one-ment—a duality to be transcended.
I fully allow that the symbolism implies that eating together
in fellowship, as the kin normally does, is incompatible with
the spirit of enmity ; so that the stranger, by being treated as
a kinsman, is miraculously transformed from a foe into a friend.
But it is only at the point at which symbolism becomes necessary
that ritual comes into existence. The commensal meal of the
kin may have provided the pattern for the rite ; but in itself it
is no rite—any more than, if for religious reasons the horns of
a bull are worn by a man, the wearing of horns is proved to
have been a religious act on the part of the bull.

If, then, I am at all right in insisting on the fundamental
disharmony which the food-rite, whether in its distinctively
totemic form or otherwise, is designed to overcome, the food-
animal, totem though it be, is not like a kinsman participating
in the common meal by natural right, but is rather like the
alien who, if persuaded to accept a gift of food, cannot in common
decency maintain the malignant attitude affected by foreign
devils as such. It is surely a matter for diplomacy—for the most
delicate handling of an international situation in which the one
party is trying to get the best of the other with as good a
conscience as it can muster—to persuade a poor beast that it
has to be killed and eaten, because that is how the world is
made. When the thing is settled—the one-sided treaty signed—
there may be rejoicings on the part of the eater ; but to force
this aspect of the matter on the attention of the about-to-be-
eaten would be bad policy and bad manners to boot. In short,
the occasion calls rather for the ceremonial lamentations that so
often accompany the death of the animal, even when it has
become domesticated, that is, has sunk to the level of a member
of the *familia*, the group of farm-chattels. Now one does not
like to think of such a show of grief as simply a piece of solemn
humbug. Indeed, man is so honestly convinced of his innate
superiority that he cannot conceive the underdog to have rights,
if these run counter to interests which, being those of so high a
being as himself, must surely be valid absolutely and for all
alike. We can call it the imperialistic fallacy, if indeed it is a
fallacy for strength to vindicate its natural dominance over
weakness. Be this as it may, primitive man is either too cautious
or too decent-minded to adopt the tone of a bully in his dealings
with those shy creatures, the game ; but is always polite, even
when he does not mean quite all he says. Indeed, when one
thinks of the very primitive hunter as essentially a man of
snares—for he has not got weapons for successful attack in the
open—one is impelled to ask whether his very ritual is not a
sort of supersnare. Facts, alas ! are facts, even if one would

prefer not to find an organized hypocrisy among the roots of religion.

Let me refrain, however, from further speculation in this unedifying direction, lest I prejudice my case. My main contention is simply that in origin the sacramental type of meal is essentially distinct from the festal, even if later religious practice sometimes tends to confuse them. The festal type is certainly to be encountered within the wide ambit of historical religion ; which includes, for instance, downright Saturnalia, when the ordinary, or profane, use of food helps to bring people together and to promote general hilarity. But, in connection with the sacramental type, no such festival spirit is endurable. As a well-known verse from the Epistle to St. Jude proclaims, " These are spots in your feasts of charity, when they feast with you, feeding themselves without fear." In the true sacrament a holy fear must preclude free enjoyment of the food as such. There need be no eating at all, as when the flesh and blood are consumed by fire ; or, if there is a meal, it must at least be sparing. For it is an act not so much of consecration as of deconsecration. Not participation but naturalization is its object. Man is not so much concerned to add to his own stock of *mana* by absorbing that of the victim, as he is to neutralize an alien *mana* which might do him harm if, like the blood of righteous Abel, the victim's blood should continue to cry aloud for vengeance. The analogy, in short, is more with a composition negotiated in a matter of blood-revenge than with any collegiate gathering— any sort of primitive bump-supper. To repeat what was previously said, the sacramental meal is not so much a feast as a fast. Nay, it often demands a previous discipline of abstinence, its ascetic quality being perhaps emphasized by the use of an emetic. It is, I would suggest, the presence of this taboo-feeling—this shrinking from the world and its pleasures— that helps to dematerialize the sacramental meal, and thus to render it the fitting symbol of a communion with the divine when approached in a truly religious spirit, namely, one that must be humble before it can become jubilant. Miss Harrison, in her clever way, perceives that in the actual cases analysed there is always a certain felt difference between the man and his totem-animal. But she thinks this sense of apartness is secondary—a faltering of the original all-embracing sense of kinship ; whereas, if I am right, it is primary, nay, integral to the very conception of the sacramental act.

The topic being inexhaustible I could go on to argue that another point made further on in the same chapter by Miss Harrison, to the effect that the idea of sacramental communion is in the middle religions supplanted by a theory of " *do ut des* ", assumes a new appearance if we identify communion with a sort of peacemaking between potential enemies. For it will be found that the savage notion of giving and receiving presents is by no means the same as our own, being largely symbolic and, in fact, embodying another characteristic method of patching up a quarrel. If so, the transition from communion to the gift-sacrifice is not so abrupt as Miss Harrison would suppose.

But, instead of pursuing this new hare, let me break off at this point with apologies for having sounded a note of criticism without at the same time expressing my genuine admiration for Miss Harrison's work. The fact is that the substance of this paper is taken from the Jane Harrison Lecture delivered by me at Newnham College, Cambridge, in 1932; and on that occasion I took the opportunity of stating how much I owed personally to the inspiration derived from her writings. Yet after all no greater compliment can be paid to her as a serious anthropologist than by subjecting her theories to critical examination. Reading her *Themis* over again carefully, I seem to perceive some slips in details, but feel at the same time that in the greater matters she exhibits an unfailing sense of direction together with an unfaltering resolution to win through. In fact, as Andrew Lang once said about her, " she has *l'étincelle* "—that divine spark which is the sign of power in art and science alike.

IBO LAW

By C. K. Meek

In the space allowed for this paper it will only be possible to refer to a few of those concepts of the Ibo which may be conveniently described as " legal ", more particularly as it will be necessary to include an account of the social and religious organization, with which the whole of the legal system is closely interwoven. For Ibo Law is not a well-defined institution by itself, but is rather the expression, when such is called for, of the innumerable latent rules governing all the tribal institutions.

The Ibo-speaking peoples number about 3,185,000 people, and are centred mainly in the Onitsha, Owerri, Benin, and Ogoja Provinces of Nigeria. It is with the North-Western groups inhabiting the political divisions of Onitsha Province, known as Nsukka and Awgu, that this paper is principally concerned. According to Dr. Talbot [1] the Ibo consist of a number of sub-tribes such as the Awhawzara and Awhawfia.[2] But these terms are primarily geographical, and the most striking feature of Ibo society as a whole is the absence of any strong tribal or sub-tribal organization. In the Nsukka and Awgu divisions there is no higher social or political unit than the " village-area ", i.e. the group of villages united by the possession of a common name and territory, the belief in descent from a common ancestor, the sharing of common customs and cults, and sometimes of a common *chi* or soul.

The village-area may thus constitute a clan.[3] But it is frequently a local rather than a kinship grouping ; for, though the component villages may vaguely claim a common ancestor, it can often be proved that there was no original relationship, and in many cases, indeed, no relationship is claimed. Such unity as they possess is due to economic and political circumstances and to intermarriage.

A village-area is known as an *obodo* or *mba* or *ala*, and includes a number of subdivisions known as *ńkporo* or *ogbwe*. The *ńkporo* in turn is subdivided into smaller groups or hamlets known as *ǫnuma* or *nchi*. The hamlet may coincide with the single kinship grouping known as *umunna* or may embrace several *umunna*. An *umunna*

---

[1] *Southern Nigeria*, iv, 42.
[2] Awhawzara means " the people of the shrub bush " and Awhawfia " the people of the thick bush ".
[3] But there is no clan exogamy.

may be composed of a single group of related families each of which consists of such close relatives as a man and his wife, brothers or first cousins and their wives and children ; or it may consist of two or more related groups of such families. Where the *umunna* consists of a single group of related families it may, for the purposes of this article, be described as an " extended-family ",[1] and where it consists of two or more groups of related families it may be described as a " kindred ".

The *umunna* is the basic social unit. Where it consists of a single extended-family it is invariably [2] an exogamous unit. Where it embraces a number of related extended-families it may or may not be an exogamous unit. Intermarriage between related extended-families is sometimes allowed and sometimes forbidden. The exogamous unit may therefore be as small as a dozen people or as large as five or six hundred. A large *umunna* differs little from a small clan (unless we are to regard exogamy as a *sine qua non* of clanship). Descent is reckoned patrilineally.

With regard to the religious conceptions of the people it may be said shortly that the Ibo believe in the existence of a Supreme Spirit known as Chuku. In his creative aspect Chuku is described as Chineke or Chukwoke or Chi Okike. He sends rain, makes the crops grow, and is the source from which men derive their *Chi* or " Soul ". He is sometimes equated with and sometimes regarded as the father of Anyanu, the Sun. He is also the father of Igwe (the Sky), Amadi Qha (Lightning), and Ale (the Earth-deity). Sacrifices are not usually offered to Chuku, but he is regarded as the ultimate recipient of all sacrifices. In the Nsukka Division every householder offers regular sacrifice to Anyanu [3] (the Sun), but in the Awgu Division there are no sun-shrines, though a man may occasionally hang up a chicken in a piece of cleft bamboo with a prayer to Anyanu that he will receive it and convey it to Chuku. Incidentally the peoples of Awka are known to those of Awgu as " The children of the Sun ".

The most important deity in the religious and social life of the people is Ale or Ala or Ane, the Earth-deity. Ale is regarded as the owner of men, whether alive or dead. The cult of ancestors is therefore closely associated with Ale, who is queen [4] of the Underworld. Ale is the source of human morality, and is in consequence the principal legal sanction. Homicide, kidnapping, poisoning, stealing farm-products, adultery, giving birth to twins or abnormal children, are all offences against Ale, and must be purged by sacrifice to her. Laws are made in her name,

---

[1] In some groups an extended-family is known as *onunne* or *umunne* (children of one mother, i.e. descendants of full brothers).

[2] With the exception of the Ache district in which marriage with close consanguineous relatives (e.g. first cousins) is permissible.

[3] The expression Anyanu means " the eyes of Anu ".

[4] Ale is sometimes regarded as a male deity.

and by her oaths are sworn. Ale is, in fact, the unseen president of the community, and no group is complete which has not its shrine and priest of Ale.

Under the control of Ale are numerous godlings or spirits, of whom the most important is Njoku, the giver and protector of yams. The ancestors of the people also live under the control and act as the agents of Ale. They profoundly influence the lives of their descendants. They are the guardians of morality, and regard any departure from custom as a breach of morality. It is for this reason that priests of cults and heads of families, who are the living representatives of the ancestors, have frequently eschewed association with the new-fangled laws of the Government.

The head of each family-group, or *okpara* as he is called, owes his authority (or such authority as he possesses) largely to the fact that he is the representative and mouthpiece of the family ancestors, symbolized by the sacred stick known as *ofo*. This stick, which is a section of a branch of a species of tree believed to have been set aside by Chuku as a symbol and guarantee of truth, is inherited and carefully preserved by all heads of families.

All priests of cults have an *ofo*, which is the recognized means of communication with the deity or spirit of the cult. But it represents also the ancestors who formerly ministered to the cult. It is the symbol of authority of the living priest, and the guarantee and means of transmission of his " Holy Orders ". And just as the priest himself tends to become identified with the god he serves, so the *ofo* becomes identified with the deity or spirit in whose service it is used. In many groups *ofos* are even specifically identified with the god or spirit of Truth and Justice. Oaths are sworn on *ofos*, and no *ofo*-holder would swear falsely by his *ofo*, unless he had become a renegade.

There is a final aspect of ancestor-worship which is of prime importance in the administration of justice, viz. the societies (secret from women) in which the ancestors or ancestral leaders are personated by maskers known as Mo. These societies act as policemen of the community, and are used particularly as a means of disciplining the female members of the community. The Mo might, on their own initiative, drive an adulterous woman out of the kindred, and banish anyone suspected of practising witchcraft, or compel him or her to submit to the ordeal of drinking sasswood.

With this brief summary we may now proceed to give some details of the manner in which law functions among the Ibo, and as law begins within the family-group or *umunna*, we shall consider first the mode by which the *umunna* is governed.

An *umunna* is composed of groups of compounds, each of

which contains one or several small or biological families closely related to each other. Each of these families is in most respects an economic unit, as each farms and trades on its own account. But each compound or household recognizes its senior member as its moral and political controller. Similarly, each group of households constituting a distinct extended-family within the *umunna*, is subject to the control of the various heads of households, presided over by the *okpara* or senior householder, who holds the family *ofo*, and represents the family in all its external relations. Where the *umunna* contains a number of extended-families, the control is vested in the whole body of elders, presided over by the head of the senior extended-family, who is the holder of the senior *ofo*. The authority of the *okpara* is based on the fact that he is regarded as living in close association with the ancestors, and is thus the chief repository of custom. He has charge of the shrine of the founder of the *umunna*, to whom he offers regular sacrifice once a year on behalf of the whole kindred, and irregular sacrifice on behalf of individuals who may be directed by the diviner to offer sacrifice. He can bring any recalcitrant member to heel by the mere threat of invoking his *ofo* against that man. To insult him is to insult the ancestors, who are regarded as ever present in his *ofo*. One guilty of such an offence would be brought before him and the other elders, and ordered to hand over a chicken, some kola-nuts, and a pot of palm-wine, that sacrifice might be offered to the ancestors, lest in their anger they should kill the offender. The advice of the senior elder cannot usually be disregarded, unless he is so old and decrepit that another has to act on his behalf. He takes immediate steps to stop inter-family fights, and, assisted by the other elders, investigates all disputes, warning those who have misbehaved themselves that if they repeat their conduct they need not look to him for assistance. If the matter were serious, such as theft from a fellow-member of the kindred, he would warn the thief that a repetition of his offence would lead to his expulsion from the village, or being sold as a slave to the Aro.[1] He might even, with the concurrence of the other elders of the kindred, order him to be tied hand and foot and placed on a platform over a smoking fire for two days without food or drink. He might threaten to drive out of the family-group any young man who had shown himself to be lazy and taken no steps to obtain a wife.[2] He might order a member of the family-group who owed a debt to a fellow-member, or to a member of another family-group, to pay the debt forthwith, under the penalty of having a taboo (a knotted palm-leaf) placed on his property. He might, in

[1] The Aro were itinerant traders and slave-dealers.
[2] But in the first instance a recalcitrant son is brought to book by his own father or the head of the small family-group.

association with the other elders, inflict a severe fine on anyone committing adultery with the wife of a kinsman, and order the poisoning of one who had committed incest.[1] He could, in former days, call on the father of twins or abnormal children to rid the kindred immediately of the " abominable thing ". When gifts, fees, or sacrificial foods are divided he, as the holder of the senior *ọfọ*, takes the first share, and when meetings are held to settle disputes he announces the decision, holding the *ọfọ* in his right hand and quoting precedents for the decision.

The head of a kindred, or family-group, is not, however, an autocrat, unless he happens to be a man of outstanding personality. If he is weak and untrustworthy he has little influence, and his functions may, by common consent, be delegated to any suitable person. Even a young successful man may be accorded the position of leadership. One who has obtained a public office or title may overshadow the senior elder, and in some communities, if there is a priest of Ale in the kindred, he may, even if he is a comparatively young man, be accorded the position of principal authority. Furthermore, if the kindred is large, there is usually considerable jealousy between the various extended-families composing the kindred, and each extended-family endeavours, for its own honour, to settle quietly any case of delinquency on the part of one of its members, without bringing it to the notice of the head official of the kindred. The authority of the head of the kindred is also qualified by the fact that he cannot act solely on his own initiative. In all important matters he is bound to consult and seek the support of the other elders and important persons of the kindred.

A well-known feature of the legal system is the collective responsibility of the family-group for the conduct of its members. The stock example of this is in cases of murder or manslaughter. Immediate retaliation was made by the kin of the murdered man on any member of the murderer's kin, and the property of the nearest relatives of the murderer was pillaged. In consequence of this rule the murderer was expected *by his own family* to commit suicide immediately, in order to save the whole family from attack and their property from spoliation. If the murderer failed to do this the whole of his kin had to seek refuge in flight.

When the anger of the murdered man's kin had subsided, the kin of the murderer could return, on condition that the murderer *or some other member of his family* committed suicide. Details will be given on this subject later, and it need only be remarked here that, in consequence of this rule of collective responsibility, the elders of a kindred constantly warned their young men to keep control over their feelings and avoid the use of lethal weapons. Further, as murder was considered an offence against

[1] But in some areas no one would take part in killing a kinsman.

Ale (the Earth-deity), the crime, if committed against a fellow-member of the same family, was not one which could be palliated or settled privately by the family itself. The whole community took action against the murderer, and his own brother might be the first to set fire to his house. Even if a man killed his brother accidentally, he had to fly and remain away for a period of one month. He was then permitted to return ; but at the first festival of Ale he had to take a goat, fowl, new basket, cloth, and some yams to the shrine of Ale where he knelt down and said : " Ale, I bring these gifts to you. I did not kill my brother by design. I went out hunting like the rest, and killed him by an accident. Ale spare my life." The various articles brought were left at the shrine. The animals were not sacrificed. The goat became sacred and taboo, and was allowed to wander about unharmed. Indeed, it was given the right of way on the road. If it bore young ones they also became taboo, being known as " Ewu Ale ". The goat was in fact a scapegoat, for it was stated that the " evil " which had moved the man to kill his fellow had passed into the goat, and that if anyone ate the flesh of that goat the inherent " evil " would cause his death. It is to be noticed that in a case of this kind (i.e. of a man killing a member of his own extended-family or kindred) no blood-money was payable, on the ground that it would be heinous to derive profit from the death of a " brother ".

The collective responsibility of the kinship group is shown also in numerous other ways. Thus (at Oduma), if a man had been summoned by the elders of the town to answer some charge, and refused to attend, the elders would send young men to bring him by force. If they could not find him they would capture any member of the accused's extended-family and keep him a prisoner until the accused appeared. This would induce the elders of the accused's extended-family to bring pressure on the parents of the accused to produce him or disclose his whereabouts. If the accused had run away to some distant town, the members of his extended-family would be called on to pay the penalty of the accused's offence. Similarly in cases of debt, if the creditor could not induce the debtor to repay the loan, he would go to the compound of any of the accused's relatives who happened to be absent on their farms, and capture goats or any other articles equivalent to or in excess of the amount of the debt. Later in the day he would send word to the owner of the property informing him of the reasons of his action. The owner in turn would bring pressure on the debtor to pay the sum he owed. If the creditor belonged to another village he might, if sufficiently adroit, appropriate property from anyone in the creditor's village, the elders of which would then force the debtor to pay. These regulations did not, of course, imply that there was any collective ownership of property or that a person was held morally responsible for the sins of his relatives. They were simply an obvious method of obtaining redress through those who were in a position to bring pressure. Nevertheless they served to maintain the kinship solidarity.

Just as the *umunna* is the basis of the social system, so the mode by which it is governed is the pattern of the mode of government of each larger group, whether it be an *ọnuma* (hamlet), *ṅkporo* (village), or *obodo* (village-area). It is government by the body of elders presided over by the senior elder. It was never government by a single individual, though a single individual might exercise a position of leadership, either on account of some special office or exceptional influence or affluence.

In using the term " government " it is not to be supposed that public notice was taken of every case which was a breach of customary law. The governing body only concerned itself with cases which were (a) an offence against religion (or, as the Ibo would say, " abominable ") and so would bring disaster on the community unless the steps prescribed by custom were taken, or (b) which were likely to break up the solidarity of the *umunna* *ọnuma*, *ṅkporo*, or *obodo*. A man might steal from another and, if caught red-handed, be sold into slavery by the owner of the stolen property, without reference to the elders or any one else. Or a creditor might recover his debt by appropriating a goat or other property belonging to the debtor, or a member of his kinship or local group. Or again two parties to a dispute might refer their dispute not to the whole council of the group, but to certain arbitrators chosen by each side.

The term " government ", moreover, was government only in a very qualified sense, for even in cases where the group solidarity was endangered the central council of elders might be powerless to intervene. The body of elders was a body of mediators and referees rather than of prosecutors and judges, and the community was a republic in the true sense of that term, i.e. a corporation in which government was the concern of all.

Instances may now be given to illustrate the composition of the councils, and the methods of procedure. Firstly, as regards the personnel of the village or village-area courts or councils, though all the elders [1] are members of the council and are nominally on an equal footing, there are particular personages or classes to whom special reference must be made. These are (a) the senior elder or holder of the senior *ọfọ* ; (b) the announcers of decisions ; (c) the holders of " staves of judgment ",

[1] The term " elders " includes all householders, but the principal elders are the heads of extended-families who are known as the Ọha.

i.e. a special class of judges or arbitrators found in certain communities; (*d*) rich or influential men who had attained a special position as arbitrators; (*e*) titled persons.

As regards the most senior elder, he generally acted as president of the council, to the extent that he opened the proceedings by a prayer to the gods and ancestors to be present at their deliberations, to enable them to arrive at a right decision, and punish any elder who attempted to pervert justice and any witness who gave false evidence.[1] It may be noted incidentally that it was permissible for either party to a case to demand the withdrawal of any elder, on the ground that that elder was a hereditary enemy of his family. There was thus a system of challenging " jurors ". Moreover, the general body of elders could by common consent call on any of their number who was known to be a bad character to withdraw from the proceedings.

The announcers of decisions were always prominent personages at councils or trials. They had usually to be men of good address and to have a sound knowledge of the customary procedure. They were commonly the holders of the senior *ọfọ*, but if the holder of the senior *ọfọ* was not a good speaker he had to delegate one of the family-group to act as his deputy. In some communities the duty of announcing decisions was not assigned to any particular person or office. Any good speaker would be called upon to perform this duty. But in other communities certain families had a special right of announcing decisions, and in some cases these families acted as principal arbiters in all disputes.

A man of outstanding wealth might in any group attain for himself a measure of chieftainship, if he was able and generous. With him rested the decision whether the group should go to war or not, for he could provide the powder and firearms. In this way he attained control over the younger age-grades, which readily placed themselves at his service for any purpose. He might even call on them to work on his farms. By rendering services to all who came to him for help he was constantly adding to the number of his free-born followers, and by demanding a major portion of captives taken in war (in return for providing powder and firearms) he was constantly adding to the number of his slaves. It is easy to understand, therefore, how a rich, generous man could become the principal judge and centre of authority. His presence would be called for in every important case, and few would care to oppose his views.

Finally, we come to the groups of titled people who, as being

---

[1] The head of the senior family in the town is frequently known as the Onyishi, and in some communities, before he is given this formal title, he is made to swear an oath that he will not adjudicate in secret, take sides in disputes, appropriate communal or other property by force, or apply public moneys to his own purposes.

the richest men in the community, took the most prominent part in its control. They included in their ranks the heads of the most important extended-families. They were in some communities the principal judges and principal executive officers, and enjoyed numerous privileges. Thus at Inyi those holding titles took the most important part in all judicial matters. Breaches of customary law were reported to the senior title-holder in the *nkporo* or quarter and he, together with other holders of the title, would go to the offender's house and capture or kill one of his goats, pending further investigation of the case. If the offence was small the loss of the goat might be considered a sufficient punishment, but if it was serious the holders of titles might order the man to be sold and divide the proceeds among themselves. If the culprit had taken refuge in the house of the priest of Ale, the holders of titles would capture and sell a boy or girl from his family. Fines were imposed on anyone who insulted a member of the order, and it is said that people were afraid even of offending a person whose brother was the holder of a title.

Among the Isu Ochi the holders of titles enjoyed numerous privileges. They inflicted heavy fines on anyone who assaulted one of their order, and if the offender was unable to pay the fine he was sold into slavery. Even to abuse the holder of a title was an offence, and it was an offence also for any non-titled person to enter the house of a titled person after dark. One who committed adultery with the wife of a titled man was sold into slavery (whereas in ordinary cases there was no official penalty unless the adultery had taken place in the husband's house, in which case the adulterer was fined). Creditors could distrain the property of debtors, but they could not do so if the debtor was the holder of a title. The holders of titles, besides taking a principal part in trials, acted as guardians of orphans and of their property, a rule which was found to be necessary, as the relatives of orphaned children had sometimes sold the children into slavery.

The holders of titles were distinguished by a spear or iron staff. Their influence has now in many areas completely disappeared, as, with the advent of the Government, they could no longer enjoy their former privileges.

In the Nsukka Division the control of the village was vested mainly in the titled personages known as Asogwa, who employed the minor titled officials known as Ndishi Iwu as their executive officers. In most villages the Ndishi Iwu used the cults of Qmabe or Qdo as the legal sanction, and, if any person broke a law or refused to obey an order of the council, the Iwu would proceed to his house with a masker of the cult and place a knotted palm-leaf in the roof, thereby interdicting the owner from touching anything until the taboo had been removed. In some localities the Ndishi Iwu were also the principal judges, but in others the principal judges were the holders of the Ọzọ title or that known as " Eze ". In a few villages, the Eze or Ezes of the village had attained a position which almost amounted to chieftainship, but this was due to the influence of the Igala tribe. For among the Ibo the indigenous form of government is essentially of a democratic or conciliar character.

LEGAL PROCEDURE

We may now give some examples of the legal procedure, and it is hardly necessary to remark that in order to understand Ibo legal procedure we must divest ourselves of many English legal conceptions, such as the rigid distinction between " civil " and " criminal " cases, or the idea that public notice had to be taken of every offence. Even in cases of " sin " no public action might be necessary, as the sinner might automatically punish himself in the manner prescribed by custom. Or, again, a criminal might be automatically punished by his own family or by the person against whom he had committed a crime. If a criminal was caught *flagrante delicto* in the presence of witnesses there was no necessity as a rule for any form of trial. Trials occurred in doubtful cases, and if, after the hearing of evidence, the matter still remained doubtful it was decided by an oath or an ordeal. It must be remembered also that there was no hard and fast code. The community reacted in various ways according to the circumstances of the case. The elders who tried cases had to consider the social position of the accused, the attitude and strength of his kindred, whether he was a useful member of society or not, and so on. Decisions were in fact judicious rather than judicial.

HOMICIDE

To commit murder was an offence against Ale, and it was the concern of the whole community to see that the steps prescribed by custom were carried out. If the murderer hanged himself forthwith (which he frequently did, either from remorse at having killed one of Ale's children, or in order to save his family from attack and the loss of their property, or because he was expected to do so) his brother was (at Owelle) required to offer sacrifice to Ale before burying the body of the murderer. He took eight yams and one chicken to the priest of Ale who, standing before the symbol of the cult, spoke as follows : " Ale, this chicken and these yams have been given to you by the brother of the man who killed your child and then hanged himself. He beseeches you to accept this atonement and to refrain from pursuing the brothers and children of the murderer. He who killed a fellow-man has also killed himself. Let his crime therefore follow him to the next world." It will be observed from this rite that the family of the murderer was considered as sharing in the responsibility of the crime unless it took steps to dissociate itself from the murder. It had to provide a cow, goat, fowl, two yards of cloth, and a keg of powder for the funeral rites of the murdered man.

If the murderer did not immediately hang himself but took refuge in flight, his family had also to fly,[1] for the kin of the murdered man (including maternal relatives) immediately made a raid on the compounds and property of the kin of the murderer. In this raid any members of the local group might join. The compounds of the murderer's family were burnt to the ground, their yams were uprooted, and their palms cut down.[2] All property found might be appropriated, but in some communities it was taboo for the patrilineal relatives of the murdered man to keep any of the raided property, on the ground that this would be " eating blood-money ". But relatives in the female line might do so, as their Ale was not concerned with the death of men in other local groups.

The family of the murderer remained in exile for a period of at least one month,[3] when they might be invited by the elders of their town to return, the consent of the kin of the murdered man having first been obtained. The murderer himself continued to remain in exile. In some communities (e.g. at Oduma) the following rite was performed before the return of the exiled family. The senior *ada* or sister of each of the kindreds concerned went together to the compounds of the exiled family and swept them out thoroughly. They then took a cock and a hen, tied them together with a palm-leaf, and walked round the compounds, saying : " Ale, do not permit such a thing to occur again. Ale, be not angry with us." They then collected the sweepings of the compound and threw them and the two fowls into the " bush of evil ". This rite of purification is known as *Eza fu ntu ochu*, i.e. " The sweeping-out of the ashes of murder ".

On the return of the exiled family [4] a public meeting would

[1] If the murderer and murdered man belonged to different local groups the whole of the murderer's local group might be forced to fly. If the murderer and murdered man belonged to two different *nkporos* a state of war might ensue between the two *nkporos*.
[2] At Mmako, in cases of accidental homicide, the relatives of the deceased went to the compound of the man-slayer and cut down one palm-tree and one bread-fruit tree only.
[3] The Ale priest and elders, usually at the end of twenty-eight days, called on the kin of the murdered man to desist from making further raids on the property of the kin of the murderer, lest a continuance should lead to another murder.
[4] In some communities the family of the murderer would not be permitted to return until they had produced the murderer or a substitute, who would be required to hang himself publicly.

be held to inquire into the matter and decide what atonement must be made by the murderer's kin. This meeting might be held in the compound of the priest of Ale, but the priest usually took no part in the discussions, from fear of making some mistake for which Ale would punish him. In some towns meetings connected with a murder were always held in an open space clear of all houses, lest the pollution of the murder should infect the houses. The proceedings were conducted principally by the elders or, in certain communities, by particular individuals who had special authority to deal with cases of homicide.[1] These would consider all the circumstances of the case, and elicit whether the homicide was accidental or deliberate, and, if the latter, whether there were any extenuating circumstances. If it appeared that the homicide had been accidental, the man-slayer might be allowed to return after twenty-eight days, and on his return would be required to offer sacrifice to Ale. But in some communities there was no difference in the penalty for accidental homicide and murder, owing to the belief that if a man killed another by what we should term an accident he must at some previous time have committed an act abominable to Ale. If there were extenuating circumstances he might be permitted to produce a substitute to be publicly killed. The substitute might be some notorious thief of whom the community wished to be rid, and the killing was carried out by a man hired from another town for the purpose, as it was considered an offence against Ale to slay a fellow-townsman, even if that townsman had been guilty of murder. Sometime later the murderer was required to go through the form of dedicating a person to the service of Ale, as a substitute for the man he had killed. He went to another town and hired a man for this purpose. He took this hireling, together with a tortoise, an *aiagere* fowl, a piece of *ofo* wood, a pottery plate, and a pot, to the shrine of the priest of Ale. The hireling was stripped naked and the priest spoke as follows : " Ale, this man has been brought to you as a substitute for your son who was killed." The murderer added : " Please, Ale, let me go free and be not wrathful with me again." The hireling then knelt before the shrine. He did not apparently remain permanently as an *osu*[2] or slave of Ale, but was allowed to return to his own town.

Whether there were extenuating circumstances or not, the

---

[1] It is noteworthy that in all investigations into homicide the judges refused to accept any form of preliminary gift such as snuff or palm-wine or kola, lest they should incur the anger of Ale.

[2] Persons permanently dedicated to the gods are known as *osu*. They are despised, and no free person will marry an *osu*. They are also feared, being regarded as dynamized by the god. If they committed theft they were not prosecuted, lest the anger of the god should be incurred. Even at the present time some Court members are afraid of trying an *osu* on any charge.

murderer might in some communities be called on to hang himself if he re-appeared in the town. Or he might be required to produce some member of his family-group to hang himself in his stead.[1] But if a substitute hanged himself, the murderer (at Owelle) had to make atonement by the following rite. He summoned the priest of Ale to his house and presented him with a white chicken and a yam. The priest roasted the yam and, holding the chicken and yam in his hand, said, " Ale, I am giving this fowl to you to appease your wrath against this man. Ale, I am going to give this man a yam to eat, and I beseech you that you will refrain from taking his life when he partakes of anything which has been touched by a man of Owelle." The murderer was then given the yam to eat. The fowl was appropriated by the priest.

It may be noted in conclusion that no person who had been guilty of homicide and had been allowed to return home was permitted to take part in any festival of Ale. During such a festival he had either to absent himself from the town or else sit on a platform, as contact of his person with the ground was regarded as a pollution of the Earth-deity. No one would eat in the company of a murderer, and a murderer's wife abandoned him.

THEFT AND OTHER OFFENCES

The procedure in cases of theft varied according to the nature of the article stolen, and according to whether the theft had been committed within or without the kinship group. But the procedure in one town might differ considerably from that in another.

If a man stole any article of property from a member of his own kinship group the owner of the property might merely warn the thief and take no further steps. Or he might report the theft to the elders, who would warn the thief and possibly order him to be tied up for several days without food. If the thief had committed similar thefts before, the elders might direct that he should be sold as a slave to the Aro.

In many localities, if a man stole an article from a member either of his own kinship or local group, he was merely subjected to ridicule and contempt. When people met him on the road they would say *Uu!* " Thief! "[2] If he was the holder of a title he would no longer be accorded any share of dues received. Even if he repeated his offence he might not (in some groups) be sold, on

---

[1] It was not uncommon (e.g. at Nengwe) for the brother of a murderer to hang himself as a substitute, on the ground that the murderer was a better man than himself !

[2] For some offences a culprit might be sung through the town by one of the age-grades.

the ground that in former times an epidemic had invaded the group as a consequence of selling a close kinsman.

But one caught red-handed stealing from a member of another local group or quarter was usually accorded different treatment —he was sold automatically by the owner of the stolen property. Under certain circumstances he was allowed to redeem himself. For if on some previous occasion a man of the thief's kindred had caught a man of the other kindred in the act of stealing his property, and had refrained from selling him, then it was incumbent on the victim's kindred in the present case to act with similar generosity.

Space does not permit of any detailed account of the legal procedure in offences such as assault, adultery, the use of black magic, or other " abominable " acts. It may, however, be noted that, while adultery within the kinship group was an " abomination " which necessitated public condemnation and a ritual purification, adultery outside the kinship group was a private injury with which the general public had usually no concern. But an adulterer was liable to be assaulted by the injured husband, and this might lead to a state of war between two groups. Or, if the adulterer refused to pay compensation to the husband, the members of the latter's group might violate women belonging to the adulterer's group, as opportunity occurred, until public peace became so endangered that the elders of the whole village-area found it necessary to intervene.

Twins, children born with teeth, children born with hand or foot first, cripples, and children who cut the upper before the lower teeth, were destroyed or handed over to Aro traders. A child who was unable to walk before he had reached the age of three was regarded as having committed an offence against Ale in his former life, and was destroyed or sold. A girl who donned a cloth like a male, or menstruated before she had taken to wearing a cloth, was also handed over to Aro traders. Her relatives and friends would wail on hearing the news, and four days after the girl's departure her mother would shave her head ; for an evil thing had fallen on her head and had to be removed.

Disputes about land were, and still are, a common source of fighting, which may continue for a considerable time before the matter is finally threshed out in an assembly of elders. In olden days land disputes between individuals of the same group were commonly referred to one of the companies of warriors or head-getters, to whom the winner of the case paid a fee. This privilege of the warriors was considered an inducement to young men to acquit themselves bravely in battle.

The decisions of judges were not always tamely accepted. An unsuccessful litigant might dispute the decision and call on the judges to swear finally on their *ofos* that their decision was in accordance with precedent ; or he might leave the assembly shouting out that he would not abide by the decision. In such a case the elders would proceed to his house on the following day, and on arrival would keep tapping the ground with their staves. This would usually cause the man serious alarm, and he would ask them to desist, promising to carry out their behests. But as the conduct of such a one had been an insult to Ale and the ancestors, he would be called on to perform a rite known as *Imfo jo Ale*, or " The appeasing of the Anger of Ale ".

Meetings held to decide disputes frequently ended in an uproar or a fight, and the dispute might drag on for years. In other cases the evidence might be so inconclusive that the elders would direct the disputants to take their case to some distant oracle, such as the so-called " Long Juju " at Aro Chuku. In such cases the loser of the suit might be sold into slavery by the priests of the oracle, or if allowed to return home would have to pay heavy damages to the winner.

LEGISLATION

Laws were passed in an assembly of all the elders of the town, and were sometimes given formal validity by a sacrifice to Ale or some other deity. Thus, if it became apparent that market brawls were becoming frequent and likely to lead to murder and intra-kindred or intra-quarter fighting, the elders of the town might meet together and decide that, if anyone in future engaged in fighting in the market, he should be heavily fined. Having arrived at this decision they would buy a goat and take it to the priest of Ale, who, holding the goat by a rope, would say, " Ale, the elders of the town have brought this goat to you in order to inform you of their wishes touching the market. They say that it is not their desire that fights should occur in the market, lest this should lead to loss of life. Ale, it is not your desire that men should kill one another, as we are your children. They declare that if anyone breaks this rule he shall pay a fine of fourteen currency rods, and they ask you, Ale, to enforce this law by dealing with anyone who refuses to pay this fine. Ale, when the elders call upon you (to assist them in dealing with a law-breaker) do you answer their call (by bringing misfortune upon him)." He would then turn to the elders and say, " Is not this your wish ? " They would all reply, " Ale, this is our wish." The priest would then kill the goat, and as he put the knife to the goat's throat would say, " Take the life of this goat and spare our lives." The flesh of the goat would be cooked and divided, and morsels of the heart, liver, and kidneys would be deposited by the priest on the cultus-symbol.

The elders would then go home, and each would inform the members of his kindred of the passing of the law. If anyone subsequently broke the law he would be arrested by young men and handed over to the head of his kindred, who would be instructed to collect the fine and bring it to the market on the following market-day. On that day the elders would walk round the market beating their matchets and saying, " Fellow-townsmen, come and take what is yours." The head of the culprit's kindred would then hand the fourteen rods to the senior elder, who would say, " Fellow-townsmen, you have seen that the fine has been paid." They would reply, " We have. Let it be handed over to the keeper of fines." The rods would then be handed to a man delegated by the elders to receive fines and hold them until they were required for some general sacrifice. The culprit would be escorted by the elders and Ale priests to the shrine of Ale. He would hand a pot of palm-wine to the priest and then squat down before the cultus-symbol. The priest would pour a little of the wine into a buffalo-horn and pass the horn round the culprit's head, saying, " Ale, I and the elders of the town have brought this man before you to tell you that he has paid his fine for ' breaking ' your market. He has brought this wine to appease your wrath. Pursue him not. A man's child may offend his father, but he is forgiven when he repents." He would then pour the libation, and the remainder of the wine would be drunk by all present, the culprit included.

The legal sanction was not always Ale. When a law was made the elders might call on the priest of any cult to bring some material object from the shrine. The priests and elders would then say, " We have made such and such a law. If anyone breaks this law may this spirit kill that person." The priest would then strike the ground with the object. If the law was broken the punishment might be left to the spirits. But the law-breaker would forestall punishment by going to the priest, who would perform sacrifice on the man's behalf, saying, " So-and-so admits that he has gone against you and he comes now to redeem himself."

In some cases rules would be made without any religious sanction. Thus the elders might announce in the market that wood was not to be cut in a certain area under the penalty of a fine of one goat. If a man was reported for breaking this rule, the elders would send young men [1] to catch a goat from his kindred or local group. If the accused redeemed the goat the money obtained was divided out among the elders and the matter ended. But if he did not redeem it, the goat would be sold or killed, and if the accused lost his case he would be called on to pay two goats to the owner of the goat. If the accused won his

---

[1] i.e. an age-grade or group of age-grades.

case, his accuser had to pay the cost of the two goats. If the accused was a woman, her fine was payable by her husband or son. But in some towns her fine was payable by her parents through the person who had acted as middleman when her marriage had been arranged.

Other instances of legislation were (*a*) that no one should visit a neighbouring town during an epidemic, and (*b*) that women should not visit the market of an unfriendly town. The elders might post young men on the roads to see that the rules were observed, and the young men were authorized to confiscate the property of anyone who attempted to break the rules. Rules might also be made forbidding the cutting of sticks (to be used for training yam tendrils) before a certain date.

In some cases an age-grade or group of age-grades might take the initiative in making rules. Thus, if it became apparent that stealing was on the increase, a group of age-grades might meet and decide that the penalties for stealing must be increased, and their decision would be announced to and accepted by the elders. Or an age-grade group might meet to fix the local price of palm-wine, or standardize the rate of the bride-price or rents chargeable for land.

This paper may be concluded by a few remarks on the changes in legal conceptions and practice which have occurred as a result of British Administration and direct contact with Western civilization.

When the British Government assumed the administration of the country, district Native Courts were established. This was a necessary step towards bringing the country under proper control and putting an end to practices which were considered inhuman or incompatible with modern civilization. The Native Courts were encouraged to administer native law as far as possible, but as most of the old legal sanctions now became illegal the native law administered in the Native Courts became a shadow of its former self. The elders, moreover, of the kindred, village, and village-area, were deprived of their judicial functions and in consequence lost much of their authority. The Native Courts in fact acted as a disruptive agent on the social structure.

Recently, however, the Government, after close examination of the ancient system, has sought to restore the power of the elders by encouraging them to settle minor cases locally, and by giving formal recognition to the village-area councils. There is a general policy of decentralization, and the old district courts are being replaced, wherever possible, by " clan " courts. The personnel of the Native Courts has been enlarged so as to include as far as possible all the most important elders of each local group. A complete return, however, to the old system, by which each village-area, or even village, recognized no higher authority than itself, would be impracticable, and distasteful also to the people, who demand a higher form of central authority than formerly existed, having acquired a wider sense of solidarity. Nor is there any general desire for a complete return to the old forms of legal procedure, even were this permissible. For the younger generation has lost faith in many of the old legal sanctions, as a result of the rapid spread of Christianity. It is said with truth that the younger people no longer obey their elders as before, and the blame for this is often laid at the door of the Government. But the real reasons are religious and economic. Children who have become Christians are often compelled to disagree with their pagan parents, and to refuse to take part in practices which they have been taught to regard as heathen. Many of them, moreover, leave their homes for long periods in search of work, and live lives of freedom from the numerous restraints imposed in their own homes. Such tend to degenerate in character, and when they return home they find it difficult to resume their former life, more especially as they have acquired new wants which cannot be satisfied in their parent village.

But the extraordinary natural adaptability of the Ibo should enable them to surmount most of the difficulties of the present period of transition.

THE ROMAN *PLEBS* AND THE CREATION OF ITS TRIBUNES

By J. L. Myres

Much of our information about early Rome comes to us through Greek writers ; and it seems certain that from the second century B.C. at least, Greek writers had found the history of Rome peculiarly interesting, because it seemed to reflect in many ways the earlier history of their own city-states ; Rome, indeed, appeared to them a " most Hellenic city ". It is likely that such resemblances were exaggerated, but not that they were wholly invented ; and we may still use Greek analogies helpfully in reconstructing early Roman history, provided that we realize what we are doing.

Rome seems to have had an abnormal structure and abnormal procedure from the first, but its abnormalities need not be exaggerated any more than its resemblances to Greek city-states. Its traditional origin in a fortuitous coalition of exiled and broken men has its parallels, in the *synoikismos* or " agreement to keep house together ", which had been giving birth to Greek city-states in the " migration period " of the Aegean world ; in its inclusion of heterogeneous elements of population ; in the strict monopoly of the privileges of citizenship by those co-partners ; and in the reserve-power to admit subsequently to co-partnership either individuals, or families, or even larger groups, who were deemed, for whatever reason, to be of the " right sort ", a public right as carefully guarded as was the complementary reserve-power to expel (or as Cicero frankly says, " exterminate " [1]) a co-partner who became a public nuisance. The foundation legend of Ephesus,[2] the incorporation of Minyan refugees at Sparta,[3] and the family histories of some great Athenians [4]— Pisistratus, Miltiades, Isagoras, Clisthenes and Pericles, and the Gephyraeans—are examples to compare with Rome's successive inclusion of whole groups of clans—after the conquest of Alba under the third king, Tullus Hostilius ; after that of Politoria under Ancus Martius ; again under the Elder Tarquin ; and

---

[1] *Exterminare* is a favourite word with Cicero, and probably his own translation of ἐξορίζειν, but *exterminus ito* was good Tertullian-slang for " Go to the
devil " (*Carm. de Sodom*, 3), and Columella (9, 15, 2) uses it for expelling drones
from a hive, a neat political metaphor.

[2] Stephannus Byz., s.v. *Βέννα*.

[3] Herodotus, iv, 145.

[4] Herodotus, v, 65, 66 ; vi, 35 ; vi, 131 ; v, 57.

228 J. L. MYRES

again in the incorporation of the Claudian house in the first year of the Republic.[1] Sometimes these new corporators were imposed on the Roman corporation by a king, or later by a *lectio* conducted by a *censor*; but the *patres* could co-opt the heads of acceptable clans.[2]

Conversely, side by side with Roman *gentes* promoted early to patrician status, and acquiring thereby eligibility for public office and representation in the Senate by their headman, there were other families who, like the *Octavia gens*, had " passed over to the *plebs* " after being patrician. How or why this happened is not clear. Diminution of numbers did not disqualify, though the *gens Fabia* lost 4,000 men at the Cremera battle and only one member survived. But loss of political influence and prestige probably did lead to effacement of some families as well as the promotion of others at the revisions of the Senate roll, which were fairly frequent. As a first element, then, in an imperfectly enfranchised populace within the citizen-community of Rome, we have original corporator-clans which had lapsed from " free and equal " enjoyment of the fullest rights of citizenship. Of the so-called " lesser clans " (*minores gentes*) we do not know enough to decide whether they mark a stepping-stone also of degradation, as they certainly did of promotion from plebeian to full patrician standing.

Further, from the details of the incorporation of Alba and Politoria in Rome, it appears that these other Latin cities had, like Rome, a fully qualified inner group of corporator-clans, and an outer mass of citizens ; and it was as natural *civitatem dare plebi*, assimilating the plebeians of Alba to the *plebs* of Rome, as it was *primores in patres legere* and thereby include the families that were patrician (such as the Tullii, Servilii, Quinctii) among the Roman *patres*.[3] And this occurred on a large scale : " the number of the citizens," Livy says,[4] " was doubled." In Greece such absorption of one city-state into another is very rare ; in early times there is the coalescence of pre-Dorian Corinth with the Dorian invaders camped on the Solygeian Ridge,[5] and there are the Hellenistic amalgamations of Medeon and Stiris and of Olymos and Labranda[6] ; but in none of these is there record of a difference of status within either of the populations concerned.

These early Latin incorporations are of interest because they show (i) that Rome's *plebs* was believed to be traceable back far into the regal period, (ii) that to have such a *plebs* was not

---

[1] Livy, i, 28–30 (Alba), 33 (Politoria), 34–5 (Tarquin and others), ii, 16 (*Claudia gens*).
[2] Livy, iv, 4.   [3] Livy, i, 28–30.   [4] Livy, i, 30.
[5] Thucydides, iv, 42.
[6] Lebas-Waddington, *Voyage archéologique* (1868–1877), inscriptions No. 335 (Medeon and Stiris) ; 336 (Olymos and Labranda.)

a peculiarity of Rome but common, if not normal, in Latium. How these observations are to be reconciled with the theory of a conquest of Rome by Sabine invaders, either before or after an Etruscan domination, it is for the supporters of those views to suggest. On the other hand, it would seem that those who have noted analogies between the Roman *plebs* and incompletely enfranchised elements in Greek city-states have been comparing, in Rome as in Greece, not an anomalous feature but one that was normal at a certain stage of civic development. Aristotle certainly refers to it as if it were common, and prescribes a remedy.[1] The close limitation of full citizenship to patrician family-groups was thus compatible, at Rome as in Greek city-states, with the co-existence of other sorts of residents who were free-men and participated in some of the functions of citizenship, including both privileges and duties. Who were these " Plebeians " ?

First, there was what Hebrew Law described in Israel as the "stranger within thy gates",[2] alien-born but accepted as an inalienable member of one of the privileged family-groups. For him that group, through its *pater-familias*, was responsible as for its own children ; on him could be conferred, for example, possession of a plot of the family land ; from him, in return, could be claimed personal services and military aid.[3] Some of these *clientes* had always been free-born ; but slaves who had received (or had bought) their freedom, and the descendants of such freedmen, remained in a relation to their former owner and his family that was practically identical with *clientela*. The *clientes* certainly were an important element in the Roman *plebs*. Mommsen thought they were co-extensive with it ; but there is an early occasion when a plebeian revolution miscarried because the patricians used their *clientes* as pickets and strike-breakers.[4] So, too, in 465 B.C. the *plebs* abstained from the consular elections—like the Venezelists in Greece in 1916—but the *patres* and their *clientes* attended, voted, and carried their candidates.

A great Roman family had thus a large body of retainers at its disposal, whose exclusion from the public rights of citizenship was in great measure compensated by the protection of their *patronus*. If a client of the Claudii or the Cornelii was in trouble with a Roman magistrate, it was not to any plebeian

---

[1] Aristotle, *Politics*, iii, 2, 1275b.

[2] Exodus, xx, 10 ; Deuteronomy, i, 16, and often ; for their legal equalit Leviticus, xvi, 29 : " One law shall be to him that is homeborn and to the stranger," cf. xxiv, 22.

[3] Authorities in Mommsen, *Staatsrecht*, iii, 54 ; von Premerstein in Pauly-Wissowa, *Realencycl.*, iv, 23 ff ; s.v. *clientela*.

[4] Livy, ii, 35, *absterrendo singulos a coitionibus conciliisque*. Cicero (*de Republica*, ii, 9, 16) certainly thought that every original *plebeius* had been assigned by the "founder" of Rome to some *gens* as one of its *clientes* ; and Dionysius (ii, 9) says (of later times, presumably) that each *cliens* had to choose his *patronus*.

tribune that he applied for *auxilium*, any more than a vassal
of the " king-maker " Earl of Warwick sought help from any
bishop or knight of the shire.

Secondly, there were free residents—at first of more transitory
habit—citizens of some other state whose business, or exiled
leisure, had brought them to Rome and kept them there as
" fellow-inhabitants " with the corporator clans—*paroikoi* and
metoikoi as they were commonly called in Greece—on customary
terms of poll-tax, house-tax, market-tax, and the like. In Rome,
moreover, from very early times, citizens of any other town of
the Latin League had treaty right (*ius exulandi*) to migrate
permanently to Rome, and these " outlanders " had all the
" private rights " of citizenship, such as intermarriage, land-
ownership, access to the markets and courts of law, which were
not reserved to members of patrician corporator-clans.   There
was probably nothing to prevent a Latin (or any other) " out-
lander " from being accepted as a client of a patrician family,
but there were many residents of Rome who had not fared so,
but formed citizen-families of their own, *plebeiae gentes*, only
differing from *patriciae gentes* in the lack of certain " public
rights " of citizenship—access to the old meeting of the corporator-
clans (*comitia curiata*), eligibility for public office, and (for what
it was worth) the right to marry into any of the families so
privileged, with the mystical rite prescribed for such unions.

Whether the members of plebeian *gentes* were admitted to
the ancient *comitia curiata* is not quite certain, nor even whether
clientes attended and voted as members of the *gens* to which
they belonged. But this uncertainty matters less, because there
is no doubt that by the Servian Reforms all plebeians of full
age were enrolled in the new military companies (*centuriae*)
and attended and voted in the *comitia centuriata*.[1] For all *clientes*
were enrolled, individually and independent of the patrician
members of the same *gens*, in that *centuria* to which they were
assigned by their wealth, not by their birth.   From this point
onwards, at all events, all plebeians, whatever their origin, were
citizens of Rome, in respect of membership of the assembly
that elected magistrates, adopted laws, and was the court of
appeal against capital sentences ; and all were alike liable to
military service, except those *capite censi* who were disqualified
by sheer poverty (not by alien birth) from " bearing arms "
at all.

Thirdly, it has been suggested, in modern times, that the
Roman state came into being by an act of conquest which
superimposed the regime of a band of Sabellian invaders on the
survivors of the previous occupants of this part of Latium. That
the Romans should have been called *Romani*, with termination

[1] Livy, i, 43.

-*ni*, like the *Sabini, Frentani, Piceni*, and other highlanders, whereas their language—the *lingua Latina*—belongs to the group of dialects spoken by tribes whose names end in -*ci*, is certainly an anomaly. But there is too good evidence for repeated admissions of previously unprivileged families into the governing class, both severally and in large groups, for this consideration to have much weight in arguments about the relation between Plebeians and Patricians in later regal or early republican times. And in the absence of literary or archæological evidence for such a conquest as is inferred from anomalies of language, it is for the philologists to decide whether this conquest occurred before the foundation of Rome as a community of corporator-families, or during the early regal period, or under the Etruscan domination, or after the expulsion of the Tarquin dynasty. They may date their own invention as they please. There were Sabine *gentes* in Rome, from the Sabellian-speaking highland, and there were people who buried their dead, as well as more numerous people who burned them ; but they shared the same cemetery, as Sabine and Latin marketed and talked politics in the same *forum Romanum* ; and it is probably not an accident that the first four kings are alternately Latin and Sabine. If, as some suppose, the burials are later than the burnings, they are nevertheless, on the same authority, themselves older than the traditional date for Rome's foundation.[1]

Fourthly, however, there is another, and historically dateable, crisis in the early history of Rome, which provided a quite different occasion for great increase in the less-privileged population. Whereas the first four kings in the traditional history are alternately Latin and Sabine, the fifth and the seventh are Etruscans, and the sixth, Servius Tullius, though a Latin himself, rose to power at the court of the Elder Tarquin. That he belonged to a plebeian *gens* is the less important, because in this he had been anticipated by the third and fourth kings, Hostilius and Marcius.

This Etruscan domination has been generally recognized as an incident in that southward expansion which culminated between the Etruscan land-attack on Cumae in Campania in 524 B.C., and the Etruscan naval defeat off the same city in 474 B.C. That the expulsion of the second Tarquin was effected by a coalition of the Latin and Sabine aristocracies is also probable ; thenceforth there were to be two consuls, and other dual magistracies are common afterwards.

There is, however, another aspect to the later monarchy. It was the usurpation of power by a foreign adventurer, who

[1] Stuart Jones, *Cambridge Ancient History* (1928), vii, 354–6, thinks that the burials succeed the burnings : Randall-MacIver, *Villanovans and Etruscans* (1924), 74–8, assigns them to the same continuous period (tenth to seventh centuries).

boasted of his transference of domicile and claimed popular support on that ground.[1] The whole story is that of one of those popular leaders who was familiarly known as *tyrannoi* in Greek city-states at this period, and it has been enriched from the Greek stock of tyrant-anecdotes. But, however enhanced, this Roman tyranny seems to be an historic fact ; and we, too, may safely supplement and interpret from the better-known tyrannies of Greece. The public works, the general prosperity and expansion of Rome, no less than the democratic reforms, attributed to the Tarquin dynasty, presume a great increase in the number of resident aliens ; and though no doubt some of these came, or remained, as *clientes* of Latin or Sabine families, most of them were attracted by the tyranny itself. They worked for the tyrant, and enjoyed his " patronage ", legal as well as economic.

An important political act of the last king of Rome is described by Dionysius as a treaty of equal citizenship between Rome and its neighbour, Gabii ; the original document was preserved till Dionysius' time. There need be no doubt of the fact ; especially as the privilege it created does not go far beyond the right to exchange one allegiance for another, which every Latin had under the terms of the League's treaty with Rome. But if a citizen of Gabii became a citizen of Rome when he entered the gates of the city, or presented himself for registration of domicile, what was his position in the event of any disturbance in the relations between Rome and Gabii during his residence in Rome, or in the event of his ceasing (by civil dissension or otherwise) to enjoy the dormant citizenship of Gabii which had been the ground of his acceptance in Rome ? The case need not have been common ; but it adds one more to the sources of a plebeian populace in a city with such varied foreign connections as are demonstrable for Rome. Moreover, it adds force to the general statement which Dionysius puts into the mouth of L. Junius Brutus at the Great Secession, that the policy of the last three kings had been democratic.[2]

While a general distinction is rightly drawn between the doings of the last three kings and those of the first four, those earlier kings had in some ways anticipated the later. Hostilius and Marcius were plebeians, like Servius Tullius ; Numa Pompilius was a Sabine immigrant, as the Elder Tarquin was an Etruscan. All alike—even the peaceable Numa—were war-lords ; and the mode of their appointment, or legitimation, by the assembly of heads of clans was conserved in the ritual of creating a *dictator* under the Republic. Archæological and traditional data, and even the discrepant traditions, are reconciled customarily by supposing that the traditional " Foundation of Rome " by Romulus in 753 B.C. represents some fresh fact in

[1] Livy, i, 34–5.   [2] Dionysius, vi, 73.

the far longer history of the Latin peoples. What if (comparing the political development of Rome with that of Greek city-states) the establishment of the kingship and the flocking of outcast men on to the Palatine, should be found to correspond with a Greek tyranny, and the whole duration of the monarchy to be an *interregnum* in a close oligarchy of corporator-clans, only terminated by a rally of the *patres*, sinking hereditary differences to expel the king ...d re-establish a government as nearly normal as the *damnosa hereditas* of a kingless populace permitted ? [1]

Having examined elsewhere [2] the contemporary experience of Athens under the tyranny of Pisistratus, I refer to this parallel incident here, only to compare in each instance the political effects of the expulsion of the tyrant. For in Athens, as in Rome, the political extinction of a patron did not involve the annihilation of his clients. But what was now their political status ? At Athens, as in Rome, the tyrant regime had lasted in to the second generation. Its adherents had acquired vested interests that could not be denied to its victims. Moreover, as we have seen, the Servian reforms had imposed on all registered residents, except the very poor, the duty of military service and the liability to be taxed, and had conceded the right to vote in elections and public business—however this may have been restricted in practice by centuriate procedure. These ex-clients of the Tarquin house were indisputably citizens of Rome ; but being without patron, they were now without remedy on the numerous occasions for oppression which the laws of debt and of military service offered. They were *plebeii* simply, no longer *clientes* of anyone.[3]

In Athens, if we may trust the brief and graphic story of Herodotus,[4] two remedies were tried in succession : Cleisthenes " first attached to his own company " the populace whose grievances he would remedy ; only " later " did he proceed to a complete regrouping of the citizen-body on the sole qualification of residence and loyal goodwill. Thenceforward it was a breach of good manners to call attention to a man's tribal antecedents : in the assembly and in the courts all were alike Athena's people. What kind of " company " [5] it was, to which Cleisthenes had first attempted to " attach the populace ", Herodotus does not say ;

---

[1] Professor H. J. Rose has suggested to me that the *flamen* in Rome may have been a pre-regal priest-king.
[2] *Mélanges Glotz* (Paris, 1932), ii, 657–666, " Cleisthenes in Herodotus."
[3] Stuart Jones, *Cambridge Ancient History*, vii, 421, assumes that whenever a patrician *gens* died out, its *clientes* were simply merged in the patronless *plebs*.
[4] Herodotus, v, 66–9 ; Aristotle, *Politics*, iii, 2–3, 1275b; *Constitution of Athens*, 20–22 and 41.
[5] The word translated " company " (ἑταιρεία) was originally quite colourless, though at the end of the fifth century it acquired the special meaning of a political " cell " for subversive talk and action. Thucydides, iii, 82, cf. viii, 65 (ἑταῖροι " comrades " in the same political sense).

but it was an obvious and tempting solution of the difficulty
for the great Alcmaeonid house, to which Cleisthenes belonged,
to offer its " patronage " to the patronless clients of the banished
Pisistratidae, in addition to its own numerous " company "
of adherents ; and, indeed, Cleisthenes himself is described as
having been at a certain point " leader and patron "[1] of the
populace. This device, however, obviously only replaced
Pisistratid tyranny by Alcmaeonid, and there was a fierce party-
struggle between the Alcmaeonid house, so reinforced, and its
political rivals. But, on second thoughts, good sense—and (may
we add) the jealousy between the great Athenian houses—
rejected that " first " remedy, and it was the Alcmaeonid leader
himself who proposed an alternative. If the patronless ones
were not to be clients of the Alcmaeonid house, what need had
they of a patron at all ? On his own merits, let every " stranger
within the gates ", like every citizen of Athens, enjoy what
Athenian citizenship had to offer. And to ensure equality of
status, as well as of privilege, the older body-politic and its
assembly, which had hitherto been constituted by traditional
groups of corporator-clans, was henceforth to include all registered
residents in the existing " townships " (demes) of Attica,
irrespective of family ties or ancient Attic descent. It is especially
noted,[2] though the precise connection between the words is not
clear, that this change enfranchised aliens who had been " slaves "
and " metics ", and in either event not of Attic origin.

Turn now to the plebeians of Rome. Here the trouble was
that, after the expulsion of the Tarquins, there was a mob of
nominal citizens whose rights were nugatory because there was
no one interested to enforce them, not against the law but against
fellow-citizens, either in administrative office or before a court
of law. That it was this lack of patron that was the practical
disability is clear from two incidents. (1) Even after the Great
Secession, in the days of Coriolanus, it was possible to split the
mass of the *plebs*, and to use the clients as pickets and strike-
breakers,[3] " scaring individuals away from meetings and con-
ferences "; and (2) even before the Secession, when the measure
of appeasement proposed by the dictator Servilius was rejected,
he warned the Senate that " the day was near when they would
long that the Roman *plebs* had patrons like himself ". This
suggests that the question had already been asked, how the
plebeians might be provided with patrons, and that Valerius
had in some sense constituted himself their patron. We have,
however, to remember that the word *patronus* was commonly

[1] The word προστάτης applied to Cleisthenes in Aristotle, *Constitution of Athens*, 20, 4, is regularly used later to translate the Latin *patronus*.
[2] Aristotle, *Politics*, iii, 2, 1275b, 37.
[3] Livy, ii, 35, see n. 4, p. 229 above.

used in Latin to translate the Greek word *prostatês* (προστάτης), and that *prostatês* may mean either the legal *patronus* or, more generally, any sort of champion.[1] But this in turn makes it all the more likely that Roman historians, compiling from Greek writers, may have missed the more specific force of *prostatês*, and deprived us of passages in which it was *patronage* not political leadership that was meant. Clearly it was as inadmissible in Rome that any one great house, the Claudii or the Valerii, should annex to itself all patronless clients in Rome, as it was in Athens that the Alcmaeonid house should " attach to its own company " the populace left patronless by the Pisistratidae. But what was the alternative ? Just this : an agreement or contract—a *lex* in its primitive meaning, a binding bargain—between the Patrician corporator-clans and the patronless *plebs*, that the *plebs* should itself create unto itself official patrons, qualified to render the same effective " help " as the head of any great house in Rome habitually rendered to his own clients ; literally to " intervene " (*intercedere*) between any plebian and any fellow-citizen or magistrate intent on impeding his personal freedom ; to rally the rest of his plebeian " clients ", in case of need, to give effect to his " intervention " ; and literally to keep " open house ", like a great Roman noble, to shelter those who ran to him for protection. The fictitious " patron " was to be as literally " inviolable " in the streets of Rome as the head of the Claudian or the Valerian house was inviolable in the majesty of his person and position ; he was literally to " take his seat " in the Senate, though not a member of it—and though he had to bring his own wooden stool to sit on—and, when there, he was to be competent to dissent from any decision of Consul or Senate ; all men knowing that without his concurrence such decision found no observance among his " company ", the hitherto patronless men, an over-whelming majority.

The precise conditions, on which the Great Secession was ended, are not preserved. We can only infer them from later descriptions of their effect :—

(1) Plebeians were to have functionaries of their own choosing ; yet these were never " magistrates of the Roman People " and are always carefully distinguished from the regular officers of state ; they had no *imperium*, and consequently no executive or judicial function, nor could they call a deliberative assembly. At most they could gather and address a crowd, and it was only gradually that their *concio* became respected as a *concilium plebis*.

(2) No member of the Senate, nor any citizen qualified to be admitted to it, should hold this function ; for that, in Athenian phrase, would be " attaching the populace to his own company":

[1] Thucydides, iii, 72, 82 ; iv, 66, applies προστάτης τοῦ δήμου to the political leader of the democratic party.

so at the end of his year his populace of clients found another *patronus*. The end, indeed, of the whole bargain was near, when it was conceived possible that a protector of the *plebs* should be re-elected ; it meant a return to tyranny.

(3) The specific function of the new *patronus* was " to bring help against the consuls ", to prevent administrative maltreatment of a patronless individual by violence or imprisonment—in cases, that is, where law is inoperative because it cannot act in time ; or act at all, to restrain its own executive.

(4) At first, apparently, these new functionaries were two for the same reason that there were two consuls ; but they were given two assessors, probably to confront the two *quaestores* who helped the consuls in domestic and especially in financial administration ; and it was probably from these that the patronless man suffered worst, especially if he were of foreign origin. The Greek equivalent of *aedilis*, too, is eloquent from the point of view of the " under dog": to the corporator-clans he was "commissioner of buildings and grounds", the dispenser of contracts and therefore of employment; to the Greekling in the forum or on the quay he was *agoranómos* (ἀγορανόμος), "clerk of the market", and looked after garbage and short-weight.

(5) Dionysius adds that the new functionaries were appointed by the *comitia curiata*, to which it may be doubted whether all or any plebeians were admitted. It is clear, therefore, that in some sense they were made as if they had been members of a *curia*. Is it too much to suggest that by a legal fiction they were created " heads of houses "—of an anonymous *curia* or *gens* ; as the dean of *non*-collegiate students ranked with the deans of colleges in the " Ancient House " at Oxford ? But if, as seems likely, the *curiae* were themselves originally local groupings of the corporator-*gentes*, which determined the parade-state of the *comitia curiata*, it may be that the plebeians' votes in these elections also were taken *curiatim*.[1]

(6) The new plebeian functionaries were as naturally nicknamed *tribuni*, as the chief magistrates whom they were to confront came to be called *consules*. The two original *praetores* or " warlords " were called *consules* because they sat and acted together. The plebeian *patroni* came to be known as *tribuni*—another adjectival form—because each kept open-door in his own " ward " (*tribus*) of the city, and among his own " wardsmen " (*tribules*). That the local " tribes " were originally meant, cannot be proved, but does not affect the fact that the *tribuni* were distributed where they would best " intervene " and " bring aid ". There were, however, already hereditary " tribes " in Rome as well as residential and territorial, and Varro[2] thought that the primitive

[1] J. S. Reid, *Encyclopædia Britannica*, s.v. " Tribune. "
[2] Varro, *De lingua latina*, iv.

clan-groups—Ramnes, Tities, and Luceres—were meant ; but he had apparently found analogy (which may be a false analogy) in those *tribuni militum* who were leaders of detachments in the primitive tribal army. The fact that the original two *tribuni plebis* forthwith co-opted three does not help us much. It dissociates them from the military tribunes, who were nine, but it does not cohere either with the threefold clan-grouping nor with the fourfold urban districts, nor with any known phase of the multiplication of tribal districts outside the city. Nor is there obvious reason to connect the *tribuni plebis* with the five classes—which are never called *tribus*—of the Servian military and economic grouping. Perhaps the anomalous total simply resulted, as Livy says, from an original two, empowered to add to their number, and actually adding three.[1] But in 456 B.C. there were already ten, two from each of the five Servian classes.[2]

The subsequent fortunes of the *plebs* and the *tribuni* are part of the political history of Rome, and do not concern us now. What has been attempted here is to discover the reason why the problems of the less privileged citizens became urgent at a particular moment, as they did, and why a unique remedy was adopted for the grievances of clients and patronless plebeians alike. For as Dionysius says,[3] what the plebeians demanded was " not only relief from their debts, but they asked also for some form of help perhaps "[4]—(he is translating the *auxilium* which a patron was legally bound to afford to his client)—" whereby for time to come they shall abide undisturbed "—(literally, " not tripped up " by unpredictable pitfalls and snags)—" for," he adds, " ever since the power [5] of the dictator [6] came along, the observance which was the warden of freedom had been undone," referring to the right of appeal on a capital charge.

(7) The peculiar provision, that the person of a tribune was to be inviolable, needs a word of explanation. When Fustel de Coulanges [7] long ago described the tribune as a kind of peripatetic altar, he was more nearly right than later scholars have been ready to admit. To say, in Roman phrase, that the tribunes were " sacrosanct " does not describe more than the

---

[1] Livy, ii, 33 ; Dionysius, vi, 89, 1.
[2] Livy, iii, 30. [3] Dionysius, vi, 58, 1.
[4] Dionysius' word βοήθεια literally means reinforcements *called up*. By Aeschylus, *Supplices*, 730, *Agamemnon*, 1349, βοή, the " cry " for help itself, is used for assistance rendered in battle. Xenophon, *Hellenica*, vii, 1, 20, uses βοήθεια for " auxiliary " troops.
[5] Dionysius' word ἀρχή (literally "initiative "—" that which makes to begin ") is his translation of *imperium*, that untranslatable word for the " competence " of any public officer within the terms of his commission (*provincia*). I have discussed the Greek notion of ἀρχή in *The Political Ideas of the Greeks* (1927), pp. 80–93.
[6] Compare Cicero, *de Republica*, ii, 34, *contra consulum imperium creatos :* but the dictator's *imperium* was *infinitum*.
[7] Fustel de Coulanges, *La Cité antique*.

procedure of investing them with an immunity guaranteed by
a fearsome penalty ; for not only was the assailant of a tribune
accursed, but every member of the *plebs* was himself under a vow
to kill such assailant.

Dionysius' Greek interpretation puts the matter in another
aspect. The office is to be ἱερὰν καὶ ἄσυλον,—*holy* in the sense
that it is filled with a power or presence ; a sanctuary or *asylum*
like a Hebrew " city of refuge ", in the sense that it communi-
cates this quality or potential to any thing or person that comes
into contact with it. Dionysius goes on to say that consequently
the very person of a tribune was holy (ἱερόν as above), and also
παναγῆ "all-hallowed", in the sense that they were charged to
the full with an *agos* ; and an *agos* in Greek is at the same time
a *pollution* which infects the person who touches what is forbidden, or otherwise breaks any kind of *taboo*—well, the word is
out ! The tribune, during his year of office, was *taboo* ; no need
for Dionysius to explain what that meant ; no need, either, for
us to explain why it was the bounden duty of every party to
the institution of such a *taboo* to obliterate the breaker of it ;
for they themselves, through his infringement, had incurred
pollution inexpiable otherwise, and lay " under a curse ", like
the fanatical Jews " until they had slain Paul ".[1]

The words of Dionysius about the person of a tribune are
closely parallel to what he says about the standards of the
Roman legions, which we know to have been images of certain
animals—eagle, wolf, boar, and the like—the largest and fiercest
animals of primeval Italy. To explain why the legionary must
defend his standard to the death, he calls them τιμιώτατα
" most venerable," and I have suggested elsewhere [2] that τιμή
stands to ἀρχή as, for example, νέμεσις stands to αἰδώς ; ἀρχή
is " initiative ", the force or quality that confers activity on
others, a *primum mobile*, like Polynesian *mana* : τιμή is the
recognition by others of the presence of such initiative ἀρχή in
any person or thing. A chief has τιμή (honour) and gold has
τιμή (value) because they get things done, as *orenda* does among
the Iroquois. But about the Roman standards Dionysius is
more explicit still, for (he goes on) " they are regarded as dwelling-
places of the gods, and holy ".[3] To mishandle a standard is
to violate an ἄσυλον, a place that may not be violated ;
so the Roman standards went into battle like the "Ark of God"
against the Philistines[4] or as the " sons of Æacus " were
brought from Ægina to help the Thebans.[5] They brought

[1] Acts, xxiii, 12, ἀνεθεμάτισαν ἑαυτούς ; " made themselves *taboo* ".
[2] *The Political Idea of the Greeks* (1927), pp. 84, 86.
[3] Dionysius, vi.   [4] I Samuel, iv, 3 ; vi, 21 ; II, vi, 6–12.
[5] Herodotus, v, 80, cf. the bones of Orestes (i, 67–8), and of Theseus (Plutarch,
Cimon, 8 ; *Theseus*, 36), ὡς καὶ τοῦ Θησέως προστατικοῦ τινος καὶ βοηθητικοῦ ;
" a kind of *patronus* and one to bring *auxilium* ".

the Divine Power itself, or the very person of the hero, into the fighting line.

All this helps us to see why plebeian officers, chosen (so our authorities agree) by, for, and from among plebeians, are nevertheless described as having been appointed by the *comitia curiata*, the " ancient house " of assembly " whither the tribes go up " in their groups of clans. For it was from the same " ancient house " that the kings, after election by the *patres*, had been endowed by a separate vote of the people, acting *curiatim*, with that *imperium* which gave their word the force of initiative authority : and from the same " ancient house ", thereafter, consuls elected in the *comitia centuriata* received the same *imperium* as the king had held, without which, strictly, they too could not function. I have given reasons (in the book already noted) for regarding this conferring of *imperium* as a formality which, whatever its origin, had a ritual and (in the general sense) magical significance. Like the golden crown, the holy oil, and other rites of investiture observed among many peoples, it conferred, as Mr. Hocart has shown in his book on *Kingship*, that " divinity that doth hedge a king ". In Rome it could only be conferred by an assemblage of the whole people in their *curiae*, which Dionysius ingeniously describes as *phratries*[1] ; and we remember that in early Athens it had been the *phratry* which had, for example, ultimate responsibility for avenging the killing of one of its members. For the *phratry* was the mystical corporation by membership of which a man became an effective citizen of the state. So, too, in Rome, it was in the assembly of the *curiae* that the essential being of the state was realized, and efficient for the " creation "—as men truly said—of its magistrates. Whether it was the *imperium* of a consul then, or the *sacrosanctitas* of a tribune, it was in the *comitia curiata* that it would be rightly conferred.[2]

Thus the remedy devised for the grievances of the plebeians was not only a quite unusual achievement of political invention, but, like many great inventions, it made use of the simplest, most obvious, and (above all) the most indisputable means, from a category of avoidances such as every Roman, patrician, and plebeian alike, was observing every hour of the day.

[1] Dionysius, vi, 89, 1, calls the *curiae* φράτραι, and the votes were taken *ex generibus hominum*.

[2] It was only in 472 B.C. that the election of *tribuni plebis* was transferred to the *comitia tributa*. As there is no mention afterwards of a *lex curiata* to confer sacrosanctity on tribunes, as it conferred *imperium* on consuls, it looks as if the election of tribunes had by this time been wholly secularized. Yet their sacrosanctity remained.

ANTHROPOLOGICAL APPROACH TO ETHNOGENICS [1]

A New Perspective

By GEORGE PITT-RIVERS

Within the ambit of anthropological discussion the scope and aim of an Applied Anthropology has been the last to receive any general attention. While the science itself was in a formative stage of development, it could hardly have anticipated the possibilities or range of its applications. As in every other science, so in Anthropology, it is safe to say that in the very interest that drove men to its systematized study was implicit the need for it in the everyday business of living.

Few anthropologists have not at times envisaged the development of the applications of their special study. It has, however, been left to the most recent times for any one worker to attempt to formulate an application of the synthesized branches of the whole study and history of Man; although previous attempts have rather concentrated on the applications of that body of knowledge dealing with the laws of heredity and the science of genetics under the name of Eugenics.

Apart from this aspect, confined principally to the physical and biological side of the study of Man, there has recently come into prominence a desire to apply, on the cultural or psychological side, the knowledge gained of the customs and social organization of so-called primitive peoples in the administration and control of subject races under the tutelage of European Empires.

Few anthropologists have shown so wide an appreciation of the possibilities of development in these aspects of the problem as has Dr. C. G. Seligman, who has reviewed under these two headings the various cultural and physical problems that are most prominent.[2]

Perhaps the first investigator to apply himself systematically to the problem of an applied anthropology with particular reference to the depopulation of primitive peoples brought into contact with an alien civilized culture was the late W. H. R. Rivers. In his work the trained psychologist and the

[1] Revised and amplified from a paper read before the Anthropology Section of the British Association, London, 1931, and published in *Human Biology*, vol. 4, May, 1932.
[2] See article, "Anthropology, Applied," by C. G. Seligman, in the *Encyclopædia Britannica*, fourteenth edition.

specialized anthropologist gives due weight to the inter-dependence of psychological and physical data, often illuminated with demographic and statistical verifications.[1]

In his 1931 Presidential Address to the Royal Anthropological Institute on " Anthropology, Pure and Applied ", Professor Myres discussed in retrospect and prospect the proper functions and legitimate aims of the Institute. Previously he has touched on the place of anthropological studies among other branches of learning, and on the claims made from time to time that anthropological research has positive contributions to make to national well-being.

If I encroach again from a somewhat different angle on ground well worn, my excuse must be that anthropological themes seem to lose their newness as little as Anthropology itself appears capable of losing the title, which it has undisputedly held for at least sixty years, of being a new science. In this year, 1931, Dr. Myres admits that " old prejudices against a new subject like Anthropology die hard . . . and systematic provision for anthropological studies, like Anthropology itself, which is still a very young science, is in its infancy ".

Should we suspect that an infant which remains for sixty years in its early infancy is arrested in its development ? And if it is arrested should we suspect lack of nourishment ?

I do not wish to anticipate the answer, but the question remains implicit in what I have to say. Speaking in 1908, on " The Scope of Social Anthropology ", Sir James Frazer called his subject " comparatively new and its limits still somewhat vague ". In the intervening twenty-six years between then and now Social Anthropology has claimed increasing, though still very inadequate, attention in our Universities, by the establishment of Anthropological Departments in some of our Dominions and Colonial Dependencies, and by the increasing volume of learned works in many departments of the subject.

If I venture to echo that comment of our great pioneer folk-lorist and social anthropologist again to-day, it is not because I ignore all the work that has been done. Yet I am tempted to repeat the excuse, or accusation, of 1908 and 1931 with even greater emphasis : the subject is still com-paratively new and its limits and scope perhaps vaguer than ever before.

APPLIED ANTHROPOLOGY

The aim of Social Anthropology remains, consistent with the aim of every other science, to discover the general laws to which particular facts conform and by which alone they can properly

[1] Cf. particularly *The Todas*, 1906, and *Essays on the Depopulation of Melanesia*, 1922.

be explained. In short, it aims at explaining what has happened and what is happening in the regulation of human history, irrespective of time or place. Consequently it must be prepared to be some guide as to how we may best conform to what may happen in the future—or our profession may be regarded as an amiable diversion of no great importance in the affairs of everyday life.

May I then not claim that the scope of Social Anthropology can no longer be restricted as it was by Frazer, and is still, I think, by Dr. Myres, to the rudimentary phases of human society ? That in spite of the limitations the former sets to the boundaries of his special studies, we can no longer avoid concern with the practical application of its results ?

The pursuit of our scientific researches into Man's social history involves a diagnosis, which leads to a demand for a prognosis ; hence to an Applied Science. Applied Anthropology has come into being ; not even the clumsy and antiquated terminology by which Social Anthropology is supposed to be distinguished from Sociology can disguise that fact. Some of our French anthropological colleagues at any rate do not attempt the distinction, and the school of Emile Durkheim and Marcel Mauss call themselves sociologists or anthropologists indifferently ; neither do they restrict themselves to the rudimentary phases of human society.

If Anthropology is still a comparatively new science, and we seem to infer it chiefly by the relatively slight influence that that discipline appears to exercise upon human affairs, and the very slow growth of any discernible influence it exerts upon human opinion, it is remarkable that it should have remained in its infancy for such a very long period. How is it that we are still discussing at its cradle, in much the same terms, such an early post-natal subject as its future career and development—its scope and methodology ?

I may go back, not twenty-six years, but more than twice that time, sixty-four years, and invite your attention to the discussion of the same subject by a former President of the Anthropological Institute. It is, I think, not ancestral reverence which makes me think my grandfather's Presidential Address in 1870 still curiously relevant.[1] It is perhaps a pity that it is so. The terminology that had come to be employed in the classification of our subjects he found at least as unsatisfactory as I venture to think it is to-day.

The term Anthropology, which he wished to reserve as the most embracing term to cover all Human Biology and Sociology

[1] Address to the Anthropological Institute of Great Britain and Ireland, on 25th January, 1876, by Lieut.-General A. Lane Fox Pitt-Rivers, President of the Institute.

with their respective subdivisions, together corresponding to
Constitution and Culture, was then customarily divided into the
four unsatisfactory departments of Ethnology, Archæology,
Anthropology proper, and general works relating to Ethnological
subjects.

If we are, after this very long interval, still willing to encumber
ourselves with such a classification, the empirical, inductive,
and the applied and dependent branches of our sciences will
become increasingly divorced, and to some extent sterilized and
narrowed in outlook.   Some were included as our proper study :
Anthropology proper.   Others, as essential to the proper study
of Man, were driven to seek the shelter of other labels and different
societies :   and   were   presumably   exiled   as   Anthropology
" improper ".

I wish, here, to do no more than suggest that the primary
classification of Anthropological *subjects*, instead of the *classification by classes and methods of workers*, may have been as injurious
to Anthropology as the polygenetic search for a fixed number of
primary human races.   Were it not for this, would not Eugenics,
Genetics, Demography, and the study of Populations, and of
Psychology,   have   their   recognized   places   as   branches   of
Anthropology ?

It is at least interesting to note that amongst the papers read
before the Anthropological Institute in 1875 we find four papers
by Francis Galton dealing with subjects now classified under
Genetics or Eugenics.   They include :   A History of Twins ;
Heredity in Twins ;   The Height and Weight of Boys in Town
and Country Schools.   The same President in his summary
observes :   " It is to be hoped we shall not have to wait until
the principle of heredity has asserted itself in Mr. Galton's
offspring before we have other contributors to this important
branch of our studies."   In addition we also find a paper on
Comparative Psychology by Herbert Spencer, and a study of
Longevity by Sir Duncan Gibb.   The infant science had plenty
of fresh nourishment in those days.

All science has its birth in Man's desire to control his
environment or to adapt his needs to its forces by seeking to
understand them.   The early Polynesian navigators, sailing
in their frail canoes across the Pacific, owed their lives to the
stars and became astronomers, and they became anatomists
in the school of anthropophagy because they found human
flesh sweet to eat.

No science can long retain the interest or spur the labours
of its devotees, let alone of its public, unless it can " deliver the
goods".   It must continually supply answers to the ceaseless
triple question whereby Man seeks illumination along the path
of survival :   " What is happening ;   why is it happening ;   then

what should we do ? " For the answers that science may give range from replies to the first question to the last, and it is the last question which prompts the inquiries which furnish an answer to the first. By the time we begin to furnish answers to the last question, " What should we do ? ", we have formulated an Applied Science. A clear vision of its applications is the best discipline in the methodology of a science. Before we can observe well, we must know what to look for and why we are looking.

On these grounds, I venture to think, Francis Galton has a foremost place amongst the greatest methodologists of his age, and a place that no mere empiricist can aspire to share. For this reason, too, we must place the science he named Eugenics first in the list of Applied Anthropologies. But the scope of Eugenics is far wider than that usually accorded to it : this is not surprising since the applications of Anthropology have so very recently begun to receive general attention.

It is curious to reflect that in respect of time far less methodical study has been applied to gaining a knowledge of the functioning, origin, and nature of human institutions, of the decay and survival of races, or of the laws governing the genetical transmission of human qualities and defects than, for instance, has been applied to the study of zoology and its practical applications in the breeding of animals and in farming, and still less to making that knowledge widely known.

CONSTITUTION AND CULTURE

The problems of Eugenics are co-extensive with the problems of Anthropology. As soon as we begin to diagnose the factors controlling the changes, increases, declines and substitution of types in the populations and races of the world, we find that Constitution and Culture are inextricably mixed. For Evolution is a process of adaptation, physical, mental, and cultural, to environmental conditions.

The progress of Anthropology must therefore increasingly depend upon the re-synthesis of all its dependent branches, biological and cultural, that together mark the changes, evolutionary and adaptive, which describe Man, singly and in his social setting. The science embraces the Animal, Man, and his environment in human populations and the link between the two, for his surroundings are continually provoking from him new reactions and fresh adaptations. The reactions are cultural, but the changes in time from generation to generation are constitutional and may be measured in the different rates of achievement in adaptation : rates of the elimination and of the survival of types. Here Anthropology must seek its verifications

in the demographic study of populations.[1]   But, as Dr. Georg
Thilenius puts it, Man, the subject of active and passive
adaptation to fresh surroundings, is further determined by his
hereditary characteristics, and is paratypically influenced by
his environment. Thus both culture and heredity determine
his Constitution : both are factors in mutation and selection.

Somatic, cultural, and psychic phenomena are thus inter-
dependently linked in the study of the time changes in Man.
From this point of view arises the newer conception of the study
of race, and race changes, or, in the phrase of Sir Arthur Keith,
of " race formation ".   Dr. Thilenius implies a similar dynamic
conception of race when he says : " To the conception of forms
was essentially added the further conception with regard to their
distribution and possible temporal limitation.   To-day we share
Scheidt's view, based on the biological conception that it is
fundamentally necessary to examine, not merely selected sections
of the nation, but the whole regional population, in its entirety."
And furthermore, " Every culture is bound up with its human
representatives." [2]

From this point of view we approach Anthropology as the
bio-cultural history of Man, and it comprehends also an ætiology
of the change or movement within a nation.   Or it may be
described as the history of populations—regionly considered—
interrelated to the history of races, or the migrations and
changes of stocks—which again is related to the history of culture
and its evolution.   Methodologically we must distinguish this
treatment of phenomena, its observation, classification, and
ætiology, from its applications.   In turning to account the study
of anthropological phenomena, so defined, we approach its
Eugenical bearings.   This will be a wider conception of Eugenics
than the traditional one by as much as the scope and direction
of Anthropological aims will also have been widened.

In so far as Eugenics transcends as an applied science, perhaps
inevitably, the rigid limitations of an exact prognosis of the
human races' changing forms, features, and morbidities, by an
insistent demand for the satisfaction of human aspirations,
ideals, and biased hopes, so far Eugenics must remain, strictly
speaking, unscientific.   To that extent, too, Eugenics must
retain something, as Galton himself maintained, essentially
akin to the enthusiasm of a religious hope or faith.   To that
extent also it will admit of both the strength and weakness of
religious conviction : the strength that leads ardent striving

---

[1] The study of the laws of racial adaptability is the main thesis of my book,
The Clash of Culture and the Contact of Races, where the conception of variational
type adaptation and its implications is first developed.

[2] Georg Thilenius, " On some biological view-points in Ethnology " (The
Huxley Memorial Lecture for 1931), *Journal of the Royal Anthropological Institute*,
vol. lxi, July–December, 1931.

after an ideal towards eventual realization in fact and achievement, and the weakness that tempts its devotees to mistake the wish world of imagination for reality. In such terms Nietzsche's *Zarathustra* voiced his dynamic, but essentially ethical and non-scientific, challenge : " Not only onward in time, but upward shouldst thou propagate thyself ! For that purpose may the garden of marriage help thee."

ETHNOGENICS

Nietzsche, profound as was his sociological insight, scorned a methodological approach ; but his time was not ripe for a methodology of the social-biological sciences. At that time Eugenics was born as an applied science of the future. The term as Galton coined it, with the value implication of the first syllable, was no more than an anticipation of a riper body of knowledge and method, to be achieved after much labour and study. The time should now, however, be ripe for a new scientific synthesis, with a defined and surer method. Out of it there emerges the conception of race, population, and culture as tripartite aspects of Man in time, conditioning, and being conditioned by his environment : the conception of race in evolution. To distinguish it from these earlier anticipations it should be profitable to introduce a newer term : a term which briefly indicates the implications of race-population change : ETHNOGENICS. The term has no propagandist colouring, for the *ethnogenist* is concerned with an exact prognosis of race, population, and culture change, and the ætiology of that change in the past.

The new synthesis will work for a correlation between somatic and psychical forms, and on the physiological side for a standardization of criteria similar to past groundwork on the side of physical measurement. Such detailed work, for instance, is already being carried on, notably by Professor Elton Mayo, in the Industrial Research Institute of Harvard University[1] ; work which correlates psychological and physiological indices and which points to striking familial and group differences in physiological capacity ; work which contributes to a newer exact ethno-sociology or ethnogenics with statistical verifications. Unlike the frequent tendency in past eugenic discussion, the use of the term " desirable ", unrelated to some measurable distinction in regard to any race or racial quality is, from this point of view, deprecated ; for ethnogenists will prefer to replace it in terms of adaptation.

[1] Cf. " *The Human Problems of an Industrial Civilization*, by Elton Mayo (1933).

RACIAL EXTINCTION

Little support is now given to theories based on the once-supposed fixity of racial types. But we have barely begun to formulate the laws underlying the decline and the increase of populations, and in the variations in adaptability exhibited by different race types in contact. Certainly, I think, we can discount those facile generalizations implying that the causes of the extinction of certain primitive races are easily recognizable in some arbitrarily selected checks to population or factors of elimination.

Examination often shows no correlation between the rate of decline and the incidence of selected mortality rates. A declining ethnic type or group often shows a low mortality rate. The approach to the problem is too often wrong, because it is forgotten that we are studying variational adaptation, and verification depends, as I have already said, upon a proper use of demographic data ; and demography is the most neglected branch of Anthropology. Races and types die out because of inner causes, provoked often by outer changes. Progressive loss of viability and extinction of human race types occur, as biologists and palæontologists know in the zoological field, when viability or growth forces fail to respond in adjustment to environment.[1]

This maladjustment may result from over-specialization, which tends to make adaptation to variations in external conditions more difficult and more rigid. But specialization and over-specialization, while conditions of racial old age, are quite different from degeneration, so that changed conditions of environment often enable a more generalized and mixed type to replace a purer, more homogeneous, more specialized and highly developed type. Race mixture or miscegenation thus plays a part in the survival and the selective elimination of types.

One of the populations I have used [2] to illustrate the operation of this process of variable adaptability is the Maori of New Zealand, where the full-blood population declined rapidly, after impact with European civilization had upset the equilibrium of adjustment with a stable environment. The rise of a new hybridized population of mixed European-Maori blood effected and is still effecting a gradual substitution of the old stock by a new, less specialized and more adaptable one. These two curves of population show opposite tendencies ; the significance of the contrast has still been insufficiently appreciated.

While this demographic verification appears to relate primarily to Constitution, Culture no less is involved in the diagnosis. For

[1] Cf. I. P. Tolmachoff, *Extinction and Extermination*, Smithsonian Report for 1929, pp. 269–284.
[2] Cf. *Clash of Culture.*

environmental factors are equally cultural, and the mechanism of adaptation, that is, the reaction to changing conditions, is a process expressible in psychological terms. Since we are dealing with innate variations of type, we touch on the subjects of Genetics and Eugenics.

A part of my verification involves an incursion into the specialized study of sex ratio variation. Here it must be sufficient to record the results of a very wide investigation, which shows a correlation between fluctuations in the balance of the sexes and an increasing or decreasing population. This variation is more marked in the reproductive age categories than the variation at birth, and is therefore brought about largely by fluctuations in the differential sex survival rate. A large percentage of males amongst the young has also been noted as a symptom of a declining stock. Increase in masculinity is correlated with a decreasing curve of population, increase in femininity with an increasing curve. Since the influence of miscegenation is reflected in the rise or fall of population, it also shows in contrasted sex ratios of the full-blood and mixed-blood stocks of populations like the Maori. To-day, Australian aboriginal and Red Indian populations furnish significant examples. Other demographic features reflect the sensitiveness of the social structure to the force of these laws, such as differential variation in the respective nuptial ages of men and women, and postponement in the male or female nuptial age.

These are problems within the scope of Anthropology, of Demography, and of Eugenics ; they constitute the material for Ethnogenic research. For all quantitative variations in population and the factors which produce them effect also qualitative changes, most conspicuous when populations are least homogeneous. Elimination and survival are selective, and evolutionary change works through variable adaptation. Inbreeding also makes for the segregation of distinctive types, while on the other hand, outbreeding militates against the specialization of types. Social customs such as cross-cousin marriage and endogamy play a part here. The inbred Fijian chieftain families showed conspicuous variations in terms of viability, survival, fertility, and other measurable distinctions. Before the catastrophe of their impact with European civilization the inbred families were superior in these respects ; afterwards they ceased to be so. The effects of monandrous, polyandrous, and polygynous matings may also be analysed by these criteria.

SOCIAL DISINTEGRATION

But all these problems may equally well be studied at home among our own European populations ; qualitative as well as quantitative changes are taking place before our eyes. There is ample work for an army of specialists, but there is still a dearth of workers in the most vital yet neglected fields. Depopulation and over-population are phenomena reflecting the same laws and processes which equally bring qualitative changes with the substitution of types and stocks. But surviving stocks are sometimes not of the type and equality capable of carrying the burden of the complex civilization created by the original stock which gave it its peculiar form. The industrial revolution in England has been an environmental revolution carried along at an increasing rate of complexity by its own momentum, bringing in its train a vast increase of population which it threatens to find increasingly incompetent to absorb profitably or healthily. While at the same time a differential survival rate is producing a change in the composition of our populations. The problem of the clash of cultures in Europe still awaits scientific investigation.

Adaptation, the price of survival, is no longer the simpler problem it was for our leisurely increasing forbears of the fifteenth century, when England had a self-supporting, mainly agricultural population of some three millions. Science, the aggregated product of a few men's brains, has produced the vast machinery which has changed the face of our world and every minute of our daily life. Do we clearly know what sort of man the machinery has produced, and is likely to produce in the future ? And what type of man is best fitted to survive in such an environment ? And which type is doomed to disappear ? And with his disappearance may not our civilization itself go with him ?

Civilization increasingly requires in its growth and sustenance variety in the men by which its machinery functions, and if the controlling factors of our changing environment operate selectively but unevenly, there seems to be evidence that they may be developing in different proportions incompatible types of men, increasingly alien to each other and incapable of the co-operative productiveness that alone ensures the cohesion, strength, and health of a nation.

This problem is beginning to force itself upon the attention of some American investigators ; for symptoms of social dis-integration are showing in the fabric of society and in its industrial life. From the racial melting-pot emerge groups intractably drawn into the economic life of the country from which they tend to withhold any collective whole-hearted allegiance. Their dawning self-consciousness is coloured far less by any economic stratifications than by their ethnic heritage and by the clash of incompatible culture trends. There are negro groups, Indian groups, southern white groups, and regionally scattered groups preserving the tongues of their diverse European heritage.

Though perhaps less conspicuous than in the new world of America, there are evidences of social disintegration in England, in perhaps a different form, symptoms of the same disease that destroys societies and brings about the collapse of civilizations and cultures. A growing consciousness that the existing political and economic structure of society is ceasing to function and is bankrupt, while it breeds disillusionment on the one hand, has fostered on the other a new determination and hope, expressed in the aspirations of the various nationalistic Fascist movements in Europe, that may ripen into a new Renaissance.

It is not only in our colonial Empire that the applications of Anthropolgy and Ethnogenics can help us to avoid disasters, promote efficiency, and effect economies ; many of the problems customarily looked upon as essentially economic or political can be elucidated only by the help of careful anthropological investigations and method. For instance, the long duration of unemployment in England since the War, with the appalling drain on the national resources involved in maintaining the unabsorbed army of our industrial life, is more than a transient problem of temporary dislocation. That it is not merely an economic but also a population problem, in which the root causes are to be elucidated by anthropological methods and in the application of scientific insight, is not generally appreciated.

When it is considered that social and economic legislation, which are determined by political exigencies in ignorance of the consequences of the influences at work, directly affect most of these factors, the importance of the right scientific training and knowledge becomes apparent. By no other means can we hope to make the world safe for intelligence.

In 1923 I was privileged to make the Presidential Address to the Anthropology Section of the Australasian Association, and I took as my theme " The Disintegration of Tribal Communities ", under the subject-heading " Mental Anthropology— the Science of Civilization ". I attempted to show that the stability and social health of any community, whether a tribe or a nation, however high or low in the scale of culture or complexity, may be reckoned by the degree of integration or disintegration it exhibits, and that every weakening of the tribal tie destroys the social purpose of each member of it. The disintegrative symptoms may even be shown and measured in such ways as the suicide rate, as Durkheim showed in his classic study of Suicide, or by the conflict of industrial, civil, and religious factions. I then enumerated some of the functions by which society achieved its cohesion.

Since that time, in later work, my studies have led me to

consider how social disintegration affects and is linked up with changes both quantitative and qualitative in a population. It was therefore with interest and gratification that I read a Presidential Address by Professor Radcliffe-Brown [1] before the Anthropology Section of the Australasian Association in 1930, and found that he also took as his theme in the domain of Applied Anthropology the " Disintegration of Tribal Communities ". My confidence in my own early essay, seven years before, was enhanced by the endorsement it appeared to receive from Professor Radcliffe-Brown's similiar treatment and conclusions. I could find, in fact, only one point in a single sentence from which to differ. But as that point concerns the theme of my present paper I venture to mention it. Our difference is, I conceive, more verbal than real.

He said : " Attempts are being made to institute generally under the name of Eugenics an Applied Science of Human Biology. These attempts are, to my mind, premature." He admitted the desirability of taking those steps as soon as possible, but added : " Our theoretical knowledge of the phenomena of heredity and variation is totally inadequate at the present time to take up the very difficult task. . . . "

Premature ! Do we not already know far more than sufficient, or suitable, to teach the teachers of the coming generation the essential, though elementary, facts about themselves, which the present generation ignores or of which it is ignorant ?

I conceive that I have in anticipation answered this previous objection. Professor Radcliffe-Brown has already gone with me so far in allotting to the scope of Applied Anthroplogy the task of formulating a doctrine applicable to the control and direction of social development and the art of Government. But I have already tried to show that it is impossible to divorce an Applied Social Anthropology from an Applied Human Biology. Human Biology thus has a concern in all the influences, cultural, physical, and environmental, that affect the extinction or the survival of ethnic variations or types. Quantitative changes bring about qualitative changes. In so far as these influences are amenable to social control or direction, they come within the domain of an Applied Science. Ethnogenics is therefore the study of those forces, amenable to social control, which may influence the fertility and survival rate of variations of type in a population : it is a necessary development of that " functional anthropology ", which has two distinguished exponents in Dr. Malinowski and Professor Radcliffe-Brown.

[1] President of Section H (Anthropology), British Association Centenary Meeting, 1931.

We are often reminded that the backward aboriginal races of the world are fast disappearing, as an urge to speed our investigations of their cultures before our material is lost for ever ; but ethnic types may disappear amongst thriving and dense populations, even here in our midst. Are we less urgently concerned in preserving those types and those races which enrich our civilization than in writing with academic precision the obituary notices of those most remote from us ; or are eschatology and the measurement of skulls the only really important branches of Anthropology ? [1]

[1] The scope of Ethnogenics or Human Ecology is further developed by the writer in " Population ", *The Journal of the International Union for the Scientific Investigation of Population Problems*, vol. i, June, 1933.

HAUSA POETRY

R. S. RATTRAY

I am about to present a translation, made from a Hausa MS. in my possession, of one of the odes of the famous pre-Islamic Arabian poet, Imruil Kais' or Kaisi, who lived A.D. 492–542. Before doing so, however, I shall endeavour to narrate briefly how this translation came into my possession and other possible points of interest in connection with my subject.

The poems or odes of this Arabian writer are not, of course, wholly unknown to European scholars.

Firstly, we have the translation of the Baron McGuckin de Slane, who, in the eighteenth century, rendered thirty-three out of the thirty-four odes, not into French, but into rather unclassical medieval Latin. De Slane's work, however, does not contain the particular ode which is given here. For a previous rendering of this into English, we have to turn to the following writers, whose names I shall merely enumerate : Sir William Jones, Captain Johnson, Arnold, Lyall and finally Lady Anne Blunt. The works of the last three are very free poetic translations, and do not serve as a very useful basis of comparison with the original.

I do not propose here to enter into any discussion concerning these translations, nor to make any comparison between them and the rendering which I present. Nor will I touch upon the life of the author of the original MS. This has been fully dealt with in de Slane's preface and also in some of the other works to which I have alluded. All of these biographies, I found, could be traced to the same source, i.e. the Arabic work, Kitab al Aghani.

I am, in fact, going to confine my remarks almost entirely to the Hausa version and to its author, Liman Alhaji Umaru, son of Mallam Abubakar Umaru.

The Gold Coast, or rather its mandated area, is fortunate in being the home of the most eminent, perhaps, of those Hausa Mallams or teachers, who have a wide local reputation.

Liman Umaru is a scribe famous for his learning throughout West Africa, wherever the Hausa tongue is spoken. As the name will imply to those who understand Hausa or Arabic, he had made the pilgrimage to Mecca, and he had also spent many years of his life wandering over Arabia. He was, of course, like all Hausa Mallams with any pretensions to learning— bilingual. He could speak and write Arabic as fluently as his own language.

Liman Umaru had in his possession a library, part of which he had inherited from his father, consisting of MSS. chiefly of Arabic.

Among his books was a MS. copy, profusely annotated on the margins, of the poetic works of Imruil Kaisi, which had been copied out by a Hausa man, Malam Salihu, of Katsena, more than 150 years ago. Liman Umaru had made a very special study, extending over many years, of the works of this Arabian poet, had collected and critically examined a considerable quantity of literature dealing with his subject, and had finally translated the thirty-four odes written by Imruil Kaisi into Hausa.

To myself, as a very humble disciple of Liman Umaru, this translation was of considerable interest. An examination of it satisfied me that the Hausa translation far surpassed in style and ability any writings which I had previously seen in that language.

I do not think that I need fear contradiction when I state that Hausa literature is almost non-existent. There are, of course, MSS. dealing with historical subjects connected with the race, and a certain number of tales and songs. These documents are, however, always somewhat disappointing, I think. They generally lack any pretensions to literary style. They can seldom, or perhaps never, be taken as specimens of the Hausa language as spoken by the more eloquent individual members of the Hausa people.

The fact, of course, is that the average Hausa scribe almost wholly neglects his own language—from a literary point of view—and not only writes Hausa in Arabic characters but prefers to use Arabic itself as a means of written communication.

Liman Umaru's translation of the Arabic MS. of Imruil Kaisi is, therefore, of very special interest, for it shows us, I think, that Hausa, when handled by one of that race determined to show its capacity for literary force of expression and beauty, becomes a medium which possesses considerable powers of poetic expression.

In working through Liman Umaru's translation, my studies were in one important respect—to which I had better confess at once—conducted under some disadvantage. I had not any knowledge of Arabic, while Liman Umaru was equally ignorant of English. Hence these excursions into the fields of medieval Latin and other works of English writers to which I have just now briefly alluded, but which do not otherwise here concern us.

In the course of these researches I discovered that Odes 2–34 had never been translated into any modern language, and that Ode 1, in the poetic version of Lady Anne Blunt, Lyall, and Arnold, had not, in my opinion, done full justice to the original.

Liman Umaru had exercised greater care than any of these

translators in striving to find the exact equivalent in Hausa for the Arabic words and phrases of the original, and I hazard the opinion that our Arabicized Hausa is at least as likely to have given us the true spirit of the original and to have set before us as vivid and accurate pictures as European scholars have been able to do working through the medium of the Latin tongue.

There is, I think, no gainsaying the fact that Arabic culture has exercised great influence on the Hausas, and consequently it is at least probable that a Hausa scholar would be more *en rapport* with the spirit of the time when Imruil Kaisi wrote than the ordinary European translator.

Semitic influences in West Africa probably date back to the tenth century A.D., when the conversion to Islam of the great medieval kingdoms of Bornu is supposed to have taken place.

Researches into the Hausa tongue show it to be a Sudanese language fundamentally though distantly connected with the language spoken between Bornu and Senigambia, upon which has been grafted some few characteristics of the Hamitic languages, as seen, for example, in the sex-distinction in the pronouns, in some of the syntax, and in a few word-roots.

In Hausa folk-lore, too, though its main characteristics are negro, a similar influence both Semitic and Hamitic is to be seen. I mention these facts to show that this Arabic master-piece which I am about to present through the medium of Hausa is being subjected to a treatment less foreign to its genius than we might suppose. I may state that Liman Umaru in his translation has not made any attempt to imitate the peculiarities of the Arabic metres or to conform to the complicated rules of Arabic prosody. His omission to do so was not, however, due to ignorance of the rules governing this particular branch of Art.

Among the MSS. which formed his library, to which I have already alluded, was an old MS. copy of a work in Arabic prosody called Uryunul Gamirati written A.H. 200 by one Shaihu Hazaraji. From this work Liman Umaru had worked out fully the forms and names of the different metres for each of the thirty-four odes in the original Arabic MS. Of the sixteen varieties of metres known in Arabic poetry, he had shown that eighteen of these odes were in that metre called Tsaili, seven in Wafiru, and the remaining nine distributed between Kamilu, Ramal, Madidi, Mutakaribu, Munsaribu, and Rajas. I only mention these facts because I think they postulate a further guarantee that Liman Umaru, who knew his subject sufficiently well to follow the scansion of the original poems, has established their true meaning and given us a scholarly translation.

I shall now, before passing on to the *pièce de résistance* of my contribution to this volume, i.e. the rendering of one ode out of the thirty-four in my possession, endeavour to draw attention to some of the outstanding points of interest, anthropological and historical, which this and other odes of Imruil Kaisi present to us.

In all these pieces, which vary somewhat in merit, a nomad people is set before us, whose chief interests are bound up in the use and well-being of their flocks and herds. I shall have to content myself, with the space at my disposal, with a few quotations only.

We constantly read in these odes of camels with their gorgeous litters conveying women and children with their belongings to new grazing-grounds and supplying them with milk and food. "The great she-camels with huge humps come homeward in the evening, they are betaking themselves behind the trees from the voices of the milkers," and again : " I have seen a man owner of many camels."

We read of a people who also possessed sheep and goats, " and as they give their owners cheese and fat in plenty and fill of food and fill of drinks that is sufficient."

Gazelles and ostriches were tamed, for we read in Ode 2 : " Salma was thinking that the time would never end when she would be tending the kids of tame gazelles or ostrich eggs at Misai where countless caravans alight."

The horse, the Bedouin's friend *par excellence*, is so constantly alluded to and praised that it is difficult to pick out quotations when so many are at hand. I will give only two, chosen at random : " Of whom (i.e. my horse) you would say I was watching over a bird with broken wings," and again : " My tall, my slender-featured one of many beauties."

We gather from these odes that manufactures were in the hands either of the people of Yemen or of the Jews or of the Eastern nations generally, for when a weapon or a fabric, or such-like is mentioned, that word is qualified by an adjective signifying the place of its foreign origin. A few examples will suffice : " Masharafian blade," " Camels' hair blankets from Hal," " Robes from Instakia," " Rudaimizan spear " ; new saddles burdened from Herat ; wines from Anata and Shibani ; " sandal wood oil from Hind."

The sports and pastimes of the people of these days are well illustrated. They were story-telling, gambling, horse-racing, hunting buffalo, antelope, and wild asses, either on horseback or on foot, with spears or bows and arrows, or with trained hunting dogs. " And here it was the son of Muri's dogs, or the dogs of the son of Simbiri came upon him (the buffalo) in the early dawn—urged on by voice and hand."

From the names of the animals constantly mentioned, we learn that those in which these people were chiefly interested were the buffalo, antelope, wild asses, the ostrich, hyena, hares, wild hunting dogs, foxes, vultures, hawks, and eagles. Little descriptive touches here and there show that the habits of these creatures were closely studied, and their peculiarities noted— " The quick walk of the wild hunting dog " ; " the swaggering (swaying) gait of the fox " ; " the hawk with his blinking eye."

When we seek for passages in these odes which would throw light on the religious beliefs of this pre-Islamic people we are disappointed at finding very few, although a kind of monotheistic idea seems to run like an undercurrent through the poems with Allah as the one High God. Not infrequently we are reminded of the philosophy of a later Eastern poet, Omar Khayam : " Take delight out of the world, for know that you are mortal, delight from wine and fair women," writes Imruil Kaisi. But again agnosticism rather than atheism seems to underlie such a passage as this : " I see us hurrying on against our wish to the unknown."

Lesser gods and fetishes were not unknown, however, and are mentioned by name. Some of these were later adapted or have survived under Islam, e.g. " the circling maidens in their white-edged robes who serve Duwari."

There are traces, too, to be found of magic, charms, and superstitions, which indeed we would have expected, but instead of such beliefs being accepted and accredited, it is a somewhat curious fact that when mentioned they are generally treated as objects of derision or dislike : " O Hindu, do not marry an owl, who has the red hair of birth upon him, which he carries rolled up on his wrist ! ", " who seeks a hare that he may place its pastern bone on the palm of his hand for fear of death."

Some general idea of the position of women may be gleaned from these odes. The pictures are those of wild love-making, passionate but short-lived, and of worship of the sex. The physical beauty of woman was adored and her character idealized. It will be seen therefore that they were not despised, or enslaved, or overworked. The attitude towards the sex seems a forecast of what was found later in the days of chivalry and knight-errantry.

It is quite evident that when these poems were composed, the people had a love of nature and could appreciate the beauty of the heavens and of flowers, which seems in somewhat strange contrast with the attitude of mind of the uncivilized African of the present day.

I recollect that on one occasion when I showed a party of Africans a garden of zinnias, balsams, and roses, their only comment was : " When will they be ready for eating ? " nor have I ever met an unsophisticated native of any part of Africa who seemed capable of appreciating the beauty in a tropical sunset.

These odes again give us an insight into the standard of

كُنْدُرُواكُوكَرْإمُرِعَالَّفْسَرِرَبُجَر

كَطُومُوكُوكَادْرُرَّتَّمَسُوِبِ دَمَسَبِّكِ ٠ نُمْ

مَجَادَارَبَرِبِ طَكَانِرُدَحُوارَدَحُومَلْ دَ

اُوضِع دَمِفْرَاتْ اَلَامَنْ بَرُطوقِبِّ دُومِنْ

اَبْدُ يَسَاكَنْ شِرِاسَكَرْكَدَنَارُوَ كَرَعَنَرْ

كَاشُرِفَرْفَرْبَرِبِ اَفَرُوَاجِيُونْ دَوَكِيْكَنْ لَا

كَانْشِ كُوسَّكَرْثُبُو كَانْدُمِرُعِ اَسَافِمَرْ

دَسَكَ دُوكُوكَايَا نَرُعْفَرْزَكِيَرْدَ نُعْ

مَرُقَاوَفَرْكَّمُووَبُنُ اَبُوكِينَ سَرْطِنْطِمَابُنْ

حُونَسُراُورِنْتَ سَرْثُواكَدَكَمْلاَ دُومَرْبَكَرْ

ثُكَ جُمْبُرَدَرُسَّ سَرِدَرُوَرْكُواللَّاحُومُونْ ٠٠

خُرُ

Facsimile page of the original Hausa MS.

ethics of these people. We see in them the good qualities that are praised and the vices that are condoned, or perhaps even gloried in. Tribal honour ran high and vengeance for the killing of a tribesman is a sacred duty for his fellows: " I swear by

Allah the blood of my ancient sire does not pass unavenged,"
the poet sings.

Drunkenness is tolerated or becomes even a matter for
boasting : " We were drinking until we thought the trees near
us were young goats, until again we thought a black horse,
a chestnut."

There are vague and somewhat shadowy references to
contemporary history and to the Old Testament : " the lamp
of the Nazarene who has cut himself off from love of women " ;
" the writings of the Psalms of David upon the date-tree board
of the Yemanite " ; " the land under Cæsar's sway " ; " a king
of Persia who stands with loins girt."

Coming within that branch of anthropology which is known
as technology, I may mention a toy referred to in the ode which
I am about to translate. This, the Hausa translator has called
by the name meaning the hyena's " potsherd " which, I think,
is the buzzer.

These then are some of the anthropological and other aspects
of this work, a sample of which I now present to the reader,
The translation given follows the Hausa version closely. With
it are given a facsimile page of the original and a transliteration.

Kundin wākōkin Imruil Kaisi, *dan* Hujuru

Ku tsaya mu yi kūkā don tuna masōyi da masabkī, -ga mafādal
rairaiyī, isakānin Dufuli *da* Haumala, *da* Tūliha *da* Mikirāta,
alāmanta bai tsūfa ba domin abinda ya sākēta, shi ne iskan kudu
da arewa. Ka na ganin kāshin farfarun bareyī afarfarjiyū nata
da fakaikanta, ka che shi kwāyaiyakin chattā *ne. Kā che dai, nī,*
asāfiyar da su ka daukō kāyā, nan ga faralkayal dengi, maifāfar
kwatōwanē. Abōkainā sun tsaitsida, abun hawansu a wurinta.
Su na chewā, " Kada ka mutu domin bakin chiki, jimrē dai." Sani
dai, warkewatā hawayē che,

A BOOK OF THE SONGS OF *Imruil Kaisi*, SON OF *Hujuru*

(1) Because of the memory of one (we hold) dear, and the place
of (her) abode (lit. the place she alighted), let us halt and lament.
(Behold she dwelt) 'twixt *Dufuli* and *Haumala*, and *Tuliha*, and
Mikirata, amidst the drifting sands.
Ageless are the ruins (lit. their land-marks have not grown old),
because of that which ever marks (lit. weaves) them out (afresh),
even the North wind and the South (on the sands, like the shuttle
of the weaver).

(2) You see the droppings of the white gazelles in their court-yards
and on their outskirts, as if they were the seedlings of the pepper tree.

(3) And as for me, standing beside the pale thorn shrub with my
kinsfolk on the morning their caravan departed, I am as he who cuts
the bitter gourds in twain.

(4) My friends drew up their mounts beside it (the pale thorn) and they are saying, " Be not overcome (lit. do not die) because of sorrow, only be patient."

(5) But know that tears heal (a heart's grieving). And when that I have caused them to flow (say), " Is there (never) a spot where I may rest amid the ruins, however brief my hours ? "

(6) 'Tis like the happenings (of long ago) from (her they called) Mother of " The Little Reaper " (lit. hoer), who was before her, and (you), her companion, " Mother of the Cloud " (who dwelt) in *Maasali*. The tears (that fall) from my eyes are shed for desire, upon my breast (they fall) till they drench the girdle of my sword.

(7) Ah ! many days were (made) sweet to you because of women, but none like that day at *Daruta* by the pool of *Juljuli*.

(8) Call to mind the day I stabbed my camel for the maidens, and you wondered to see its saddle borne aloft, while they, they passed the live-long day, tossing the meat from one to the other, and the fat was like the twisted tassels of a silken robe.

(9) Call to mind the day I entered a palanquin, *Unaizaki's* palanquin, when she cried, " May *Allah* bring woe upon you, verily you will be the cause of my having to go on foot (if you do so)." And she is saying, " You make my camel weary, get you down *Imruil Kaisi*."

(10) And all this time the house swayed with us both. (And) said I to her, " Let us on, leave its reins free, and do not push me far from your ripe fruit, that is so smooth for me."

(11) "I have come to many such as you by night (and some were even) great with child. (Others) again with infants in their arms I caused to forget the little one, decked with charms, that was all too soon to have a little companion (shame on the mother of two babes unweaned)."

(12) And when the infant (she had set) behind her cried, she would turn towards it just one half of her body, the other half was ours and was not turned away.

(13) Call to mind a day behind the sand dunes, when one unwillingly (came) with me, vowing with irrevocable oath (she would never yield herself to me) (Till I grew weary, saying), " O *Fatsima* ! gently now, put aside half this your coyness, or if it be you wish indeed to leave me, let it be a kindly parting."

(14) "And know, that if my nature has angered you, then pluck my heart from out your heart that it may be free, for was not love of you my destroyer ; it is that which caused you to despise me ? (But know) because of you, whenever you would call on it (lit. instruct) (again) then will it follow."

(15) " Your two eyes did not shed tears except to pierce me with your two arrows in a heart already slain."

(16) Many eggs (lie) in the litters that are not sought for in their tents (by others), but as for me, I find it sweet to toy with them, and hurry not away. I pass and repass many guards and hosts of dangers all lusting to destroy me, and had the killers seen me, then had they slain me.

(17) When the " hen and her chicks " (the Pleiades) appeared in the sky above, like a necklet, strung with beads of varying size, then

I have come, and of a truth already she hath unrobed for sleep and (stands) in the screened-off chamber of her tent, clad only in little shift.

(18) And then she spoke :—

" By *Allah*, you have little wisdom, and as for me I cannot think that the blindness of (your) heart will ever be removed from you."

(19) And out I passed with her (into the night). She trails the fringes of her cloak behind (to cover up) our footprints on the sands.

(20) And when we had passed behind the dwellings of her people, (then) among the sand dunes, firm (and) mounting one on top of the other, was our quest.

(21) And as she inclined towards me, her scent was wafted (o'er me) like the winds from out the East, that come perfumed with the camphor tree.

(22) And when I said, " Bring, give to me." She would bend towards me her soft waist ; (her limbs), swelling where bracelets and anklets encircled her, (but) with fair little body and belly which never was big. Her breast smooth as the face of a mirror, (and her skin) like the egg of a young hen ostrich shaded white and brown. Her repasts she made of purest water, undisturbed.

(23) (As she turns) she displays an oval cheek, (and) darts terror from her eyes like a cow buffalo of *Waujurata* with her young.

(24) Her neck (was poised) like the gazelles, for ever beautiful, and when she raised it, lacked not ornaments.

(25) (As) branches, her jet black locks, thick, like clusters of dates with unripe fruit, covered her back. On the crown of her head her (locks) were braided, twisted, (and) the ornament (that held fast her hair) was lost among the tresses.

(26) Her waist was smooth as silk plucked from the cocoon, and her ankles were like the supple withies (that are fastened to the gourd cups) that are caused to drink the water.

(27) She stretches forth palms that are soft, without roughness, (soft) as the maggots of the midden heap, or the tooth stick of the *Ashali* tree.

(28) She gives light to the darkness of the early night, like even to the lamp of the Nazarene, who has cut himself apart from love of women.

(29) The scent of powdered musk lingers o'er her couch until morning is far advanced, her couch from which she does not rise until the sun is high.

(30) She talks not idly. As she stretches forth her arms in relaxation, (clad) in some garb mid-way between a woman's cloak and a young girl's short garment, even the cautious man looks upon such an one with desire. The blind passions of men's hearts are soon removed from play (with common loves), from love of her the folly (of my heart) cannot be plucked out.

(31) Often one who would have spoken with me concerning you, strong bitter words of admonition, I turned (him) aside from speaking the truth, but the slander was not little.

(32) Often *Night*, like the froth (hiding the surface) of a river, let down its curtain upon me, and every kind of doubt to weigh me (on the scales).

(33) I said to him, as he thrust out his breast, as he buttocked with (his) buttocks, as he leapt forward with (his) chest, " Hail to thee, O thou long *Night*, is it not that thou art coming to an end because of *Dawn*? Is not *Dawn* more powerful yet than thou?

(34) O Night how wonderful thou art! One would say that his stars had been bound with every twisted rope to the body of the mountain of *Yazbula*.

One would think that the " hen and her chicks " (the *Pleiades*) had been hung across his horse-pegs on a hempen rope, (and fastened to) a solid rock.

(35) Of a truth, I rose up very early in the morning—even the birds were in their nests—with my great short-clipped steed, (so fleet) that you would think that the full-grown beasts of the jungle had been tethered (lit. so fleet as (to seem) to tether, etc.).

(36) As a smooth rock—which the torrent has brought down from the hills—he would advance, flee away, face you, present his back ; (as it were) at one and the same time.

(37) A bay he was. The saddle-cloth would slip from off his back as the descending waters glide over a smooth rock.

(38) Gallop (lit. swim) he would gallop when all were weary, (and) would spurn up the dust from the hard places, boiling even when weary, with a roar in his belly like the rumbling in an iron pot.

(39) He would throw the light youth from off his back and shake the cloak from off the heavy fool.

(40) His turning is like the hyena's piece of broken gourd, pierced and spinning on the twisted thread, which boys revolve between their palms.

(41) To him have been given the flanks of the gazelle, the slender legs of the ostrich, the quick walk of the wild hunting dog, and the swaggering gait of the fox.

(42) One would say that his shoulders were the stone mortar (in which the incense) of a bride (is mixed), or the juice of the bitter gourd.

(43) Saddle and bridle rested (ever) upon him, nay, he slept even with his two eyes (open) and stood fastened ever ready (lit. stood, not loose).

(44) Herds of buffalo would come nigh us, all unknowing, and you would say that their cows were the (circling) maidens in their white-edged robes (who serve) *Duwari*.

(45) (And on a sudden) they turn back, strung out, even as a string of beads of different sizes, on the neck of one, with many kinsfolk both on father's and on mother's side.

(46) He, (my steed) caused us to overtake the foremost, and behind him lagged the weaker ones, which did not disperse.

(47) He galloped and galloped among the bulls, and cows, and overtook them.

He sweated not, nay he did not even have to be groomed.

(48) Then the cooks spend the whole day, roasting or partly boiling the great lumps, or drying them in the sun.

(49) We return again in the evening, and the great horse too turns homeward and prances of his own accord, and those whose eyes (alight upon him) look him up and down (in wonder).

(50) You would say that the blood of the foremost (buffalo) upon his chest is the powdered henna on a combed-out silver (beard).

(51) (And for) you when you would pass behind him, he is wont to fill the space between (his flanks) with flowing hair that reaches to the ground, and hangs so gracefully (lit. which does not bend outwards).

(52) Oh *Hari*! do you see the lightning which I show you with its shimmering like the waving of two hands among the banks of clouds?—it is shedding its light even like the lamp of the Nazarene recluse who has poured oil upon the twisted strands of wick.

(53) I dwelt amid such (storms) while my friends were (safely camped) between *Hamiri* and between the hills. You see how far my gaze was set.

(54) It was early morn, and raining every hour, and (the storm) was casting the great trees prone (lit. on their chins).

(55) Even to *Taimaa* it had a thought to go, and left not even the stumps of its date trees standing, nor any wall, save only those built up with stones.

(56) You would say, the peak of *Mujaimiri* in the morning, because piled with flotsam, was the whorl that tops the spindle.

(57) Like a great man lying huddled up in his blanket is the mountain of *Abana*, among its many waters.

(58) (The flood) throws its chest towards the *Gabitsi* (jungles), (and settles itself down upon the land) like a rich *Yemanite* whose bags are full of wealth.

(59) You would say that the lions, floating upon its farthest flood in the early dawn, were the root-bulbs of the frog's wild onions, dug out (of the earth).

(60) On the right, its floods pour forth on the summit of *Kutsumi* and on the left on *Satari*, and *Yazbula*, and along with Night it throws its chest to *Busyani*, carrying down the wild goats from every (peak) whereon they stood.

MOTHER-RIGHT AMONG THE CENTRAL BANTU [1]

By AUDREY I. RICHARDS

The Babemba of North-Eastern Rhodesia have always been classed as one of the typically matrilineal, matrilocal, tribes of Central Africa—part of that solid mass of Luba-Lunda-Bemba peoples which stretches from the Central Congo on the west to Lakes Tanganyika and Nyasa on the east. These warrior groups of Bantu seem to have spread in successive waves from the borders of Lubaland, occupying the open expanses of forest land to the east. The Babemba themselves apparently crossed the Lualaba River over 200 years ago, gradually expanding over the whole of what is now known as the Tanganyika plateau of North Rhodesia—the territory between the four great lakes, Mweru, Bangweulu, Tanganyika, and Nyasa. All these agricultural, hunting peoples, such as the Luba, Lunda, Bemba, Bisa, Lala, Chewe, etc.,[2] show great similarities of speech and culture, and of these a strongly matrilineal kinship system, associated in some cases with matrilocal marriage, has been reckoned as one of the most characteristic features.

It is for this reason that a detailed study of the matrilineal elements of Bemba culture is one of the anthropologist's first tasks. I say detailed, because we are coming more and more to realize that the summary classification of primitive peoples as *patrilineal* or *matrilineal* is not only inadequate, but actually misleading without careful descriptive notes of the use of the terms in each case.[3] Dealing with the problem of authority alone, Radcliffe-Brown has shown us how widely the power of the father varies in relation to that of the maternal uncle, the male head of the family, from tribe to tribe, even in those

[1] The material for this article was collected during a year's work among the Babemba, 1930–1, for which I am indebted to the generosity of the Cape Town University, the Rhodes Trustees, and the Percy Sladen Trust. I should like to add it to this collection in honour of Professor Seligman, because it was at one of his seminars at the London School of Economics that it first saw light, receiving as all other work I have brought to him, his most ungrudging criticism and help. As an account of Bemba kinship it is necessarily provisional and incomplete, since I am, at the moment of writing, again at work in the field, correcting and checking previous observations.

[2] Classified by the late Mr. Emil Torday as the forest-dwelling Bantu, in *Descriptive Sociology, African Races*, London, 1930, and by Dr. I. Schapera, in " A Working Classification of the Bantu People of Africa ", *Man*, May, 1929, as the Central Bantu.

[3] See, e.g., *Notes and Queries on Anthropology*, fifth edition, London, 1929.

parts of South Africa which are reputedly most patriarchal in type.

Moreover, the recent emphasis on the psychological aspects of primitive kinship has revolutionized our whole conception of such institutions as mother-right and father-right. Malinowski, in particular, has shown us very clearly that native ideas and beliefs as to sex and kinship, and the traditional emotional attitudes towards the different sides of the family, paternal and maternal, are just as integral a part of the social system as the legal rules of descent and succession on which the classification of primitive peoples used to be made. He maintains that this very legal over-emphasis of the rights of one side of the family as against the other is often responsible for an emotional tension between the two kinship groups, and resultant compensatory mechanisms for the satisfaction of the losing side. The terms matrilineal and patrilineal must in fact be defined, not only in terms of the legal rules of kinship, but also by an analysis of the emotional ties which unite the members of the two groups. It is just this balance between the conflicting interests of the paternal and maternal kinsmen, sometimes more, and sometimes less satisfactory in its working, which we have to try to estimate in any particular case. What in fact do we mean by the term *matrilineal* as applied to the Bemba tribe ?

To begin with the facts most familiar, what are those elements of Bemba culture which have led to the classification of these people among the matrilineal Bantu ? At first sight the list is impressive. Descent, clan membership, and the chiefly succession follow, with few exceptions, the maternal line. The mother's brother, the *nalume*, seems to play a very important part in deciding the destinies of family or home. Marriage, at any rate for a certain period, is matrilocal ; and anyone observing day to day the independent behaviour of the Bemba women, their easy rights of divorce, the evident power of the older women in village life, and the unique position of the royal princesses, or *banamfumu*,[1] is inclined to suspect that here at last something like real matriarchy actually obtains.

But it is necessary to keep an open mind on the question, until we have made a preliminary analysis of the rules of inheritance, succession, and descent and the exercise of authority in family life. Now to estimate the relative importance of these different aspects of kinship, we require some knowledge of the economic and political structure of the tribe, and the functions which various groups of kinsmen have to perform in it. Thus among the Babemba, a people which have not yet reached a very high level of agricultural development, and live moreover

---

[1] Cf. *The Great Plateau of Northern Rhodesia*, by C. Gouldsbury and H. Sheane, London, 1911, for a first description of these facts.

in an area poor in natural resources, the inheritance of material property is of relatively little significance in determining kinship ties. It might be said in fact that the average Mubemba inherits little from his maternal uncle besides his hereditary bow, and possible rights over the distribution of the crops of the dead man.

Among the Babemba wealth really consists in the power to command service, whether this be from subject to chief, son-in-law to father-in-law, slave to owner, or youth to age. Such services were used formerly in the conquest and subjection of surrounding tribes. Even at the present day a chief reckons his assets in terms of the number of villages he possesses and the number of men who can be relied on to do *mulasa*, or tribute labour in his fields.

Moreover, the question of succession applies not only to the case of chiefly office and positions of rank. Every Mubemba must be succeeded at death by the appropriate heir, who takes not only his name, his bow (or, in the case of a woman, the girdle or *mushingo*), but also his status, social obligations, and *mupashi* or guardian spirit as well, with the resultant right and duty of approaching this spirit in prayer. This form of succession, known as *kupyanika*, is not of course unparalleled among other primitive tribes, but in this case the identification between the dead man and his heir seems to me to be unusually complete. It invades every aspect of daily and ceremonial life. Whether as regards legal status, kinship terms and attitudes, or everyday behaviour, the heir newly appointed actually is the dead man, and I shall treat this custom of *kupyanika* under the heading of succession rules.

The rules of descent among the Babemba are equally important from a functional point of view. This colonizing tribe cannot boast long generations of attachment to one particular geographical region. Its people are by temperament travellers, and their form of social structure makes for constant change of residence from one part of the country to the other.

Among many primitive societies cultural integrity is maintained by a strong sentimental attachment to a certain tract of land, but among the Babemba this feeling is replaced, I think, by a reverent, sometimes almost passionate interest in the question of descent—usually traced from the first ancestors to leave Lubaland in search of new worlds. This is particularly the case, rather naturally, among the members of the royal clan and the hereditary officials attached to the Paramount Chieftaincy itself. It is, moreover, in my opinion, the basis of tribal cohesion in this large and scattered tribe. Let us see then in greater detail how far these two institutions—succession and descent—follow a decidedly matrilineal **or a** patrilineal type.

As regards descent the Babemba are definitely matrilineal.[1] Membership of the clan, or *mukoa*, follows that of the mother. Clan membership is of course more or less important in determining kinship sentiment according to its function in tribal life. Among the Babemba it would seem at first sight that this is not a very great one. With the clan there are associated no totemic taboos of the type common among other Central Bantu peoples. Clan names often refer in fact to essential human foods such as millet, or to parts of the human body, or to natural phenomena such as rain. Nor does a man look to his fellow-clansmen for help in time of trouble, as we are told is the case among the Ba-ila further south.[2] To obtain hospitality or support it is necessary for a stranger to trace his lineage on both sides of the family, as well as giving his clan. In all the actual difficulties of life it is to the *lupwa*, a bilateral group of relatives, to which he turns—a fact which is in itself a hint that the matrilineal emphasis in this tribe is not as strong as we should have at first believed. Nor, in the eyes of the native, does the clan regulate marriage, since he always maintains emphatically that he can marry those of his own clan. He is only forbidden, he says, to marry to those he calls *nkashi yandi*, or " my sisters," which means in fact his parallel cousins on both sides. He cannot, therefore, in reality marry a near relative of his mother's clan, although he himself regards the prohibition as an extension of the brother-sister incest rules rather than as a clan taboo.

Nevertheless as regards formal descent the clan is important. Even a young man will remember the legend of his clan origin. Clan membership among the Babemba also determines to some extent social status, especially in the case of the *benangandu*, or crocodile totem, the royal clan.

Descent, apart from clan membership, is also reckoned in the matrilineal line in the first place. The average Mubemba remembers four generations of his relatives on his mother's side, and then records a blank till he reaches the original ancestors, men and women, of the matrilineal side. On his father's side he will remember fewer or more relatives according to the latter's rank. In the case of those holding chiefly office the contrast is more striking. I have met hereditary councillors of the chief who could give me thirteen generations of male relatives on their mother's side, and only two on their father's ! The Paramount

---

[1] Reasons of space compel me to omit most of the evidence for this and similar statements in the sequel. I shall have to beg the indulgence of my readers on this score, as my aim is not to demonstrate the existence of " matriliny " and " mother-right " among the Bemba, but to examine its functional relations with " father-right ".

[2] *The Ila-Speaking Peoples of Northern Rhodesia*, by E. W. Smith and A. M. Dale, London, 1920.

Chiefs are reckoned as twenty-seven or so, and of course, in the case of a chief, the paternal ancestors are merely the consorts of the royal princesses and as such, from the point of view of descent, practically do not exist! We see, therefore, that though the matrilineal clan plays little part in everyday life, yet the formal rules of descent, crystallized most clearly in the case of the royal family, are typically matrilineal.

In succession, too, the formal legal emphasis is matrilineal. A chief is succeeded by his brothers, then by his sister's sons, and then by his sister's daughter's sons. But besides those actually succeeding to the chieftaincies, all *benangandu*, that is to say all members of the royal clan, have chiefly rank, whether men or women.

This matrilineal line of succession is associated among the Bemba with a glorification of the function of motherhood in the royal line. Each *namfumu*, or royal princess—the sister, uterine niece or grand-daughter of a chief—is the potential mother of a ruling head, and is brought up from her earliest years to feel that the production of sons and daughters for the royal succession is her proper function in tribal life. These *banamfumu* occupy an extraordinarily privileged position. They are above all tribal laws, especially in matters matrimonial, and are backed in all their actions by their brothers, or uncles, the chiefs. Certain of the *banamfumu* also reign over territory in their own right, although always under the ægis of some chief who wields for them their political and legal power. The mother of the Chitimukulu (Paramount Chief) is the most important of these ruling chieftainesses. She has rights of decision in the selection of the Paramount Chief himself, and receives presents and help from nearly all her sons, the sub-chiefs. Succession to such chieftaincies is of course strictly matrilineal, first to the dead woman's sisters, and then to her grand-daughters.

The important position of the *namfumu* in tribal life is reflected in a cult of the dead mothers of the chiefs. Legend tells how the first Chitimukulu and his brothers, on arriving in Lubemba, sent back messengers to fetch *nkashi yesu* "our sister", stealing her from Lubaland after untold adventures on the way. The site of her first village is still one of the most sacred spots in the country, and here start the big sacrificial rites (*Kupepo*), which are then successively carried out at all spirit centres throughout the land. In the chief's relic-house is kept the flour-basket which she is said to have brought with her, and at some of the chiefs' villages is a house kept sacred to the spirits of the royal women. In certain rites performed at these capitals the chief himself salutes to the ground in front of this house and prays to "our mothers who bore us and suckled us and carried us in skins on their backs."

This reverence of the ancestral mother is associated very naturally with an idealized picture of the brother-sister relationship in legend and folk-tale. In daily life the husband and the father intervene, make their demands and take their dues, but in myth the supplementary figures fade away, and the essential structure of the family—grandmother, mother, mother's brother, and brother and sister remain alone on the stage. It is interesting, too, to note that this system of succession has never yet been questioned, even in areas where the white influence has been particularly strong. This pertinacity of the belief in matrilineal succession does not seem to be at all incompatible with wide changes in the *patria potestas* in the course of daily life.

So much then for the question of descent, succession, and inheritance—though to the question of descent we shall have to return again. What about that more complex aspect of kinship—the leadership and authority in family life ? In a primitive society the power of the father as against the male head of the family, the maternal uncle, is manifested usually in certain well-defined ways—actual authority in the household and charge of the education of the children ; the legal possession of the children in case of divorce or dissolution of the marriage ; the power to arrange the marriage of the children themselves, or to share in the marriage payments made on such occasions ; and in general the mutual obligations of father to son, or maternal nephew to uncle, as regards general support.

The question of authority in the household must be largely determined, of course, by the rules of residence at marriage. Among the Babemba marriage is matrilocal. The girls are betrothed usually before puberty, and after making his first symbolic presentation to his parents-in-law (*nsalamo*) the bridegroom, often himself a mere boy, will move to the bride's village, build himself a hut, and start to work for a period of two, three, or even up to seven years for his father-in-law. During this time he is fed by his mother-in-law, and his bride, as she grows older, will come to sweep out his hut and to draw water for him. She may also, if she wishes, sleep with him at night, since pre-pubertal intercourse is permitted provided the girl is returned to her mother as soon as there is any danger of her conceiving (a terrible calamity if her *chisungu*, or initiation ceremony, has not been performed). The husband, in the meantime, is responsible for various further marriage payments—the *mpango*— and formerly fulfilled this part of the contract by the provision of two or more bark-cloths, or sometimes hoes and arrows, usually fetched from the Lunda country to the west. But such payments could almost be considered symbolic in the old days. There is nothing comparable to the considerable transfer of wealth in the form of cattle which we find at marriage among the Southern Bantu. The period of service for the bride's father was formerly the essential element of the contract.

But with the payment of the *mpango*, and the completion of the *chisungu* ceremony, the husband is not allowed to move his wife to his own village until one, two, or even more children have been born, and until his good and steady behaviour has reassured his parents-in-law. The length of this probationary period will depend on the relative social importance of the husband's and wife's families, and of course in the case of a *namfumu*, the husband could never expect to remove his wife at all.

It will be seen that these marriage customs have important bearings on the question of paternal authority in the household. Matrilocal marriage means in general the absence of the younger men of the family who are probably away working for their fathers-in-law at a village somewhere else. There is a resultant concentration of authority in the hands of the elder people of the bride's family, her mother and father if they still remain married, or her mother and maternal uncle if the former is a widow or has been divorced. This situation is the more pronounced since the early marriage of the girl makes her exceedingly dependent on her female relatives in daily life. She spends her day at her mother's house, eats there with her other married sisters, and, when her first baby comes, relies entirely on her mother for advice, and is, in fact, hardly fitted to do much else. It is not surprising, therefore, that during the first years of a typical marriage the father is a person of little account. The biological family of man, woman, and child exists. Husband and wife sleep in their own hut, and perform together the ritual acts necessary for the rearing of their child. But custom decrees that the child should go to sleep with its grand-mother as soon as it is weaned. Sex taboos between husband and wife are then at an end, and contact with sexually active persons is magically dangerous to the young child. For the next five years or more the grandmother is the most important person in its life. She looks after him, feeds him, and often becomes more to him than the mother herself. Nowadays, when parents both go down to the mining centres, it is quite common to find children who do not remember their mother at all.

Again, though husband and wife are economic partners, and make a joint garden, yet the agricultural work is usually done in groups, the mother helping her daughters and sisters and *vice versa*, and the son working for, and with, his relatives in law. Moreover, sex taboos and etiquette, and the rigid sex division of labour of a primitive society set a barrier between husband and wife at their meals, their play, and their work; but on one

T

side of this is the wife amidst a solid phalanx of her own relatives, while on the other is the father, isolated, often a stranger in the village and prevented by the stringent in-law taboos from joining many of the groups of men who eat in the men's shelters at night. The situation is of course altered where inter-village or cross-cousin marriage has taken place, but the picture I have tried to draw is typical of the old-fashioned marriage and the one that is illustrated, moreover, in proverb and song.

The position of the father is very much altered when he can remove his wife to his own village later in life. He will then probably choose to go to live with his own most important relative on either side, either his grandfather, his *nalume*, or even his father if the latter has a village of his own. Here he will stay until he is in a position to build up his own settlement —the dearest aim of every Mubemba—or until he is called upon to succeed his *nalume*, and may go to become the headman of a village which is, so to speak, already made.[1] In either case, unless family intermarriage has taken place, the wife has to leave the support of her own people and live as a stranger in her husband's village. If the marriage has been in any way unstable, it is not uncommon for divorce to take place at this time. A woman thus left alone, whether by her own wish or by necessity, naturally looks to her own brother or to her *nalume* for support, and goes to settle with him.

If on the other hand the marriage endures, and these cases are after all in the majority, the wife will follow her husband to his home. If he has young daughters, married or about to be married, his position is at once greatly strengthened. As a father-in-law, and later a grandfather, his position is triumphant, even if as a father it is a poor one. This is what a Mubemba means when he says that with the birth of his daughters *ninsanga chifulo*, " I have found a permanent place of abode." A man with many daughters is envied, and the children of his daughters are of course particularly his own.[2] A man's sister, the *nyina senge*, has also peculiar powers over his daughters.

---

[1] The average village contains about thirty huts, but a man might start with a group of ten or so relatives and hope to attract others until about seventy huts had been built.

[2] In the royal family matrilocal residence is of course more continuous, and the husband of a *namfumu* will remain so to speak an outsider all his life. As in many other cases, the kinship system of the *benangandu* is the extreme instance of a rule which is greatly varied in the case of the ordinary men and women of the tribe. The *namfumu* chose their *lumbwe*, or consorts, usually in quick succession, according to eugenic principles, and a *lumbwe* had really no other job than to provide strong sons and daughters as heirs, or mothers of heirs. These consorts lived in the old days a precarious life, liable to be dismissed on the slightest pretext, and to suffer mutilation or death if a difficult or fatal childbirth caused suspicion that they had committed adultery during the pregnancy of the *namfumu*, their wife. Only a *lumbwe* of great distinction, or himself a *mwinangandu*, could expect his wife to follow him, even temporarily, to his own village.

The question of the possession of the children of any marriage is more complex, and here great changes are noticeable at the present day. Formerly it was of vital importance, since the elder relatives had the right to give the younger as slaves in compensation for blood guilt or as wives to fulfil a marriage contract which had been broken for any reason. This right lay almost exclusively in the hands of the maternal side of the family, and in particular the *nalume*. Nowadays we have to consider chiefly the question of the legal possession of the children in case of divorce. Technically this right belonged to the maternal relatives, but recently the position has very much changed. Then, and now, a man who had paid a large *mpango* could thereby increase his rights over the children, but at present the demands of the wife and the children for clothing and European luxuries are growing rapidly, and with them the power of the paternal relatives. In fact if divorce has taken place by mutual consent, a man can maintain his rights over the children by sending occasional gifts or clothes for their support. Divorce cases heard at a native court consist largely in the weighing-up of the contributions made to the marriage at various times by the father and the *nalume*.[1]

In the case of the division of the *mpango*, we may note very much the same tendency towards an increase in the father's power. An old man will tell you that the *nalume* should get all the *mpango*, but that he should give something to the father and to the *nyina senge*, especially if the father is a person of rank and means. Nowadays the father claims the right to divide the payment, although he will give something to the *nalume* or maternal grandparents. Even if divorced from the mother he can claim half the money given at his daughter's marriage. In reality, I think, the mother or maternal grandmother is the owner of the *mpango* and that she hands it to the male relative, whether father or *nalume*, who is the acting guardian of the girl.

It will be seen, therefore, that as regards the possession of the children, the balance between paternal and maternal relatives is fairly evenly maintained. The child moves from the care of his maternal grandparents to that of his father, according to circumstances, or his own free will. It must be remembered also that the permanent village does not exist among the Babemba. Sites are changed every four or five years with shifting systems of agriculture, and kinship groups are constantly dissolved and reformed. But in spite of wide possibilities of

[1] In actual practice it may be added that the phrase "custody of the children," used in the white man's order, is largely a meaningless expression in the case of the Babemba because of the freedom allowed young children. Whatever the decision of the European court, the children in practice move from relative to relative very much as they like.

individual variation, the legal rule to this day remains the same. A Mubemba is emphatically associated with his mother's kin. The clan system, inheritance, and succession pass in the maternal line, and this identification of a man with his mother's relatives is made closer by the *kupyanika* system of succession to the spirit and social status of the dead *nalume* or maternal grandfather. Matrilocal marriage and the customs of child-rearing make for the authority of the maternal grandparents, while the *nalume* is the official guardian and educator of the child, formerly with power over the life and marriage of his uterine nephews and nieces. It is perhaps significant, too, that the injured spirit of a maternal relative, particularly the mother or the *nalume*, can be expected to return and afflict the neglectful child at death, whereas the father, however much he may have given to his children, of his pleasure, during his lifetime is not, according to formal dogma, permitted to return in this way.

But this seemingly matrilineal organization is twisted, and sometimes even deformed in actual fact. The father is constantly making inroads on the maternal family's prerogatives, and we shall see that there is almost a balance of rights maintained in the course of daily life. The first factor which alters the strong matrilineal emphasis is the native theory of procreation. According to Bemba theory it is technically only the woman who can pass on the blood to her children, although this statement will be immediately qualified by most natives. "If a man begets children," an old native of rank will say, "what are they? Things of no value. But if his sister bears children they are of his blood and he must look after them." And in this way the first chiefs married their children to their sisters' children to create *bufyashi*, or seed. But the Babemba are perfectly aware of the physiological function of the father in the conception of the child, and this very rôle is made the basis of important paternal rights. ⌜In Trobriand society the facts of physical paternity are ignored.⌟ In South Africa they are known, but the sociological fatherhood established by the payment of *lobola* is made of more consequence in tribal life ; but in Bemba culture it seems to be the actual fact of physiological fatherhood which is recognized as the basis of the father's rights over his child, and the attitude of respect with which he is treated. Divorce is frequent among these people, as we have shown, but the father is never forgotten. It is extraordinary to see grown men and women, children of parents long since divorced and parted, making long journeys to visit their father and to give him presents. Extraordinary, too, to listen to the calm assurance of the father, living perhaps some 300 miles away, " They will come back one day. How can they forget their father ? " And in both cases the explanation is apparently the same. " Would my mother have conceived without my father?" said a man impatiently, in answer to my continued questions. I have had the same answer offered as a reason for giving half the girl's marriage payment—*mpango*—to a father who had contributed little to her maintenance during her youth. So also in the case of the royal clan, the *lumbwe* or consort, who is typically an object of pity and derision, may be rewarded and honoured by a chief, "Because he was a good man. He begat many children for our mothers."

Further there is in native belief an intimate magical connection between a man and his wife and his child. The lives of the three are mysteriously entwined by the very fact of the sex act, and their common association with the fire of one hut. The sex behaviour of one partner affects the life and health of the other and the birth and safety of any children of the union— especially in the case of a man's head wife. It is for this reason that a father has a very important part to play in the ritual life of the young child. The young father, as we saw, has not much power over his first children, but even he, isolated in a strange village, is hailed by the omnipotent grandmother as the *mwine*, or owner of the child, called by the child's name, and considered absolutely essential to the safety of the baby's life.

It is surprising to find, too, that in this matrilineal tribe a man is called by his father's name and not by that of his *nalume*. The first name given to a child is that of the spirit which has been found by divination to be its guardian, but to this name is added, as a kind of surname, that which the father has taken later in life. Thus even a member of the royal clan, a *mwinangandu,* is known by the name of his father, the despised *lumbwe*—cases being on record of a slave *lumbwe* having so given his name to the child. Moreover, the guardian spirits, or *mipashi*, are inherited bilaterally, and a man may go through life protected by a spirit of his father's line.

Moreover, besides native theories of procreation we have to consider the actual sentiment attaching father to son. Malinowski has shown us very clearly, in another typically matrilineal society, the conflict between the legal duty to the maternal nephew, and a man's natural desire to benefit his own sons. In Bemba culture something of the same phenomenon can be seen. Between father and son there is a freer, more casual and affectionate relationship than that between uncle and uterine nephew. Not only is the *nalume* the ultimate legal guardian, but as the boy grows up he begins to feel the shadows of approaching restraints. His preferential marriage is with his cross-cousin, the daughter of his mother's brother. The *nalume* is a potential father-in-law, and already treated with stiffness and uncomfortable respect. The boy knows also that he may have to assume the name of his maternal uncle and also to inherit the latter's wife. The possible future identification between the two relations sets up a barrier between those who are legally next of kin—a man and his sister's son. This is particularly the case in the chief's family where the question of inheritance is of greater importance, A *mwipwa* (or " sister's son ") of a chief must stay at his uncle's court, entirely at his service, but may not eat or drink with him, joke, or touch his person—all this in marked contrast to the behaviour of the royal sons. It is significant, too, that a chief, or a man holding high office, is helped in his duties by son or grandson rather than his uterine nephew. " Why may my *mwipwa* not see my sacred relics ? Because he will succeed me. He is the same as me (*alelinga ine*). It would be a slight to the spirits while I am still alive. Besides, why should I show things to him who will one day get everything of mine ? I am not going to teach him. I shall teach only my sons. My *mwipwa* can learn from other people when I am dead. How do you suppose I learnt myself ? " This statement by one of the chief's hereditary councillors sums up the typical attitude of the *nalume* well. In this uneasy relationship between *nalume* and *mwipwa* the father sometimes plays a part as a kind of neutral. At a *kupyanika*, or an accession ceremony, it is the father who has to hand the heir the bow of succession ; the father's sister who gives the *mushingo* to the girl. Thus in the case of succession to the chieftainship, the father, himself a nobody, has to play an important part. There are cases on record, too, where the father's relatives were put in charge of a chief's sacred relics when the fighting between two rival heirs was acute. Conversely, in the case of the chiefs, the desire of the father to secure benefits for his sons as against his sister's sons meets with a large measure of success. In this matrilineal society the *banabamfumu*, or sons of the chief have definite rank, though not membership of the royal clan of course. In youth they live at their father's court, care-free, irresponsible, and spoilt in every way. As they grow older they are given villages in their father's territory, live near him, and get his constant support. There are even large tracts of land which are regularly inherited by sons of chiefs. The Makasa, for instance, one of the biggest of the sub-chiefs, is always the eldest son of the Paramount Chief, and fulfils an important rôle in tribal affairs, while the headmen of his territory are always sons of former Makasa and their succession is therefore practically patrilineal.

We see, then, that the strength of the institution of chieftainship can override the matrilineal principle and find in tribal organization a place for the chief's sons, and that, therefore, in this decidedly matrilineal society there

was, even in former days, a strong admixture of patrilineal right. The legal rules of kinship could be overruled
by a man of superior rank, and a man of royal clan could
probably claim successfully both his *bepwa* and his sons.
Conversely, a man whose father's rank was superior to his mother's
would unhesitatingly attach himself to the clan of the former.
Similarly a man of substance, by dint of the size of the *mpango*
given for his wife and the contributions given for her support
and that of the children, could *ipso facto* increase his control.
In the case of the children of a slave wife his rights were naturally
complete.

Contact with white civilization has further tilted the balance
to the father's side. This has been due in part to the ignorance
of white administrators and teachers and their prejudice against
the matrilineal system, and partly to directly economic factors.
The exodus of men to work in the Rhodesian copper mines has
greatly diminished marriage by service, and also largely put an
end to matrilocal marriage itself, The increasing demands of
wife and children for cloth and objects bought by money has
placed a further weapon in the father's hand.

As against this we have to set the greater instability of modern
marriages, and the enormous number of deserted wives driven
back on their maternal relatives for support. To this cause
we have to attribute also an increase in interfamily and cross-
cousin marriage. A near relative is less likely so to desert a wife.

When the balance of patrilineal and matrilineal rights is so
intricate, it is no longer useful to accept the old rough and ready
classifications as an end in themselves. It is our task rather to
make comparative studies among a series of kindred peoples
in order to get some general conception of the way in which
this balance is maintained. Again, though it appears that in
Bemba society a change is taking place very rapidly from
matrilineal to patrilineal, yet this change is in itself dependent
on so many factors that it is ludicrously inadequate to try to
account for it by any facile belief in the universality of such
an evolutionary change.

THE STUDY OF CHARACTER DEVELOPMENT AND THE ONTOGENETIC THEORY OF CULTURE

By Géza Róheim

Psychology and anthropology, in fact all the various methods of studying mankind, seem to be converging towards one essential problem. We want to know more about human character, about the reasons that induce human beings to act in a certain way. Under similar conditions different people or different groups of people will act and feel differently to each other, but consistently to themselves. People are avaricious or liberal, witty or dull, kind or the opposite, brave or full of anxieties, i.e. they show certain typical attitudes. Popular belief also attributes a certain character to whole nations, regarding, for instance, the German as methodical but slow, the Frenchman as witty but unreliable, the Englishman as eminently a man of common sense, the Spaniard as proud and brave, and so on. There are, of course, very great differences in the opinions nations form about themselves and in the views held by others regarding their neighbours. We shall have to inquire into the question as to how far this idea of a collective or group character is justified, by which I do not mean to ask whether the French or the Germans are really what they are alleged to be, but whether and how such a thing as a group character can exist.

It is, of course, possible to choose all sorts of characteristics and use them as a basis for the classification of mankind.

Kretschmer's famous attempt to correlate constitution with certain mental types is built up on psychiatry and popular opinion. The author sides with Julius Cæsar when he says :—

> "Let me have men about me that are fat,
> Sleek-headed men and such as sleep o' nights.
> Yond Cassius has a lean and hungry look,
> He thinks too much : such men are dangerous."

But when he accepts Kraepelin's grouping of psychotics as either mania-melancholiac or schizophreniac (*dementia præcox*), and then extends this classification to non-psychotic individuals and correlates it with the " asthenic " and the " pyknic " type of constitution, it is doubtful whether he has given the anthropologist a tool that he can use.[1] His " asthenic " type agrees mentally more or less with Jung's idea of an introvert, the

---

[1] Cf. E. Kretschmer, *Körperbau und Charakter*, 1926.

" pyknic " or " cyclothymic " with that of an extrovert. It seems very doubtful whether thin and tall races are in general more likely to adopt an introvert attitude than broadly built, fat people.

Jung's well-known classification has been applied to anthropology by Professor Seligman. In a very interesting paper he arrives at the conclusion that the civilization of India and China should be regarded as mainly introvert, while all so-called primitive people as well as the representatives of Western Civilization are extroverts.[1]

Another classification is contained in Barbara Aitken's study of North American religion. The author distinguishes the individualistic and the social temperament both in individuals and in societies or tribes of North America.[2] Although the paper refers only to North American societies, the psychoanalyst will be the first to acknowledge the applicability of this point of view to characterology. The " Catholic " type of mind would be the result of the acceptance of the father as an ideal, while the " Protestant " or critical or individualistic attitude corresponds to what Lorand has called the reactive character, that is, character development in opposition to the father-imago.[3]

A division of human beings based on their dominant tendencies has been put forward by Freud in one of his recent papers. Our psyche consists of three constituent factors, the Id, the Ego, and the Super-Ego. There are also three types of human beings according to the predominance of these three factors. The erotic type of personality represents the demands of the Id, and for people of this kind their interest in love is the predominant trend of their life. To love and to be beloved makes life worth living and the loss of the love of the opposite sex is the great anxiety in life.

In the obsessional type the demands of the Super-Ego outweigh all other considerations. There is a great tension between Ego and Super-Ego, a strong tendency towards cultural activity and anxiety is connected with conscience.

The third type is mainly negative in its characteristics. There is no predominance of Super-Ego or of Ego considerations and the main interest is centered in the Ego-activity. Narcisstic individuals are more likely to be leading personages and to give new directions to culture, while the activity of the obsessional type is mainly conservative.[4]

In his earlier writings Freud has taken the first great step

---

[1] C. G. Seligman, " Anthropology and Psychology," *Journal of the Royal Anthropological Institute,* 1924, p. 54.

[2] Barbara Aitken, " Temperament in Native American Religion," *Journal of the Royal Anthropological Institute,* 1930, p. 363.

[3] S. Lorand, *The Morbid Personality,* 1931, p. 74.

[4] Sigm. Freud," Über libidinöse Typen," *Zeitschrift für Psychoanalyse,* vol. xvii.

towards understanding human character on a dynamic basis,
In clinical practice we see a human being in the making, or.
rather, we can go back to early events in human life which have
provoked certain reactions in the immature Ego. These reactions
have become displaced to other aims and stereotyped, and thus
constitute what we now call the character of the adult. Freud
noticed that a certain group of patients were so exact in their
behaviour that we might call them pedantic or peculiar, so saving
with their time and money that this amounted to morbid forms
of avarice, and finally so true to themselves in everything that
we might call it obstinacy. Analysis could always demonstrate
that this was an acquired character. The development of this
character was shown to be due to the attitude of the parents,
to the care they took to make the child defecate and urinate
according to their regulations. The child resented this
interference and desired to dispose of the pleasure-giving material
according to its own whim. As an adult it carries over this
infantile obstinacy to the world in general. Money becomes
a symbol of the excrements, a process of symbol formation in
which the contrast element has a large share. Colour, cohesion,
and value of the symbol are in exact contrast to the original,
although at least as far as value is concerned this contrast is
really a restoration of the original libidinal valuation. Gold
represents excrement because gold means the most valuable, and
excrement the least valuable material, but also because the
infant originally loves every particle of its body and is far from
regarding fecal matter as worthless. Freud's researches were
afterwards carried on by Ferenczi, Jones, Abraham, and others
till we find that the evolution and nature of the anal character
is one of the subjects that has received the greatest attention
in clinical analysis. What we usually call anal character-
formation ought really to be called a reactive anal character, for
there is also another type of anal character-formation in which
Ego-trends are based not on inverted, but on direct libidinal
trends.

From the frequency of anal characters in clinical analysis
it was only one step to the conclusion that our culture or the
type of our social organization in general was based on
sublimations or reaction formation of anal trends.[1] Where
else can we find such an organized system of caring for the future,
such a far-going possibility of " retaining " food-stuffs in a
symbolical form ? The infant receives nourishment from the
mother and messes her with its excrements as a symbol of love.
Civilization has invented a form in which the equivalent of
nourishment can be retained for any length of time (money)
and by means of which we can organize this retention (savings

[1] A. Stärcke, *Psychoanalyse und Psychiatrie*, 1921.

bank). No other group of human beings has such exaggerated
ideas of hygiene and cleanliness, and whoever first said that the
amount of soap used by a people was a sure indication of their
level of "civilization" was not far from the truth. Soap,
money, and regulations.

On the other hand, I found that a certain happy and careless
infantile attitude characterizes primitive mankind in general.
Food forms the bond of union between human beings, and they
are continually reciprocally reviving the mother-child relation,
i.e. giving each other food as a sign of goodwill.   Our civilization
is anal, whereas more primitive forms of society are oral.[1]

But the real significance of all these considerations was only
brought home to me in the course of my field-work.   I had an
intuitive feeling that there was a salient feature in the civilization
of each area with which I came into contact.   The Somali are
the people who perform the operation of clitoridectomy and
the sewing together of the labia, and open their wives on the
bridal night with the aid of a knife ; the Central Australians
are characterized by the *churunga* cult and the *alknarincha*
women ;   the people of Duau (Normanby Island) by the *sagari*
and other food-distribution festivals.   The Yuma Indians
appear to be characterized by the creation-legend, the mortuary
festivals (Karook), and their vocation dreams.

The initiation ceremony in Central Australia consists of two
operations performed on the boy, and as a compensation for
what he has to undergo with his penis he receives two *churungas*.
The *churunga mborka* or body *churunga* is connected with
circumcision and the *namatuna* (grass-hitter) with subincision.
Both types of *churunga* have a definite purpose.   The larger
type of body *churunga* is the link that connects the boy with
his totemic ancestors, while the small *churunga* enables him to
win the love of an *alknarincha* woman by performing an *ilpindja*.
An *alknarincha*, i.e. "eyes turn away" woman, is a woman
who runs away as fast as her legs will carry her at the sight of
a man.   *Ilpindja* means "blocking" or inhibition, and is
the name of the love magic or incantation without which the
namatuna has no value.   The two concepts, however, i.e.
the *alknarincha* and the *ilpindja*, belong together in a peculiarly
ambivalent fashion.   For a woman is made an *alknarincha*,
i.e. a woman who resists the advances of the male through
having been "sung" by an *ilpindja*.   On the other hand, one
must sing an *ilpindja* in order to gain the love and to conquer the
resistance of an *alknarincha*.   Thus, the idea of resistance is
linked up very closely with that of sexual desire.   Moreover,
the ordinary vocation of the *namatuna* is to announce the advent

<hr>

[1] G. Róheim, "Die Völkerpsychologie und die Psychologie der Völker,"
Imago, 1926.

of the initiate and frighten the woman away, but in connection with the *ilpindja* it is a means of attracting an *alknarincha*.

For the present all we can see is that ambivalence has contributed its share to the formation of the *alknarincha* idea. Nor could we get very much further if it were not for the aid brought to field anthropology by psychoanalytic technique. As I have explained elsewhere,[1] my method of work represents an approach to clinical analysis as far as this is possible in field-work. One of my main "informants" or "patients" is old Yirramba (Honey ant), a blind old man who was initiated at the *inkura*[2] held by Spencer in 1896, and who speaks of Spencer as a personal friend of his.

On the 14th March, 1929, he had the following dream[3] :—

"Yesterday night I saw a lot of women. They were very pretty and they were decorating themselves with *alpita* (rabbit tail or bandicoot tail) and *kanta* (circular string ornament). They had *uritchas* (pitchis) on their heads. We went up a hill and then we ate grass-seed together. A man came and brought some lizards and erected a *natandja* (ceremonial pole).

"There were two *knarrentora arakutya* (big or old women) who sat in the middle, performed *quabara* (ceremonies), and had *churunga* on their head. We all ran round the two old women. Then we went down a mountain as I kept whirling the *namatuna*."

Two days later Yirramba had the following dream :—

"*Alknarincha* women called me to come and sit down with them. But I refused. They killed *kurra* (kangaroo-rat) and got bush-seeds. I dug yams. My father sat in the middle at a flat stone called Pulja (Navel). A tree arose where the old man was seated. The *alknarincha* women went hunting and came back while the old man performed ceremonies. I was making string, some of the women were getting the *kanta* (circular ornament) ready, others were making *alpita* (bandicoot tail). We all whirled the *namatuna*. Then we were all making *walupanpa*.[4] We all gathered round the old man, I and all the *alknarincha*. We all held the *tingari* (ceremonial pole) and went down into the ground at Pulja with the old man. We all went down and became *churunga*."

In connection with the first dream he explains the use of the *uritcha* and other wooden dishes. The thing the women had on their head was an *alpara*, the kind of pitchi used for carrying children.[5] When the young men swing the *namatuna*

[1] Cf. "Psycho-Analytic Technique and Field Anthropology," *International Journal of Psycho-Analysis*, xiii, 6.
[2] Written by Spencer *engwura*.
[3] For reasons of space I give only an abbreviated version of the dreams and the association material.
[4] The string worn by the *maliara* (novices).
[5] First he said it was an *uritcha* (for water).

their *alchera* (ancestral spirit) enters the girl's womb. She feels suddenly sick and then goes to sleep and dreams of the *maliara*. When nobody observes her she runs away and follows the *maliara*. Then after a time she vomits and again she dreams of the boy, of his *alchera,* and the *namatuna.* This time she is pregnant.

The two *knarrentora arakutya* are like two Aranda women at the mission who are both his *ankalla* (cousins). He loves them both (*kankama*),[1] when he meets them he kisses them and is very happy.

But the context of the dream shows that his desires regarding his two *ankalla* women are not as innocent as they seem to him. For these women are carrying the troughs on their heads that serve as a receptacle for the new-born baby and he is whirling the *namatuna,* i.e. making them fall in love with him and inpregnating them. Moreover, the woman who is gained by means of the *namatuna* is an *alknarincha,* and this links up the women of the first dream with the *alknarincha* women in the second dream. These, he tells me, were fair like white women, they had red hair, and they were very pretty. When he woke he looked round but he could not find them. She is, of course, much younger than the old man, but he calls her *mia* (mother) according to the classificatory system of relationship, and he remarks that he was present when she was born. Then he goes on to talk about his own mother and about the *arunkulta* (evil magic) which killed his brother and sister on the same day at Alice Springs.[2] Then he asks me about my wife. When is she coming back? *Konja, konja* (pity) that she went away, she was like a mother to him.

The conclusion to be drawn from these remarks of Yirramba is quite obvious. The woman who averts her eyes, who is yet desired by all young men is the mother, who appears to be the most desirable woman in the world from the infantile point of view, but who remains an *alknarincha* because she refuses to grant the incestuous desires of her son.

The next thing that strikes us in these dreams is the rôle attributed to the *alknarincha* women. In one of the dreams we see the two " old women " in the centre of the scene with a *churunga* (phallic symbol) [3] on their heads that is, in a position that can only be occupied by the old *knaripata* (fathers) in actual ritual. The dreamer identifies himself with the young women who run round the two old women. In the second he is with the *alknarinchas,* i.e. in the position of an *alknarincha* with

---

[1] The expression *kankama* means rather sublimated than direct genital desire.

[2] The influenza epidemic.

[3] The phallic meaning of the *churunga* has been shown in my *Australian Totemism,* 1925. The proofs I obtained in my field-work are conclusive.

regard to his own father. But what is the father doing ? He
is kneeling near a flat rock—and kneeling is the position both of
coitus and of the ceremonies. Moreover, when he kneels a tree
grows out of the earth and a ceremonial pole is erected. The
place-name means navel, and navel in the sacred songs is a
frequent euphemism for the vagina or the womb. I was much
interested in the ending of the dream, in which the dreamer, like
the heroes of the myth, is transformed into a *churunga*. " What
does it feel like ? " I asked. He described the sensation as a sort
of feeling of sinking into something soft, like soft earth. O yes,
it was splendid—he felt *chipa-chipa*. What is *chipa-chipa* ?
Then he explained that *chipa-chipa* meant great pleasure,
supreme happiness, for instance the sensation of coitus.

The many *alknarincha* women are a series-formation derived
from the mother-imago. The situation in which we find the
father (kneeling at the vagina), and in which he is afterwards
joined by the women and the dreamer, clearly shows that the
latent content of the dream is the primal scene, i.e. the coitus
of the parents. The child represses what he has observed
because of the phantasies provoked by the scene. One of these,
as we see from the contents of the dream, is to steal the mother
from the father and to have intercourse with her, i.e. to do as
the father does. For the man in the first dream, he tells me,
looks like Pukuti-wara, a mythical ancestor whose story begins
by his stealing a woman from another man. He has nothing
to say about his father, the only thing he keeps repeating is that
he was present when the old man died and tended him in his
sickness.

While these elements of the dream (death of the father, use
of the *namatuna* in connection with the mother, the vessel in
which babies are carried on the woman's head), clearly indicate
the positive Œdipus trends as one of the dream elements, we
also see that the child identifies itself with the women in their
relation to the father. Finally, the dream represents a compromise between the two aspects of the ambisexual Œdipus
conflict; the boy, the father, and the mother all become *churunga*,
all sink into the ground, i.e. all have intercourse together.

This explanation of the dream fits well with the moment in
which the boy receives the *namatuna*. He is now separated
from the mother and aggregated to the society of fathers. At
the same time society offers him a phantasy substitute for the
beloved mother of his infancy in a woman who turns her eyes
away, but then after having been enchanted by the *ilpindja* she
rushes to him from some distant country. The mechanism of
symbol formation is very familiar to all those who have analysed
dreams ; the unknown woman coming from a strange country
means a woman we know very well and with whom we have

lived in close proximity—the mother. The two *knarrentora arakutya* of the first dream are the cross-cousins of the dreamer, and marriage with the cross-cousin here as in other primitive societies is just on the border between incest and exogamy. However, although the resisting mother as represented by the *alknarincha* is what every boy is trying to get, when he whirls the *namatuna*, yet there are large quantities of anxiety connected with this concept, or at least with a sub-species of the *alknarincha* idea called *labarindja* or *allaparinja* by old Yirramba.[1]

Both from songs that I have recorded and from Spencer's description of *illapurinja* we see that the concept of dangerous and " shy " women, who are therefore specially desirable as wives, plays an important part in the life of every young Aranda. We can also conclude with a fair degree of certainty that the unconscious equivalent of this idea is that of the mother with male attributes. One day while I was talking about the significance of certain typical dreams with Mulda and Wapiti I learnt another important detail regarding the natural history of *alknarincha*. In a dream an *alknarincha* always appears in the shape of a *nyurpma* (illicit, incestuous) woman, and if you dream of an *alknarincha* you must awake immediately. If the dreamer does not awake the *alknarincha* woman will have intercourse with him in the inverted position, she will sit upon the man's penis. The dangers to be avoided in this are both the incestuous nature of the coitus and the female position occupied by the man. But the concept of the mother in the male rôle is not merely a phantasy due to the negative aspect of the Œdipus complex, it is also an experience, an actual fact in the life of every Central Australian male. One of the Ngatatara women told me a dream in which her brother was " chasing her " with an axe. She concluded the narrative by saying : " I woke up and I was lying on Nyiki." If a woman is chased by a man that can only mean that he is trying to have intercourse with her and the word *kula-kula* means both to run after a woman and the act of coitus. Then they explained that it is the custom of the women to sleep so that the body covers that of the child, in fact she sleeps on her child like a man who is having intercourse with a woman. She will go on doing this till the child is about seven or eight years old, especially when the nights are cold.

We can easily understand what this custom means in the life of an Aranda or Pitchentara. There is no latency period, and both the boy and the mother are naked. Evidently the child had an erection as a response to the physical contact with her body but she would certainly not permit an immission.

---

[1] *Allaparinja* is *Aranda choritcha* (Eastern Aranda), and *labarindja* is *Aranda ulpma* (Finke Aranda).

The Central Australian native therefore gets as near to the realization of his incestuous desires as any human being can, without actually having intercourse with the mother. This is exactly the kind of trauma which is so familiar to us from clinical analysis. The child is confronted by a situation which contains an overdose of libido for the immature Ego. Repression is called to the rescue, and the original experience continues to exercise a strong, but unconscious, influence on the destinies and character of the individual till it is brought back into consciousness and abreacted in analysis. The important difference between the Central Australian native and our individual neurotic is that in the former the libidinal shock or infantile trauma is conditioned by custom. It is an habitual trauma, a common experience, and will also be abreacted or dealt with collectively. What I contend is that it is this collective abreaction of infantile traumata which gives the specific features of each civilization. The typically " male " organization of Central Australian tribes, in which ritual consists in keeping the women as far away as possible, is a reaction formation against the erotic sensations conditioned by the infantile situation, by the proximity of the mother. The woman who " runs away " was once the woman who was in closest contact with the child. The exaggeratedly " male " attitude of the *mbanja* (marriage by rape) is the over-compensation of the original infantile passivity with regard to the mother. The *churunga* itself, which may well be called the leading symbol of Central Australian totemic society, represents this original situation while at the same time it is also an effort to deal with it by means of sublimation. For the first *churunga* was the penis of the mythical hero, Malpunga, and the concentric circle which covers the surface of the *churunga* symbolizes the vagina or womb.[1] In the *churunga* cult the men are united and the women excluded—in the infantile situation the boy is in the closest proximity to one woman. But the *churunga* itself is a penis covered by the vagina and thus represents the situation which it represses. Moreover, we should not forget that the *churunga* and indeed the whole complex of Central Australian totemism form an inextricable unity with the puberty ritual.[2] When I was working among the Pitchentara and other western tribes speaking " Luritja " dialects I found that the climax of their ritual, the great mystery of initiation, a word which they would only pronounce in whispers and which even Strehlow had never heard, was *ngallunga*. This means both a definite kind of myth and a definite form of ritual. Initiation cannot be carried out with any kind of totemic myth, but only with a *ngallunga* story.

[1] Cf. *International Journal of Psycho-Analysis*, xiii.
[2] My field-work has shown me that this unity goes considerably further than I could guess in *Australian Totemism*.

A *ngallunga* story is always a myth of the kangaroo (or associated) totems, and the typical heroes of the narrative among the Yumu are Unami and Yurgna, that is Semen and Testicles. *Ngallunga* in ritual means the part of initiation when the men run backward and show the bleeding[1] subincision wound to the child by jerking the penis upward. Finally the word *ngallunga* means " we two are friends ". Taken in connection with the psychology of initiation it is obvious that the formula refers to the relation of the initiators to the initiated, of the fathers to the sons. The function of initiation is to separate the boy from the mother and to aggregate him to a male society. How is this to be attained ? By showing him the subincised penis or the subincision wound of the men. Now we have not merely the skeletons of the *ngallunga* myths, but also the flesh and blood that is the mythical songs. In these songs both the subincised penis and the subincision wound are called " *kunna* ", that is, vagina. If we connect this with myths of the *alknarincha* women in which these women appear with three phalloi, moreover, with the tradition that the *namatuna* (bull-roarer) was owned by the *alknarincha* women in mythical times, and it was from them that the phallic hero Malpunga obtained it, we can see clearly what might be called the function of initiation. Instead of the " phallic mother " of their infancy the boys are now to love a " vaginal father ". " We two are friends " means " Leave the women and come to the men, we have also got vaginae ". Lack of space makes it impossible to go into further details or to give other instances from my field-work. What I believe is that there is such a thing as a group character, and that it is based on the collective sublimation of customary traumata, although, of course, not without individual deviations from the standard type. A primitive society might be defined as a society in which these deviations are small, i.e. in which the behaviour of the parents is more uniform than in an advanced society. When we shall have more workers in the field trained in the use of analytic technique we shall probably find that the leading symptoms or characteristic features of primitive tribes can be explained as being derived from the infantile traumata which habitually occur in these societies. This is what I mean by an *ontogenetic theory of culture*. While the old ideological view of history regarded men as actuated by ideas, that is by the Super-Ego, while the Marxian view of history believes in economical conditions, that is in the Ego, the ontogenetic theory of culture interprets humanity in the terms of the Id, and regards our impulses as conditioned by the first experiences which the infant makes in life as the basis of everything else. In my opinion the greatest objection to a Marxian interpretation of history

[1] Blood has been made to flow by using minute stone knives or little chips.

lies in the clinical experience of psychoanalysis. To say that
the ideas of a society are a superstructure built up on the economic
conditions implies that these economic conditions determine
our actions, even when we are not aware of the fact, i.e. that they
are unconscious. But when we investigate the unconscious
we do not find economical conditions. Our ideas or beliefs are
derived from our infantile impulses ; they are all sublimations
or reaction formations of the Œdipus complex. " Economic
conditions " are not supernatural beings derived from the stars,
but the result of a compromise achieved between man's primary
impulses and environment. On the other hand, the ontogenetic
view of culture differs from the phylogenetic interpretation of
culture, put forward by Freud in the *Totem and Taboo*, since
it seeks a less ambitious goal. I think we ought to be able to
understand culture first in the psychology of the present bearers
of culture, as the collective neurosis of a group, before we can
correlate it with the process of psychical transformation which
took place at the dawn of humanity. I do not mean to say that
we should give up all hopes of a psychological reconstruction of
the past, but it seems obvious that a culture, like a neurosis,
should be traced to its ontogenetic roots before we invoke the
shades of phylogenesis. This view of culture means an approach
to theories put forward by the modern anthropological school
(Malinowski, Mrs. Seligman) who like myself believe that the
specific determining factors for the development of each type of
civilization, and also for the character development of the
individual, can be found in the family situation.

But we have not replied to the question we started out to
investigate. How can we regard a group as having a common
character ? Or how far can we regard culture and character
as identical ?

The great problem for a civilized middle-class child is the
choice of a vocation or a job in life. He can sublimate his
infantile conflicts or traumata in various ways. We have in
clinical analysis abundant proofs for the assumption that our
occupations are determined by the unconscious. But in a
primitive society there is one path for all and there is a relatively
greater degree of homogeneity, both as regards the infantile
trauma and in the Super-Ego sublimation of this trauma, i.e.
in their culture or group character.

I do not mean to say that there are no individual differences
in a Central Australian society. Certainly Pukuti-wara and
Yirramba and many others had an individuality of their own,
and to a certain measure I can also trace the sources of this
individual character development in their analysed dreams.
The task of the future field anthropologist, trained in the use of
psychoanalytic technique, will be to investigate the infantile

roots of collective and of individual character formation in primitive societies.

There is, however, one objection to be made to the ontogenetic view of culture. It explains the adult in the terms of his own infancy, and especially in so far as that infancy was conditioned by behaviour of the previous generation of adults. Then that behaviour again remains to be explained, and here we may be compelled to call for the aid of other factors, either psychological or constitutional. If these factors are constitutional we shall have explained how they become psychologically and sociologically effective through the medium of infantile receptivity. But if these factors are also psychological we seem to be moving in a vicious circle, for we have then explained the adult as conditioned by the child, and the child as conditioned by the adult.[1] Even in this case, however, something will be accomplished in finding the psychological formulae of the different primitive societies.

[1] Further conclusions are contained in my forthcoming book, *The Riddle of " the Sphinx."*

ORAL SORCERY AMONG THE NATIVES
OF BECHUANALAND

By I. SCHAPERA

The conceptions of sorcery and witchcraft held by the Bantu of South Africa vary considerably. The most clear-cut distinction between these two forms of nefarious activity appears to exist among the BaVenda and the BaThonga. The BaVenda apply the term *vhaloi* (sing. *muloi*, from *u loya* " to bewitch ") to all those people who employ magic in order to inflict injury or death upon others. But there are two quite separate classes of *vhaloi* : those who act unconsciously, and those who deliberately seek to harm their enemies through the use of magic. The unconscious *muloi* has a dual personality. By day she is an ordinary individual, completely unaware of the dreadful powers she possesses. But at night she becomes an evil creature. It is said that her spirit leaves her body when she is asleep and goes out into the world to carry on its destructive mission in company with its fellows, for these *vhaloi* are believed to associate together in a sort of professional guild. On the other hand there is the *muloi* who, consciously and deliberately, either alone or with the aid of a *nganga* (magician), attempts to encompass the death of an enemy by magical means. The black magic employed is termed *madambi*. Many magicians are acquainted with this means of destruction and are willing, for a large fee, to help the *muloi* carry out his designs.[1]

A distinction almost identical in nature is found among the BaThonga. It appears further from Junod's account that the evil powers of the " unconscious " *baloyi* are hereditary. " This dreadful power," he says, " is sucked in at their mother's breasts when they are still infants, but it must be strengthened by special medicines in order to be really efficient." And again, " it is well known that all the sons of a *noyi* woman are equally *baloyi*." [2] Although he does not go fully enough into this point, it is apparent that these *baloyi* may really be regarded as persons with a peculiar biological endowment. Adopting the terminology used by Evans-Pritchard in his discussion of Zande sorcery, we can, then, speak of the unwitting *baloyi* as " wizards " and of the deliberate malefactors as " sorcerers ".[3] It should be noted,

---

[1] Cf. H. A. Stayt, *The BaVenda*, Oxford, 1931, pp. 273–8.
[2] Cf. H. A. Junod, *The Life of a South African Tribe*, London, 1927, ii, 504 ff .
[3] E. E. Evans-Pritchard, " Sorcery and Native Opinion," *Africa*, iv (1931), esp. 26–8.

o

however, that the distinction he makes in regard to the methods employed by these two classes among the AZande is not entirely applicable to Venda or Thonga society.

The BaKxatla, of Bechuanaland Protectorate, appear to have merged into one the conceptions of witchcraft and sorcery kept distinct by the BaVenda and the BaThonga.[1] They speak, it is true, of *baloi* who go about at night in groups trying to kill or harm other people. In many respects their beliefs about these *baloi* correspond to those held by the BaVenda and the BaThonga, especially in regard to the animal familiars associated with their activities. But it is also maintained that the *baloi* go about in the flesh, not in the spirit, and are always fully aware of what they are doing. Moreover, they do not inherit their evil powers, but have to learn from the other *baloi*, and any man or woman can become one of them. There are still other *baloi* who do not belong to the fraternity or practice the black art habitually. They are content to employ magic solely in order to secure vengeance against a particular enemy, and would therefore correspond closely to the " sorcerers " found amongst the BaVenda and BaThonga. All *baloi* must as a rule obtain their medicines (*dithlare*) from the *dingaka* (professional magicians), and on the whole they all practice similar methods of destruction. Magicians themselves may be hired to work destructive magic against one's enemies, and may do so too against their own hated rivals. In such cases they are also said to practice *boloi* (sorcery). There is always the idea of deliberate intent behind the activities of the *baloi*, and their motive is invariably one of vengeance, envy, or greed. Nothing appears to exist corresponding to the purely physiological condition of witchcraft found amongst the BaVenda and the BaThonga.

The Kxatla *moloi* who wishes to harm an enemy may accomplish his purpose by any of the following methods. He may simply put some poisonous substance into beer or porridge or other food which he persuades his enemy to take. This method is not often employed, although I have actually come across several instances of genuine poisoning. It is far more usual for the *moloi* who chooses to use food as his medium to put into it some substance which he has previously " doctored," i.e. treated with his medicines. When the unfortunate victim swallows the food, this substance (*sejeso*, " that which is fed ") changes into a miniature crocodile or lion or some similar animal which gnaws away persistently at his bowels until he dies. This particular form of bewitching is greatly feared, for its cure

[1] The information upon which the following notes are based was obtained in the course of several trips to the BaKxatla during the years 1929–1931. I am gratefully indebted to the University of Cape Town for financing this work.

is said to be almost impossible. In consequence, many of the people, when they go to feasts where they are likely to encounter it, " doctor " themselves before leaving home as a protection against it. Again, the *moloi* may enter the hut of his victim late at night, and after throwing him into a dead sleep will cut him on various parts of the body, into which he introduces small stones, fragments of meat, and other particles which have also been " doctored." These foreign elements (*dilokwa*) cause the victim to fall ill, and unless a magician is able to extract them in time he will die.

In these three instances, the *moloi* acts directly upon the body of his victim. On the other hand, he may sprinkle " doctored " blood over the court-yard of his enemy's *lapa* (household enclosure), the blood as a rule being that of the latter's *seano* (totem animal) or of some member of his family. Should the victim step upon the blood, his feet become affected, and he will either die or lose the use of his limbs. Sometimes the *moloi* conceals a bundle of rags containing " doctored " roots and other substances in the eaves of his victim's hut, or buries them in the ground at the entrance to the latter's *lapa*. The mere presence of these substances (*sebêela* or *sefêfa*) about the *lapa* will bring illness or death to one of its inhabitants.

Again, the *moloi* may take some dust from his victim's footprint and work upon it with his medicines ; or he may blow some prepared powder in the latter's direction, at the same time calling upon his name ; or he may send an animal, such as a snake or leopard or ox, to inflict direct bodily injury upon him. This last form of sorcery, known as *xo nêêlla* ("to give over ") is said to be very commonly used. Again, the *moloi* may use the lightning as a destructive agent. By working with his medicines he can either direct it so that it strikes his victim, or else he may go up into the air himself and descend upon his victim disguised as the lightning ! This method, known as *tladimothwana* (" little man lightning ") is much favoured by magicians in settling their grievances against a colleague.

All these different forms of sorcery are classed together as *boloi ba dithlare*, " bewitching with medicines." The name indicates the one great feature they all have in common. For their efficacy reliance is placed primarily upon material substances of some sort. My informants, whether magicians or laymen, all stressed the material substances or " medicines " (*dithlare*, a word whose primary meaning is " vegetation " or " trees ") as being by far the most vital element in their magic. The rite itself is occasionally important, as is also the spell, but this does not apply to all forms of magic. In some magical rites no spell at all is used, e.g. in love magic and in certain forms of agricultural magic ; while on the other hand the rite actually performed is almost always subject to a good deal of variation in detail, which does not matter so long as in the main the medicines are correctly applied. But the correct medicines must be used, otherwise the magic will have no effect at all. As a rule, also, no stress is laid upon the condition of the performer, save in such exceptional forms of magic as rain-making and the destruction of animal pests, which involve the observance of certain taboos. The emphasis laid upon this aspect by Malinowski and Evans-Pritchard in their general analyses of magic does not therefore apply altogether to Kxatla magic.

In contradistinction to *boloi ba dithlare* there exist certain forms of sorcery known as *boloi ba molomo*, " bewitching with the mouth." Here the material element is entirely lacking. The potent factor is the feeling of malevolence, anger, or bitterness cherished against a person by someone else. The latter makes no use of *dithlare*, he utters no spells, he performs no special rites, nor does he have to observe any taboos or other special usages. All the normal ingredients of magic are lacking. The only thing necessary is for him to have a bitter heart against his enemy. As we shall see later, there is some difference of opinion as to whether this really constitutes *boloi* or not. But the name by which it is generally known seems to suggest that on the whole the BaKxatla are inclined to class it in the category of sorcery together with other forms of malevolent activity against the well-being of a person.

This particular variety of *boloi* may assume two different forms. In the one, known as *xo hutsa* " to curse ", a person definitely threatens his enemy, or expresses the wish that some evil will befall him. For instance, when two men quarrel, the one who feels affronted may say to the other : *ke tla xo hutsa*, " I shall curse you," or *o tla ipônna*, " You will see for yourself (what will happen to you)," or *se ê nao*, " May it (misfortune) go with you," or he may even say outright, " I hope that you die, because I don't want to see you in this tribe." He is then said *xo bua maswe*, " to be speaking evilly." He remains cherishing in his heart a feeling of bitterness against his enemy. Then should the latter meet with any sort of misfortune, such as being gored by an ox, or being badly knocked about in a fight, or run over by a wagon, or falling ill, it is believed that he suffers this misfortune because of the curse put upon him. The following case illustrates a simple form of the curse and its consequences. Two young men, Masilo and Raditladi, quarrelled about a girl in whom they were both interested. A stand-up fight took place in which Raditladi was worsted. As he got up from the ground, he said to Masilo : " Well, you'll see what will happen to you, because you are no good, I shall curse you." He remained very depressed, would not eat his food, and always spoke very bitterly of Masilo. A few weeks later Masilo broke off a toe against the side of a sled in which he was going to fetch water. When this was told to Raditladi, he brightened up considerably, saying to the other boys : " You see, I said that something would soon happen to him." This certainly does not seem very much like sorcery, but the young men with whom I discussed the case all agreed that Masilo had been hurt because of the curse put upon him by Raditladi.

There is a classic instance of *xo hutsa* in the history of the tribe. Masellane, one of the early chiefs of the BaKxatla, was abandoned by his sons when he was already very old. He called them back, and in the hearing of the people said to them : *ka le seke le rata kxosi e xola, xo xodile nna, xa le nke le thlwe le xolelwe ke kxosi epe moraxo ya me, ya re le fuduxa le mo tloxele,* " Since you do not like a chief to grow old as I have grown old, you will never have any chief grow old on you after me, so that you may abandon and leave him " (free translation). It is for this reason, say the BaKxatla, that, with only two exceptions, none of the many chiefs who followed after Masellane had a long reign.

Another occasion which may give rise to *xo hutsa* occurs when a boy consistently refuses to marry the girl chosen for him by his parents. At last they express the hope that he will meet with harm. Should any misfortune then come to him, it will be attributed to their curse. Or if he marries a girl of whom they disapprove, they tell him to his face that they hope he will not rear any children, that all his offspring will die. Again, if a child is naughty, his parents as a last resort threaten to curse him, in the hope that this will induce him to amend his conduct. So, too, if a boy finds some object in the veld and does not bring it to his *malone* (mother's brother), whose rightful due it is, then should the latter come to hear of it he will *hutsa* the boy. " He thereby tells you straight out that his heart is bitter against you, and that if anything happens to you it is because his heart is working actively against you."

It must be emphasized that there is no direct action on the part of the person who inflicts the curse. He merely tells you that he feels bitter against you, and that he wishes you harm, but he does nothing further. If he is not satisfied to let the matter rest there and wait for the realization of his threat, he may go to a magician and ask him to work against you, e.g. by *xo néélla*, by sending an animal to injure you. But in this case he becomes a *moloi wa dithlare,* " a sorcerer of medicines," and is no longer *moloi wa molomo,* " a sorcerer of the mouth."

Analogous to *xo hutsa,* and known by the same name, is the action of a person who points his index finger at you. He need not utter any threat, but you know by his action that he is wishing you evil. In effect he is saying, *o tla ipónna*, "You will see for yourself." Then if any misfortune does overtake you, he will be held responsible.

I tried to discover what the reaction is against a person whose curse has brought misfortune upon another. No legal action can be taken, such as is permitted with *boloi ba dithlare*. The victim is fully aware, or the diviner will tell him, that his misfortune is due to the curse of his enemy, but the tribal court does not regard this as an actionable wrong. The only remedy is for the victim himself to use sorcery against his enemy, and this generally appears to be done. On the other hand, it is possible to avert the threatened evil by attempting to restore friendly relations before it is too late. If the breach is healed, and you are once more on good terms with your former enemy, his curse will no longer have effect. Among the other Chwana tribes there is a special ceremony of reconciliation performed in such cases, but in spite of careful inquiries I have so far been unable to find anything of the same sort among the BaKxatla. You try to conciliate your enemy with gifts or with fair words, but if he does not respond to your overtures nothing can prevent misfortune from falling upon you.

In the type of *boloi ba molomo* just described, the threat or hope is actually expressed that evil will befall the person with whom one has quarrelled. On the other hand, the person offended may merely brood over his grievance, without uttering any curse at all. But his attitude of mind is in itself sufficient to bring harm to his enemy. This is known as *kxaba* (sing.) or *dikxaba* (plur.). Willoughby, speaking of the BeChwana in general, summarizes *kxaba* as follows : " The anger of a living father, grandfather, uncle, or elder brother, as well as that of the dead, is thought to be physically injurious to its object ; and immature members of the offender's household are more susceptible to its malign influence. If a child fall ill soon after a family quarrel, the diviner is apt to discover that the cause of the illness is the anger of the father's elders in family or clan. There is no cure for such illness till the anger of the offended elder has been assuaged, and he washes the child with ' medicine ' and recites the formula over it : ' If it was I, let him heal ! ' " [1]

"*Kxaba*," commented one of my informants, " is something incomprehensible. It can happen to anybody with relatives, for it is caused by the wish of a relative who is angry with you. After the quarrel the *medimo* (spirits) up above will help his angry heart and pray their great ancestor to help on his wish of harming the person with whom he has quarrelled. *Dikxaba* always happens after a quarrel in which one person nourishes a sore heart against his opponent. *Kxaba* is not necessarily intentional.

[1] W. C. Willoughby, *The Soul of the Bantu*, London, 1928, p. 194.

Even if you don't intend to attack the other person, the fact that you feel anger against him is sufficient.   Hence if someone comes to tell you that you have sent *kxaba* on to a person who is now sick, you need not deny it ; it may be that your heart was sore against him long ago, and this has caused evil to fall upon him.   Hence you must try to avoid quarrels, lest you be suspected of sending *kxaba*.   Even after your anger has cooled down, and you feel better, thinking that all is now well again, it will take effect all the same."

It is obvious from this description that the mere feeling of anger or injury on the part of a person with whom one has quarrelled is sufficient to bring about *kxaba*.   This name is not applied to any specific form of disease, but to any misfortune which may overtake one after a quarrel.   *Kxaba* takes effect in many ways.   The victim may fall ill, the distinctive feature of this illness being that it comes suddenly, not gradually. Violent headache, or stomach trouble, or perpetual sneezing suddenly attacks him, or sores break out all over his body, or he feels unaccountably miserable and wretched, or he breaks a leg, or a wagon runs over him, or an ox gores him—any of such misfortunes may befall him.   The magician summoned to divine its cause will cast his divining bones (*ditaola*), and after scrutinizing them will say that it is due to *kxaba* emanating from such and such a person.   *Kxaba* need not necessarily fall directly upon the person with whom one has quarrelled.   It may affect a very near relation instead ; but, as one of my informants remarked, " The effect is as bad upon the person with whom you quarrelled, for the sick person is of his blood, and he therefore feels as troubled as if it had fallen directly upon himself."

The following case-histories illustrate some of the manifestations of *kxaba*.   In February, 1932, an unmarried girl named Manthso Pilane, who had become pregnant by her lover, suffered greatly from protracted delivery and ultimately gave birth to a stillborn child.   The magician attending to her consulted his divining bones, and reported that her illness and the death of her child had been caused by *kxaba* emanating from her father's father, who was known to be furious with her for disgracing the family name.   Again, in June, 1931, a small girl of *kxôro* Makxôphaneng died of a swollen stomach.   The diviner said that her death was due to *kxaba*.   It was then learned that her father had quarrelled with one of his sons, but the *kxaba* instead of passing on to the son had affected the daughter instead. So, too, a certain widow of the same *kxôro* (lineage group) sold one of her cows to a neighbour.   The cow died soon afterwards, and the purchaser complained bitterly that he had been cheated. A few weeks later the widow's daughter began to bleed profusely through the nose.   The magician called in to attend to her

consulted his bones, which revealed that her illness was due to
kxaba emanating from the man to whom the cow had been sold.

Kxaba, no matter in what form it takes effect, is cured by
washing the body of the patient. This washing must be done by
the person whose feeling of anger or injury has caused the
misfortune to occur. The magician, after consulting his bones,
attributes the misfortune to *kxaba* emanating from a certain
person. The latter is then sent for and asked to wash the patient
with a lotion prepared by the magician. Should he refuse,
on the ground that he does not feel responsible for the patient's
condition, the other relatives will accuse him of wanting the
patient to die ; and they will warn him, *thloxo di tla lekane,*
" The heads will be just the same," i.e. " Just as he dies so will
you die." " And it is true—after a while that person will also
die." If he nevertheless persists in his refusal, the magician
may himself wash the patient, but this is not regarded as equally
effective.

The medicines with which the patient is washed are the
roots of the bulb *thlathsana tsa ramere* (also known as *kxaba*
because of its use in this connection) and the blades of the
sanyane grass. These are cut up, ground down to powder, and
put into a pot of water. The patient, who is inside his hut,
then has to strip completely, and the person said to have
" seized " him with *kxaba* (*yo o mo thswereng kxaba*) washes him
all over the body with the mixture which has been prepared in
the pot. As he does so he repeats the following prayer to the
ancestors after the magician : *bontatê lesang ngwana ka pelo
tsa lona, xe e le rona re mo loketseng bolwetse ka xo bua xa rona,*
" My fathers, release the child with your hearts, if it is we who
have caused his illness by our speech " (free translation).
Another form of prayer used on the same occasion is as follows :
*ntata, ke nna ke lwatsang ngwana o, o ne a nkutlwisitse bothloko,
ka re ke baya diatla tsa a ka mo xo ene, modimo o mo thuse, ke
inêêtse mo pelong xe ke rate ngwanakê xe a ka nthswêla a a mpolle,*
" My father, it is I who have caused this child to fall ill, he made
me feel aggrieved, I tried to place my hands upon him, may
God help him, I give in to my heart that I like my child, that
he may come out (of his illness) for me, may he get well for me "
(free translation).

Occasionally, however, the treatment is unavailing, and the
patient dies. Then it is said that the magician has used the
wrong medicines, or else has made them too strong, " so that
they burn out the life of the patient." Or, again, the magician
may simply have caused the patient to be washed, without
calling upon the ancestors to help in the curing. Their help
is essential. " They heard the quarrel on earth and will have
to give healing, because the two who were quarrelling on earth

did not know what they were doing." Or, of course, *kxaba*
may manifest itself in the form of a fatal accident, and only
after the death of the person will the diviner discover from his
bones that the fatality was due to *kxaba*.

Sometimes *kxaba* emanates from a deceased person. The
diviner says to the patient, "You are sick because your father
died with a sore heart against you, you did not carry out his
last wishes," e.g. in regard to the allocation of the inheritance,
or some other last request. This variety of *kxaba* is distinguished
by the name of *kxaba ya badimo*, "*kxaba* of the ancestors."
It is cured by the sacrifice of an ox or goat at the grave of the
offended ancestor. The magician, the patient, and the latter's
near relatives all go to the grave of the dead person, whether
it is in the cattle-pen or in the more modern cemetery. As they
go along, driving the sacrificial animal before them, the patient
carries with him some *mothlodi* in a *sexo* (calabash scoop).
(*Mothlodi* is a vegetable substance used in cooking *boxobe*, native
porridge.) At the graveside the magician tells the patient to
put some of the *mothlodi* into his mouth, bend over the headstone
of the grave, spit out the *mothlodi* on to it, and then call upon
the deceased : *ntatê, kea utlwa xe o utlwile bothloko, mme ke tla
ka kxomo ke e, ntatê ke tlile xo xo rapela ka yona, xe ke xo utlwisitse
bothloko nthswarele,* "My father, I hear that you feel aggrieved,
and I have come with this ox, my father, I have come to pray
to you with it, if I have caused you pain forgive me." One
of the men present then cuts the throat of the animal. It is
skinned on top of the grave, and the flesh cut so that the *moswang*
(chyme) falls on to the branches which have first been put on
the grave. The magician cuts small pieces of meat from various
parts of the animal's body, and lays them out on the branches.
Then he prays to the dead person : *re xo bexêlla kxomo ke e, le
dinama ke tse o di je, ngwana wa xaxo wa xo rapêla, mme o le
kopanya babothle bomaxomoxolo le bana ba xaxo babothle o je nabo
kxomo e,* "We bring this ox to you, and this meat, so that you
may eat it ; your child is praying to you, and all his maternal
relatives and all your children have come together so that you
may eat this ox with them" (free translation). He then takes
up all the pieces of meat from the grave, and cooks them on a
fire which has been made near by. When they are done, they
are eaten by all those present. The rest of the meat and the
skin are taken home, but the *moswang* is left lying on the grave.
All the bones of the dead beast are also first gathered together
and then burned on the fire. The meat taken home is cooked there,
and all the neighbours are invited to come and eat it. The
magician takes the *letsoxo* (foreleg) as his perquisite.

This sacrifice of a beast (*kxomo ya medimo,* "beast of the
spirits") may be done on the grave of any dead relative, including

brother and sister and even wife, who is indicated by the diviner as responsible for the *kxaba* by which the patient has been affected. No further treatment is applied to the patient. It is held that the sacrifice is sufficient to remove the anger of the dead person and thus effect a cure.

It may be noted that not only in *kxaba ya badimo*, " *kxaba* of the ancestors," but also in ordinary *kxaba*, the misfortune affecting a person is believed to arise from the offended hearts of the ancestors. In the case of *kxaba ya badimo*, the connection is direct. In the case of ordinary *kxaba*, it is said that the quarrel on earth between the two relatives is noticed by their ancestors, who take the part of the person affronted. It is through their agency rather than his that *kxaba* takes effect. The significance of this doctrine may perhaps be more clearly understood when it is remembered that *kxaba* can emanate only from one's senior, not from one's junior. It is only when you have quarrelled with an older relative that there is a possibility of *kxaba* affecting you. The underlying idea obviously is that the offender has violated the respect due to his senior relatives, a feature of considerable importance in all Bantu society, and therefore has merited punishment. The prayers to the *badimo* used in healing both varieties of *kxaba* show definitely that it is they, as the senior relatives *par excellence*, who must be appeased, rather than the living person with whom you have quarrelled.

The association of *kxaba* with the ancestors is all the more interesting in that the BaKxatla have long abandoned ordinary ancestor-worship in favour of the Gospel. For the past forty years the official cult of the tribe has been Christianity, and most traces of the old ancestor-worship have long ago disappeared. At the present time few if any of the old people still pray regularly to their ancestors, while none of the younger generation appear to have more than a very vague and sketchy idea of the former tribal religion. *Kxaba* is one of the very few instances in which the ancestors are still believed to influence their living descendants. Even the younger people know that in the case of *kxaba* the right treatment involves a prayer to the ancestors, but none of those with whom I discussed the subject could say why it should be so, or how the ancestors actually cause *kxaba* to work.

The attribution of *kxaba* to the anger of the ancestors is hardly compatible with the equally common view that *kxaba* is a form of *boloi*. My informants differed considerably about the connection between *kxaba* and *boloi*. Some of them denied altogether that *kxaba* is a form of *boloi*, others were positive in asserting that it is. Some light upon this confusion is thrown by the following statement made to me by one of them : " There is a certain custom which our people agree causes sickness. This custom is called *kxaba*. I refuse to call this *boloi*, because many people are indicated in the bones of our magicians as having caused it, although it is said that they do not bewitch ; that is why I refuse to call it *boloi*. It is said that *kxaba* is caused by a sore heart, or when a person envies another because of his wealth or happiness ; also that a father when he is not satisfied with the conduct of his son will send *kxaba* upon him. Nevertheless, it is said that there are people who when they see that another person works hard and progresses favourably envy him, and their jealousy will cause him to fall ill, and that person becomes sick and often dies. This form of *boloi* can be cured."

The refusal to regard *kxaba* as *boloi* because so many people are shown by the diviners to have sent it upon others is rather naïve. But apart from this, it would almost seem as if there has developed a confusion between the misfortune produced by the malevolent feelings of other people, and the *kxaba* caused by the anger of an older relative. Both Willoughby's general statement and the prayers to the ancestors among the BaKxatla suggest that *kxaba* was originally restricted in its application to members of the same family or lineage group, while the true *boloi ba molomo* was the hatred or jealousy felt against a person by anybody, including an outsider. But I was unable to obtain a clear discrimination between these two forms of mental attitude. Both were described to me under the name of *kxaba*. I found, however, that my informants, when given a hypothetical case of a man's envious feelings causing another to fall ill, immediately termed it *boloi ba molomo*, whereas when asked about *kxaba* of an offended relative they almost invariably hesitated to do so. Probably the marked decay of ancestor-worship has contributed greatly to the popular assimilation of *kxaba* with the original *boloi ba molomo*.

Psychologically both *kxaba* and *xo hutsa* are of considerable interest. They are not actually forms of *boloi ba dithlare*, i.e. of " sorcery " in the common sense of the word. But the association between a quarrel and consequent misfortune is so obvious in a society where the fear of sorcery is still a dominant factor that it is easy to appreciate why the tendency to regard them as minor forms of *boloi* should arise. On this point Junod has some illuminating facts to record. Speaking of the BaThonga, he says : " . . . should a serious case of illness occur, one of those evils which are generally attributed to the *baloyi*, the first thing to do is to *detect* the culprit. Who may he be ? The patient's relatives have most probably already some idea on this point, because, at the beginning of most *buloyi* cases, something happens which arouses *suspicion*, and this is a very important point to be noted if we wish to find the psychological explanation of these customs. Perhaps there has been a quarrel between two persons, and one of them, in his anger, has said to the other, *N'ta ku bona*, i.e. ' I shall see you.' On hearing this the people immediately say : ' This man is a *noyi*. He has revealed by daylight his crimes of the night.' The man himself had perhaps not the slightest idea of such a thing. The same conclusion will be drawn if he points to another person with his index finger. An imprudent word which at first sight would appear quite innocent may have the same result if hostile feelings already existed between two persons. Jealousy alone is sufficient to give rise to the suspicion even without a word having been uttered ".[1]

This description applies equally well to the BaKxatla. It brings out very clearly how, in a case of misfortune, suspicion of having caused it fastens upon a person with whom you have quarrelled or who has a grievance against you. But the BaThonga do not appear to share the Kxatla belief that a mental attitude alone is sufficient to produce this misfortune. A man's known feelings against you suggest that he is probably the sorcerer, but if so he must have bewitched you by one of the recognized methods of sorcery akin to the Kxatla *boloi ba dithlare*. The BaKxatla, on the other hand, distinguish clearly between *boloi ba dithlare* and *boloi ba molomo*. They are on the whole rather hazy as to the exact mechanism of *boloi ba molomo*, they cannot say just how *kxaba* and *xo hutsa* operate to cause misfortune, but they are quite convinced that the mental attitude alone is sufficient to harm one. Their argument is one of *post hoc ergo propter hoc*. You quarrel with someone, misfortune befalls you, therefore he must be regarded as responsible for it.

Boloi ba molomo is not held to be an actionable wrong, there is no legal redress for it, but its effects upon the life of the people are well described in the words of an informant. " Many people die of *kxaba*, hence there is no peace in the tribe. You quarrel with your relatives, then they fall sick and say it is due to your *kxaba*, then they begin to hate you, because you have sent *kxaba* on them, and they stay with sore hearts, which adds fresh fuel to the flames of their hatred." Even if *kxaba* is not itself always regarded as *boloi*, it may therefore easily become one of the motives for the practice of *boloi*. Its association with consequent misfortune leaves a feeling of bitter injury which often results in the attempt to obtain vengeance through *boloi ba dithlare*. By doing so, the injured person lays himself open to punishment as a *moloi*. His only lawful remedy is to have himself " doctored " by a magician. Then if anybody again tries to bewitch him, the medicines with which he has been inoculated will fight against the sorcerer and perhaps even kill him. It is

[1] Junod, op. cit., ii, 524–5.

then said that the sorcerer has brought about his own death, and his intended victim is not held responsible. *Kxaba* in its original sense of being an injury caused by the anger of an older relative would certainly not have given rise to the practice of *boloi* as a form of vengeance. The fact that nowadays sorcery with medicines is often resorted to by people who have been affected by *kxaba* shows that the tendency to regard *kxaba* as a form of *boloi* is becoming stronger, and that the old idea connecting it with the ancestors is gradually dying out.

THE PART OF THE UNCONSCIOUS IN SOCIAL HERITAGE

By Brenda Z. Seligman

It is with peculiar pleasure that I contribute to this volume. For twenty-nine years I have been so closely associated with Professor Seligman and his work that it is quite impossible for me to discover what I owe to his precept ; for though I have never been his student in the academic sense, we have worked together and have agreed and disagreed on so many subjects that there can hardly be one concerning which I have remained uninfluenced.

For this reason I feel that no apology is needed for the choice of my subject. Professor Seligman has himself dealt with some aspects of it recently in his Huxley Memorial Lecture, and I cannot do better than begin by a quotation from that lecture :—

> " We may well be prepared to accept as actually demonstrated the claim that the savage mind and the mind of Western civilized man are essentially alike ; for what holds of one mental function may be taken to hold of any other, since no mental function can be isolated from the organic whole which we call the mind." [1]

Even Professor Levy Bruhl, whose work emphasizes the difference between primitive and civilized mentality, considers that there is no gulf between the two and hazards the suggestion that in all human beings, however highly developed, there persists an ineradicable basis of primitive mentality.[2]

In every group, even the most primitive that have been described, society demands certain norms of behaviour ; how far such norms are formed by repression arising within the individual and how far the individual is repressed by society is a distinct problem. It is the work of psychology to inquire into the contents of these repressions, it is the part of anthropology to deal with their social expression. Perhaps the most remarkable demonstration of repression is the split or divided personality, which in its developed form is recognized in our own society as abnormal. I suggest that the cultural regulation of the manifestations of the divided self is a most powerful factor in culture. We may then ask in any given culture : (*a*) What

---

[1] " Anthropological Perspective and Psychological Theory " (The Huxley Memorial Lecture for 1932), *JRAI.*, lxii, 1932, 219.
[2] *La Mentalité Primitive*, The Herbert Spencer Lecture, 1931, p. 26.

are the manifestions of the divided self ?   (b) What scope does social heritage [1] give for their expression ?

Briefly stated, dreams, mystic conditions, and dissociated states are phenomena experienced when the whole self is not completely integrated, and though all these are essentially individual experiences, all are capable of becoming socialized in varying degrees. In our Western European social heritage dreams have no important social function ; as a legacy from the Bible the prophetic dream has its place, yet public opinion regards anyone making use of this concept as odd, though not abnormal.

Mystic experience, important in medieval times, plays a lessening rôle in our social heritage. I am aware that the distinction between mystic states and dissociated states is somewhat artificial, but for the purpose of defining culture their end results make it convenient to separate them. The mystic may or may not become dissociated, but during his experience motor activity usually plays no important part.[2] Moreover, the aim of the mystic is to be at one with some super-natural power, and the sensation of merging the personality with this, or a loss of identity in some cosmic entity, is a common feature of mystic experience. In the dissociated states with which I wish to deal, common in savage society and also occurring in our own, the subject usually believes that an alien personality takes possession of his body.

Conditions of dissociation are from the cultural point of view by far the most important manifestations of the unconscious, for they easily become socialized. In these states in savage society motor activities play an important part, as they do in a number of pathological cases in our own culture. In our social heritage precedents for dissociated conditions exist, and one of the most obvious conditions of dissociation, that attributed to demoniacal possession, formed an integral part in the beliefs of the whole Western civilization until well into the eighteenth century. The belief is defended by the Roman Catholic Church, which maintains that spiritualistic mediums are the victims of demoniacal possession, but at the present time in the West

[1] Graham Wallas divides nurture into two parts. The first part consists of that which each one of us acquires for himself. The second part consists of the knowledge and expedients and habits which were originally the acquisition of individuals but which have afterwards been handed down from one genera-tion to another by the social process of teaching and learning (Our Social Heritage, London, 1921, p. 16).

[2] William James describes the essentials of mystic states. There is intense feel-ing, insight, or knowledge ; moreover, they are of relatively short duration, and are characterized by passivity : " When the characteristic sort of consciousness once has set in the mystic feels as if his own will were in abeyance, and indeed sometimes as if he were grasped and held by a superior power. This latter peculiarity connects mystical states with certain definite phenomena of secondary or alternative personality, such as prophetic speech, automatic writing, or the mediumistic trance " (The Varieties of Religious Experience, London, 1907, p. 381).

spiritualists form the only organized body of any importance that definitely encourages the practice of dissociation. The ritual is conventional and usually follows a definite pattern. It is notable, however, that dissociation is as a rule only induced in the medium ; the votaries remain as interested spectators and rarely themselves become dissociated. Dissociation as practised by the spiritualists has but a limited influence on the general public ; anyone who feels interested in either their beliefs or practices must make a personal effort to get in touch with a group of believers or experimenters. On the whole it would be fair to say that public opinion does not encourage either the beliefs underlying spiritualism or its practice, that orthodox religion upholds the former while it condemns the latter, and that science is inimical to both.

When we come to the direct outcropping of the unconscious in ill-health, public opinion is positive. It will have none of it. Of the loss of conscious control and the manifestation of the divided self under the influence of infection or alcohol, public opinion is fairly tolerant. These are recognized as deliria, important as symptoms but in themselves regarded as insignificant. When, however, an individual without such recognized causes acquires the habit of dissociation, public opinion is alarmed—his conduct differs so widely from that of the mean that he is considered queer or definitely mad, and society must be protected from him. Persons in such states being excluded from normal society, their behaviour has no influence on public opinion and remains merely individual experience.

Similar behaviour, and the mental state accompanying it, is, however, part and parcel of many of the lower cultures and may constitute a powerful element in their social heritage. For this reason analyses of statements occurring and of dramatic acts performed in such conditions in our own society should be important in throwing light on savage behaviour, and I therefore record the following case.

M. was in rather poor health when the responsibility for X., an hysterical subject, was thrust upon her. After some days she considered it better to put X. in charge of someone else. It was after leaving X. with a responsible person that she was aware of an overwhelming fear. Something in X's case had started a train of thought, and M. began to fear that she might have harmed the person in life dearest to herself. For about thirty-six hours she was obsessed with this fear, while at the same time suffering deeply from the general anxiety due to the War. M. had had very little sleep for some time, possibly for about a week, and this may have been a contributory cause to the lack of higher control which ensued. The dramatic act took place in a flower-shop, where she had gone with a companion.

She became interested in choosing the flowers, not for themselves but for the intense emotional value which she attached to them at the moment. She rejected certain flowers for this reason, and asked for others that reminded her of her childhood ; up to this time she was perfectly aware of her thoughts and the motives for her speech and actions, though afterwards she recognized that such symbolism was unusual in herself. Then at a certain moment—as she stated—she ceased to be master of her actions ; she was intensely aware of her muscular move- ments and her emotions, but not of any motivation. The ordinary associations with shops, such as asking for objects and paying for them, vanished. She seized a bunch of flowers from the staging in the window, grasped it firmly in her right hand, buried her nose in the blossoms and inhaled deeply. She can remember how tightly she grasped the flowers, how repulsive their colour was to her, but that at the same time their sweet scent gave a great sense of comfort. She walked quickly out of the shop on to a crowded pavement, with every breath taking comfort from the scent. Suddenly she raised her head and became aware only of the abhorrent colour of the flowers. She then released her grasp, and straightened her fingers with a jerk. The flowers fell to the pavement ; her companion, who had followed her from the shop, bent to pick them up, but she signed to him not to do so. She longed passionately for him to put his foot on them, but she did not speak. In another minute she said to him, " I am all right now, let us go and have tea." Her inward comment was, " Now *that* will never worry me again." She did not, however, analyse what *that* was, but she knew, and vaguely realized, that she had disposed of a worry in an unusual manner. For the rest of that day, she said, she felt normal.

The colour of the flowers symbolized X., and at the same time they represented the aberration from which X. suffered. It was clear that X's aberration was closely connected with, if not directly due to, the conduct of Y. and X's reaction to Y. The fear in M's mind was whether her own beloved N. could have been injured by herself in the way that X. had been injured by Y. She explained that she did not throw away the flowers, but that her hand opened, and that with the palm flattened and the muscles of her hand tense she felt that a definite cleavage between herself and the flowers had taken place. At that moment the flowers only symbolized the abhorrent idea, X's aberration. When she became aware of her companion, M. supposed that he understood the meaning of her action, and she was disappointed that he did not crush the flowers and give finality to the drama. The idea that he might pick them up and give them to her had filled her with misgivings.

Though M. accepted with gratitude the relief that she had

gained from this dramatization, she recognized that her behaviour was entirely outside the accepted norm in her own social heritage, and even during the few weeks of illness which followed, when symbols had peculiar importance to her, whenever she was aware of a tendency to use them dramatically she checked herself. When she had regained normal health she was impressed by the fact that without any unravelling of the worry her behaviour with the flowers had given complete relief. She recognized that the idea of N. having suffered harm through her was really absurd, and that the analogies in X's case which had suggested it were due to superficial coincidences, but, in the condition in which she had been, either rational thought did not occur, or was not accepted as it gave no emotional satisfaction.

M. had drawn her satisfaction mainly from very simple muscular activity. She was aware of her deep breathing when she inhaled the scent of flowers, and derived joy from it. The intensity of her grip on the flowers was important to her, as was the jerking open of her hand. Each of these activities expressed strong emotion. The self, relieved of conscious control, seized upon a primitive and satisfactory method of dealing with the emotion—that of dramatization.

Certain negative aspects of M's actions must be noted for comparison both with S. W. (to be described later) and with " shamans " in savage society. M. was aware that her own volition ceased, yet she felt that it would have been impossible for her to act otherwise than as she did ; the command was imperious, and seemed to come from without. She did not believe in supernatural agencies, but in discussion she said that it would have been easy to suppose that some external force, might have been in command of her actions. M's companion did not understand her actions, and it did not occur to him to take part in the drama. M. was entirely unaware of this, and when he bent to pick up the flowers she supposed that he understood all they symbolized to her and that he wished her to shoulder again something which she considered an intolerable burden ; her divided self thus inferred social cognizance of her behaviour.

S. W., described by Jung,[1] came of a family with neuropathic inheritance. She was of average intelligence, her education somewhat neglected and her interests limited. She heard about table-turning and began to take interest in it, at first as a joke, but was discovered to be an excellent medium.

" In somnambulic dialogues she copied in a remarkably clever way her dead relations and acquaintances. . . . She also . . .

---

[1] "Psychology of Occult Phenomena," *Collected Papers on Analytical Psychology*, second edition, London, 1917, pp. 16 et seq.

closely imitated persons whom she only knew from descriptions.
... Gradually gestures were added to the simple speech, which finally
led to *attitudes passionelles* and complete dramatic scenes. . . .
At the end of the ecstacy there usually followed a cataleptic
state with *flexibilitas cerea* which gradually passed over into the
waking state. . . . At first the attacks occurred spontaneously,
afterwards S.W. could provoke them by sitting in a dark room
and covering her face with her hands. . . ."

During times of divided personality her grandfather was her
" guide " and her spirits took complete possession of her.
S. W. firmly believed in her " spirits " and resented any explanation, moreover regular believers attended her séances. After
some time she became stale and was caught cheating. She then
gave up working as a medium, the somnambulic attacks ceased,
and she became an industrious and responsible person. In other
words, she failed to retain her enhanced social status in a limited
group, and returned to the larger community as a normal member.

These typical cases indicate the scope our Western social
heritage has to offer to the dissociated ; their experiences either
remain individual and abnormal, or are accepted as desirable and
are conventionalized and accepted by small groups which are themselves regarded as abnormal by society as a whole. Turning now to
the manifestation of the divided self in savage society, I shall
pass over briefly the part played by dreams and mystic experience,
and shall contrast the rôle of the dissociated state in savage
society with its treatment in our own culture.

The part played by dreams in savage society is undoubtedly
important. Current beliefs concerning dreams will assuredly
influence the dreamer, and the connection between dreams and
the belief in life after death is well known. The dream *per se*
is essentially an individual experience ; although the meaning
attributed to it may be accepted and acted upon by society, yet no
man can see another's dream, nor can his dream personality come
in contact with the dream personality of another. Even so,
the individual experience of the dream can form the basis of
a rite and possibly of a cult, and the accompanying ritual may be
conventionalized.[1] The mystic state and the dream, though
capable of ritual and social treatment, are both essentially
individual. Neither of these conditions, convincing as they may
seem to the re-integrated individual, has the advantage of the
dissociated or semi-dissociated state for socialization. In the
latter the inner experience is expressed by gesture and dramatic
action, and symbols may be used. The phenomenon can be

[1] For an interesting discussion of " Winnebago " type of religion based on
personal experience, and the more obvious social and ritualistic Pueblo religion,
see Barbara Aitken, " Temperament in Native American Religion," *JRAI.*,
vol. lx, 1930.

observed and interpreted by onlookers, whether accompanied by words or not. These states satisfy repressed emotions in the observer and tend to be contagious.

In savage society, ritual, which gives full scope to the divided personality of its leaders, fulfils the function of releasing emotion into socially recognized channels, thus preventing individuals from discharging it erratically or anti-socially.[1]

In Vedda culture the experience of its prominent members during dissociation is completely integrated into the social organization of the community, and thus constitutes an excellent example of the social function of dramatization. In 1908 (the date of our Vedda investigation) a few hunting Veddas, entirely dependent on the chase and the collection of wild food-stuffs, still existed. Their communities were small, consisting of a few closely related families. The leader of the group, who was at the same time head of the family, was the priest or shaman, trained in methods of dissociation. Vedda beliefs centre round the cult of the dead, associated with that of culture heroes whose lives are dramatized in ritual dances. From infancy Vedda children with their mothers watch the ceremonies in their group, so that dissociation and the significance attributed to it become familiar to all.

" The method of invocation of the *yaku* [spirits] is essentially the same in all Vedda ceremonies ; an invocation is sung by the shaman and often by the onlookers, while the shaman slowly dances, usually round the offering that has been prepared for the *yaku*. . . . As the charm is recited over and over again the shaman dances more and more quickly, his voice becomes hoarse and he soon becomes possessed by the *yaka*, and, although he does not lose consciousness and can co-ordinate his movements, he nevertheless does not retain any clear recollection of what he says, and only a general idea of the movements he has performed. . . . The shaman . . . surrenders himself to the dance in the fullest sense, and it is this, combined with a high degree of subconscious expectancy, which leads him to enact almost automatically and certainly without careful forethought the traditional parts of the dance in their conventionally correct order. Further, the assistant, who follows every movement of the dancer, prepared to catch him when he falls, may also greatly assist by conscious or unconscious suggestion in the correct performance of these complicated possession dances." [2]

The ceremonies are performed for definite consciously determined purposes, and the shaman begins his performance in a fully conscious condition ; the invocations are traditional, and there are certain traditional objects, mostly arrows of a

[1] All ritual cannot be looked upon in this light. Much is little more than the recognized correct way of doing things, and has little or no emotional significance.
[2] C. G. and Brenda Z. Seligman, *The Veddas*, Cambridge, 1911, pp. 133–5.

ceremonial type, which are associated with particular spirits and are looked upon as their emblems. Shamanistic dances are performed after a death, during pregnancy to ensure safe delivery, and to bring good luck in the search for food, hunting, honey-collecting, and gathering of yams ; when the spirits are present questions are asked them concerning the health of members of the community who may be ailing. Close association with the spirits is maintained. Not only are they invoked when the people need their help, but when in luck, e.g. when a sambur deer is killed, a dance is held and offerings made to the spirits.

Besides the shaman, spectators who are emotionally involved also become possessed. In a ceremony performed after the death of a man his two brothers became dissociated ; the spirits of the dead spoke through the shaman to their relatives, showing them favour by feeding them or smearing food on their bodies.

In spite of a definite pattern adhered to in every dance, in the communities we visited there was considerable variation in the incantations and the preparations made for the dances ; in the latter especially, contact with Sinhalese neighbours in certain localities had led to elaborations. Besides this the shaman, though he followed a traditional method, gave individual messages to some of the onlookers, and there can be little doubt that when in a dissociated state ideas that originated in his divided self became expressed.

Tension, especially obvious in a brother of the dead man, was present in the Vedda community for several days after a death, before the performance of the ceremony and during the ceremony there was a great release of emotion. The brothers of the dead man became possessed by the spirit, and all the children and near relatives were fed ceremonially by the spirit in the person of the possessed shaman. After the ceremony calm again reigned ; emotion had been released into recognized social channels, and not only had those immediately concerned been relieved but the whole community had taken part.

Among the Veddas we see the abreaction of anxiety expressed by behaviour closely similar to that of M. Higher control is lessoned or entirely disappears. Gesture and action largely take the place of speech, and symbols (or emblems [1]) are used. But the anxiety of the individual is given social significance, and the satisfaction that follows the abreaction is felt by the whole community. The head of the family is the social and religious leader ; he is therefore emotionally concerned (to a greater or lesser degree) in every ceremony that he performs for a birth or death in the community, while for obvious reasons ceremonies

---

[1] Psychoanalysts limit " symbol " to a symbol chosen by the unconscious, regarding consciously recognized symbols as " emblems " (Ernest Jones, " The Theory of Symbolism," *British Journal of Psychology*, vol. ix, 1918).

for success in hunting must concern the whole community. The lack of specialization within the group makes it possible for any manifestation of the dissociated individuals to become completely socialized.

Among peoples whose social organization is more developed, priests and medicine-men who practise dissociation are more definitely specialists than they are among the Veddas ; though their influence may be great—where women and children are not permitted to witness their performances nor the uninitiated to take part in them—it can hardly be so uniform as among the Veddas.   Still, among the majority of savage peoples this mode of expression is legitimate and is socialized in ritual channels.

In the Sudanese battalions, which in 1909 were all officially Muslim, we were able to observe some interesting adaptations from tribal to regimental life. A company of Diga, a tribe calling themselves Azande, had been recruited from one locality and were accompanied by their own women. Like many other units they held a *zar* on Fridays. *Zar*, performed in the harems in Egypt [1] and many other Muslim countries, form a special outlet for the abreaction of emotion, but are unorthodox, and disapproved by the Ulema. The ceremony is practised by a confederacy of persons who may be regarded as hysterics. Women who have suffered illness or shown some idiosyncracy or other symptom of " possession " meet under the direction of an expert, who is herself a woman possessed by a spirit. Under the influence of her own familiar she controls the spirits of the other women, who pass into dissociated states, when their spirits make their own demands and complaints.

The Diga *zar* was not confined to women ; the chief dancer and master of the ceremonies was one Farag, a corporal, said by his English officer to be very efficient. As an infant in his own country Farag had been unable to suck and had been fed by his grandmother, who chewed sugar-cane and spat the juice into his mouth ; a medicine-man had been called, and the child was found to be possessed by the spirit of an ancient Zande king. The spirit showed no further sign of its immanence until Farag was twelve years old, when he fell ill ; a ceremony was held and a sacrifice made. Later a second spirit, related to the first, also became immanent in Farag, and this was regarded as a sign of favour. It was of vital importance to Farag to hear the drum occasionally, so that he could dance and give his familiar spirits

[1] We did not find *zar* practised by the Kababish—a nomad Arab tribe of Kordofan—and Mr. Bertram Thomas states that in Arabia they do not flourish in the desert but are common in the coastal fishing villages in Oman. The Umm az-Zar (mother of the *zar*, mistress of the ceremonies), is usually a negress, and the participants chiefly women (*Alarms and Excursions in Arabia*, 1931, p. 261).   See also Niya Salima, *Harems et Musalmanes d'Égypte*; Brenda Z. Seligman, " On the Origin of the Egyptian *Zar*," *Folk-lore*, xxv, 1914.

occasion to express their wishes, yet on parade he was able to control his familiars and did not dance. Farag's performance has been described elsewhere.[1] He passed into a genuine auto-hypnotic state, and in this condition performed dramatic actions, all probably based on tradition, though certain incidents showed that at least some of these were adapted to the occasion, as when he stopped his dance to inquire the reason for our presence.[2]

We witnessed another *zar* of a different type in a Sudanese battalion at Kodok. This battalion had been recruited from the Khalifah's prisoners ; they were a mixed lot, including persons of varying ages, many of the younger having been born in captivity. Here, though men were present and played the musical instruments, while we watched women only became possessed. One after another they left the crowd of onlookers, fell on their knees, jerked their bodies violently, became possessed by their spirits, and made various requests and announcements, often asking for some particular tune. When the music ceased the spirits departed ; as a rule the women remained inert in a sitting posture, whereupon an old woman came and crossed and recrossed their arms and bent their necks, after which most of them would get up and quietly go away.

In both these *zar* there were a number of objects of various kinds placed on a stand which had been rigged up for the occasion ; most of them had been specially demanded by some person when possessed. Both *zar* present interesting adaptations to changed circumstances. There is little doubt that had Farag remained among his own people he would have fitted harmoniously into his surroundings and become a person of social importance. He was well balanced enough to become a corporal, and the alien Muslim practice of the *zar* gave outlet to his tendency to dissociation, while his associates looked up to him as an individual in personal contact with their tribal spirits and thus fit to be consulted on matters of importance concerning the members of the company. In the other *zar*, as well as those in Cairo described by Niya Salima,[3] the condition is different. Certainly the older women, who claim to be possessed and, as experts, preside at the meetings, gain social and pecuniary advantage. But their clientele is not the community at large, as in untouched savage society, but individuals of hysterical tendency. The spirits are usually regarded as unfriendly, are often foreign, and may sometimes need exorcism. In fact two deaths have been recorded in the Sudan due to the violent

---

[1] Brenda Z. Seligman, op. cit.

[2] During the dance Farag was the complete " savage " ; his movements were violent, his expression furious and strained, betokening great release of emotion and contrasting with his conventional and unemotional demeanour when later he came to talk to us, the correctly attired corporal of his company.

[3] Op. cit.

methods adopted by the exorcists.[1] In the battalion at Kodok
it is probable that all the women from the married quarters
may have attended the *zar*, while from Niya Salima's description
it would appear that spirit possession flourishes chiefly in the
large harems, especially where negress slaves are found.   So here
we find the " possessed " forming cliques in the social milieu,
within which the phenomenon is doubtless contagious, a condition
in many ways similar to that of spiritualists in Western society.
The practices are tolerated, though disapproved by the upper
section of society.

To sum up : In savage society the behaviour of persons in
dissociated states is in harmony with belief and custom, moreover
the persons subject to this condition are far from being reputed
unstable members of the community ; on the contrary, they
are frequently leaders.   There is usually an elaborate system of
myth and ritual, which is familiar and on which behaviour
during dissociation is based.   There is thus a reservoir of material
upon which the divided self can draw, and to which it constantly
adds.   The social significance given in this way to unconscious
material becomes a very powerful factor in culture ; its
importance in the savage's social heritage and its relative
insignificance in our own may possibly account for much of the
difference between savage and civilized behaviour.   Further,
when we consider that persons in dissociated states alter or
add to their ritual, and take into account the widespread capacity
for dissociation and the varying forms of belief connected with
this, it seems legitimate to assume the beginning of
shamanistic ritual in spontaneous personal dissociation.   If the
emotions which are given dramatic form by the divided self
are of a type that might be experienced by any member
of the community, and are in harmony with the existing social
heritage, then the satisfaction drawn from the action is complete, and suffices for the initiation of fresh ritual.

[1] " Two Murder Trials in Kordofan," *Sudan Notes and Records*, iii, 1920,
245.

INDIGENOUS EDUCATION IN AFRICA

By EDWIN W. SMITH

I

An African, Mr. Julius Ojo-Cole, has put forth the claim that whenever Europeans set out to do anything for his people they should " search first for the African conception about it ". There certainly was, he says, a system of training youth for the responsibilities of manhood before the advent of white men, and the educationist should ask : What is the principle underlying this system, and what is the method ?[1] It seems a reasonable claim. Until recently the people responsible for schools in Africa have, in general, worked on the assumption that Africans have no culture that is worth perpetuating and no method of transmitting it that need be taken into account. When Dr. C. T. Loram wrote his standard work, *The Education of the South African Native* (1917), it was the schooling by Europeans that he had in mind ; the African's previous experience was dismissed in a sentence or two.[2] The Phelps-Stokes Commission, which gave a distinct impetus to the development of educational policy, scarcely hinted that Africans trained their children before Europeans appeared on the scene. The latest review of the subject, contained in a bulky volume issued by the International Colonial Institute,[3] is content to notice that the young of whole races were " before our arrival . . . generally left in ignorance ". Some advance was made by Mr. Victor Murray who recognizes that there were two sorts of education among Africans : " vocational," the training in use of tools ; and " liberal ", found " in the initiation ceremonies and other mysteries which concern the life of the person as a member of a society, mortal and at the same time immortal". Neither type goes very far, he thinks, and their bias is conservative and communal ; but he sees that they make for discipline, self-restraint, and other virtues.[4]

It appears then that educationists are at last coming to realize that there is something in African education which is worthy of their attention. Apart from Dr. Mumford's experiment

[1] *West Africa*, 24th August, 1929.
[2] " Before the coming of the white man the education of the South African native consisted in his adjustment to the narrow environment of his tribe through direct imitation of his elders," p. 28. On p. 7, he allows that the " almost superstitious reverence for the chief " was accompanied by strong family discipline.
[3] *L'Enseignement aux Indigenes* (1931), p. 30.
[4] *The School in the Bush* (1929), p. 84.

at Malangali, in Tanganyika Territory, I know of no school where the principle is deliberately adopted of building on native tradition and making the training continuous with that which existed prior to the advent of the European.[1] The comparative negligence is all the more surprising in that, as General Baden-Powell has acknowledged, the Boy Scout movement, the most fruitful of modern educational developments, owes a great deal to Africa.

Hitherto ethnographers in the field have not adequately explored this subject. No scientist has done for the juveniles of Africa what Margaret Mead has done for those of Samoa and New Guinea.[2] Mr. Hambly's *Origins of Education among Primitive Peoples* (1926), reveals only too clearly the wide gaps in our knowledge. Much further investigation is necessary before the values in the indigenous system can be known and applied universally.

2

It is more than possible that the comparative neglect of the subject is due to a restricted view of the nature of education. So long as it is defined in terms of school the observer has nothing to study, for the pagan Africans had no such institutions. But to think of education as if it were or could be given only through schools is to take a part for the whole. Schooling and education are not synonymous terms : some people, like Bernard Shaw, may complain that their schooling did them a great deal of harm and no good whatever—that, indeed, it only interrupted their education. J. S. Mill claimed that education comprehends even the indirect effects produced on character and on the human faculties by things of which the direct purposes are different : by laws, by forms of government, by the industrial arts, by modes of social life ; nay, even by physical facts not dependent on human will, by climate, soil, and local position. Recognizing that for practical purposes this description is too wide, Mill restricted education to " the culture which each generation purposely gives to those who are to be its successors, in order to qualify them for at least keeping up, and if possible for raising, the level of improvement which has been attained ".[3] Others define education as the influence of the environment upon the individual to produce a permanent change in his habits of behaviour, of thought, and of attitude.[4] They recognize, however, that while the whole of the environment is the

[1] W. B. Mumford, *Africa*, vol. iii, No. 3 (1930).
[2] *Coming of Age in Samoa* (1929) ; *Growing up in New Guinea* (1931).
[3] Quoted by John Adams, *The Evolution of Educational Theory* (1922), pp. 10, 11.
[4] G. H. Thomson, *A Modern Philosophy of Education* (1929), p. 19.

instrument of man's education in the widest sense, certain factors are distinguishable as being more effectively operative ; and of these factors the school is only one. There is, indeed, conscious and unconscious education, and the conscious type may be formal or informal.

In this paper I regard education as the whole process by which one generation transmits its culture to the succeeding generation. If this broad view be accepted, it is impossible to deny that Africans educate their young. Their culture consists of a whole complex of institutions, handicrafts, industries, manners, customs, laws, knowledge, beliefs, values, language. Each generation as it comes along does not begin *de novo* ; it takes over all these things as its social heritage and passes them on in its turn, more or less modified. In this matter, Africans do not differ essentially from ourselves. We have our social heritage, which is of no less importance than the biological inheritance. The African's differs in its elements, but radically is of the same kind. His mechanism of transmission is not of an entirely different sort from ours. The point of divergence lies in the fact that we have a system of writing and that the school, which seizes our youth continuously from early age to adulthood, has as its unique and essential (though not its most important) function to teach its pupils to read and to know good books.[1]

3

Since education is the transmission of culture, to describe the content of African education would be to describe the whole life of the peoples. To do that here is obviously impossible. We must be content to say that the five essentials may be postulated for Africa equally as for other parts of the world. " Let it be granted, as Euclid would say, that a child, that anybody, must know something of the world of things, the world of people and the world of ideals, that he must have tools to use, and that he must develop his æsthetic and creative sense." [2]

The environment into which the child is born consists first of the land upon which his people dwell : the plains, forests, mountains, rivers, springs, and lakes ; the pasturage, the arable areas, the hunting and fishing grounds. It includes the wild and domestic animals ; the forest fruits, the grasses, the edible and other plants. There are the heavens too, and the weather. All these things set the conditions in which the Africans live. About them a certain degree of knowledge has accumulated ; certain emotional attitudes, certain sentiments have grown around them ; and upon his adjustment to them the African's existence depends. The younger generation must be given

[1] G. H. Thomson, op. cit., p. 39.   [2] V. Murray, op. cit., p. 155.

that knowledge, brought to adopt those attitudes, taught to make that adjustment. They must learn to make and use the tools which the experience of the past has evolved : spear and axe and hoe ; baskets and pots. The child is born, too, into a human environment : his family, clan, and tribe ; and the wider circle of friends and foes. He cannot live alone : every act, thought, and emotion is conditioned by other human beings. He must learn to live in his group, to maintain it, to defend it, to propagate it. To this end he must be disciplined into control of his instinctive impulses. The manners, customs, laws, inhibitions which the experience of the past has proved necessary to the integration of the social structure must be made bone of his bone, flesh of his flesh. Decency of speech and behaviour, respect for his superiors in age and rank, a diligent sharing of the common tasks, must be inculcated. In particular, social life involves regulation of the commerce of the sexes ; the canons of correct behaviour as understood by the tribe must be learnt : a complicated system of avoidances, taboos, permissions, must be acquired and passed on. In all these matters there is constant tension between natural impulses and the welfare of the community, and only a rigorous code of morality backed by strong sanctions can avail. Moreover, the African community consists not only of the individuals who live visibly in the flesh but also of those whom we civilized folk name " the dead ". The newly-born infant is the reincarnation of a person who after passing through all the stages of mundane existence went to sojourn for a time in the world of the invisible. Between the " living " and the " dead " there are certain obligations upon the right observance of which the welfare of both depends. And beside these ancestral spirits there are other mysterious powers to which the living must adjust themselves, whether to use or to avoid. Ideals of physical form and quality, of intelligence, of moral character, are involved in the process of standardization to which the young are subjected. The Africans have very definite ideas as to what constitutes good citizenship and they seek to mould their offspring in accordance therewith. They also have their own standards of beauty in natural forms, in art, and in language. They find joy in the making of things that in some measure satisfy their sense of what should be. Music and the dance take a large place in their culture. And all these component parts of it are handed on. The Africans, that is to say, educate their children.

4

Passing from content to method we have to ask by what means the education of the Africans is effected. In brief we may

say there are three ways : the formal, as when a boy is apprenticed
to a trade, or when the traditional rules of conduct are impressed
upon boys and girls during the initiation rites ; the informal,
as when young people learn by imitation ; and the unconscious,
as when children in their play unknowingly obey impulses which
have a social end and which are stimulated by the actions of
their seniors. Oral instruction is only one means, and it is not
the most important. The young African learns chiefly through
participation in the activities of the community. Boys and
girls are introduced into a succession of ever-widening circles
which overlap in some degree ; and as they enter one circle
after another they acquire, partly by precept but chiefly by the
example and pressure of their fellows, the standards of conduct,
the emotional attitudes, and the knowledge appropriate to the
stage which they have reached.   Each circle brings an enhanced
status, with corresponding duties and responsibilities. In this
progressive manner they arrive ultimately at full membership of the tribe, emerging as socialized persons with knowledge
of what is required of them and fitted to the emotional and
active life that awaits them.   Their character is formed through
the relationships established in the various groups which together
compose the well-knit African community.

    Some writers who recognize the existence of education among
Africans appear to consider that it is confined to the puberty
or initiation " schools ". These are indeed of very great
importance, marking as they do the transition from juvenility
to adulthood. Attention has been centred upon them in
educational circles by the largely successful attempt by Bishop
Lucas and other missionaries to adapt them to Christian uses—
a process of sublimation that might well be made more universal.[1]
Among certain tribes, we are told, no definite instruction is
imparted during these rites. This is said, for example, of some
Xosa-speaking peoples [2] ; it seems to be particularly true where
circumcision has come to be the chief feature of the boys'
initiation, though it is not so of the Basuto. It may be that
the boys and girls are not taught a great deal that they do not
know before they enter the " school " ; but it is the manner
rather than the amount that is of importance. Mr. Hambly
is right in saying that the tutors are revealed to be good
psychologists. At this period of peculiar plasticity everything
is done to heighten the temperature so that the youthful minds
may receive an indelible impression. The seclusion in a camp
of their own, the atmosphere of mystery that is thrown about
it, the ritual, the special costumes, the terrifying monsters

[1] See Bishop Lucas's contribution to *Essays Catholic and Missionary* (1928),
pp. 138 sqq.
[2] P. A. W. Cook, *The Bomvana* (1931), pp. 51 sqq.

(represented by men) like the Selwana of the Bakhaha that are let loose among the initiates, the symbolical putting to death and resurrection, or second birth, as in the Nzo Longo and Kimpasi rites of some Congo tribes ; the rough treatment, the floggings, the tortures, the exposure to cold, the fatiguing dances, the abnormal sexual practices, the obscene songs—all these things induce a state of nervous super-excitation. The stamp which the metal receives in this malleable condition remains for ever. The boys and girls emerge as new beings, the new names they bear being a witness and pledge thereof to the whole community.

Important as this rite is in the African's life it must not be regarded as the sole occasion for educating him. Puberty or initiation rites are not universal in Africa, and the transmission of culture goes on where they are absent. Where they exist they do not stand alone but form one of a series of progressive *rites de passage* which introduce the African youth into the stages of his career. To understand how he is trained it is necessary to follow him through these stages. These are more strongly emphasized by some tribes than by others, but would appear to be universally recognized.

The most elaborate system is found among the Didinga, one of the Nilo-Hamitic tribes, who initiate the boys into successive stages at the ages of eight, thirteen, eighteen, and twenty-eight ; and Mr. Driberg tells us that there are degrees beyond that age.[1] At eight they are removed from their mothers' influence and formed into a group, the members being drawn from all the clans and are henceforth age-mates for life. At this earliest stage they are instructed in the use of the spear and in the treatment of spear-wounds ; they are taught the rudiments of cattle-husbandry, and the names, appearance, and uses of a number of plants ; manners and etiquette are inculcated, particularly the duty of subordination to the elders ; they learn something of ritual, tribal traditions, and religious belief. Dances are an important part of the training, not only by emphasizing and establishing the unity of the group, but also by their dramatic representation of animals and events. Rigorous discipline is enforced and the boys are hardened by exposure and exercise. After this primary initiation the boys live at home until the second stage is reached at the age of about thirteen. After taking part in training the group junior to themselves they enter the school and are taught largely by members of the group next in seniority, under the elders' guidance. The earlier instruction is carried a stage further, and new subjects are introduced : elements of agriculture and astronomy ; the technique and magic of hunting ; the meaning

[1] J. H. Driberg, *At Home with the Savage* (1932), pp. 232 sqq.

of the rain and other ceremonies. In the third stage, bee-keeping, weather-lore, clan and tribal law are taught ; the regulation of sexual conduct is especially enforced ; and the use of arms is perfected. The young men now enter upon ten years of military service, at the close of which, and in preparation for their new status as married men, there is a fresh initiation : marital and parental obligations are insisted upon at this stage, and they are rigorously prepared for civic duty.

Among the Bantu it is rare to find a continuous or even intermittent course of formal instruction that corresponds in any degree to our schools. An exception is offered by the Bavenda, of the Northern Transvaal, who have, or had, an indigenous school, named *thondo*, through which all young boys passed. It was, Mr. Stayt says, essentially a military institution for the purpose of training warriors. Boys entered when they were seven or eight years of age and left only at the first sign of pubescence to go through the tribal initiation rite of *vhutamba vhutuka*. During this period they were not wholly withdrawn from ordinary life ; they repaired to the school after completing the daily duty of herding. Our information about what took place is meagre ; we are not told what they were taught ; but it seems that severe discipline was the rule, that tribal etiquette and rules of politeness were enforced, and that certain tasks, such as mat-making, were set.[1]

The institutions described by Driberg and Stayt are for the purpose of formal instruction and discipline. We are not to imagine, however, that whether among Bavenda and Didinga or any other African peoples the beginnings of education are deferred to the age of eight. Educationists now recognize that the period of active habit formation from two to six is by far and away the most fateful in a human life. Unfortunately our information in regard to the African child at this age is extremely vague and meagre. Yet the main outlines may be discerned.

Africans generally distinguish by name the various stages of human life. The Ila word *mwana* " child " is applied generically to all the young of both sexes up to the age of puberty. This period is subdivided. From birth to weaning the infant is in the state of *bucheche* and this is marked off into degrees. *Busahana*, say the Bathonga, is the child's condition while it and its mother are in seclusion : it ends after the first seven days of life in a ritual act by which the father acknowledges his paternity and formally receives his child into the biological family. Another ceremony at the end of three months removes certain taboos from the parents ; and when the child begins to crawl a further ceremony advances it to another degree—

[1] H. A. Stayt, *The Bavenda* (1931), pp. 101 sqq.

Junod says it thereby becomes a regular member of the community : it is now an *nkulu* " a grown-up " and no longer *khuna* " an incomplete thing ".[1] Weaning marks a definite step forward ; in some tribes a religious act of prayer and sacrifice brings the child definitely into relation with the unseen kin ; and it may also bring it into touch with the larger family when it goes to live with its grandparents.   Entrance into later childhood, which at about the age of eight is marked physiologically by the cutting of the second teeth, is not always through a *rite de passage*, but in many tribes the boys, and perhaps the girls, leave the parental roof and sleep in dormitory huts set aside for them separately.

Each stage of growth is attended by an enlarged experience as the child is introduced into a wider circle.   In its earliest years it is in constant touch with mother and father, and probably brothers and sisters older and younger than itself.   This is the biological group, the family, of supreme importance in African society.   For the child in its earliest stage the mother is the most important member.   She provides its nourishment, watches over it with solicitude, by her croonings and lullabies evokes its powers of speech.   The earliest and most enduring sentiment is formed in regard to her : " You may have many wives," the Baila say to a bridegroom, " remember always you can have only one mother."   In some of her maternal functions she is assisted by her daughters, if she has any : elder sisters early come to act as nurses.   The father plays his part in the care and training of the child ; but probably his influence becomes potent only when the child walks and talks.   His duties, though perhaps not his responsibilities, are hardly affected by the rules of descent.   In so-called patrilineal tribes he is, of course, paramount.   In so-called matrilineal tribes, where (as among the Ashanti) the child belongs legally to the mother's clan and his right is distinctly inferior to that of the maternal uncle, the father's position is strengthened by the fact that his children inherit the *ntoro* spirit through him and it might resent high-handed actions on the part of the *abusua* who share with the children in the mother's blood : they are held in awe of the father's spirit.   His legal power may be weak, yet he is strongly attached to his children by natural affection, and the bringing-up of the boys falls to him, the uncle having little to say during the early years.   If the father orders his child to do one thing and the mother another, the father gets his own way.   Rattray gives a list of some of the first lessons taught to an Ashanti child in olden time, apparently by the father : to use the right hand for eating and gesticulation, the left for toilet purposes, and both in receiving a gift ; not to stare in any person's face unless he

[1] H. Junod, *Life of a South African Tribe* (second edition, 1927), i, 57.

is actually addressing one ; to say *ago* on entering anyone's house and not to enter until the reply *ame* has been given ; and so on. " Even in the nursery," he says, " the Ashanti child is trained to avoid those pitfalls which in later life constitute his chief danger of coming within the arm of the law, i.e. he has been admonished to avoid sexual offences ; to be careful to guard his tongue ; to respect other people's property ; he is also at an early age instructed in the matter of taboos." [1]

It is probable that all African children are taught this kind of behaviour by their parents. But the quick African child learns more by using ears and eyes in observation of what goes on around him. He sees how father and mother, elder brothers and sisters behave towards each other ; and through their manifest approval or disapproval comes to know how he is expected to behave towards them. Ridicule, that most powerful of sanctions, is early brought to bear upon him. The importance of meals has been pointed out by Dr. Richards : it is largely by training in the manners of the " table " that the African child gets his sense of the status and functions of his different kinsmen.[2] African children are not treated roughly : leniency rather than harshness is the rule ; with their belief in reincarnation the parents live in dread that the young child may at any time make up its mind to return whence it came. The drastic punishment for pilfering by the use of red peppers, mentioned by Rattray, is quite exceptional. Yet we have seen a very small boy soundly thrashed by his mother for telling her a lie. In one way or another, the child acquires the proper attitudes towards those who are in a position of authority over him ; and this is the most important thing he learns, for upon these patterns he will base his behaviour to others when he leaves the family group for a larger circle. The respect he has learnt for his mother's and sister's sex will be extended to all those women whom he comes to address as " my mother " or regard as " our sister ". The incest taboo is implanted in him for life. The reverence for his father will in due course be extended to his uncles and to the elders and chiefs of the tribe. One of the chief things he learns is how to address the persons he meets, those related to him by blood or marriage, and those not so related. He learns

[1] R. S. Rattray, *Ashanti Law and Constitution* (1929), pp. 13. 14.
Since writing this paper I have read Bruno Gutmann's *Die Stammeslehren der Dschagga* (1932), in which the instruction of the Chaga children is exhaustively treated.
[2] Audrey I. Richards, *Hunger and Work in a Savage Tribe* (1932), p. 68. Kinship usages are well appreciated even by a child of six or seven years. " He becomes early acquainted with the grouping of the family at mealtimes, and the rules governing the ownership and distribution of cooked food. It is by lessons such as these that the whole kinship structure is felt rather than explained. Family sentiment is imprinted by a series of daily habits rather than taught by any definite lesson or rule," p. 66.

this not from a table of kinship, such as figures in ethnographical treatises, but by instruction, direct or indirect. If he hears his father address a person as " my child " he will know that he should speak to him, and of him, as " my brother ", and treat him accordingly.

How or when young Africans learn the many taboos to which they are subject is obscure. The forbidden foods of childhood, such as fat, eggs, and certain fish, are certainly withheld from the beginning ; the child thus becomes familiar from a very early age with the fact that certain things are simply not done because of the inevitable disaster that would follow the doing.

The family group continues to govern the African's conduct long after he has ceased to be a child ; but when he can walk and talk he is brought into association with other groups which influence him. There would seem not to be in Africa that severe dichotomy between juvenile and adult life which, according to Margaret Mead's description, obtains in New Guinea where the children spend their formative years " in a good-natured vacuum ".[1] But undoubtedly the young folk have a world of their own into which they enter joyfully whenever they can escape from the tasks imposed upon them by their elders : a world in which distinctions of age and rank are recognized, and in which strong character early shows itself in leadership. The youthful playmates of the Thonga chief are taught to respect him ; he is surrounded in his games by a miniature court, from which he chooses his favourites ; some of his companions act as councillors and reprimand those who fail to treat him with due respect.[2] They play at court. In this and other respects the young show themselves interested in the life of their elders and imitate it. They have an infinitude of games which they play with zest and in which the serious pursuits of adults figure largely. Tiny toddlers will be seen prodding gleefully with stems of stout grass into the ground where a sweet potato is hidden— their first lesson in the use of the spear. Larger boys fight fierce battles with longer stems of thick grass as spears, practising all the casts and parryings, feints, charges and retreats used by the warriors of the tribe. Girls play with " dolls " and early begin to fashion pots and baskets. Thus by imitation the energies of youth are canalized in the direction of adult activities. This is seen particularly in the small villages of miniature huts (*amashanshi*, the Lamba call them) erected by the children of some tribes. The girls may play the game by themselves, choosing a " headman ", pairing off as " husband " and " wife ", grinding corn, cooking, all according to the habits and rules

---

[1] *Growing up in New Guinea*, p. 107. " Manus children live in a world of their own, a world from which adults are wilfully excluded."

[2] Junod, op. cit., i, 369.

of their elders.   Or the boys and girls may live together during the day in the toy-village as husbands and wives, even to the point of going to bed in the huts.

Boys and girls are introduced early into the economic life of the community.   This is a valid part of their education. Children of both sexes at the age of five or six are set to herd goats or small calves in the vicinity of the village.   They have plenty of time for playing together, for the task requires only casual attention.   At about ten the boy may be promoted to accompany the cattle herds, and at certain seasons this may involve absence from home for several months.   He learns to manage the beasts, the good and noxious grasses, the diseases, how to milk, and so on.   Africans never work so hard as during their later childhood when they are under the dominance of boys older than themselves ; and from these petty tyrants they acquire a great deal of miscellaneous knowledge.   They come to have a minute and extensive acquaintance with the names and habits of animals and insects, with the names and uses of plants and trees.   Anyone who has collected with the assistance of young Africans will testify to this fact.   The accuracy with which they learn to count (in tens) is also noteworthy : they begin early, by being taught little ditties, to know numbers ; where cowries were in use there were names up to a million.[1] In the village the boys begin early to take part in the building of the huts.

Girls are brought at a tender age to share in the occupations of their mothers and sisters.   Almost as soon as she can walk the girl begins to carry a little receptacle by balancing it upon her head, and very soon she will come back with her mother from the river or water-hole bearing her little water-pot in this manner : it induces to strong muscles and an upright carriage.   She learns by her mother's example all there is in the production and preparation of food after the native manner : long before the time she is married she is expected to be proficient in these arts.

So both boys and girls are brought into close association with their elders and mould their lives unconsciously or consciously after their pattern.   Where the father is skilled as an iron-worker, wood-carver, or in other trades, he may teach his son deliberately.   Some tribes have a system of apprenticeship, with a course of two or more years of training and the payment of fees.   In other instances the boys watch the skilled workman—there is always a group of interested youngsters around the forge—and some will begin to do little jobs for him and gradually pick up his skill.   Among the riverine peoples, boys are taught to handle canoes and paddle with agility, gracefulness, and accuracy.   The Congo father will give his

[1] J. Roscoe, *The Baganda* (1911), p. 41.

son a toy paddle and teach him to backwater, to steer, to move his paddle in unison with others. Very soon the boy will be familiar with fifty phrases regarding the craft. He is also taught to make fish-traps and nets, the best places to put them, and how to bait and cast a hook. Lads of fourteen and fifteen know the names of innumerable fish in the rivers and creeks, their habits and the best way of catching them.[1] Boys are also initiated early into the art of hunting : to track various animals according to their habits ; the spears to use for various purposes ; the ways of cutting up ; and all the magical and religious practices peculiar to the hunter.[2] When a lion has been mortally wounded near a village small boys are brought near and made to spear it before life is extinct. Thus they are brought up to face the fiercest beasts without fear.

5

The remainder of this paper will be devoted to what might pardonably be called the literary education of Africans : that is to say, to the educational function of folk-tales. Did space permit I might deal in the same way with the proverbs, in which much of the traditional wisdom is expressed and conveyed, and with the riddles which serve an educational purpose in stimulating the wits of the young.

In recent years the educative value of story-telling has come to be recognized by teachers. Tales are seen to be the natural forms for revealing life, the natural carrier of racial tradition, of information and ideals. They are declared to have two functions : they are an illuminator of facts, and they are a moulder of ideals. What is now appreciated by modern educationists has always been realized by Africans. They teach very largely by telling stories.

Experts in child psychology say that each period of the young person's life demands a particular set of tales. From three to six the child dwells in a realm of realism, is interested in familiar things ; stories like that of Mother Hubbard and her unfortunate dog, stories that contain much repetition and introduce the cries and calls of animals are appropriate to this period. From six to eight the child passes through a stage when the imagination is very active and he craves fanciful tales that picture a larger experience than he has attained to. Then he emerges into another realm of realism, when barbaric instincts manifest themselves, and he looks for true tales of heroic deeds. And from twelve or thirteen onwards he wants

[1] J. H. Weeks, *Among Congo Cannibals* (1913), pp. 143–5.
[2] This must be modified in regard to tribes where hunters form a guild to which young men are admitted by initiation.

stories of a higher type of heroism, stories of chivalry and romance. Africans tell tales that fall into all these categories ; but whether the African child passes through the same psychological stages in this respect as our children, and whether the tales are graded accordingly I, in common with other collectors of these tales, have neglected to inquire. There is here an interesting and profitable field for study.

The tales are, first, an illuminator of facts about the mother tongue. We know very little about the process by which African children learn their complicated and beautiful language ; but we do know that they rapidly learn to talk it with fluency and accuracy. Of the Mpangu child Father Van Wing says : " A quatre ans il parle mieux sa belle langue Kikongo qu'un Europeen de douze ans ne parle la sienne." [1] So far as my experience goes it is very rarely that a grammatical solecism can be detected in the everyday speech of adult Africans. They have no books of grammar ; there is no formal instruction in language. It appears that they learn by the natural method of listening and imitating ; and I am confident that the tales told around the fire in the evening play an essential part in the process. Like our own children, African small folk do not object to the repetition of a story ; indeed, they call often for their favourites ; but they like it retold in the same words ; little Tories as they are, they dislike revolutionary changes. Forms of expression are heard over and over again until they become thoroughly familiar. When one has collected a large number of tales told in the hearing of the young, one ceases to wonder at the very extensive vocabulary that Africans grow into possessing. Many of the words occurring in the tales are but rarely used in everyday conversation ; but the context gives the meaning, and once they are ingrained upon the young person's mind they are there for use when occasion arises. The same applies to grammatical forms : all the tribal usages in speech are conveyed to the young through tales.

Some of the stories are told to draw attention to particular modes of expression and to ridicule people who make mistakes in regard to them. " Take care of your nasals ! " is very necessary advice to anyone who studies a Bantu language. Instead of formulating a rule about it, or merely uttering a precept, the Baila tell a tale to impress it upon the memory. Certain travellers, they say, were hospitably received in a village and were told by their hosts : " When you have eaten this dish *mukandile,*" i.e. " you shall eat with milk." As soon as they had finished their dish the travellers arose, took their spears, and began to charge up and down as if they were at a funeral. The astonished villagers asked : " Who is dead ? Whom are you

[1] R. P. Van Wing, *Études Bakongo* (1921), p. 262.

mourning for ? " And the visitors replied : " We are mourning because you said, ' When you have eaten this dish *mukadile*,' " i.e. " you shall weep ". " No," said their hosts, " we said *mukandile*, not *mukadile*." Mind your nasals ! Similarly tales are told to impress the necessity of correct intonation of words and phrases.

Tales also convey to the new generation much of what their forbears learnt (or think they learnt) about the world around them. A large proportion of them is made up of what Rudyard Kipling called " Just-so stories " ; in more erudite language, etiological myths. They explain how things came to be what they are. That they are abreast with modern science, nobody would pretend ; but they convey in the most fascinating manner the elders' observation and reflection upon the facts of their experience. Such a tale as the Ashanti tell to explain why the spider has a bald head—and there are hundreds with the same *motif*—may not be zoologically exact, but at least it draws the children's attention to natural facts and helps to make the animal world interesting.

The great facts of human existence and the origin of things are also illuminated by stories. How did death come into the world ? how did divorce, murder, incest originate ? How did the practice of taking a friend—a great thing in the African's experience—arise ? What is the genesis of heaven and earth, the sun, moon, and stars, and of man himself ? I agree with Mr. Cardinall [1] that the stories told in response to such questionings are not mere fairy tales or imaginative yarns to the African, but are absolutely real. They form the background of his thought about the universe. I think that of many of them it can be said they possess real religious value. Some are told openly on any occasion ; others are the sacred and guarded possession of a few selected elders of a tribe and constitute what Rattray calls " the African's Old Testament ".[2] But they all go to forming the young people's attitude towards their environment and are therefore educative.

It is not too much to say of many African stories that they are moulders of ideals. Moral instruction is conveyed in precept, in maxims or proverbs ; but a still more sure way of instilling social rules into the mind of the rising generation, and of holding before them ideals of conduct, is to embody them in tales which are at once interesting and rememberable. " When some member of your family accidentally spoils or loses something belonging to you, do not claim or accept compensation " ; " When anyone at all is engaged on any work and he asks for help, help him " ; tales which drive home such excellent

---

[1] A. W. Cardinall, *Tales Told in Togoland* (1931), p. 9.
[2] R. S. Rattray, *Akan-Ashanti Folk-tales* (1930), p. xiii.

instruction are found in Rattray's collection, and others might easily be enumerated. The moral is not always explicitly stated. Africans are very much like the little English girl who said : " I like the preacher's stories, but I don't like his morals ! " A wise story-teller does not force his lesson upon his listeners : he tells his tale, and lets it work. To point the moral may excite resentment : as if people were not intelligent enough to see what the story means ! Africans show wisdom in this matter ; the tales are often didactic in intention, but the teaching is not obtruded. A multitude of stories suggest, without being offensively explicit, that hasty judgment is likely to be false, that the weak should not be treated with contempt, that you cannot transgress with impunity.

The popular animal stories which are told primarily for entertainment often seem to commend the anti-social vices of double-dealing, falsehood, and deceit. That merry person, Mr. Hare, is the embodiment of cunning ; we ought to ostracize him, but we do not ; he is so variously and infinitely droll that we cannot but join in the African's enjoyment as we listen to his wonderful adventures. The stories of Mr. Hare and the other animals, if they are not of the highest moral tone, at least demonstrate that brain is more than brawn : it is always wit that vanquishes brute strength. The lesson may have its dangers ; but there is a salutary side to it. Besides this, the human qualities which the African detests supremely are sometimes associated in these tales with the most loathsome animals : greediness with the hyena, for example. The child links the two together to the reinforcement of its parents' precepts.

6

From the obscurities that for us still hang about African childhood, the fact emerges that Africans do educate their children. It is a genuine education. To our minds its limitations may be obvious enough, but these should not blind us to its value. What the African sets out to do, namely, to prepare the new generation to take its place in the community and carry on the tribal tradition, he accomplishes with a very considerable measure of success. If it be objected that the education given is conservative and not creative, it may be readily admitted that it is designedly conservative, but African society is not static ; there is movement in it, and change, whether produced by external stimulus or by spontaneous variation within, and these modifications or improvements, when they meet with general approval, are equally with the more remote tradition handed on in the manner we have described.

What Mr. Bryant has said of the Zulus may be said of some other African tribes : " Through the ages this admirable system of forming character and imparting knowledge continued, until at length was evolved a Zulu race noble of heart, dignified of bearing, refined of manners, and learned in natural science— qualities, alas ! rapidly dying out before the destructive and demoralizing advance of European civilization." [1] The concluding sentence applies to many a tribe.   No small part of the demoralization is caused by the disturbance of the family through the prolonged absence of the senior males at work on European mines and plantations and through the flocking of boys to European towns ; it is in the family life, as we have seen, that the most vital discipline and instruction are given. It becomes a problem of urgent importance, how, while introducing the European system of schools, to conserve the very real values of the indigenous African system.   The problem awaits solution.

[1] A. T. Bryant, *Olden Times in Zululand and Natal* (1929), pp. 77, 78.

SOME CHINESE CHARACTERISTICS IN THE LIGHT OF THE CHINESE FAMILY

By L. K. TAO

It has been the usual practice of writers on China to take as representing the national character certain qualities of its people which they discovered either through personal contact or in books. Thus the Chinese have been variously described as faithful and untrustworthy, docile and restive, cruel and humane. While many of these characterizations, no matter whether they be merely personal whims, fleeting impressions, or deep convictions, are doubtless interesting and suggestive, and may perhaps be considered valid in a limited way, yet it is certainly erroneous to accept them as depicting the Chinese national character, something that is inherent in the race. The number of publications on racial or national psychology notwithstanding, it appears that they are in most cases merely facile generalizations without any scientific basis.

The character of the Chinese people, it seems, must be studied in their social institutions. If it is admitted that various peoples are more or less the same in their natural endowment, the differences of their national character must then be accounted for by the divergence of their cultural traditions and social environment. What one finds as the character of a race or a nation is but a product of its tradition and social environment as they act upon human nature. There would be no mystery in any national character if we could analyse and understand the social conditions under which the people live. To affirm that there are mental or moral traits that are innate and ineradicable among the people of a nation shows only our ignorance of their nature and our incompetence to analyse the particular conditions under which they grow and develop.

There is no doubt that the forces affecting and contributing to the making of personal character must be very complex. For instance, education, occupation, sports, government, church, and other social institutions are all influential forces in moulding character, stimulating it in one way and retarding it in another. An accurate and exact estimation of the influence of each force is of course most difficult, if not impossible. Yet it seems reasonable for us to say that certain forces are dominant in moulding certain aspects of character or mentality.

Now, in a study of the character of the Chinese, our attention must be drawn to their family system, which is of all their institutions the most powerful and important. The family not only forms the basic unit of Chinese society, the whole nation being a collection of families, but also supplies an important principle for the organization of many other associations, such as the store, the workshop, the school. It may be assumed that practically all Chinese are born and bred in families and their life continues in family groups. Under such circumstances the influence of family life on individuals must be very great ; it tends to determine the behaviour patterns and moral ideas of the young, when their minds are plastic, and it further supports and reinforces the persistence of these patterns and ideas once they are set. This, it should be noted, is not to deny the influence of other institutions on the life of individuals, or to attempt to make family life entirely independent of them. What is contended here is that family life either directly or indirectly must have a predominant influence in moulding the moral and mental characters of the Chinese. Hence it would seem necessary to examine certain aspects of Chinese national character in the light of their family system.

Before proceeding, it would be well to define properly the term " Chinese family." First of all, the family must not be confused with the sib, though the latter has been and still is in existence feebly and in a very limited way in China. The sib, as is well known, is an association of persons bearing the same surname, including those female members married into it, and worshipping the same ancestors. Its distinctive features are that its members do not as a rule live in one house, and that they have no common economy except some form of property for ancestral worship and education of the young. In view of the fact that the sib organization is not universal and that it is hardly influential even where it persists, too much importance must not be attached to it. The forces that tend to undermine its existence or its power may perhaps be mentioned. In the first place, an excess of deaths over births in a sib, through natural or social causes, would of course reduce its membership. Secondly, migrations or the dispersal of its members also make for its decay. Thirdly, impoverishment through various causes would either weaken its solidarity or reduce its size. In short, the sib organization appears to be constantly subjected to a variety of factors which tend to diminish its membership and weaken its structure. There is no doubt that the family organization would be similarly affected if these factors were at work. But it seems reasonable to maintain that the sib organization must suffer much more easily from untoward influences, since the sentiment of kinship on which it is based cannot extend very far, and the lack of a common economic organization deprives it of one of the important factors of solidarity. On the other hand, it is comparatively much easier for the family to retain its solidarity and cohesiveness, since it has not only important common interests, but also those of the members of the nearest kin.

Thus, the sib organization is confined only to certain parts of China where natural and social conditions are favourable, or to certain classes, such as the propertied and the gentry, whose economic status enables them to afford the luxury of propping up kinship relationships even of a remote kind, and whose conception of conventional morality is gratified by doing thus.

So much for the sib. The family in which almost all Chinese pass their lives must vary in individual cases, but considering its broad features alone, it may be either of two types : the small family of parents and their children as one finds in the West, and the joint-family which consists of the members of more than two generations, including wives married to its members. The former is comparatively rare, unless the family membership is reduced to that extent, while the latter appears to be the prevailing type. Among the latter, a family of four generations may comprise only eight members, that is, the great-grandfather and the great-grandmother, the grandfather and the grandmother, the father and the mother, and the son and the daughter-in-law, but its membership may grow to twenty, thirty, forty, or even more, if each generation has a number of brothers with their wives, and sisters who are unmarried. On the whole it may be said that the family of three generations is quite common in this country while that of more than five generations is comparatively rare.

It may be observed here that the Chinese family is an economic unit for consumption and very often, as in farming and handicraftsmen families, also for production purposes. All members work for the whole family and their material and other wants are supplied from the estate, treasury, or income of the family, administered by the paternal head. No member, therefore, is allowed to amass any fortune for his own benefit. Thus a Chinese moral tenet enjoins, " When parents are living, their offspring dare not keep any wealth in secret." In a well-ordered family this tenet is no doubt carried out to its full extent, each member either having no private income or, if he has, giving it up to the paternal head for family expenditure. It is in this respect that the Chinese family is sometimes considered as communistic in character.

One of the important features in the Chinese family that must first attract our attention is that it comprises a great number of persons. The very facts of overcrowding and the intimate contact of so many members in one house must have important

z

effects on the members. Although there are, under such circumstances of conglomeration, traditional codes and observances according to which individual behaviour must be adjusted, yet there are bound to be friction, misunderstanding, maladjustment, and incompatibility of temperament among the members. At any rate, it must be admitted that the problem of living together, which is entirely bound up with sentiments of kinship, is a difficult one even for members of the near kin. In the Chinese family this is solved by mutual forbearance, each member trying to put up with whatever comes. Forbearance, it appears, has become a cardinal virtue owing to which family life in China has been made possible. Thus Chinese moralists of various ages have unanimously extolled forbearance as the key to preserve perpetual peace in family life. Amongst others, the virtue of forbearance has been well analysed in a treatise on family codes by Ssu Ma Kwang, a distinguished historian and official in the eleventh century, as follows :—

" Forbearance is sometimes construed as nursing resentment in our heart. I can keep my resentment in the heart when I am offended only for once or twice, but it will burst out uncontrollably like a torrent if it is accumulated for some length of time. Preferably any resentment will be explained and cleared from our heart, by taking every offence as due to unthoughtfulness, ignorance, mistake and narrow vision, and considering it as harmless. One will not show it on his face, even if the offence is repeated more than ten times. Then the important consequences of forbearance will be manifest. This is forbearance at its best."

This interpretation of forbearance, it seems, is in no way different from the well-known maxim, " Tout comprendre, c'est tout pardonner." The following story is often quoted as illustrating the importance of forbearance in Chinese family life. Chang Kung Yih, a native of Shantung in the seventh century, was living with nine generations in one house. When asked by the Emperor, who visited him in A.D. 666 on his way to Taishan, as to the secret of his keeping so many members together in one house, Chang wrote the ideograph of forbearance one hundred times as a reply. While Chang's family is no doubt extraordinary in having so many as members of nine generations, who must amount to well-nigh a hundred and form a sib rather than a family, the moral of the story clearly shows how necessary and also how successful is the practice of forbearance in maintaining a big family organization.

That forbearance should form a cardinal virtue that is required of members living in families is evident. While there are traditional codes determining the reciprocal relationships between members of the elder and the younger generations, such as the father and the son, or the aunt and the niece, the reciprocal relationship between the members of the same generation, such as brothers and cousins, is somewhat loose and difficult to determine. It must be borne in mind that the pivotal relationship in a Chinese family is that between parents and their children, while other kinship relationships may be said to be dependent upon or projected from it. Now if a father has three sons, each son with his own children would form three distinct lines or branches of descendants in the family; in other words, its members seem to cluster on three different lines by lineal descent. As the parent-child relationship is pivotal in a family, filial piety towards the parents therefore plays a dominant and all-important rôle in Chinese family life, and consequently the deference paid by the young to the aged and the elderly is merely an extension or projection of filial piety towards those who are of the same age or of the same kinship status as the parents. Thus, while relationships between members of different kinship status, whether they be lineal or collateral, may be easily adjusted as a projection of the parent-child relationship, those between members of the same kinship status would lack any such-like strict and definite regard for each other. Hence the necessity and importance of forbearance in adjusting the relationship between members of the same kinship status.

Forbearance is no doubt a fine virtue in Chinese family life, if it is a conscious effort as a result of complete understanding and enlightened trust of fellow-creatures. Yet there can be no doubt whatsoever that forbearance is not always desirable, for as has been pointed out by Burke, there is " a limit at which forbearance ceases to be a virtue". What is worse is that it may easily degenerate into an unhealthy mental attitude, such as resignation or passive submission to what is simply intolerable.

In this connection one may perhaps be allowed to speculate whether or not filial piety, which is always required of every one towards one's parents, and forbearance, which is always required towards each other in regard to all kinds of behaviour, make the whole atmosphere of the family life excessively oppressive ; whether or not in this atmosphere of oppression the Chinese, at least those who are of a timid nature, have during the ages acquired a great capacity to endure, to resign themselves to what comes? It would also be interesting for us to inquire whether or not this oppression of family life is also the main cause of the backwardness of the Chinese in trying to understand and control their natural environment. In short, is it possible that the family arrangement of the Chinese, together with its accompanying patterns of thought and behaviour which they should follow, have made them the

most docile of races, conformist in nature, lacking even a spark
of revolutionary spirit, and totally disinclined or unable to
kick against what is untoward in nature and man ? These are
all questions of very great interest and an elucidation of them
would no doubt help us to understand more clearly the nature
of the history of the Chinese people.

From another point of view, forbearance means a repression,
if not annihilation, of personality or individuality and, consequently, that the Chinese family is possible is due mainly, if
not entirely, to a repression of personality. Every member
of the family is required to fall in with his or her status in
relation to other members, and acts according to conventional
family injunctions regarding definite rights and duties. It is
not for a person to doubt and inquire why certain duties are
enjoined. He is not to ask why, but to observe what is prescribed by convention. Thus instead of the constitutional
convention " The King can do no wrong," as has been adopted
in some countries, the Chinese take for granted that " Parents
can do no wrong." (Literally the maxim is that " There cannot
be in the world any parent that is in the wrong.")

The repression of personality deprives the Chinese of the
opportunity of developing such traits as self-expression,
originality, creativeness, an adventurous spirit of exploration
and pioneering, inventiveness, etc. Hampered in development, the mentality and behaviour of the Chinese are
greatly stereotyped and trammelled, and whatever is new and
departs from the stereotyped pattern of thought and action is
therefore tabooed. As a consequence, their views of life, their social,
political, and economic systems, and their material conditions
—in short their whole culture—have not throughout the ages
undergone such fundamental innovations as have been found
in European civilizations. Now, one may perhaps ask, If the
stereotyping of the mind and action of the Chinese, as a result
of their family system, has denied to them social and cultural
development, has it not gained for them in compensation a
degree of stability and conservation that few peoples enjoy ?

Another aspect that is noteworthy in Chinese family life is
that it encourages or is at least indifferent about the dependence
of its members. As the head of the family is responsible for the
well-being of the whole family, an unnecessarily large share
of the burden is put on him while all the other members will
do as much as they cannot avoid doing, but no more. The
lazy, the indolent, the ne'er-do-well, have good conditions
for survival under Chinese family conditions. It is perhaps no
exaggeration to say that Chinese family life cultivates laziness.

It is true that all the members of a family ought to take part
in the economic provision for the whole family. Every member

must have his or her part to play under the high authority of the head of the family. Yet it must be remembered that unless the organization is strong and the paternal head exercises his power over all impartially, some members may try to shirk their responsibility, in order to escape the hard toil that is required of them. If the family is engaged in pursuits other than farming, then to earn a living must depend on the one hand on one's ability to work, and on the other hand on conditions of employment. When neither of the two conditions obtains, it is futile to make any member work. And it is interesting to note that the paternal head is liable to be partial to his children ; he is usually inclined to protect the incompetent, the lazy, the weak, who must be taken care of by the members that are able. If it happens that all are incompetent to earn any living, it then remains for the paternal head to make every effort to support the whole family and his lot will be a very strenuous one. He it is that should be responsible for the sustenance and livelihood of all the family, and he can in no way escape the burden except by death. Thus while it sounds very well in theory that the Chinese family is a communistic organization of the people of the same kin, there are plenty of cases in which an extremely unequal distribution of labour among the members is evidenced. It is always the paternal head or some such competent member of the family that is made the beast of burden to feed and clothe the whole family. It is likely that in every society there must be a number of the indolent and the weak whose living and welfare will have to be taken care of by their fellow-creatures, and that the difference between Chinese and European systems is that in the former they are kept in the family and supported by members of the same kin, while in the latter they are thrown out on the streets and are maintained by public or social agencies. It seems that there is not much to choose between the two. Nevertheless, one is inclined to believe that the Chinese system is the more harmful, for under it not only is the indolent not stigmatized, but his irresponsibility and dependency is often taken as a matter of course ; thus, the unproductive member takes his daily allowances free from his kin simply as a right and feels no shame about it. But a family comprising unemployable or unproductive members is constantly in danger of breaking up on the disability or death of its bread-winner. And it seems that the strong economic pressure that is being felt everywhere in China must lead further to the total disruption of all joint-families.

A third aspect of Chinese family life is that it hinders the development of the capacity for organization among its members. The kinship principle on which family organization is based is a strongly discriminating principle, stressing blood-relationship on the one hand and kinship status or generations on the other. While blood-relationship discrimination must have softened somewhat in the course of ages, in view of the development of political and other organizations in China, yet it appears that owing to the dominance of the family system, the kinship sentiment and kinship loyalty still remain to claim the most important consideration in one's thought and action. Since the life of every Chinese is circumscribed in the narrow limits of the family and his upbringing is deeply stamped by the family hall-mark, it is evident that his outlook and interests throughout life would manifest a strong family-centred egoism.

It should be pointed out that the Chinese respect for age is not so much for age itself as for the status of kinship of which age is often a symbol. For instance, a person in a lower status, such as the son, the daughter, the nephew, the niece, or the daughter-in-law, has to pay due respect to one in a higher status, such as the father, the mother, the uncle, the aunt, etc. Thus, persons belonging to the same status form one generation, to whom persons belonging to a lower status would pay due respect, and from whom persons of a higher status may exact due reverence. It is important to point out that this status principle is not limited to the family and relatives alone, but is extended to many other relationships. For instance, friends of one's father are called " uncles," and those of the same kinship status as one's mother, " aunts." In schools the teacher occupies the same status as the father, while the teacher of one's teacher is accorded the reverence similar to that given to one's grandfather. Even among those who have passed government examinations, successful candidates of earlier years are considered as belonging to former generations, to whom reverence is shown by later arrivals. In short, the whole conception of kinship status is shot through all human relationships in China, and applied universally.

It is evident that the kinship principle and, more particularly, the status principle are incompatible with any effective organization of free individuals for other than kinship purposes. As soon as a few persons get together, kinship relationships are established and a hierarchy consisting of various statuses formed. It is extremely difficult, if not impossible, for them to stand on an equal footing and exchange ideas and act freely as equals, Here again, as in the observance of the virtue of forbearance, full expression of one's individuality is seriously hampered and any development of effective organization is checked. Under such circumstances, none is regarded as an active agent, but each forms only a part in the whole of the family or kinship structure. Thus, the value of the individual is entirely lost, as each is regarded only as in some kinship relationship with somebody else and his position is not determined by what he is but by what kinship status he has. A junior occupying a lower kinship status is therefore required only to follow his elders ; but his turn of becoming a leader will arrive in course of time. Personal intrinsic merit will have slight effect when kinship considerations predominate.

Lastly, it is possible that the family organization whose solidarity is maintained by artificial and forced circumstances has an undesirable influence on the character of its members. In its ideal the family represents an harmonious organization in which each has a part to play and in which the welfare of each is cared for. The harmony, as may be gathered from the above, is maintained by the authority of the head of the family, and the sentiment of kinship and forbearance on the part of every member. It is based on the alleged community and unity of interests of the kin, which transcend those of every individual member. Yet in spite of the various forces that attempt to foster family solidarity and harmony, it is evidently impossible to expect complete harmony among a great number of persons grouped together on the basis of kinship considerations alone. Age and sex, occupation and association all tend more or less but inevitably to disrupt family harmony by creating sectional interests. What appears outwardly as unified family life may therefore be, inwardly, no other than a constant ferment of discontent and factional dissensions. If the paternal head is an upright character, blameless in conduct and strong in his rule over all the members, family solidarity may perhaps be maintained. But as soon as such a power is withdrawn, personal bickerings may develop into open quarrels, and secret nursings of discontent may explode into ferocious outbursts and storms. Thus it often happens that on the death of the paternal head, who may be the maker of family fortunes, the sons would at once begin to quarrel over a division of heirlooms. Notwithstanding the edifying efforts of sages and moralists to promote family solidarity and to consolidate family property, there always exist more powerful forces tending to disrupt the family. It is true that the degree of harmony or disharmony must vary a good deal in different families. In some it may be merely an atmosphere of incompatibility or mutual indifference, while in others it may develop into a conflict of a very intense kind. At any rate, the younger generation brought up under such circumstances of stress and strain must suffer. It has been demonstrated that children, in homes where there is parental conflict, often suffer from mental maladjustment in the form of a neurotic or unstable character ; so also, where there is disharmony in the joint-family, this must also produce correspondingly unhappy effects on the natures of its individual members.

In this connection we need not deal with the families in which concubinage is practised, for then the complications would be greater and the children reared under such conditions would be more liable to develop erratic temperaments.

It has been shown very briefly in the foregoing pages that such characteristics as endurance, suppression of personality, dependence, incapacity for organization, and instability, which are usually found among the Chinese, may be attributed to the nature of their family system and the conditions of their family life. It is not claimed that all characteristics can be so interpreted, but it is firmly believed that a great deal of light may be gained on the character of the Chinese by a close examination of their family system. It may be recalled that Chinese moral philosophy maintains that a good world order must be achieved through having well-disciplined families, which on the one hand depend on the cultivation of the self, and on the other hand lead to the good rule of the state and finally to the peace of the world (to our ancients the world was much smaller, as it was circumscribed by seas in the four quarters). However well conceived, the theory has unfortunately not been proved in practice. It may be doubted if the ideal family has ever become universal, although moralists of all ages have emphasized its importance and preached its maintenance by all means. It may still be doubted that even if Chinese family life is made to approach what is idealized by moralists, either a good state or an international order of peace can be the result. It seems that too much emphasis on family life brings with it an accentuation of kinship over other social and broader interests. As has been pointed out, the Chinese family fails to help to develop those aspects of personal character which are desirable and necessary for a higher form of social organization. In the course of time, not only has the Chinese family not attained the perfection Chinese moralists have aspired to, but it has been actually and continually breaking down in face of economic and other forces. Perhaps with the passing of the power of the family, the Chinese may in time be able to discard their narrow familial outlook on life together with its accompanying characteristics which are good only for family organization, and begin to develop those valuable qualities which are required for nation-making in this world of struggle for existence.

ADVENTURES OF A TRIBE IN NEW GUINEA
(THE TJÍMUNDO)

By RICHARD THURNWALD

Professor C. G. Seligman's book on British New Guinea makes frequent mention of tribal migrations. It has been generally very difficult to gather reliable stories on the subject, especially since the establishment of white rule. The memory of details vanishes rapidly or is sometimes retained with legendary dimness. In working with the Tjímundo people on the banks of the Kerám the " Potters' River ", a tributary of the Káguia (mistakenly called " Sepik ", and previously named the " Augusta River "), in the former German New Guinea in 1913 and 1915, I was able to ascertain the history of the latest wanderings of the Tjímundo people. Let us call them a tribe, since in this region every village may enjoy the honour of such an appellation. Each village has its own peculiarities of speech, of cultural equipment, even of physical type and social deportment. This is explained by their relative isolation and, sometimes, the considerable distance between settlements.

I found that excellent opportunities for information were afforded by asking the history of individual men and by investigating the short popular songs about accidents or various happenings. It was on such an occasion that I came across the story to be related later. These songs often reveal more concerning the customs and mind of the people than myths and legends, as, for instance, the song which runs :—

| *Mi oréma* | *bidjémoa ?* | *ame Moándī-dobje* | *Móto-ne.* |

You name which child from where I Moándī village-belonging Móto-called.

The verse cited hints at a whole story which is not described. The event referred to is not related specifically, so that it may be recognized only by one who knows it. These phrases hint at the situation in such a way as to be symbolic of the whole. The particular song is occasioned by a man who goes hunting pigs with his dog, on the way meeting a man named Móto. He is asked whence he comes and how he is called. His village is found to be Moándi, a small place half-way between Moim and Angórum.

But the song which led me on the track of the Tjímundo runs thus :—

ibuē orémoa	*numboáma ?*
their name which	village which

amè   Mátaro númboa   Imboándo—Tamlĕende
I am   Mátaro village-belonging   Imboándo   our home

When I asked about these phrases, I learned from Tírgaui, through my boy Yérabe, that the people of the Tjímundo on the Potters' River had formerly lived at Mátaro, somewhat above Imboándo, where to-day many coconut trees and betel-nut palms may still be found. These are invariably a land-mark in New Guinea, for they rarely grow in the bush. Consequently trees of this type indicate the site of a former settlement. And this is the only sign, for houses rot quickly and disappear. At Mátaro many people had died, and the rest had moved to Imboándo.

The Tjímundo people had originally lived in Amébonum on the main River Káguia at the point where to-day the Catholic Mission " Marienberg " is situated. When these Tjímundo were building their new village they cut a number of Limbum-palm trees for their houses. This was resented by their neighbours from the villages of Boánam, Tjuk (Tjigéndo) Mangán, and Manbér, who allowed them to cut the big trees but not the small ones. These people attach great value to the products of the forest, and they did not want the new growth exterminated. The natives of the place, then, festooned some spears and stuck them in the ground, telling the Tjímundo that the hill-people had made this sign of their desire to fight. The Tjímundo were not taken in by the trick, and said immediately, " It is you who have done this." Then began the dispute leading to hostilities in which the Tjímundo drove away the others. In spite of their success, however, they did not want to risk settling there again for fear the original inhabitants should return, so they migrated to Mátaro.

Here they had a similiar experience, occasioned by a woman who went for fuel to a house in the old village of Mátaro. The man of the house attempted to rape her. She fled, weeping, and complained to her husband who at once harangued the Tjímundo. They seized their weapons and ran for fire which they threw into the houses of the Mátaro people. Suddenly they became conscience-stricken and retreated. Afraid of the revenge of the Mátaro people, they fled that night to Angórum, and the next day went on to the mouth of the Potters' River. There they built up their village at a place called Yáguinan, where in 1915 five old coconut trees could still be found.

This site, in its turn, belonged to the people of Moágendo with whom they found they could not come to terms. The hostility originated in this event. Two Tjímundo women were visiting the Moágendo, and made fun of the sores on the body of a man named Ago. Ago angrily asked, " Why do you laugh ?

Have you never had any sores yourself ? I shall kill the women of Tjímundo. I do not care if the Tjímundo do come to take revenge on the women of Moágendo." And he killed them with one of his fish-tail paddles (*tjagrábudja*). The Moágendo people put the two corpses in their own canoes and let them drift down the river. When these were seen by the Tjímundo and the corpses were discovered, the latter were wept over and buried. In the meantime, not knowing what had happened, a couple from Moágendo had arrived, intending to call on friends. But the Tjímundo, excited as they were by recent happenings, stirred

FIG. 1.—Situation of places in Central North New-Guinea, mentioned in this paper.

up a quarrel, killed the couple, and buried them immediately. Ago himself, by the way, later married a woman of the Tjímundo called Yábo, who not long after the first killing ran away from him and stayed with her people, the Tjímundo. These happenings aroused the Tjímundo people so that they sang and danced the whole night through.

In the morning the Moágendo men made a surprise attack on their camps. The Tjímundo jumped for their dug-outs, and the fight was waged from canoe to canoe. The Moágendo were driven away, and a number of their canoes seized. But they returned not much later to play a trick. It was at the time of the high water after the rainy season, and they went over the Moágendo lagoon at Kumbrágumbra. By certain of the creeks passable only at high water they reached the Kerám, the Potters' River, above Yáguinan, and hid there in the forest. The move was explained to me in this way :—

Kerám-buda	*ategrábera*	*údjigum*

Kerám river gaining in a right angle to the river they break through

yógam

their way.

Two Tjímundo men, Ínango and Moándjimali (elder cousins of my boy, Yérabe) happened to go up the river by this route. They were shot by the Moágendo people, who seized the corpses, took them in canoes to Yáguinan, and showed them to their people. Ago, one of the Moágendo men in the party, called up for Yábo, the wife who had run away from him, crying out : " O Yábo, Yábo :—

" *Yóo uréma*	*amè-lígane*	*imboára*	*kiglíno*	*wéiaga*
me what kind	I have shot	pig	cassowary	come quick

orboategánum ! "

fetch them back for yourself

By this cry he called one man a pig and the other a cassowary, a common method of abuse. When he said, " Get them back," he of course implied, " If you have the power or the courage to do it." The remark was highly sarcastic.

The Tjímundo, aroused by the taunt, ran to their canoes and took possession of the two corpses. They struck and wounded many of the Moágendo, and also captured several of their canoes. At that point the Moágendo retired. Then they tried to get the help of the Moim, Kamblínto, and Támbunum people. The plan was to lay fire to the village of the Tjímundo. As usual, they planned their attack for the early morning. At first dawn on the chosen day the triton shell (*yuáring*) was blown :—

" *Num*	*àmbugon-boága*	*órda !*	*trímo*
village	they are going to burn	with fire	surprise attack

boàn-údjiga ! "

they are undertaking

exclaimed the Tjímundo people. At once they rose and fought to defend their place against fire. The Moágendo and their allies had to retire. There were wounded on both sides.

The attack, however, had warned the Tjímundo people that, amidst all these hostilities, they could not remain at this place. They decided to migrate to a spot farther up the Kerám, to Máyenum. This was somewhat above the creek by which the

PLATE XIX

THE VILLAGE OF MOÁGENDO

TJÍMUNDO PEOPLE

Moágendo people had come on their recent attack from the lagoon of Kumbrágumbra. The taking of this route was described by saying :—

" *Kendúmbudo*   *atiagum*
along the bank   they break through in the same direction
yógam   *Kerám-buda.*"
their way   the Kerám along.

Once settled in Máyenum they lived there quietly for about two years, apparently on friendly terms with the Moágendo and the Moim, with both of whom they exchanged visits. Then one night a woman named Tábo heard canoes approaching. At first dawn they heard the Moágendo people blow the triton shell and beat on their canoes as if they were drums :—

When they came up to the point somewhat below Máyenum where the river curves, the Moágendo threw spears and shot arrows, spitting and shouting : " Now we will eat the bones of men and the flying fox ; now let us finish up our affair with the Tjímundo people." The Tjímundo people, on their part, were exceedingly frightened as they had not expected the others to come so far up the river. Their frequent saying had been : *bòbō—Yágenama* " They cannot ascend (the river) ". The Tjímundo people finally ran away trembling, after an intense fight in which several people were killed and some of their houses in Máyenum burned. One man of the Moim people fell, shot in the arm by Kámle of the Tjímundo. One man named Guémo of the Kamblínto was shot in the shoulder by the arrow of Kítugur and killed at once. Of the Moágendo people three were killed, one by Kálambi, hit in the belly, another man who was struck in the knee by Agáu, and a third, shot in the stomach by Kágleb. Three of the Tjímundo tribe fell : Moándan, wife of Tjágume ; Yésan, daughter of Moándan ; Kēgo, father of Tírgaui, father's brother of Yérabe. This was considered a big battle. On the whole the conflict was surprisingly successful for the Tjímundo people, but both claimed the victory, and the Moágendo, as well as the Tjímundo, danced, sang, and fêted (*boànumbligírga* " made a victory fête "). The killing of Guémo occasioned a warrior verse :—

Guémo anàia   *watàmboa*   *kábutu-*
Guémo uncle totem symbol on the war canoe   when he broke it
yàbugunu   *anàia*
he fell down, uncle

As many of their houses were burned, and the people did not feel safe, even thus far from the Moágendo, they left Máyenum.

They moved still farther up the Kerám to a place that bore the name of Orúmonum, where again they built houses and planted coconut trees. (It may be mentioned here that the various places in the bush bear traditional names, transmitted from former inhabitants. Villages were generally built on the banks of the river for various reasons, particularly communication and easy fishing, although they were thus more exposed to attack than if hidden in the forest.) At first they kept deep in the forest. When they came to Orúmonum they hoped to settle there for a long time, so they arranged their houses and sept-halls carefully. (A " sept " is a " clan-moiety "—*intámboar*.) The houses of a sept-settlement (*garágum*) were arranged in two rows at right angles to the river, two rows for each *garágum*. The

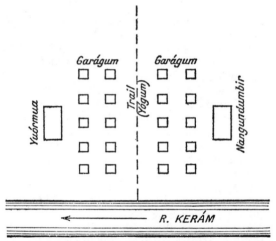

Fig. 2.—Pattern of settlement of the Tjímundo Tribe.

two septs were separated by a road running between them (*yógum*). Outside and opposite the middle of the two rows of houses were the two festival halls of each sept: down-stream the one called " Yuórmua ", and upstream the one called " Nangúndumbir ". These hall names refer to the whole sept and are repeated at other settlements of the Tjímundo. They used to have a saying: " Yuórmua goes first in going down-stream, and Nangúndumbir follows behind." (*ang-garágum: Yuórmua, Nangúndumbir kéibigum*).

This distinction gives the impression that the whole village was floating down-stream. Also, the one moiety gets its women from the other moiety. The saying for this is: *Mi omámlega!* " Go in the upper village ! " *Mi wádjinaya !* " Go in the lower village ! "

Here in Orúmonum they succeeded in remaining for many years. The coconut trees matured. Kaib, Yérabe, Orábu, and Kúbule were born there. The Tjímundo begot many children and had many feasts. In Orúmonum Kaib and Yérabe were first introduced to Kagúmali, the first stages of puberty rites.

In the meantime the Moágendo tribe had become embroiled with the Kumbrágumbra people, some of whom they had caught in the outside lagoon on the site of a former settlement. The Tjímundo about the same time had discovered a new trail connecting with Kumbrágumbra, leading from beyond Máyenum through the Iáginio forest, abundant in breadfruit and Limbum trees. On the banks of the Kerám, where this trail went off,

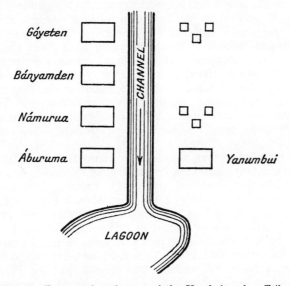

FIG. 3.—Pattern of settlement of the Kumbrágumbra Tribe.

one day some old men of the Kumbrágumbra people were waiting. A man named Kabádje, of the sept Áburuma, who had just come by, was shot by a Moágendo man. Somewhat later two married women passed by. Both were of Námurua, one of them named Mági. Then came a man named Tjándabui, of the Góyeten crowd. All were killed.

It should be noted that on the inner lagoon of Kumbrágumbra, on the right bank of the channel the houses of the septs were arranged in this way: Uppermost is the hall, named Góyeten, with a few houses of the same sept opposite on the other bank. The next houses below are those belonging to the hall of Bányamden. Somewhat farther down comes the hall Námurua, faced by houses of the same sept. The fourth hall is Áburuma. Opposite to it, on the mouth of that channel of the lagoon, lies the hall of Yánumbui. It should be remembered in this connection that the Yánumbui people used to be on fighting terms with the Moágendo. And it should also be mentioned in passing that the Bányamden group came from Lémbot, the Áburuma from Irádj, and the Yánumbui from Tjóutam.

After killing these three persons the Moágendo people cut off their heads, put them in the canoes, and went home, beating their canoes and singing a song of victory. Previous to this event the Moágendo had arranged with some of the Tjímundo to act as go-betweens in the buying of pots. They had given rings (*guíning*), shell money (*tangátening*), and tobacco (*tjógwi*). The Tjímundo people had brought the pots to Moágendo. Irábu, Máli, Bógai, and other men and women had gone there to barter fish and help with the building of canoes. They were in the midst of this when the Moágendo came back from their raid with the head trophies. The Tjímundo were frightened and hastened to return, afraid of the revenge of the Kumbrágumbra. For if they had remained and participated in the feasting the Kumbrágumbra might assume their co-operation. To the Moágendo men they said : " You have drummed on the canoes and you have sung the victory song, *yuårini*. We know all about it."

The Kumbrágumbra people later reproached the Tjímundo with having betrayed them by informing the Moágendo of the trail, which they had not previously known. The Kumbrágumbra came almost to the point of shooting the Tjímundo for it, in spite of the fact that they had formerly lived in peace together. After this squabble, in order to apologize to them, the Kumbrágumbra brought pigs and yams to the Tjímundo.

When a certain man of the Tjímundo died, one named Máliga, an uncle of Kaib, the rumour was spread that the Moágendo people had poisoned him (*bóidjir[tar] arebígen*). Consequently the Tjímundo people again became angry with the Moágendo and made allies with the Kumbrágumbra against the Moágendo. Thus the Kumbrágumbra men became the political friends (*tjámun*) of Tjímundo, as was already the village of Kambót. Then the Kumbrágumbra people called on the Tjímundo, and it was agreed that Bági, uncle of Yérabe, should go to Moágendo with certain selected men. They said :—

> " Bági wågirga   Moágendó-bunai "
> Bági should go   [in the] Moágendo direction

Bági had very often visited among the Moágendo people, at the home of a son of his friend. They therefore conferred with him, saying, " It is better that we make our attack when the Moágendo are pulling upstream, for they are thus handicapped by the current. This is better than if we should come to their village. Try to lure them up the river."

Bági then went to Moágendo and told the people : " The Tjímundo have now come with pots, bananas, pigs, sugar-cane, and all the things which they have long intended to bring you. They are, however, afraid to come to your village for you killed some of the Kumbrágumbra people recently, and so they are waiting down the river." The Moágendo people were glad to hear this news and many of them went to their canoes. Bági led them down the Káguia and up the Kerám. The Tjímundo waited in the " Bragen " forest, somewhat below Máyenum, but still above the place where the trail branches off at the point where the Moágendo people had ambushed the Kumbrá-gumbra. The Tjímundo waited in their dug-outs, while the Kumbrágumbra who had joined them hid in the woods. They were shouting to each other :—

" *Trìmo-voága* *anándi !* *tavórabi !* *tjínaga !* "
attack-crowd keep together ! look out ! they are coming !

Before this the allies had offered sago to each other, saying :—

" *Buē wátiaga !* *boàg-voagá* *buē worbótega !* *wátiaga !* "
sago get for you ! guest-crowd sago take for you get for you !

First came the canoe of Bági, with his friend Atáni, a leader among the Moágendo, and his brother, Ámbeb. After them followed the rest of the Moágendo people in their small dug-outs, each holding only two or three men. Among those were Ámuno Kónge, Kárak, Káimbo, and others. When they got the first glimpse of the Tjímundo, Atáni and Ámbeb tried to get on shore. Kándi, Kaib's father, was hidden in the woods, preparing to shoot at Atáni. Ámbeb became aware of Kándi's intention and seized him by the hands, but Kándi wrenched himself free, and pushed his opponent so that he tumbled into the water. Then, getting hold of his spear, he struck Ámbeb from behind in his loin, and then pulled him, dying, out of the water into his canoe. Wéyabu, father's brother of Yérabe, flung his spear upon Ámuno, who was hiding in his dug-out, in which he tried to reach the other bank of the river. But, felled by three spears, he crumpled like a crocodile. Kárak received a spear from Dáduli, Irábu's father, but only in his arm. He fell into the water, and was carried away by the current, but managed to save himself and is still living. Káimbo, who was just arriving in his canoe to see what was happening, was hit in the eyes by two spears, thrown by Moáno, father's brother of Kaib, and by Tjámbe, father's brother of Yérabe. He fell into the water and was drowned. Kónge received a spear from Kirádji and was hit in the back just as he was trying to crawl on to the banks of

A a

the river. Even as he was crying aloud in his death throes he was hit by many more spears. Atáni had hid himself in the water, where at last he was discovered by Kangándja, Yérabe's cousin, and Máli, and Moánale, also Yérabe's cousin and brother-in-law of Kaib. They threw their spears after him and at last Kangándja hit him. The Kumbrágumbra people also shot arrows at him. He tried to hold fast to the Limbum tree on the banks of the river, but, as its roots were washed under by the current, the tree began to fall. Trying now to climb higher up on the trunk, he received still more spears. Just when Andúali and Dor of the Kumbrágumbra in their canoes caught Ámbeb and Kónge, Atáni succeeded in catching one of the spears meant for him, and returned it to Andúali and Dor, but without hitting them. Before long, however, this most important man of the Moágendo had received so many spears and pointed throwing sticks that he succumbed.

The victors began to gather all the corpses into their canoes. The Kumbrágumbra people were willing to leave Atáni, Ámuno, and Kónge, the human spoil, to the Tjímundo, since they had killed them. The Tjímundo people in their turn said generously, " No, they belong to you. You killed them, you take them." This was meant as a courteous opening for revenge for the recent loss in the Kumbrágumbra tribe. The Tjímundo took only Ámbeb. Atáni, Ámuno, and Kónge went to the Kumbrágumbra. Ámbeb's head was cut off, and the body dried on the fire. It was carved, and parts were then given to each of the villages with whom the Tjímundo were on friendly terms, so Kámboa, Kauguyánum, Góropa, and Kumbrágumbra, all got pieces. They were delighted, and roasted their portions to eat with sago. The skull was deposited in the sept-hall of the victors. In a similar way the Kumbrágumbra dealt with their spoil.

After all this the Tjímundo, of course, were again afraid of the revenge of the Moágendo. They remained only two days more in Orúmonum. On the third day they decided to go further up the river. Accordingly, without delay, they sent their women on ahead with the big drums. In Bobónarum they settled and built new houses. One house was still standing from a previous settlement. The hall of Yuórmua was built first and then that of Nangúndumbir. Their fear for their situation in Orúmonum had been increased since they knew that the Moágendo had become acquainted with the character of the wood and the trails on the lower banks of the Kerám. It would thus have been quite possible for them to be surrounded and killed by their old enemies.

One day when they were just finishing putting the rafters on a roof, the Moágendo appeared around the lower bend of the river where they had put a trap (*tjále*) for pigs and a decoy (*kádje*) for fish or eels. Yánua, Kaib's brother-in-law, got the first glimpse, and Wéyabu, father's brother of Yérabe, standing behind him, saw them also. Yánua made a sign to Wéyabu, who ran off and tried to get on the other side of the river. In this way he exposed himself to the throwing-sticks of the Moágendo, who hit him. They seized him and got him into their canoes. Then they beat their dug-outs as a sign of victory. This beating of canoes was heard by the villagers who began to shout, " *Trímo* ! *Trímo* ! " (surprise attack) thinking both Wéyabu and Yánua had been killed. The Moágendo people threw lime in the air after they had caught Wéyabu. But now Yánua appeared among his tribesmen who quickly turned about, shouting, " Here he comes ! Here is Yánua ! " The Tjímundo then hurried to their canoes and chased after the Moágendo. However, they were not able to get any of them or to get Wéyabu back. Their pursuit was hampered, since, in their hurry, they had taken only their small canoes. With the Moágendo people there was only one man of Kamblínto, none of Moim. The houses which stood in Orúmonum the Moágendo burned. It was not long after this skirmish that my motor-boat appeared for the first time at Bobónarum. Thus ends the adventurous migration of the Tjímundo, though, of course, my story has taken them only to 1915.

In addition to this, it may be mentioned that the Moágendo had formerly invited the Karadjúndo people, farther down the Káguia river, to fight with them against the Tjímundo, promising many pigs. They had also tried to win the Tsíngali and the Imboándo for their enterprise against the Tjímundo. Once the Moim refused their support, a dispute broke out between the Karadjúndo and the Moim, and the father of Mátawei, one of my boys, was killed by the Moim. The Karadjúndo took the part of the Tjímundo by saying, " Where do all the pots come from ? They come by the trade of the Tjímundo on the Potters' River."

This story was obtained from discussions such as those mentioned in the introduction. As the interpreters had stayed with me for nearly three years, sharing my life in the bush and learning my lack of sympathy with white man's " prejudices ", they were not reluctant to communicate to me whatever they could gather from our main informant, even details of their cannibalistic usages. Admittedly, the occurrences are somewhat highly coloured because the informants and their interpreters were involved, but it must be maintained that from their point of view the events had happened as depicted, and are subjectively true. I do not believe that their stories are more distorted or prejudiced than any similar reports of Europeans.

The cause of the enmity between the Tjímundo and the

Moágendo could perhaps be gathered from a complementary report on their side. This would undoubtedly run differently. But the historical truth we do not know. The details of our story are particularly fascinating. We are struck by the restlessness of the Tjímundo tribe. Their first quarrel originated in the using of the cord of palm trees which were considered to belong to another community. Also characteristic is the fact that these people value the old trees and take care of the young ones. It indicates that a mere predatory attitude does not prevail in such measure as we often suppose.

Incidents with a woman are never lacking, first with the Mátaro, and later when the women of the Tjímundo visit the Moágendo, particularly in the case of Ágo.

The use of scorn is also a very human failing, an impulse bound to excite resentment and lead to future complications. It is a trait met in all societies, only in a more direct and naïve form among Papuans. Scoffing is a particularly dangerous enterprise in these societies, and disdainful remarks are never forgotten. For the number of persons with whom one comes into contact is not considerable, and daily life becomes monotonous in that it offers few possibilities for diversion. Insults thus grow deep roots and are cherished for years. It seems in this case as if the primary offence of scornful remarks was a starting-point for the chain of blood-feuds between the Tjímundo and the Moágendo people. This is by no means extraordinary. We know of similar starting-points in many old sagas. In Montenegro, as late as the nineteenth century, a scoffing remark of a young man to a girl at a well led to not less than seventy-seven cases of blood revenge. In fact, blood-feuds among the Papuans are one of the main topics for activity and gossip, and always provide interest unless a feast is in preparation. These two are the great excitements of life, since hunting and trapping in these parts of the world are neither particularly dangerous nor challenging. Honours and prestige cannot be acquired in this way.[1]

Of course, there is the desire among feud-bearers to get aid from other settlements if possible. This is, in general, gained by relatives, particularly by means of wives secured from the other village. In our case, Moim, Kamblínto, and Támbunum appear as allies of the Moágendo tribe. The Tjímundo in their turn, try to draw the people of Kumbrágumbra, the lagoon tribe, to their side. But only one clan of these had a special grudge against the Moágendo, so they were not particularly successful.

[1] A number of stories are reported in my *Forschungen auf den Salomo-Inseln &c.*, Berlin, 1912, iii.

Alliance is finally established with the Kumbrágumbra people and with the Kambót, who, however, belong to a tribe of another language and culture. Such differences do not prevent friendships between villages. A symbol for declaration of war mentioned is the festooned spear. The ever-present tendency to all kind of deceitful practices leads to complaints and squabbles.

The beating of the drums or the dug-outs may be heard a long distance, particularly at night, reverberating along the river, canyoned between the high walls of the forest. Then these rythmical tones sounding through the air seem to one half-asleep as coming from a nearby village.

The manner of fighting, the way a man meets death, and the wounds received, are accurately described by the " experts " just as in the old sagas.

Occasionally a kind of " sea-battle " occurs. The men are good " sailors " of their craft. Canoes, sometimes rather small dug-outs, are paddled standing. Destruction of enemy villages and pillaging coconut trees play an important rôle in warfare. Laying fire to the houses of the hostile village is not always an easy task on account of the moist climate.

Exchange of products, even lending aid, goes on even among old foes such as the Tjímundo and the Moágendo. In fact this precedent was used by the Tjímundo to play a low trick on the Moágendo. There is no shame in luring the others into a trap as did Bági with his renowned friend Atáni.

Over all deeds of violence hangs the Damocles' sword of revenge and punishment. In particular did the Tjímundo expect it immediately after their last successful slaying of the Moágendo. Consequently they hurried away to look for another settlement which they found at Bobónarum.

The triumphant Moágendo did not refrain from immediately announcing their success by beating canoes, thus with the impulsive action exposing themselves to the attack of the Tjímundo. The throwing of lime in the air meant realized revenge.

The seizing of the corpses is a point of honour. For the cannibalistic orgies of devouring the slain are considered a grave insult to the losing party. They hardly ever remain unclaimed in a vendetta.

Worthy of remark is the delicate way in which the Tjímundo let the Kumbrágumbra people get their human spoil as due revenge. Earlier the Kumbrágumbra had apologized with donations of pigs for the squabble with their friends.

A man's death is always connected by these natives with the malignant device of an enemy. Quite as a matter of course the rumour spread that Máliga had been " poisoned ", or, in other words, bad magic had been played against him, and their old enemies, the Moágendo, were considered by the Tjímundo to be responsible. It is a recognized trait in human social attitudes to imagine " in the blue " some sequence of events, and paint it as fear or hope may dictate. This was the case with the death of Máliga. Mere phantasy or imagined danger acts as a stimulus for a new chain of happenings of disastrous consequences. There is no difference between the so-called primitive and the civilized in such behaviour.

From the Kumbrágumbra, for tomahawks and knives, the Tjímundo got two of their wives.

Before the advent of the Europeans, who brought tomahawks, calico, and knives as late as 1913, the gifts offered for women were large arm-rings and tobacco, at that time still fairly scarce. (They would dry the tobacco leaves in the sun, but did not know how to make them ferment.) Actual buying of women was still rare ; the taking of women in general amounted to an exchange between villages.

Ábayu, Kaib's little sister, had been seized by the Kumbrágumbra people without recompense. At the time when this information was given to me it was said : *yabánuaga nabíruboatig Kaib-ben nabíruboatig*, " He shall get recompense, Kaib (with) shall get a wife from there."

From Kambót, the neighbouring village with which the Tjímundo were on good terms, they got women without paying for them, in exchange for some of their own girls. Two sisters of Yérabe, Kábui and Tjéngamo, were given to men of Kambót when they were still children. Búi and Báua were the ones to get them. A third woman was Tábo, sister of Wangewá. Also two young men were seized by the Kambót for their girls. The Tjímundo had to submit to it, as the Kambót people were stronger and the Tjímundo were anxious to keep peace with them in order to maintain a protected rear against the Moágendo in front.

Nevertheless, when the Kambót people had seized Tábo, the Tjímundo tried to get her back on the occasions of her visits, avowedly to see her relatives. It was Ángem who finally came back with her from Kambót at the time when the Tjímundo said, " We shall not permit her to return." When she failed to arrive in Kambót, some of their men came down and made a " row " with the Tjímundo. In their position the Tjímundo were not able to keep her and they had to relinquish her to Kambót. But retaliation did not fail. The Tjímundo decided to get a girl from Kambót.

The Angórum people also got women from the Tjímundo, but did not think of paying for them. Tátuli of Angórum got two of the Tjímundo women, first Kángerema, later Yáyo. Kángerema died after she had borne a child named Bráui, at

ADVENTURES OF A TRIBE IN NEW GUINEA 359

present working in Dalip with a mission. Yáyo is living and
has children.

If a woman marries between the villages of Tjímundo and
Angórum nothing is paid for her, since each is on good terms with
the other. The father does not interfere. Thus it happened,
for instance, with Tátuli, who first courted the girl and then
went away with her.

There is no rigid rule as to where the new couple shall live.
Sometimes the woman goes to the house of the man. In other
instances the contrary occurs, depending on whether a village
needs men or women. No festivities accompany marriage or
the birth of a child, since most of the ceremonies are mainly
associated with puberty rites. Only when the first child is
old enough to laugh when it is stroked on the cheeks is it assumed
that its soul has entered. Then the hair of father and mother
is cut above the ears and around the head so that only a crest
remains. The shorn hair is thrown into the water. A small
feast is then prepared of coconut and yams, and coconuts
are planted on the place where the child was born. The coconut
trees from these belong to the child during its lifetime. On
this occasion the mother sits down on the place where the child
was born and the father throws on her a pudding (*kándjin*)
of coconut and yams, whereupon she rises and sits in another
place. The idea is that the ghost responsible for the birth of
the child resides on the place where it was born. The pudding
is thrown out for that ghost, and is supposed to dwell thereafter
with the placenta (*kabunbanbálida*). These meals, with much
eating of yams, are for the women, and not for the men.
They say :—

> *Moándeg atigóragle amúgone*
> child yams-eating big

For comparison the method of acquiring women in Kambót
may be mentioned. A man does not talk with the father of
the bride if he wants to get a woman, although the father always
pretends to be angry afterwards.

> *Yámbe   mátirima   mĕtirima   fándurubma*
> for nothing he catches her, he caught her [and] brought her into the house.

There is no festivity at marriage, only after the birth of the
first child a ceremony takes place in the eating of a special sago
meal, similar to that of the Tjímundo just mentioned. The mother
prepares *ang*, which is a sago stick, rolled in leaves and roasted.
The father makes *tjai*, a pudding of sago cooked in water.
The *tjai* is to be eaten by women and the *ang* by men,
the friends and relatives who come to visit the parents. Coconuts
are also served. The women with the mother assemble in the

agreement *bab umur*, or guarantor of the compact. Should any member of the dead man's family break the truce (*lhĕna*) by killing the homicide or one of his relatives, the *bab umur* would have to pay a fine of a hundred and twenty ewes. Should he be seen taking aim at the enemy but be prevented by someone else from firing off his gun, the fine would be sixty ewes. Should he discharge his gun without being seen aiming at anybody and without killing anybody, it would be thirty ewes. The *bab umur* would exact the fine from the party who broke the truce ; but in any case he would himself be responsible for the payment of it. Should he fail to pay he would be disgraced for ever. His grave would be dug at a market-place or a high-road : he would be socially a dead man and avoided by everybody. He would be unable to get a wife. At weddings the women would sing lampoons about him. He would no longer be called by his own name, but be referred to as " the traitor ". It is not necessary that the guarantor should be a man : instead of a *bab umur* there may be a *läll umur*, or female guarantor, with the same liabilities and the same punishment in store for her if she fails to fulfil her duty. For her also a grave would be dug, and called " the grave of the traitress ".

The promise of the injured party to refrain from taking vengeance, and the security given for it, only imply that the homicide and his relatives are safe for the time being if they keep at a certain distance from the dead man's village, whereas they may be attacked with impunity if they go beyond the stipulated border. This border is also preserved in the new agreement which is apt to follow on the first one. Shortly before the time agreed upon expires the homicide or his relatives ask a shereef or a few other influential men to go to the dead man's village and put *'ār* upon his kindred by sacrificing a sheep or cutting the sinews of a bullock's hocks as *am'arqab* (a most awful form of *'ār*) at their house or tent or outside the mosque of the village. Then negotiations are opened with a view to extending the truce, and if they are successful a *bab umur* is again appointed. The same ceremony may be repeated on subsequent occasions, until the relatives of the deceased at last relinquish their revenge altogether, accepting *ddīt*, or blood-money, in its place. If they are few in number and weak they may be willing to do so before long. But it is hardly considered proper to come to an agreement of this kind until a year has passed after the perpetration of the crime.

Before blood-money is accepted the relatives of the man-slayer may on their own behalf make terms with the family of his victim in order to prevent the vengeance from being wreaked upon them. They commission the shereef or the other men employed as negotiators to arrange about the so-called *abĕrra*, which each of them has to pay as a price for their safety. It may amount to two Moorish dollars or ten, or even a hundred dollars if they are well off and the injured party appears implacable ; and it may be paid either with money or with a silver ornament or a gun. After it has been paid the relatives of the man-slayer go to the family of the deceased, accompanied by the shereef or the other negotiators, kiss the head of each member of the family, and entertain them with a meal, of which everybody present partakes. When they arrive there the women of the household cry and complain of the agreement which has been made. The women generally play an important part in the negotiations, and not on the side of peace. When their relative was killed they scratched and tore their faces and breasts in a terrible manner—more so than on an ordinary death in the family ; and they cut off their right plait, or their left one as well, as they otherwise do only when they have lost somebody who is very dear to them. If the proposal to pay *abĕrra* seems to them to be made too early, they say that it cannot be accepted before their wounds have healed. The *abĕrra* is taken by the male members of the dead man's family—his father, brothers, and sons—not by more distant relatives ; and a *bab umur* again assumes responsibility for their faithfulness to the agreement.

The life of the man-slayer himself is made safe only by the payment of *ddīt* and the guarantee given by one or more *idbäb imurr* (plur. of *bab umur*). If he is too poor to pay his share of the *ddīt*, he tries to raise the necessary sum by putting '*ār* on people or in other ways, and if he fails he will probably leave his tribe for ever. When the *ddīt* has been paid he goes, accompanied by a shereef or a few other men of importance and some relatives, to the family of his victim with a dagger between his teeth and his hands behind his back, kisses the men of the family and other male relatives of the deceased who are present, as also his mother, on the head, and says, "We are repentant for the sake of God ; O brothers, God laid it upon me according to his decree." Then a meal is served with *afttäl* (the Arabic *sĕksu*) and meat of an animal slaughtered for this occasion ; and henceforth the man-slayer can go wherever he likes without running the risk of being killed.

Ddīt and *abĕrra* are not the only expenses he or his relatives have to pay in order to come to a satisfactory agreement with the enemy. A *rrshut* (from the Arabic *reshwa*), or " bribe ", must be given to the persons who were asked to prevail upon the family of the deceased to accept *abĕrra* and *ddīt* instead of taking vengeance. It is offered secretly, and its amount varies according to the circumstances. Moreover, if the people are loyal to the Sultan and his government, a *dd'äirt* (in Arabic *d'äira*), or "fine", is paid to the governor of the district. Again, if the tribe is in

kills a woman, not he but one of his kinswomen is to be killed, and if a woman kills a man, not she but a man belonging to her kin shall die. So strictly is this rule observed that if a woman who is with child is killed in a fight between tribesmen, her body is cut open so that it can be ascertained whether the child in her womb is a boy or a girl and the vengeance, or the amount of the blood-money, can be regulated according to its sex.

Revenge may be taken even for manslaughter which has been committed on strong provocation. If a husband finds another man with his wife and slays the adulterer, the kindred of the latter are allowed to avenge his death, though they may perhaps content themselves with accepting one-half of the ordinary *ddīt* ; and the killing of a robber, even when he is caught at night, leads either to vengeance or payment of the full *ddīt*. Accidental homicide is attended with the same consequences as intentional homicide, even when committed by a child. It is argued that otherwise lack of intention might easily be pleaded as an excuse for voluntary manslaughter or wilful murder ; for who can exactly tell what is accident and what is not ? Not even the last wish of a dying man can prevent a feud. My informant's sister's son had been killed by a man belonging to the kin of his maternal uncle. Before he died he expressly forbade his kinsmen—that is, relatives on the father's side—to take vengeance on his maternal uncle (my informant) or any of his brother's sons ; but nevertheless one of the latter was killed. This, again, shows that homicide is looked upon not merely as an offence against the individual, but as an offence against his *ljma't*.

There may be a feud also in the case of an act that does not immediately lead to a person's death. If someone who has been wounded by another but has recovered, at any time afterwards falls ill and dies and, before his death, declares that his illness was due to the wound he received, the person who inflicted it is treated as a man-slayer, and it matters not how many years have passed since the infliction of the wound. The same applies to anybody who beats a pregnant woman if she subsequently gives birth to a stillborn child.

Killing in war leads to the same consequences as any other kind of homicide if the war is intra-tribal, but the case is different if it is carried on with another tribe. If a person is killed by a member of a strange tribe, there will be a feud not merely between his kinsmen and those of the man-slayer, but between the two tribes ; and in this case the rule of a life for a life is not observed : peace may be concluded though the number of lives lost on one side is not equal to that lost on the other. It is brought about by the leading men of both tribes, who after some preliminary negotiations agree to meet on a certain day at a certain place. There they exchange their cloaks (*izĕnnarr*, sing.

azënnar) or, if they have no cloaks, their turbans or the cotton kerchiefs of their wives ; and if the meeting is held in a village they have a meal in common. These proceedings are acts of covenanting, which lay restraints on those who perform them on account of certain native beliefs.[1] To partake of a common meal is a frequent method of sealing a compact, because he who breaks it thereby exposes himself to the other party's conditional curses which are embodied in the eaten food : it is said that " God and the food will repay him ". The exchange of cloaks or turbans or kerchiefs, again, is based on the idea that the promisee will be able to avenge a breach of faith on the part of the promiser owing to the magical connection between a thing and its owner. This idea also underlies another custom that may be mentioned in this context. When the Ait Yusi are going to fight another tribe, the man who has been elected chief secures the cloaks of the leading men of the tribe as a pledge for their appearance at a certain place on the day and at the hour fixed by him ; and if any of them fails to appear, he blackens his cloak and sends it to different parts of the tribe to be shown to all the people. The blackening of the cloak of the faithless man is not merely a means of disgracing him, but is supposed to cause him misfortune, black being a colour that contains *bas*, or evil.

There are cases of homicide in which no vengeance is taken nor blood-money paid, namely, when a person has been killed by a member of his own family. In explanation of this I was told that the family does not like to lose another member besides the one it has already lost. A son who has killed his father or mother—such cases are by no means rare—runs away, not to return for a few days, if he has grown-up brothers, and then nothing is done to him ; but if he has no grown-up brother he may not have to leave his home at all. If a man kills his brother there is, for the moment at least, no question either of revenge or blood-money, unless the brother has a grown-up son ; but if he has a son who is still young, the fratricide may later on have to pay for his deed with his life. If a husband kills his wife her kindred will avenge her death on a woman of the husband's kin, or blood-money has to be paid to them.

A person who has been accused of homicide, but has not been proved guilty, can clear himself of the charge by oath, if forty-nine other male members of his kin, all of whom need not be grown-up, also swear to his innocence. Ten of them are chosen by the accuser. If any of these refuses to swear, the suspected person is considered guilty of the crime ; hence it frequently happens that by bribery the accuser induces some kinsman of the latter to refuse to act as conjurator. This

[1] See my *Ritual and Belief in Morocco* (London, 1926), i, 564 sqq.

limbs and reeled about the villages, one man involuntarily following the example of another until almost the whole population of a village might be affected at the same moment. The condition was known as *haro heraripe* "one's head is turning round". It is as obvious that these symptoms were involuntary among the masses as that similar symptoms were deliberately affected by certain leaders for their own purposes. While they indulged in these antics the leaders frequently poured forth utterances in "Djaman", or "German", a language composed mostly of nonsense syllables and pidgin English which was wholly unintelligible. But at other times they took care to make themselves understood by words and actions, and thus the movement was invested with real significance.

The main teaching was that the old customs and ceremonies must be done away with. The bull-roarers and the masks worn in the *Hevehe* and *Kovave* ceremonies were cast out of the men's houses and burnt while women and uninitiated children looked on. Personal adornment was banned ; feathers were snatched from the heads of vain unbelievers ; and the forbidden lime-pot was dashed from their hands. In some communities the people, or certain influential men among them, were strong enough to resist the invasion and preserve their possessions and customs. But in most they were completely overpowered : they caught the *haro heraripe* and themselves joined in the work of destruction. There can be no doubt that misunderstood Mission teaching had something to do with this aspect of the Madness.

But besides mere iconoclasm there was some positive doctrine. The "bosses" declaimed against thieving and adultery. (There was no originality in this, and it certainly had no great effect, for sexual standards were noticeably relaxed for the time being.) Some of the preachers were perhaps quite sincere, though by claiming to detect wrong-doing they continually extracted atonement from the wrong-doers in the form of pigs. Further they insisted on cleanliness ; on the equality of women ; and, as the most important duty, on the necessity of offerings to the dead.

It is to certain prophecies and beliefs, however, that I wish to draw special attention. It was foretold and everywhere believed that the spirits of the dead would return ; in some quarters they were expected to appear as white men, and indeed some Europeans were actually welcomed as the ghosts of Papuans. Universally it was believed that a steamer would come to the Gulf. The original idea was certainly that it would be full of the spirits of the Papuan dead, though many of those who looked for the vessel were not quite clear as to the nature of its passengers. The leaders were in continual communication with the dead, receiving messages in various forms, sometimes by papers that fluttered down from the sky or were held out by invisible hands, but mainly through the agency of flagpoles, the message being caught at the top and transmitted to the base, where it was received by those who had ears to hear. Everywhere preparations were made for the welcome of the dead. Food was accumulated and ripe coconuts were stacked in readiness for loading on to the steamer. In the meantime the spirits were supposed to come in invisible form and eat of the offerings that must be set out for them ; and in many villages there were tables ready laid with knives and forks and floral decorations. It was principally from these offerings to the dead that the " bosses " or leaders were enabled to make their profits ; for they posed as go-betweens and had sole access to the *ahea uvi*, or " hot houses ", to which the spirits resorted in order to partake of the offerings made by the more simple-minded. By methods such as these, and by continuing to make or allow their heads to " go round," the leaders kept the Vailala Madness alive long after the masses had ceased to show any nervous or physical symptoms.

THE LEADERS

It is important to get an idea of the personal character of the leaders. Unfortunately the more prominent of them (at this western end of the Division) have since died, so that it is not possible to add much that would be reliable to what has already been said in " The Vailala Madness ". Biere alone remains from among the real leaders ; and further acquaintance confirms the impression that he is a strong character and a man of high intelligence ; it also makes clearer the fact that he was an impostor. I think he may stand as an example of that class of leaders who deliberately used the movement for their own gain. Ua Halai, of Arihava, was, I believe, of the same class.

While some leaders, however, were cool impostors others were evidently to some extent sincere. Harea, who played a highly important part, I never met personally. He eventually became a lay preacher, but the Rev. R. A. Owen, under whom he worked, informs me that he was a strange character, fanatical in the extreme, and liable even as a lay preacher to verge upon unintelligibility. The record of Evara, to whom as an individual it is plain the movement owes its origin, has already been mentioned in " The Vailala Madness ", with the significant item that he had been subject to ecstatic seizures before ever the Madness began. I have since learned that as a youth he was marked by extreme nervousness ; he avoided the men's house ; he would fly to the bush on the least sign of a quarrel between two villagers ; and he would never come near to look on a corpse at a native funeral. When he married, his " inside hardened ",

or a number of visits, did take place even if the spirits did not materialize.

Thus a young man who was house-boy to the Magistrate at Kerema tells me how he once heard cries of " Sailoh! " from the village of Karaita just below the residency. He went out to see what boat was coming and found some of the " bosses " and others affected by the Madness running about the beach in great excitement, clapping their hands and shouting " Hippu! Hippu! " They were welcoming the Phantom Ship. My informant looked out over the calm waters of Kerema Bay and saw the wash of the steamer as she approached. He heard the pounding of her engines, then the rattle of her anchor-chain. He heard the dinghy lowered noisily into the water and the sound of her oars as she was rowed ashore. And not only he but all the others present (so he says) heard the same sounds, for they were communicating their impressions to one another. Soon their ears informed them that the dinghy was returning; the anchor was heaved up, the engines started, and the Phantom Ship sailed out of hearing. Not once had she been seen.

Again, one hears how a steamer (the prophecy is not nailed down to one only) entered the Vailala River at night. She had three masts and an imposing red funnel, though these perhaps were not very clearly observed; more emphasis is laid on her lights, which many saw as she passed quickly upstream. None of the passengers were visible, but when Evara paddled out alone in a canoe and came alongside they threw a token into the dug-out. It was a medal which he subsequently wore round his neck like the badge of a Village Councillor. (When I met Evara, nine years before I heard this story, I noted his Victory Medal, 1919, but he did not tell how he had come by it. I do not know that he himself professed to have received it from the steamer.)

Here at Orokolo and Arihava the steamer was sighted one morning at about 11 o'clock. The smoke was seen, but before the vessel came properly into view it was obscured by clouds. To the majority of people in Orokolo (who had escaped or resisted the Madness) the steamer was not so clearly visible, but the *haro heraripe* men would clutch them by the arm crying, " There, can't you see it? " and my informants appeared to have no doubt that it had really been there.

The Resurrection of Ua Halai

When at the end of 1922 I was first inquiring into the Vailala Madness at Arihava one of my best informants was Ua Halai. He was still, so to speak, practising, and was the most influential of the " bosses " in a village of some 1,500 people. I did not know then that he had been the hero of the remarkable exploit which is here recorded ; perhaps everyone conspired to keep it secret, for there was a well-grounded feeling that the Vailala Madness was not viewed with favour by the Government. The exploit was nothing short of resurrection from " death ".

It transpires that Ua Halai had complained of indisposition one morning, and by midday he was " dead ". He had apparently foreseen this eventuality, for he had issued instructions that when his body was laid out in the usual fashion it was not to be closely approached. Further, he had said that no grave should be dug for him ; his friends and relatives should wait and see what they would see. Ua Halai was so " dead " that the rats gnawed his ears. (This point is made by all who tell the story, and the disfigurement of the ears is vouched for by eye-witnesses. Some also say that his toes were attacked.) But at noon of the third day he came back to life, issued forth from the house, and began to preach in a voice of thunder, using the " German " language. Next he caused a litter to be carried from end to end of the long village of Arihava while he lay reclined upon it, waving a cassowary-plume switch and crying out that his litter was the steamer of Lavara, a legendary ancestress, come back to Papua. During his period of " death ", as he gave out, he had been to the land of the dead, whence he had brought back more warnings against stealing, adultery, etc., as well as the idea of the *ahea uvi*, or " hot house ", which was to be shared as a place of resort by the spirits and the " bosses ".

To us, of course, it appears almost self-evident that Ua Halai's " death " was a carefully prepared hoax. It would seem likely that he had accomplices among the other " bosses ", for it is said they stood guard, allegedly looking for signs of returning animation, but also enforcing their superior's wish that none should approach too near. Yet with the rank and file the hoax was a complete success ; I have heard no one express any doubts, and in answer to a direct question one will be told seriously that for three days the man was dead. Had I known of this exploit when I met Ua Halai in person it would have been possible to examine his ears and see to what extent he or his accomplices had gone to provide this grisly evidence. That the ears were in some way disfigured is beyond doubt. It is, of course, conceivable that they were actually gnawed by rats during a trance, but the careful staging of the whole affair is strong evidence for the other interpretation.

Maivake's Ghost

The third incident is of a different kind in that it represents a failure on the part of the " bosses " to carry out their pretence. In Vailala West the principal " boss " was Biere, whom we have seen to be a man of outstanding intelligence and personality.

of nearly all established legends the historical antecedents can only be conjectured, but it need not follow that we are always wasting our time when we try some historical reconstructions from the evidence of legend as we find it.

The part played by individual leaders in the movement is obviously of the greatest significance. The attribution of its origin to Evara has been amply verified by my later inquiries ; but some of the other " bosses " had their own gleams of imagination. It is obvious that movements of this kind have their starting point in the mind of an individual, viz. in his personal reactions to those antecedents, large and small, which may be regarded as more ultimate causes. Then other individuals begin to exert their influence, like so many buds on an original stem from which new branches may develop. We have briefly examined the character of a few of these leaders. Some of them were undoubtedly cool schemers with a gift for leadership or organization and an eye to their own interests. But it seems that this class have in some measure proceeded by exploiting the ideas of men who were not so well balanced. In fact it is not too much to say that the most important ideas of the Vailala Madness emerged originally from visions or delusions. It is certainly easier to believe that they were the product of fevered imagination than of cool planning.

The reaction of the populace to such ideas is in primitive society the test of their permanency. We have seen some amazing examples of suggestibility and credulity. While in some villages the people stood firm against the destruction of their customs, there must have been few out-and-out unbelievers. The most extravagant claims were not too much for primitive gullibility, and prophecies were accepted as facts even after they had manifestly failed. The delusion or the pretence of one man may thus easily become the belief of thousands and eventually appear in the guise of legend. Indeed, it is not improbable that the miraculous exploits of many culture heroes are no more than their delusions or pretences which have been accepted as facts.

I have pointed out that there are degrees of scepticism and credulity among different informants. But provided there are sufficient believers I do not think that at the primitive level a leavening of unbelievers can prevent this kind of legend-making. There are, in fact, varying moods of scepticism and credulity in every individual ; or to put it another way, there are moments when the native's critical faculty, such as it may be, is awake, and others when it is sound asleep ; in truth, it seems almost that he deliberately puts it to sleep. Now, when a native is story-telling he and his audience are in the mood of credulity ; they willingly discard the trammels of fact, and the more the miracles the better the story.

This coming and going of credulity is familiar in the native's attitude toward his ceremonies as well ; and certain features of the Vailala Madness serve to throw light on the growth of ritual as well as legend. It might fairly be claimed that the offerings at the *ahea uvi* and the receipt of heavenly messages at the flagpole had the makings of genuine ritual ; but it is the experiment of Maivake's Ghost that provides the best instance. Here the " bosses " of Vailala, and those of Arihava who were about to follow their example, had all the materials at hand for the creation of a new kind of masked ceremony, one which might have replaced the *Hevehe* and *Kovave* that they themselves had cast out. There may have been other doubters besides the man who unmasked the ghost, but there were certainly a great number who believed ; and had the cult but lasted long enough to develop a more liberal policy, absorbing into its midst all who paid the necessary pig, then it might conceivably have become permanent. No doubt many similar experiments have failed in the past : the circumstances attending one such attempt, however, may throw a light upon those masked ceremonies which have had a more successful run.

If the present paper has any claim to interest it is because it deals with culture on the move. The Vailala Madness came as a violent shock to the societies of the Gulf Division, and the adjustments and reactions afford material for the study of culture in a state of unusually rapid metabolism. Incidentally we have been enabled to trace with some particularity the origin of a number of beliefs and of certain practices which might have become permanent. It may be idle to speculate upon origins in a static culture ; but there are more than enough native societies undergoing change at the present day, and the study of these has, I believe, a special importance, for here if anywhere we shall have a chance of discovering how elements of culture begin and how they grow.

Dudgeon, and P. N. Panton) : *Proceedings of the Royal Society of Medicine, Pathological Section,* i.

" An Example of Incomplete Glandular Hermaphroditism in the Domestic Fowl " (with S. G. Shattock) : *Proceedings of the Royal Society of Medicine, Pathological Section,* i.

1908. " On the Occurrence of new Growths among the Natives of British New Guinea " : *Third Scientific Report Imperial Cancer Research Fund.*

1910. " The Influence of Oöphorectomy upon the Growth of the Pelvis " (with S. G. Shattock) : *Proceedings of the Royal Society of Medicine, Pathological Section,* iii.

" Attempts to produce Chondromatous or Osteomatous Growths by the Grafting of Fœtal Bones " (with S. G. Shattock and L. S. Dudgeon) : *Proceedings of the Royal Society of Medicine, Pathological Section,* iii.

1914. " Observations made to ascertain whether any Relation subsists between the Seasonal Assumption of the ' Eclipse ' Plumage in the Mallard (*Anas boscas*) and the Functions of the Testicle " (with S. G. Shattock) : *Proceedings of the Zoological Society of London.*

ANTHROPOLOGY

1901-7. Contributions to *Reports of the Cambridge Anthropological Expedition to Torres Straits,* ii (1901) ; iii (1907) ; and v (1904).

1902. " The Medicine, Surgery, and Midwifery of the Sinaugolo " : *JRAI.,* xxxii.

" Note on the Preparation and Use of the Kenyah Dart-Poison Ipoh " : *JRAI.,* xxxii.

1905. " Note on a Skull prepared for Purposes of Sorcery, from the Mekeo District, British New Guinea " : *Man,* v.

1906. " Physical Anthropology and Ethnology of British New Guinea " (Hunterian Lecture) : *Lancet.* i.

" Anthropogeographical Investigations in British New Guinea ' (with W. M. Strong) : *Geographical Journal,* xxvii.

" Note on a Trephined Skull from New Britain " : *Man,* vi.

" Notes on the Tugere Tribe, Netherlands New Guinea " : *Man,* vi.

1907. " On Prehistoric Objects in British New Guinea " (with T. A. Joyce) : *Anthropological Essays presented to Edward Burnett Tylor in honour of his 75th Birthday,* Oct. 2, 1907, Oxford, Clarendon Press, and *British Association Report.*

1908. " Note on Totemism in New Guinea " : *Man,* viii.

" The Vedda Cult of the Dead " : *Transactions of the Third International Congress for the History of Religions* (Oxford).

" Note on recent Work among the Veddas " : *Journal of the Royal Asiatic Society, Ceylon Branch,* xxi.

" The Veddas " : *British Association Report.*

1909. " Linked Totems in British New Guinea " : *Man,* ix.

" A Classification of the Natives of British New Guinea " : *JRAI.,* xxxix.

" A Type of Canoe Ornament with Magical Significance ' from South-Eastern British New Guinea " : *Man,* ix.

1910. *The Melanesians of British New Guinea,* Cambridge University Press, pp. xxiii + 766, illustrations, and map. With a chapter by F. R. Barton, C.M.G., and an Appendix by E. L. Giblin.

" A Neolithic Site in the Anglo-Egyptian Sudan " : *JRAI.,* xl.

" The Physical Characters of the Nuba of Kordofan " : *JRAI.,* xl.

1911. *The Veddas* (with Brenda Z. Seligman), Cambridge University Press, pp. xix + 463, plates, text-figures, and map. With a chapter by C. S. Myers and an Appendix by A. Mendis Gunasekara, Mudaliar.
" Note upon an Early Egyptian Standard " (with Margaret A. Murray) : *Man*, xi.
" Note on the ' Sa ' Sign " (with Margaret M. Murray) : *Man*, xi.
" An Egyptian Holy Man " : *Lancet*, i.
" The Divine Kings of the Shilluk " : *British Association Report*.
" The Cult of Nyakang and the Divine Kings of the Shilluk : *Fourth Report of the Wellcome Tropical Research Laboratories*, Khartoum.
" An Avungara Drum " : *Man*, xi.
" Dinka " : *Encyclopædia of Religion and Ethics*, iv.

1912. " A Cretinous Skull of the Eighteenth Dynasty " : *Man*, xii.
" Stone Adze Blades from Suloga (British New Guinea) as Chinese Antiquities " : *Man*, xii.

1913. " Ancient Egyptian Beliefs in Modern Egypt " : *Essays and Studies presented to William Ridgeway on his 60th Birthday*, Cambridge University Press.
" Some Aspects of the Hamitic Problem in the Anglo-Egyptian Sudan " : *JRAI.*, xliii.

1914. " The Cheddar Man " (with F. G. Parsons) : *JRAI.*, xliv.

1915. " Note on Bisharin " : *Man*, xv.
" Note on an Obsidian Axe or Adze Blade from Papua " : *Man*, xv.
" Note on a Wooden Horn or Trumpet from British New Guinea " : *Man*, xv.
" An undescribed Type of Building in the Eastern Province of the Anglo-Egyptian Sudan " : *Journal of Egyptian Archæology*, ii.
" Presidential Address to Section H.—Anthropology " : *British Association Report*.

1916. " A simple Form of Reaping Knife from Northern Kordofan " : *Man*, xvi.
" Dinka Arrows " : *Man*, xvi.
" Stone-headed Club from Southern Kordofan " : *Man*, xvi.
" An Australian Bible Story " : *Man*, xvi.
" Lime Spatulæ from Rossel Island, British New Guinea " : *Man*, xvi.
" The Uas Sceptre as a Beduin Camel Stick " : *Journal of Egyptian Archæology*, iii.
" Ceramica sudanese impressa a traliccio " : *Revista di Antropoligia*, Roma, xx.
" Ethnic Relationship of the Vanquished represented on certain Proto-Dynastic Egyptian Palettes " : *Annals of Archæology and Anthropology*, vii.
" A Prehistoric Site in Northern Kordofan " : *Annals of Archæology and Anthropology*, vii.

1917. " The Physical Characters of the Arabs " : *JRAI.*, xlvii.
" Nuba " : *Encyclopædia of Religion and Ethics*, ix.
" Canoe Prow Ornaments from Netherlands New Guinea " : *Man*, xvii.
" A Bongo Funerary Figure " : *Man*, xvii.

1918. " The Kababish, a Sudan Arab Tribe " (with Brenda Z. Seligman) : *Harvard African Studies*, ii : *Varia African*, ii.

1920. " Shilluk " : *Encyclopædia of Religion and Ethics*, xi.
" Bird Chariots and Socketed Celts in Europe and China " : *JRAI.*, l.